The Law of Emergency Powers

Abhishek Singhvi · Khagesh Gautam

The Law of Emergency Powers

Comparative Common Law Perspectives

Springer

Dr. Abhishek Singhvi
BA (Hons); MA (Cantab); PhD (Cantab)
Senior, Third term Member of Parliament
Senior Advocate, Supreme Court of India
Former Chairman, Parliamentary Standing
Committee on Law & Justice
Former Additional Solicitor General of India
Supreme Court of India
New Delhi, India

Khagesh Gautam
Jindal Global Law School
O. P. Jindal Global University
Sonipat, Haryana, India

,

ISBN 978-981-15-2996-2 ISBN 978-981-15-2997-9 (eBook)
https://doi.org/10.1007/978-981-15-2997-9

This Springer imprint is published by the registered company Springer Nature Singapore Pte Ltd.
The registered company address is: 152 Beach Road, #21-01/04 Gateway East, Singapore 189721, Singapore

"To my late father, for being an inspiration, an exemplar & my legal guru; To my mother, for being the *only* one who did *not* think that a law PhD would be valuable time lost from an early start in the legal profession; To my wife, for uncomplainingly standing by me as a young bride in Cambridge on a shoe string budget and for typing 200,000 words on a 1983 IBM transportable;"

Prolegomenon

All prolegomena are trips down memory lane, a recollection of the journey from the inception of an idea to its delivery as a final work of authorship. But this one exceeds the normal length and depth of that journey down memory lane, since it rewinds over 35 years to the mid-80s, when I conceived, labored, and delivered a bonny baby of a 200,000-word Ph.D. thesis in 1985 at Trinity College, Cambridge, UK. Its publication as a book after so many decades is as much a matter of joy as an admission of lethargy, coupled with a recognition of the undeniable exigencies which overtake the life of a busy practitioner, and, still worse, someone who strayed into public life in India. Let me reflect on the journey of this work from its conception as an idea to its publication as a book.

I. My Cambridge years and the conceptual evolution of this work

I am struck by the recollection of how I approached, in 1981, the forbidding persona of Sir William Wade (then Prof. HWR Wade), Master of Gonville and Caius, with a proposal to do Ph.D. on "due process," a phrase to which I had inexplicably taken a fancy in my youth. It is a supreme irony that after meandering through a humongous forest of materials on the heavily trodden path of "due process," and frequently getting lost and depressed, I ended up revising my proposal to the *obverse* of "due process," viz. *suspension* of due process, which is virtually another name for emergency powers!

My youthful ambitious zeal to write the definitive and most comprehensive *comparative* work on emergency powers caused me much anxiety and grief before I realized that I would need to educate myself for many years in the French and German languages, and possibly many more European languages, before I could do justice to even a *partially comparative* work subsuming *civil law* constitutional systems. I then settled for a fairly wide comparative *common law* sweep and chose four meaty and large jurisdictions, viz. UK, USA, India, and the international human rights jurisprudence.

The idealistic desire to achieve maximum coverage made me include international law treatment of emergency powers, more commonly referred to as derogations from human rights in the thesis, including a detailed analysis of case law on the subject of derogations spawned by regional human rights fora like the European Court of Human Rights, the European Commission on Human Rights, the Inter-American Commission on Human Rights, and some other international fora. That has been excluded from this book, and hopefully, in the not too distant future, shall receive separate book length treatment as a companion volume two to the present work.

II. Thematic examination and the pursuit of research and writing

My original intent in the thesis was to deal with issues and sub-issues (e.g., martial law, military acting in aid of civil authority, statutory emergency powers, wartime powers, etc.), thematically, subsuming jurisprudential materials from the UK, USA, India, and International law under each of these conceptual sub-heads. Sadly, the width of coverage of my thesis did not permit me to use this thematic and conceptual format and I was compelled to compile the research materials country wise and jurisdiction wise in the thesis, though within each jurisdiction, the arrangement of multiple headings and subheadings was entirely conceptual. Happily, by choosing some topics (e.g., International law, as explained above) and adding new sections and headings in the present book (e.g., Judicial Independence and Economic Emergency), we have been able to largely achieve a conceptual layout for the table of contents, though inevitably there is some jurisdiction wise treatment (e.g., Chapter five titled Emergency Powers in India), due to the historical context peculiar to a particular jurisdiction.

I reminisce about the terror I went through, when my 3 years of penance and solitude at Cambridge were put to the test in a viva voce lasting half a day in a London in 1985, with an intimidating set of two super eminent examiners in public law, viz. the redoubtable Prof. Graham Zellick, then Editor of Public Law (the most well-known journal on the subject in the Commonwealth) and Prof. DGT Williams, then President of Wolfson College, Cambridge and later Vice-Chancellor, Cambridge University. I had already been given a special extension of the word limit from 80,000 words to 1,00,000 words but in view of the huge wealth of jurisprudence from four jurisdictions (case law, articles, etc.), I had put out a second *additional* volume of an additional 1,00,000 words comprising footnotes! It was a catharsis when I learnt after several weeks that I had cleared the viva, despite the pure horror suffered *during* the viva when asked by the punctilious examiners to explain the citations, for example, in footnote 348 in volume two of footnotes volume relating to Chapter three in the second volume of 1,00,000 words!

III. The saga of publication seeing the light of the day

I fondly recall the venerable old Mr. Trivedi and the doughty Mr. Majumdar, both from the then most reputed Indian law publishers, Tripathi & Co, visiting me on a monthly basis in Delhi from Bombay (now Mumbai), after my return to India in late 1985, imploring me to either allow them to convert the massive thesis to a publishable book or to do it myself, before the lapse of much time. Ignoring my father's sage advice not to let the perfect become the enemy of the good, I told Mr. Trivedi and Mr. Majumdar that I wanted to *personally* try and convert the thesis into a book and that I would have it done by 1987 at the latest. Each passing month drew me into the vortex of law practice in India and although the fragrance of professional success (including designation as a senior at age 34) was sweet and enticing, the publication of my thesis as a book became the casualty. Time passed and after the death of both Mr. Trivedi and Mr. Majumdar, Tripathi & Co. also folded up, but my idealistic and unreal dream of redoing my thesis *personally* persisted for many years. It is only two years ago that my interactions with Vice-Chancellor Prof. C. Raj Kumar of O.P. Jindal Global University reignited my desire for a quick *redelivery* of the "Bonny baby," now a middle-aged being!

VC Prof. Raj Kumar, with his usual dynamism and optimism, found Prof. Khagesh Gautam, just the right person for the job at the right time. Khagesh has the academic's curiosity for ideas backed by the discipline for relentless research. When we sat together for hours over several sittings, after he had spent almost a year updating the references, I found that, astonishingly, there were hardly any book length treatments of the subject, none with a comparative common law approach and certainly none of this width and length. The intervening years, the subject of some misgiving and doubt in my mind initially, did not prove to be the insurmountable hurdle I had feared. Indeed, not even any obstruction.

IV. The jurisprudential foundations and constitutional imaginations of the book

This book is a comprehensive legal and constitutional study of emergency powers in a comparative common law perspective, the *first* such study of three jurisdictions and the first one dealing in such detail with varied forms of emergency powers, constitutional, statutory and common law, martial law and military acting in aid of civil authority, wartime and peacetime invocations, and several related themes like judicial review of emergency powers (existence, scope, and degree). A study of the legal propositions on this subject, especially in a comparative perspective, is useful for any body politic, which aspires for democracy, along with constitutionally controlled aberrations to protect that democracy.

Even today, there are few book length contributions to the growing discourse on emergency powers. This study attempts to bridge the following gaps in published book length legal scholarship and (a) remains the only comparative study of the three jurisdictions discussed, (b) covers the largest population within the common law world, (c) provides the maximum representative diversity, (d) covers virtually every form and methodology of emergency powers as stated above, (e) remains the only study (to the best knowledge of the authors) to have gone vertically into comparable depth of each form of emergency powers within the common law context, (f) is the most heavily footnoted, and (g) has the highest granularity of detail. To give one example, specific subheadings in each chapter address questions like—what is the true meaning of "martial law"; who can invoke "martial law"; when can it be invoked and suspended; what happens when military is called in to aid civilian authorities; can marital law be deemed to exist or coexist when the latter happens; what is the extent to which the state may go when an economic emergency is invoked, and, above all, can, and if so when and how much, can courts judicially review emergency powers? The asking of such hard questions in a Dworkinian sense is itself important, and, howsoever imperfectly, they have been attempted to be answered.

V. Expression of gratitude and a deeper sense of appreciation

My indebtedness to a large number of individuals and institutions is, I hope, more fully reflected in the copious footnotes contained in this book, but some debts of gratitude require special mention. Prof. Sir William Wade had been much more than my supervisor for this thesis. He had been a friend, philosopher, and guide. His vast knowledge and experience, his attention to detail, his helpful and kind disposition, and his ready availability at crucial moments had proved invaluable and indispensable in the 1980s. I had been in intermittent touch with him till his death at 86 in 2004.

The librarians and staff of the Squire Law Library at Cambridge University, the Institute of Advanced Legal Studies, London, and the Indian Law Institute, New Delhi had extended themselves beyond the call of duty to assist me in my research. The first, now shifted from the venerable old building near Trinity College, was my first, not second, home. I have had the privilege (and misery and fear) of being the only human being sitting in this huge and ornate building through many nights, with a special key given to me as a special exception by the intrepid Mr. McVeigh, its Head Librarian, to enable entry into the building 24x7. Occasionally, I had to ask my newly wedded wife to sleep nearby on a few chairs bundled together, while I researched, because that was the only way to shore up Dutch courage to enter this colonnaded building at midnight amid the possible company of ghosts!

A Trinity College graduate studentship had funded a substantial portion of the study. My former supervisor and director of Studies at Trinity College during my undergraduate years, Philip Allott, had always been a source of inspiration and made valuable suggestions after reading parts of the study. Now well into his 80s at Cambridge, I regret losing touch with this introvert, soft-spoken bachelor philosopher, the archetypal academic, a man ever so kind, compassionate, and helpful, who wore his humongous versatility as an erudite master of constitutional and international law most lightly. My tutor at Trinity College, Michael Proctor, made the task of coping with the college and university bureaucracy much easier and, being a mathematician, provided a welcome contrast from the company of lawyers. Najmi Waziri, now Justice Waziri of the Delhi High Court, spent many hours on a word processor to transform a series of illegible handwritten sheets of paper into a presentable thesis and also to prepare caselists, bibliographies, and appendices.

Some acknowledgments are foundational—more personal in nature and even deeply existential. To my late father, Dr. L.M. Singhvi, for being an ideal to inspire and to follow and for making numerous stylistic and substantive suggestions in respect of the thesis; to my mother, Kamla Singhvi, for suggesting that I forgo some years of law practice to complete the thesis; to my wife, Anita Singhvi, for toiling ceaselessly in Cambridge at the then newly invented IBM transportable computer (all of 3 feet by 2 feet and weighing 20 kgs) to ready my thesis for printing, while uncomplainingly (she was different then!) sacrifice the many hours and days that were justly hers, especially as a 3-year-old bride; and to my Cambridge born, then 20-month-old elder son, Anubhav, for being an endless one-person entertainment machine. In that sense, this thesis and book has been my oldest and most laborious love: I still remember a nightmarish first week of December 1984, when I used to attend to my pregnant wife (who delivered Anubhav on December 8) for half a day, travel from Cambridge to London to attend for the balance day to my father undergoing his first bypass at London (in those days, a rather intimidating medical procedure) and spending the night at Squire Law Library back at Cambridge, finishing chapters of my thesis! Traumatic as these experiences were, in retrospect I would not miss them for anything, for they make me as a person more than anything else.

Last, but not the least, let me reiterate my gratitude to my co-author Prof. Khagesh Gautam (and to VC Prof. Raj Kumar for finding him and providing all institutional support to him), not only for updating of legal literature of the intervening years 1985–2019 (as reflected in the footnotes), but also for spending long hours of exciting and productive discussions with me when we rewrote large parts of several chapters and tailored it for 2020. Above all, for his rigorous discipline in completing things on time. I am deeply obliged to the publishers, a most reputed international brand in the realm of law publishing, for prompt and efficient midwifery for redelivery of my "baby" as a book in this new avatar!

Sonipat (Haryana)
March 7, 2020

Abhishek Singhvi
Supreme Court of India New Delhi India

Preface

In the world that we live in today, it would be very difficult to find any written Constitution that either expressly or impliedly does not provide for some kind or type of emergency powers. Supreme Courts around the free world, while interpreting these written constitutions, have usually referred to these express or implied provisions in order to locate the source, and more importantly articulate the extent, of emergency powers in their respective constitutions. Perhaps one of the oldest surviving written constitutions establishing a democratic and republican form of government in the modern world, the U.S. Constitution does not expressly provide for any emergency powers. But that did not prevent the U.S. Supreme Court to interpret the U.S. Constitution in a manner, whereby emergency powers were embedded in several constitutional provisions thereof. That doctrinal and scholarly debate continues in the pages of law reports, and law reviews in the U.S. even today. In one of the most important and influential democratic and republican constitutions drafted after the Second World War, the Constitution of the Republic of India, an entire chapter is dedicated to emergency powers. India, however, is no stranger to the concept of exceptional powers. They have been a part of ancient Indian tradition and only their extent and manner of their exercise was changed by the Indian Constitution. The Supreme Court of India, perhaps the first apex court in the world, has articulated the standards of judicial review whereby any excessive or arbitrary use of these exceptional powers could be checked. In the U.K., a democratic country with a constitutional monarch but not a written constitution (like the U.S., or India), the existence of emergency powers to be used in exceptional circumstances has never been denied, and several judicial and political methods to check any abuse of these powers have evolved that are consistent with legal and political traditions of that country. These three, i.e., U.S.A., India, and the U.K., provide an interesting comparison set in the study of emergency powers.

This work was originally prepared in the form of a doctoral dissertation by Dr. Singhvi in completion of his Ph.D. in Trinity College, Cambridge, U.K. in 1985. This was the same year I was born. I first became aware of this work via a YouTube interview sometime in 2010, where Dr. Singhvi mentioned this work and challenges that it presented. I was a young lawyer practicing in Punjab & Haryana High Court in the chambers of my learned senior, Pt. Avneesh Jhingan (now, his lordship Mr. Justice Jhingan, P&H High Court). If someone would have told me then that before the decade ends I would be Dr. Singhvi's co-author, I probably would have just smiled and ignored such a statement. After finishing my LL.M. from Columbia Law School, New York, I joined the faculty at Jindal Global Law School in 2013. One fine afternoon Vice-Chancellor Prof. (Dr.) C. Raj Kumar inquired if I would be willing to be a part of this massive project. I requested for a copy of the manuscript and was handed over a massive two-volume work a few days thereafter. I immediately recalled the YouTube interview and realized that the task ahead was going to be long and challenging. After much hard work, long and intense discussions and readings of chapter drafts with Dr. Singhvi, this work was born. I am very glad to have been a part of this long and worthwhile journey. As Dr. Singhvi and I rewrote large parts of his original work, it became clear to me that Indian history (legal and otherwise), and especially ancient Indian history is a goldmine for an emergency scholar. There is much work to be done on the subject, and this work also opens up many lines of further scholarly inquiry. We hope that this work will inspire other scholars to carry this scholarship further.

Working with Dr. Singhvi also allowed me the opportunity to develop some arguments of my own that I had been working on. The discussion on the constitutionality of the controversial Armed Forces Special Powers Act, 1958 builds on a previous work, and is taken to its logical conclusion in this work. The historical reading of article 34 in light of the peculiar historical circumstances of that time (i.e., the martial law imposed in Hyderabad after independence) was also a novel addition to this work. The chapter on economic emergency was originally prepared as a law-review article (while working on this book). When I mentioned this side-work to Dr. Singhvi, he immediately inquired as to what I had written, and after a brief discussion suggested to expand it into a chapter and make it a part of this work. The segment on post-*Bommai* developments is a crucial element of this work that provides not only a legal and brief statistical analysis of emergency proclamations made under article 356 of the Constitution, but is also informed by the lived experience of the very senior counsel who has argued some of these important cases.

Over a span of five chapters that follow, this work attempts to make a comparative study of emergency powers as they have been provided for and practiced in these three countries. There are domestic, and cross-jurisdictional lessons in the use and abuse of these exceptional powers that emerge from this study. They deserve closer inspection across the globe. We hope that this study will be found useful by judges and politicians, lawyers, and law professors alike. Law students at an advanced stage of the study will also find this work helpful. Though every effort has been made to ensure there are no errors, if the reader locates any, they remain entirely ours. The case law cited in this work is current till 2019.

A word of thanks for those without whom this work would not have been possible. The first, of course, is to the lead author of this work, Dr. Abhishek M. Singhvi, Sr. Adv., without whose original work this work itself would not have been possible. Throughout the preparation of this work he took time out of his extremely tight professional and public schedule, and our meetings and readings on several occasions went for hours on a stretch. A huge thanks to Vice-Chancellor Prof. (Dr.) C. Raj Kumar, Founding Vice-Chancellor, O.P. Jindal Global University (JGU), who invited me to be a part of this project. From the very first day, Raj put the full weight of the resources of JGU behind this project, and constantly provided moral support and encouragement. This project faced a lot of challenges but the lack of resources was never a part of those. A special thanks to my research assistant Raunaq Jaiswal for outstanding, painstaking, and unfailing research assistance, without which this project would have taken much more time. Throughout this project, my own ability to work efficiently was very often the result of Raunaq burning the midnight oil.

A huge thanks is also due to my wife Shelja who provided constant support, encouragement, and care that allowed me to focus on finishing this work in time. Thanks also to my father, Mr. Prithvi Nath Gautam, Adv., who understood the importance of this work from the very beginning, and provided constant guidance and encouragement throughout the preparation of this manuscript. I am also grateful to my mother, Mrs. Meera Gautam. If I am able to read and write, and constantly engage with complicated ideas, it is only because she inculcated these habits of mind in me from a very young age.

A huge vote of thanks is also due to all my students in my elective "Advanced Constitutional Law: Emergency Powers." Rigorous class discussions during this course allowed me to develop and test some ideas in this book.

And lastly, I am grateful to Prof. NAP, whose life is a constant source of guidance and encouragement for me, and to whom I would like to dedicate this work.

Sonipat (Haryana) Khagesh Gautam
March 17, 2020

Endorsements

"Two particular challenges have faced those who, in the course of millennia, have sought to organise the good life in society. A human society is constructed on the basis of its collective consciousness but also on the basis of a constantly evolving legal system. Who is to have the last word on the interpretation and application of the law? How can a legal system respond to events that may challenge its very existence? In conventional modern discourse, these have come to be called the problem of the independence of the judiciary and the problem of emergency powers. It may be that these two problems have never before been present as acutely and as widely as they are in our present troubled world. It is a rare thing to be able to respond to them with high scholarship and historical erudition, but also with a lively sense of the profound practical consequences of the answers that you offer. This book could not be needed more, or more urgently, than it is at the present time."

- ***Professor Philip Allott***, *Professor Emeritus of International Public Law, Cambridge University, UK; Fellow, British Academy*

"This work by Dr. Abhishek Manu Sanghvi and Professor Khagesh Gautam, inspired and supported every way by Vice Chancellor Professor C. Raj Kumar, offers a provocative treatise on emergency powers in the Constitution of India. It bristles with comprehensive historical narratives and contemporary insights and helps us better understand the location and the vocation of authoritarian power to sustain as well as destroy the letter and the spirit of a living constitutionalism. The analysis at every phase is analytically cogent and juristically conscientious. The treatise also shows how the power of analysis can deflate varied forms of populist authoritarianism.

There is no doubt that this only full-length treatise on Indian emergency power and process will be hailed and held as a contemporary classic on constitutionalism."

- ***Professor (Dr). Upendra Baxi***, *Professor of Law, Jindal Global Law School, O.P. Jindal Global University, Sonipat, India; Emeritus Professor of Law, University of Warwick, Coventry, U.K.; Former Vice Chancellor, University of Delhi, India*

"In the 'Law of Emergency Powers', Dr. Abhishek Manu Singhvi and Professor Khagesh Gautam, provide a timely and rigorous comparative analysis of emergency law in India, the United States, and the United Kingdom. In response to COVID-19, governments around the world have used their powers to declare emergency and abrogate civil liberties and human rights. This book engages with important questions that will be asked for many decades after the pandemic ends—when is it appropriate for governments to utilize their emergency powers, how can we determine if the government has overstepped its powers, and who determines when the extraordinary circumstances have changed? Anyone who cares about these questions should read this book."

- ***Professor Sital Kalantry***, *Clinical Professor of Law & Faculty Director, Cornell India Law Center, Cornell Law School, USA*

"This work provides the first comprehensive analysis, supported by rigorous research and intellectual discipline,of concepts in emergency law that have not been addressed in this manner before in India. Many questions, heretofore unanswered and urgently needing an answer, have been addressed and in my opinion have been laid to rest in this work of unparalleled scholarship."

- ***Justice R.C. Lahoti***, *former Chief Justice of India*

"Emergency provisions in any democratic constitution is antithesis to constitutionally guaranteed rights and institutional checks and balances but they are necessary in times of extraordinary urgent situations and public emergencies. The problem arises when emergency provisions are used not as a reasonable response to genuine emergencies but to concentrate power in the hands of an individual. The edifice of this book—The Law of Emergency Powers—rests on the work prepared as PhD thesis by Dr. Abhishek Manu Singhvi few decades back. The most interesting aspect of this book is that a comparative study of Emergency Powers has been carried out of three democracies, one of which has no written constitution (U.K.), the other mentions Emergency Provisions in Part XVIII of the world's longest constitution (India). The discussion on the topics such as 'Can Martial Law be Proclaimed Under Article 34' and 'President's Rule: A Sui Generis Emergency Power' is thought provoking. Everyone serious about the emergency provisions prevalent in India and U.S.A—the two biggest democracies in the world—and U.K. needs to read this book."

- ***Justice R.M. Lodha***, *Former Chief Justice of India*

"In 2020, the comparative law of emergency powers in India, the U.S. and the U.K. conjures thoughts of the crackdown in Kashmir, enhanced interrogations in Guantánamo, and police arrests under the Emergency Coronavirus Bill. This book is not about those burning issues of the day. It is rather a brilliantly written and deeply scholarly legal history of the doctrine of emergency powers, starting with ancient India and Greece and focusing on judicial independence and preservation of legislative powers in the three countries, drawing primarily on events up to the mid-1980s, when the work was first drafted as Dr. Singhvi's Ph.D. thesis at Cambridge University. He and his co-author, Prof. Gautam have provided essential reading for anyone interested in emergency powers in common law jurisdictions. Hopefully a subsequent volume will address the international law and contemporary dimensions of this critical issue of law and governance."

- ***Professor (Dr.) Stephen P. Marks***, *François-Xavier Bagnoud Professor of Health and Human Rights, Harvard University, Cambridge, U.S.A.; Member, Committee on Human Rights in Times of Emergency, International Law Association*

"Singhvi and Gautam provide an indispensable service with the publication of this book. The first of its kind, 'The Law of Emergency Powers' presents a foundational analysis of a critical topic for any country's legal system. However, the authors' comparison of the British, Indian and American common law systems' approach to emergency powers is a triumph both in deep legal investigation of each country's particular approach, as well as broad description of important common challenges these regimes and many others face. The authors further situate this analysis in the context of international humanitarian law, and thereby help draw lessons from these 2 common law systems that all countries should learn."

- ***Professor (Dr.) Nathaniel Persily***, *James B. McClatchy Professor of Law, Stanford Law School, Stanford University, USA*

"'Amidst the Clash of Arms Laws are Silent' despite Lord Atkin's exhortation to the contrary. Emergency powers of the state are just another attribute of sovereignty. In this brilliant work 'Law of Emergency Powers', Dr. Abhishek Manu Singhvi who commands a large practice in Constitutional and Public Law litigation in India and his scholarly co-author Khagesh Gautam dig into the depths of 'Constitution's Dark-Matter' to trace emergency powers and the legal limits of the concept. Courts have defined the over lapping boundaries of Law and Order, Public Order and Security of states. In search of the legal limits of the State's authority. English Common Law grew in 'rugged isolation' from the systems across the British channel, greatly influenced the Liberal American Constitutional tradition. The way the other jurisdiction, including India, dealt with the issue is equally fascinating. This work examines and lights up larger issues which have democratic and civilisational implications. Great reading."

- ***Justice M.N. Venkatachaliah***, *Former Chief Justice of India*

"In this timely and important book, Abhishek Singhvi and Khagesh Gautam trace the history and contemporary uses of one of the most consequential—and controversial—actions that can be taken by any government: to declare a state of emergency. With all of the analytical rigor and theoretical sophistication that one would expect from a book written by one of India's leading advocates and an equally distinguished scholar, the authors catalogue and dissect the justifications that have been offered for this extraordinary suspension of the normal rules of governance from ancient Greece to the Indian Constitution. At a time in which governments of all stripes are increasingly resorting to "emergency" measures to combat everything from terrorism, to mass migration, to global pandemics, this thoughtful and balanced assessment should be required reading by all those who care about the future of democracy."

- ***Professor David B. Wilkins***, *Lester Kissel Professor of Law, Vice Dean for Global Initiatives on the Legal Profession & Faculty Director of the Center on the Legal Profession, Harvard Law School, Harvard University, USA*

Contents

About the Authors

Abhishek Singhvi is an eminent jurist, senior third-term parliamentarian, visible media personality, well-known columnist, author, thinker and commentator. He was the youngest designated Senior Advocate, Supreme Court of India (at age 34); the youngest Additional Solicitor General of India (at 37); and is a former elected Vice President, Supreme Court Bar Association (at 39). He is a former Chairman of the Parliamentary Committee of Law, one of the seniormost national spokespersons of the Congress Party & former Chairman of the AICC Law and Human Rights Department. He has been a member of the Indian Supreme Court, where he created and administered bilateral legal forums, including the Indo-British, Indo-US, Indo-Canadian and Indo-Israel forums. After obtaining his B.A. (Economics) degree from St. Stephen's College, New Delhi, Dr. Singhvi went on to complete his Masters and PhD at Trinity College, Cambridge, UK. He also taught at St. John's College, Cambridge, and joined a brief summer program at Harvard, USA. He has lectured to student/faculty groups and general audiences at Stanford, Harvard, Yale, Boston, MIT and George Washington Universities, as well as NGOs and think-tanks. He was a visiting Trumbull Lecturer at Yale University, USA, in 2011 and is currently an Honorary Adjunct Professor at O.P. Jindal Global University.

Khagesh Gautam is an Associate Professor of Law at Jindal Global Law School, O.P. Jindal Global University, Sonipat, India. He received his LL.M. from Columbia Law School, where he graduated as a Stone Scholar. He teaches core courses on Constitutional Law and Evidence and elective courses on Comparative Constitutional Law and Forensic Evidence. He has also taught at the China University of Political Science and Law, Changping, Beijing, and at William S. Richardson School of Law, University of Hawaii, USA. He is also a member of the Editorial Board of the *Africa Journal of Comparative Constitutional Law*. His work has been published in e.g. *the Columbia Journal of Asian Law*, *Indiana International and Comparative Law Review*, *Southwestern Journal of International Law*, *Boston University International Law Journal*, *Vienna Journal on International Constitutional Law*, *Journal of Comparative Law*, *International Tax Journal*, and *Economic and Political Weekly*.

Table of Cases

Chapter 1
The Concept of Emergency Powers in History and Political Thought: Greek, Roman and Indian Paradigms

1 Ideas Underlying the Concept of Emergency Powers

The phrase "emergency powers" or "state of emergency" is used in the sense of a "suspension of or departure from legal normality in response to a political, economic or social crisis."[1] "Being a crisis situation affecting the population as a whole and constituting a threat to the organized existence of the community which forms the basis of the State,"[2] a state of emergency involves a temporary suspension of ordinary law and its substitution by a set of extraordinary legal rules, which may collectively be grouped under the general rubric of "states of exception."

A number of overlapping philosophical, political, and legal ideas underline the concept of emergency powers. Chief among them is the idea that the preservation of the State is of overriding and fundamental importance. The view that a temporary departure from the values and ethos of a social and legal system is justified, if done to ensure its survival in future, was pithily expressed by Lincoln:

> By general law, life and limb must be protected, yet often a limb must be amputated to save a life; but life is never wisely given to a save a limb.[3]

---

[1]*See* O'Donnell [1].

[2]Questiaux [2]. For a different approach in the American context, *see* Miller [3] who defines emergencies as "not only the conditions suggested above—those of an urgent nature—but also perceptions by political (and group) officers of actions necessary for the well-being of the entity (that means the well-being of the state broadly defined)." Later, he refers to emergencies as "that set of conditions perceived by political officers, frequently the executive acting alone but often in concert, actual or tacit, with the Congress to require actions which under basic constitutional theory are extraordinary, even extra-constitutional," *id.* at 48. *See also* Jenkins [4] (reviewing Miller's book).

[3]Nicolay and Hay [5] (writing particularly of the power to emancipate).

A. Singhvi and K. Gautam, *The Law of Emergency Powers*,
https://doi.org/10.1007/978-981-15-2997-9_1

His emphasis on the preservation of the State is age-old. Aristotle cautioned against complacency upon the establishment of a democracy for "a far greater difficulty is the preservation of it."[4] Machiavelli classified republics as "good" on the basis of their longevity[5] and justified actions contrary to charity, humanity and religion on grounds of preservation of the State and the ruler.[6] Marsilius of Padua thought that "The destruction of the city or state…[is the] consequence most to be avoided."[7] Hobbes emphasized that the institution of the Commonwealth is in vain if its members have not "the purpose or the courage to preserve" it.[8] John Locke asserted that "the end and measure of …power …[is] the preservation of all … society."[9] Rousseau emphasized that "the primary intention of the people is that the state should not perish."[10] Spinoza opined that "the chief good is the preservation of the State."[11] Implied in the goal of the preservation of the state is the idealization of the State as the key source of life and spirit and as the end and rationale of human activity. Closely akin is the view of the monarch or the State as the *parens patriae* of the people, in return for whose protection the people enter into the social contract

---

[4]Aristotle, Politics 196 (Benjamin Jowett trans., Oxford Univ. Press 1885). In book 6, Aristotle notes—

> The mere establishment of a democracy is not the only or principal business of the legislator, or of those who wish to create such a state, for any state, however badly constituted, may last one, two, or three days; a far greater difficulty is the preservation of it. The legislator should therefore endeavour to have a firm foundation according to the principles already laid down concerning the preservation and destruction of states; he should guard against the destructive elements, and should make laws, whether written or unwritten, which will contain all the preservatives of states. He must not think the truly democratical or oligarchical measure to be that which will give the greatest amount of democracy or oligarchy, but that which will make them last longest.

[5]Machiavelli [6, pp. 19–22].

[6]Machiavelli [7].

[7]Gewrith [8].

[8]Hobbes [9].

[9]Locke [10, p. 80]. In Chap. XIV of his treatise, on prerogative powers, Locke observes—

> Nay, it is fit that the laws themselves should in some cases give way to the executive power, or rather to this fundamental law of nature and government, viz., that as much as may be all the members of the society are to be preserved.

[10]Rousseau [11, p. 109].

[11]Spinoza [12].

and pay taxes and other exactions.[12] Similarly, the view of governance as a (sacred) trust emphasizes the duty of the trustee to protect and preserve the State to the best of his ability. On the other hand, the public good inherent in emergency action is emphasized by those who view it as "the power to act according to discretion for the public good, without the prescription of law and sometimes even against it."[13] Another view expounds the doctrine of necessity as the overriding and most sacrosanct principle during the times of adversity. Loosely encapsulated in epigrams like "necessity knows no law"[14] and "no law can abandon man from his own preservation,"[15] the idea is a legal recognition of the harshness of reality and an affirmation of the principle of pragmatism. Cicero expressed the view that the "laws are silent amidst the clash of arms."[16] As John Stuart Mill said:

> I am far from condemning in cases of extreme exigency, the assumption of absolute power in form of a temporary dictatorship.[17]

Indian references to "appadharam kale" (the law of crises) in the world's longest epic *Mahabharata* and Kautilya's *Arthasastra* which recognizes extraordinary steps in extraordinary times (both dealt with hereinbelow), predate and mirror the same sentiments and similar legal doctrines.

Finally, the idea of a regulatory constitutional prescription for emergency situations and the dangers inherent in the inflexibility of a republican legal order which is driven to resort to extra-constitutional measures in the absence of such constitutional prescription was formulated by Machiavelli:

> And when a Republic lacks some such systems, a strict observance of the established laws will expose her to ruin; or to save her from such danger, the laws will have to be disregarded. Now, in a well-ordered republic it should never be necessary to resort to extra-constitutional measures; for although they may for the time be beneficial, yet the precedent is pernicious, for if the practice is once established of disregarding the laws for the good objects, they will, in a little while, be disregarded under that pretext for evil purposes. Thus no Republic will ever be perfect if she has not by law provided for everything, having a remedy for every emergency, and fixed rules for applying it. And therefore I will say, in conclusion, that those republics which in time of danger cannot resort to a dictatorship, or some similar authority, will generally be ruined when grave occasions occur.[18]

---

[12]Hobbes [13, p. 163]. *See also* Calvin's Case (1608) 1 St. Tr. 659, where Coke, C.J., states that allegiance and protection are two sides of the same coin.

[13]Locke [10, p. 80].

[14]Hobbes [13, p. 239].

[15]Hobbes [13, p. 232].

[16]Cicero [14] (*circa* 52 B.C.).

[17]Mill [15]. *See* essay titled *Considerations on Representative Government id.* at 371.

[18]Machiavelli [16, p. 203].

In a similar vein, Locke and Rousseau warned against the inflexibility of laws and stressed the need for latitude to the executive power because human foresight has its limitations.[19] Let us now turn to a brief examination of the embryonic idea of emergency powers in the Greek period, the more fully developed concept of emergency powers in Roman times, and the even more philosophical approach to the subject in ancient India.

2 The Greek Period

The emergencies affecting the Greek State varied from war, rebellion, revolution and public disorder to natural calamities. Plato and Aristotle both reflect on the causes underlying revolutions[20] and emphasize the paramount importance of the preservation of the State.[21] Around the seventh century B.C., after the fall of the Greek kingship, the various governing institutions and offices of Athens (a major Greek city-state) included the Council of Areopagus and the offices of Archon and Polemarch.[22] The Council "was the hub and center of the Constitution," controlling the administration of state affairs, safeguarding the Constitution and the laws, inflicting penalties without the right of appeal, transferring fines to the state treasury and acting as final court for many religious matters.[23] The Archon was the civil magistrate who also exercised judicial powers over many civil matters. The Polemarch was the military magistrate. These three bodies exercised various functions during an emergency situation. In his "Constitution of Athens," Aristotle states that

---

[19]Locke [10, pp. 80–81].

> …[A]nd because also it is impossible to foresee, and so by laws to provide for all accidents and necessities that may concern the public, or make such laws as will do no harm if they are executed with an inflexible rigour on all occasions and upon all persons…therefore there is a latitude left to the executive power to do many things of choice which the laws do not prescribe.

See also, Rousseau [11, p. 108]

> The inflexibility of the laws, which prevents them from being adapted to emergencies, may in certain cases render them pernicious, and thereby cause the ruin of the State in a time of crisis…A thousand cases may arise for which the legislation has not provided and to perceive that everything cannot be foreseen is a needful kind of foresight.

[20]ARISTOTLE, POLITICS 190, 195, 198 (Jowett trans., 1985); 1 DIALOGUES OF PLATO 325 (Jowett trans., Oxford University Press, 1871) (*circa* 387 B.C.).

[21]ARISTOTLE, POLITICS 246–47 (Jowett trans., 1985); 1 DIALOGUES OF PLATO 421–24 (Jowett trans., Oxford University Press, 1871) (*circa* 387 B.C.).

[22]*See generally*, for Greek history of that period, Bury [17], Hammond [18], Powler [19].

[23]Hammond [18].

the office of Polemarch, a supreme military magistrate, was "added because some of the kings turned out unfit for war"; this by the way is why Ion (presumably an early Polemarch) was sent for, in an emergency.[24] There appears to be a parallel between this office of Polemarch and that of the Roman dictator, both of whom were entrusted with a particular role for the preservation of the State in emergency situations. Similarly, the Council of Areopagus earned high repute for taking certain measures during the Battle of Salamis when the generals did not know how to deal with an emergency and made a public proclamation that everyone should care for his own safety.[25] Aristotle also mentions the emergency committee of ten or the "committee of the Probuli," consisting, according to Thucydides, of ten elder statesmen who, immediately after the news of disaster in Sicily reached Athens (in 413 B.C.) and were elected to prepare measures to meet the emergency.[26] Aristotle's descriptions of these measures are illustrative of the effects of an emergency:

> After this, they established the following principles for the new political order: that the public revenue was to be used only for the war; that the public officials, with the exception of the nine Archons and the Prytanes in office, should serve without pay for the duration of the war; that these officials should each receive three obols a day; that, for the rest of the administration, the whole state should be entrusted, until the end of the war, to those of the Athenians who were most capable of serving the state with their persons and their property, to the number of not less than five thousand. These men should also be empowered to conclude treaties with whomever they wished.[27]

The Greek institutions and procedures relating to emergency situations did not, however, reach the proportions of a system. That conceptual development emerged in the case of Roman dictatorship.

3 The Roman Dictatorship

The Roman dictatorship is undoubtedly the most outstanding example of normative order to contain the concept of emergency powers. It illustrates in a remarkable manner how conventional restraints were markedly effective in achieving a transient and temporary deviation from the established legal order, formally and consciously made, solely to meet a genuine crisis, reverting to normality as soon as the necessity for its existence subsided, and avoiding its institutionalization.

In 501 B.C., during the war, the consuls, who were the annually elected chief magistrates, elected a *magister populi* with royal title and powers,[28] who afterwards

[24] Aristotle, Constitution of Athens 70 (K.V. Fritz and E. Kapp trans., 1950).

[25] *Id.* at 93.

[26] *Id.* at 100, 173–74.

[27] *Id.* at 101.

[28] Greenidge [20, p. 84]. Rossiter [21, p. 16], quoting Cicero, suggests that this first dictator was a certain T. Larcius Flaccus, appointed about ten years after the establishment of the first consuls.

came to be called dictator.[29] He was to remain in power only as long as the danger lasted; as the danger was originally military, a single campaign of six months was held to be the maximum duration of the office.[30] During this time, the dictator was to exercise the full *regal imperium* and the accompanying military jurisdiction without appeal. The office of dictator never fully lost its original military character but it was part of the republican constitution rather than a suspension of it.[31] As Greenidge puts it:

> A small, struggling, and essentially military society, such as that of early Rome, contemplated martial law as an occasional necessity; there were times when the peril of the state was so great that it was felt that the citizens' ordinary guarantees of protection should sink into abeyance if they were thought likely to interfere with the safety of the commonwealth. The dictatorship had an internal as well as external side to its military character; it was even, perhaps, on its earliest institution, meant to control disobedient citizens as well as to oppose the enemy …Its true merit was the unity of administration which it created …The dictatorship was an integral part of the original republican constitution …the right of the consul to declare martial law, as he did by appointing dictator, was never questioned …But the appointment of dictator was supposed to be due to exceptional circumstances.[32]

3.1 Appointment of Dictators

The power to appoint a dictator appears to have been vested in the Senate or in the consuls.[33] Rossiter's view is that while the Senate could initiate a proposal for the appointment of a dictator, the consuls could also propose the same, but the approval of the Senate was necessary.[34] The dictator appointed to meet an emergency of war or revolution bore no special designation referring to the emergency, but was

---

[29]*See* Mommsen [22] (arguing that the original title was probably "praetor" but that "dictator" was later adopted in deference to republican sentiment. One of the many meanings of the word is he who issues edicts.).

[30]Greenidge [20, p. 84].

[31]*Id. See also*, Mommsen [22].

[32]Greenidge [20, pp. 84–85].

[33]However, Montesquieu and Machiavelli differed on the issue as to who had the power to appoint a dictator. *See* Montesquieu [23] (noting that the Senate created a dictator). *Cf.* Machiavelli [16, pp. 203–04] (observing that the consuls primarily had this power).

[34]Rossiter [21, p. 20]. He also appoints out that the power of appointment resided constitutionally in the two consuls, who might act jointly, in consultation with the praetor or separately, in which case the Consuls who made the appointment were chosen by lot.

described as a dictator *rei gerundae causa*, i.e., for carrying on the business of the State.[35]

Various natural causes, including "large scale emigrations…floods and epidemics,"[36] were common causes for the appointment of the Roman dictator. Nor were emergencies lightly proclaimed. Adjectives signifying a high degree of deviation from normality were used to qualify situations requiring emergency treatment. Thus wars had to be "grievous,"[37] and civil unrest "serious"[38]; danger had to be grave and "pressing."[39] Rousseau conveyed the same idea when he spoke of a nation "inflamed by civil war" amidst "epochs of violence."[40] It is a tribute to the statesmanship and self-restraint of the Romans that in the absence of formal safeguards like judicial review or a written constitution containing criteria for the declaration or existence of an emergency, "never in the three hundred years of the office was this unshackled display of power used to subvert the constitutional order."[41] Fraudulent declarations of emergency on imaginary and specious grounds to institutionalize tyranny appear to be a gift of modern times.

---

[35]Greenidge [20, p. 192]. However, it is interesting to note that the various trivial needs and tasks of peacetime also led to the appointment of a bewildering variety of dictators; thus there were dictators appointed for holding elections, for making out the list of the Senate, for celebrations of games, for the ordering of festivals and for the ritual of driving the nail into the temple of Jupiter. (*Id.* at 193) As a writer on the subject puts it:

> In each of these instances, an unusual act of state to which no official was considered competent or for which the regular official was temporarily incapacitated demanded performance…(and) the dictatorship was chosen to fill the breach.

See Rossiter [21, p. 23].

[36]Saint Augustine of Hippo, The City of God 118–19 (Marcus Dods ed. and trans.1948) (*circa* 426 A.D.).

[37]Rossiter [21, p. 19].

[38]*Id.*

[39]*See* Machiavelli [16, pp. 202–03]. *See also* Rousseau [11, pp. 110–11] (commenting on the Roman dictatorship, Rousseau opined that "only the greatest danger can outweigh that of changing the public order and the sacred power of the laws should never be interfered with except when the safety of the country is at stake.").

[40]*Id.*

[41]Rossiter [21, p. 24]. However, Machiavelli refers to the case of Manlius Capitolinus who was angry at the honors bestowed upon Furius Camillus and alleged nepotism and maladministration. "These statements produced a great impression among the people …This greatly displeased the Senate, who, deeming the occasion momentous and perilous, created a dictator who should take cognizance of the facts and repress the audacity of Manlius." *See* Machiavelli [16, p. 135]. ("In proportion as accusations are useful in the Republic, so are calumnies pernicious."). The dictator summoned Capitolinus to a public peace, asked for details of the alleged misappropriation, and upon getting an inadequate and evasive reply "had him incarcerated." *Id.*

3.2 Limitations of Time

Perhaps no other political or legal system in the world has ever applied limitations of time on emergency under regimes so successfully as the Roman system. Roman dictators laid down their offices and their awesome and limitless powers with almost clockwork precision after the lapse of a fixed period of time without any of the prevarication or brute force often used by many present-day emergency regimes to perpetuate themselves. The basic precondition of successful emergency government —temporary nature, brevity of duration—insisted upon by all present-day scholars of constitutionalism[42] was fulfilled almost to perfection in ancient Rome. There is the legend of Cincinnatus, the aged Roman farmer called from the plough by his embattled countrymen and given despotic authority to repel the threat of alien tyranny who laid down the sword after sixteen days of absolute power and went back to the plough.[43] Nor did Saint Augustine exaggerate in suggesting that the dictator Hortensius' prolonged stay and death in office after having met the emergency was "an event without precedent in the case of any dictator."[44] The fact that "dictators were appointed only for a limited term, and not in perpetuity, and their power to act was confined to the particular occasion for which they were created"[45] was the primary and substantive limitation on their enormous and otherwise unfettered powers. Rousseau underlined the brevity of the emergency office as the cause of its success and the reason for the absence of abuse:

> …[I]n whatever way this important commission may be conferred, it is important to fix its duration at a very short term which can never be prolonged. In the crisis which cause it to be established, the state is soon destroyed or saved; and the urgent need having passed away, the dictatorship becomes tyrannical or useless. In Rome, the dictators held office for six months only, and the majority abdicated before the end of this term. Had the term been longer they would perhaps have been tempted to prolong it still further, as the Decemvirs did their term of one year. The dictator only had time to provide for the necessity which had led to his election; he had no time to think of other projects.[46]

Various reasons have been put forward to explain this inviolable and sacrosanct convention. It has been suggested that the six-month term was chosen as the Romans fought only in summer. Montesquieu, however, supplied another more political rationale. Comparing the administration of emergency or the "magistrates invested with extraordinary power" in Rome, and in Venice respectively, he says:

> But how comes it that these magistracies are so very different in these two republics? It is because Rome supported the remains of her aristocracy against the people; whereas Venice

[42] *See* Watkins [24] ("…no reason why absolutism should not be used as a means for the defence of liberal institutions if it be of temporary character involving prompt return to normalcy."); Mill [25]. *See also*, McIlwain [26], Friedrich et al. [27], Friedrich [28].

[43] Rossiter [21, p. 26].

[44] Saint Augustine of Hippo, The City of God 68 (Marcus Dods ed. and trans. 1948) (*circa* 426 A.D.).

[45] Machiavelli [16, p. 202].

[46] Rousseau [11, pp. 110–11].

> employs her state inquisitors to maintain her aristocracy against the nobles. The consequence was, that at Rome the dictatorship could be only of a short duration, as the people acted through passion, and not with design. It was necessary that a magistracy of this kind should be exercised with lustre and pomp; the business being to intimidate, and not to punish, the multitude. It was also proper that the dictator should be created only for some particular affair, and for this only should have an unlimited authority, as he was always created upon some sudden emergency. On the contrary, at Venice they have occasion for a permanent magistracy; for here it is that schemes may be set on foot, continued, suspended and resumed; that the ambition of a single person becomes that of a family, and the ambition of one family that of many... In a word, the latter is designed to punish suspected crimes; whereas the former used rather menaces than punishment even for crimes that were openly avowed.[47]

Although the duration of the dictatorship was usually limited to six months, or, occasionally, a year, shorter periods were not wholly unknown. As Montesquieu says:

> In all magistracies, the greatness of the power must be compensated by the brevity of the duration. This most legislators have fixed to a year: a longer space would be dangerous, and a shorter would be contrary to the nature of government; for who is it that, in the management even of his domestic affairs, would be thus confined? At Ragusa the chief magistrate of the republic is changed every month, the other officers every week, and the governor of the castle every day. But this can take place only in small republic environed by formidable powers ...[48]

Whatever be the duration conventionally prescribed, the dictator's "greatest glory consisted in promptly laying this dignity down again."[49] Indeed, it has been pointed out that were the dictator to attempt to violate this rule—an event of the rarest frequency—the tribunes could force him to resign if the emergency had clearly terminated, and if he failed to do so, could prosecute him for having illegally prolonged this tenure of office.[50]

3.3 *Non-derogable Areas*

Modern emergency law recognizes certain non-derogable and inalienable rights as a limitation upon wide-ranging emergency powers. This, however, is not a latter day invention. The Roman dictator, in spite of his awesome powers, was similarly circumscribed, inter alia, by two non-derogable and inviolable conventions. He could not alter the basic form of government and he could not make laws. The former limitation was premised upon the view that the "sacred trust" of the dictator was to maintain the constitutional order, and although to this end he was competent to resort to any measure, the republic which he was chosen to defend could not be altered or subverted. Machiavelli put it succinctly when he said:

---

[47]Montesquieu [23].

[48]*Id.*

[49]Machiavelli [16, p. 195].

[50]Rossiter [21, pp. 23–24]. He gives the example of L. Manlius Imperiosus who, when called up in 363 B.C. *clavi figendi causa* (for "driving in the nail"), regarded his selection as due to military rather than religious reasons and assumed the role of a full-fledged dictator, but in the face of the unanimous opposition of the tribunes was forced to resign from his office.

> But the dictator could do nothing to alter the form of the government, such as to diminish the powers of the Senate or the people. Or to abrogate existing institutions and create new ones.[51]

It is interesting to note the parallel between some sophisticated modern constitutional law theories and the Roman view on the inviolability of the basic structure of the Constitution.[52] It is also doubtful whether the large-scale amendments made *en masse* by modern governments during so-called emergencies, fundamentally altering the constitutional polity of the nation, would have been permitted more than two thousand years ago. The other limitation—the prohibition against making laws—is mentioned by Rousseau when he says:

> In this way the suspension of the legislative power does not involve its abolition; the magistrate who silences it can make it speak; he dominates it without having power to represent it; *he can do everything but make law*.[53]

It is certain that this limitation, expressed by Rousseau in such sweeping terms, did not preclude the dictator from ruling as the executive head, through decrees and appropriate orders, and with the power to disregard existing laws. What he was deprived of was formal legislative power, exercised as such by the legislature. This denial was no more than what it is commonplace in modern constitutions.

3.4 Other Limitations

Emergency administrators in earlier times functioned under the general limitation that they could exercise their powers only for the public good and not for private purposes or irrelevant considerations. This flowed from the view of all power as a trust. At the time when emergency powers were conceived as part of prerogative power, Locke expressed this inherent limitation thus:

> This power to act according to discretion, for the public good, without the prescription of law, and sometimes even against it, is that which is called prerogative ... This power, whilst employed for the benefit of the community, and suitably to the trusts and ends of government, is undoubtedly prerogative, and never is questioned: for the people are very seldom or never scrupulous or nice in the point; they are far from examining prerogative, whilst it is in any tolerable degree employed for the use it was meant, that is, for the good of the people, and not manifestly against it ... for in so doing, they have not pulled from the prince any thing that of

---

[51] Machiavelli [16, p. 202].

[52] The theory of the "basic structure of the Constitution" enunciated by the Indian Supreme Court in Kesavananda Bharati v. State of Kerala, AIR 1973 SC 1461 states that while the amending power of the Parliament in its constituent capacity is wide and untrammeled and subject only to article 368 of the Indian Constitution, Parliament cannot, in the exercise of its amending powers, alter the basic structure of the Indian Constitution. Minerva Mills v. Union of India, AIR 1980 SC 1789 extended the doctrine by making judicial review an integral part of the basic structure. This has never been fully defined, although some elements of it like republican democratic nation and free and fair elections have been enumerated. *See*, Seervai [29], Palkhivala [30], Basu [31].

[53] Rousseau [11, p. 109].

> right belonged to him, but only declared, that power which they indefinitely left in his or his ancestors hands, to be exercised for their good, was not a thing which they intended him when he used it otherwise.[54]

Machiavelli, similarly, said that the dictator could do no harm to the Republic.[55] The Roman dictator was further limited by his dependence on his creator in financial matters. This was because of the constitutional prohibition against withdrawals from the public treasury without Senatorial consent. He was not given the right to declare wars, which right was reserved by the Senate. Finally, he had no civil jurisdiction as a judge, being limited in his judicial powers to dealing with such criminal cases as might affect the safety of the State.[56]

3.5 Some Additional Effects of Use of Emergency Powers

To modify somewhat the words of a well-known writer on the Roman dictatorship, if collegiality was the distinctive mark of the normal state, unity was the distinctive mark of a state of exception.[57] Emergencies often arise due to divisiveness and a multiplicity of decision-making centers of power: they are met by the antidote of unitary decision making and a display of unity, solidarity and integration. This was the effect of the Roman dictatorship, which, through its one man (dictatorship) executive risked absolutism. Moreover, parallel to the increasing centralization resulting from an emergency is the vast increase in executive power and discretion. The logical origin of the Roman dictatorship is attributed, inter alia, to the multiplicity of its executive authorities, which led to atrophy of decision makers. The strong executive was almost as alien to normal Roman government as a unitary executive: the absence of the latter accounted for the absence of the former and vice versa. It was therefore not surprising that the dictator as replacement possessed full and wide executive powers. He was not fettered by the "tribunician veto, the appeal from his sentence to the people, the responsibility after leaving office for his acts and particularly the presence of a collegial official."[58] Machiavelli outlined the dictator's executive and judicial powers thus:

> [Their] powers consisted in being able to decide alone upon the measures to be adopted for averting the pressing danger, to do whatever he deemed proper without consultation, and to inflict punishment upon anyone without appeal.[59]

54Locke [10, pp. 80–81].

55Machiavelli [16, p. 202].

56Rossiter [21, p. 24].

57*Id.* at 20.

58*Id.* at 24.

59Machiavelli [16, p. 202]. According to Rousseau, he could never "silence all the laws and suspend for a moment the sovereign authority." Further, said Rousseau, the dictator could not be called to account or be reproached for what he had done, as could, for instance, be Cicero, who was a consul.

3.6 *The Decline of the Dictatorship*

The beginning of the end of the dictatorship commenced with the weakening of its powers, the emergence of a multiplicity of power centers and in some cases, the ineptitude of those who called upon to fill the office. Around 300 B.C., the right of appeal from the dictator's sentence came to be accepted and sometime later, the power of the tribune to impose its veto was also accepted.[60] Around the time of Hannibalic War, two further weakening elements were introduced into the office of the dictatorship, viz., popular election and colleagueship.[61] In the year 217 B.C., when the consul Fabius Maximus was elected dictator, the distrust and misplaced confidence of the people raised M. Minucius, the Master of the Horse, to an equality of command with Fabius. It is opined that "both acts were the signs that the office was felt to be an anachronism, and the next year (216 B.C.) marks the last instance of the military dictatorship,"[62] although a dictator to conduct elections was appointed in 202 B.C. Thus ended "the most unique and successful constitutional emergency institution in all recorded history."[63]

4 Ancient and Medieval India[64]

Often, the supremacy of the king was considered synonymous with the supremacy of the State, partly because of an "almost pathological fear of anarchy"[65] which characterizes the ancient Indian literature in the composite field of political science, statecraft, public administration, and diplomacy. A king was created or appointed "to hold the State" and was expected to remain firm without faltering.[66] Kautilya

---

[60] Rossiter [21, p. 26], Greenidge [20, p. 194].

[61] Greenidge [20, p. 194].

[62] *Id.* at 195.

[63] Rossiter [21, p. 28].

[64] For further discussion under this heading *see infra* Chap. 5, part I.

[65] Compared by many to Machiavelli and by others to Aristotle and Plato, Kautilya is alternately praised for his sound political wisdom and knowledge of human nature and condemned for his ruthlessness and trickery. All, however, agree that it was because of Kautilya that the Mauryan Empire under Chandragupta (reign c. 321 B.C. to 297 B.C.), to whom Kautilya was advisor and counselor, became a model of efficient government. The best translation of Kautilya's book is to be found in the book by Shamasastry, who discovered the lost treatise.

[66] Spellman [32]

> The fear of anarchy was almost pathological. Underlying every concept of kingship was the doctrine of Matsya Nyaya, the analogy of the big fish eating up the little fish.

likened the king to the hub and axle of a wheel.[67] Republics were faulted and berated because of their lack of unity and strength and their inability to cope with situations of war, rebellion and natural calamities. The supremacy of the king was synonymous with the supremacy of the State.[68]

There was a strikingly Lockean-Hobbesian emphasis in India on the duty of protection as the supreme function of government and the payment of taxes as a "quid pro quo" for the discharge of this duty.[69] Finally, the doctrine of necessity, justifying normally unsupportable actions in times of adversity, finds repeated articulation in early Indian texts. As a writer on the *Mahabharata* says:

> When face to face with dire adversity, government could do anything. The justification of it all is that abnormal times have an ethics of their own, Apaddharma as it is called. It must be clearly understood, that in days of distress, all the ordinary rules of morality and custom are suspended...The whole chapter of Apaddharma reminds one of Machiavelli. There are sentences written with the point of a stiletto (sic). Which may pass for the Prince...The section as a whole may be styled... 'The circumstances under which it is right for a prince to be a scoundrel.' In both, the purpose is the same... the secular state, supreme self-interest

---

[67]Atharva Veda VI. 87–88. Also Rig Veda X. 173 (slightly codified).

> [R]emain firmly without faltering... be you firm like the mountain and may you not come down. Be you firm here like India; remain you here and hold the state... firm as the heaven, firm as the earth, firm as the universe, firm as the mountains, let this raja of the people be firm ... Vanquish you firmly, without failing, the enemies .... And for firmness the Assembly here creates (appoints) you.

See also Jayaswal [33, pp. 186–87], Prasad [34, p. 16]. The Vedas are the sacred hymns and oblational verses of Indo- European peoples on a pre-Sanskrit language and are widely regarded as the oldest literature in the history of mankind.

[68]Rao [35, pp. 165–66]. *See also* Hassan [36].

> The existence of the people, their happiness, the institutions of society and the rules of morality and religion depended upon the king's office. Hence there is no wonder that the king's importance is emphasized. He becomes supreme in his sphere.

[69]*See, inter alia,* Prasad [34, pp. 51–52] ("The ... idea of protection as embodying the supreme function of royalty or government runs through the whole of Indian political speculation"). *See also* Jayaswal [33, p. 321]

> The theory that taxes were wages to the king for protection was so ingrained in the constitution that even partial failure of protection was deemed to entitle the subject to claim refund of wages in proportion to loss.

The king has been described as "*preeminently the protector of this people...*"; i.e., "gopa-janasya" (Rig Veda III. 43) and as "Dharampravartaka." *See* Rao [35, p. 123]. *See also*, Pratap Chandra Ray, Mahabharata, Book XII Santi Parva, CXXXIX, 459 which states that according to Manu, one of the seven attributes of a king include "protection," the other six being "mother, father, preceptor, fire, vaicravana and Yama." It sanctions abandonment of a king who fails to protect, as a leaky ship is dangerous and ought to be abandoned. To the same effect is Hobbes. *See* Hobbes [13, pp. 169–70] (Leviathan, XXI).

> and self-regard, avowed as the single principle of state action…here is the salvation of states…[70]

The kinds of emergencies faced by early and medieval Indian rulers were of a pattern and included wars with neighbors and foreign powers, attacks on the life of the rulers[71]; subversion, sabotage, intrigues, conspiracies and rebellion by princes or army commanders or provincial governors and disturbances of the peace; and providential visitations, like "fire, floods, pestilential diseases, famine, rats, tigers, serpents and demons."[72] There are also references to a large-scale decline in probity, morality and righteousness[73] and "extreme, frightful… drought,"[74] "fire, floods, pestilential diseases" and "famine and hunger." These hotch-potch reasons illustrate the lack of fine distinctions and elaborate juristic formulations relating to

---

[70]Prasad [34, p. 16].

[71]2 Beveridge [37]. There is the example of Akbar who, in 1564, wanted the slave Fulad put to death immediately for firing an arrow at him.

[72]KAUTILYA, ARTHASASTRA, 294 (Rudrapatna Shamasastry ed., trans., 1915) (*circa* 300 B.C.).

[73]Yudhishtir uses graphic language in *Mahabharata* to describe seasons of distress:

> When high righteousness suffers decay and is transgressed by all, when unrighteousness assumes the form of its reverse; when all wholesome restraints disappear, and all truths in respect of righteousness are disturbed and confounded; when people are oppressed by kings and robbers, when men of all the four modes of life become stupefied in respect of their duties, and all acts lose their consequence of lust and covetousness and folly, when one another in their mutual dealings, when houses are burnt down throughout the country, when the Brahmanas become exceedingly afflicted, when the clouds do not pour a drop of rain, when every one's hand is turned against every one's neighbor, when all the necessaries of life fall under the power of robbers, when, indeed such a season of terrible distress sets in, by what means should a Brahmin live who is unwilling to cast off compassion and his children?
>
> How, indeed, should a Brahmin maintain himself at such a time? Tell me this, O grandsire? How also should the king live at such a time when sinfulness overtakes the world? How, O scorcher of foes, should the king live so that he might not fall away, from both righteousness and profit?

See PRATAP CHANDRA RAY, MAHABHARATA, Book XII SANTI PARVA, CXLI, 467–68.

[74]*Id*. at 468. Described in the *Mahabharata* as follows:

> [E]xtending for twelve years… (when) the thousand eyed deity of heaven poured no rain… (when) agriculture and keep of cattle were abandoned, stakes for teethering sarcrifical animals disappeared, … festivals and amusements perished… the cities and towns … became empty of inhabitants…. Brahmins began to die on all sides, protection was at an end; herbs and plants were dried up; the earth became shorn of all her beauty and exceedingly awful like trees in a crematorium; … when righteousness was nowhere… men in hunger lost their senses and began to eat one another….

states of exception,[75] which were regarded as "seasons of distress" and were governed by pragmatic expediency within the framework of a modified moral code and astute administration. Responses to seasons of distress varied also according to the form of government. Within monarchical systems, there were differences of style and approach.

Internal problems and dangers were often accorded prime importance in ancient India. In the *Mahabharata*, Bhishma puts his finger on "internal dissension" as the besetting malady of Republics.[76] The *Arthasastra* sees internal troubles as more serious than external ones, and amongst the internal troubles, those of internal origin with internal abetment as more serious and dangerous than those of external origin with external abetment. In Kautilya's hierarchy of internal troubles, those of internal origin with external abatement come third and troubles of external origin with internal abetment take the last place.[77]

Examples of non-derogable principles during "seasons of distress" spanned the material, spiritual and religious spheres of life. Thus, while the strict rule of caste duty and function could be modified substantially in an emergency, no Brahmin could ever "form a connection either through the Vedas or by marriage" with the people of the other three castes who had not been initiated and had not received the sacrament at the proper time.[78] "Even at the time of dire distress a teacher of Vedas should rather die with his knowledge than sow it in barren soil"[79]; i.e., should not disseminate knowledge where there is neither merit nor wealth nor obedience. A shudra woman (of the lowest caste) could not be taken as the first wife of a Brahmin or a Kshatriya, though they lived in the greatest distress.[80] No Brahmin, "even in the times of distress," must cause an injury to any creature which is not sanctioned by the Vedas[81] and no king, "though fallen into the deepest distress," should provoke Brahmanas to anger.[82] The *Mahabharata* had the same conception of non-derogable rights: while the king may practice the laws for emergency situations and while he may expropriate and levy extraordinary taxes at such times,[83] he could not oppress Ritwijas, Purohitas, preceptors and Brahmins.[84] Nor could

---

[75]Indeed, the *Arthasastra* deals with "*alasya*" (laziness and inertia in the body politic) and "*premada*" (hedonism) as factors which undermine and subvert the foundation of the social and political order and must be combated. *See* Rao [35, p. 155].

[76]Prasad [34, p. 66].

[77]Kautilya, Arthasastra, 449 (Rudrapatna Shamasastry ed., trans., 1915) (*circa* 300 B.C.). *See also*, Ramaswamy [38].

[78]Manusmriti, supra note 4, II. 40.

[79]*Id.* at II. 13.

[80]*Id.* at III. 14.

[81]*Id.* at V. 43.

[82]*Id.* at IX. 313.

[83]Pratap Chandra Ray, Mahabharata, Book XII Santi Parva, CXXXIT, 425.

[84]*Id.* at CXXXII, 423; CXXXII, 460; CLXVI, 531.

such expropriations be directed against "persons who are given to the performance of sacrifices, as also the wealth dedicated to the deities …".[85]

The effects of an emergency could be wide-ranging. In the ancient Indian context, few things could be more far-reaching than a substantial modification of the laws regulating professions, caste duties and caste functions, which embraced the entire spectrum of life. The *Mahabharata*[86] narrates the episode involving the eminent sage Vishwamitra, a great Brahmin, who, "urged by pangs of hunger"[87] and driven from pillar to post in search of food during a "frightful drought"[88] was forced to eat dog's meat illegally taken from a "Chandala."[89] Indeed, the great rishi (sage) Agastya, sent to the south of India by Lord Shiva himself, is said to have devoured the demon (asura) Vatapi to survive a great famine,[90] while the sage Agigarta, suffering from hunger, attempted to slay his own son and "was not tainted by sin since he only sought a remedy against famishing (sic)."[91] These stories are perhaps meant to dramatize the underlying point of the law of the state of exception and emergency (Apaddharma). Bhishma justifies such actions by saying that "theft is allowable in a season of distress even by an eminent person."[92] The moral of the story is summed up by him thus:

> Even thus, when the end in view is the preservation of life itself, should a high souled person possessed of learning and acquainted with means rescue his own cheerless self when fallen into distress, by all means in his power. By having recourse to such understanding, one should always preserve his life.[93]

The whole morality of adversity was different. Expediency tempered by wisdom was the call of the hour; foes could temporarily become friends when confronted by

---

[85] *Id.* at CXXXVI, 431.

[86] Pratap Chandra Ray, Mahabharata, Book XII Santi Parva, CXLI, 468 *et. seq.*

[87] *Id.* at 470.

[88] *Id.* at 468.

[89] *Id. See also* Manusmriti X. 106 & 107, which tell of Vandeva and Bharadwaj, the former trying to eat dog's flesh to save his life.

[90] Pratap Chandra Ray, Mahabharata, Book XII Santi Parva, CXLI, 473.

[91] Manusmriti X. 105.

[92] Pratap Chandra Ray, Mahabharata, Book XII Santi Parva, CXLI, 471. *Cf.* Hobbes [13, p. 232].

> If a man, by terror of present death, be compelled to an act against the law, he is totally excused; because no law can oblige a man to abandon his own preservation…. When a man is destitute of food, or other thing necessary for his life, and cannot preserve himself in any other way but by some act against the law; as if in a great famine, he takes away the food by force or steals…or in defense of his life snatch away another man's sword, he is totally excused.

[93] Pratap Chandra Ray, Mahabharata, Book XII Santi Parva, CXLI, 477.

bigger and more dangerous enemies.[94] Further, "a Brahmin who has fallen into distress may accept (gifts) from anybody"[95]; he may beg food from the king[96] and practice usury by lending "to a very sinful man at a small interest."[97] But no one could "perform his duties according to the law for times of distress… 'without being in distress'."[98] In short, the individual and the king may deviate from the path of righteousness, but only in times of distress.[99]

Extraordinary situations justified extraordinary taxation. The *Manusmriti* permitted expropriation of up to a fourth of the crops produced by citizens, "in times of distress…if he (i.e. the king) protects his subjects to the best of his ability."[100] The *Arthasastra* put this figure between one-third and one-fourth.[101] Sometimes kings became supplicants before "paura Janapada," i.e., the general assembly of the cities and the countryside for such exceptional taxes in seasons of distress. The *Mahabharata* provides a graphic account of how this was done:

> Here a danger has arisen. A large enemy army. They forebode our end…In this serious difficulty, and in the nearness of this grim danger, I beg of you money gentlemen, for your safety. When the crisis is over, I will repay, gentlemen in full…Money is desired only for the sake of the citizens, the children and wives. In crisis, this honourable assembly should bear the burden. You should not value money very much in a crisis.[102]

Financial relief was equally common during natural calamities. During such "emergent occasions," Kautilya directed that "remissions of taxes shall be made.[103] "Similarly fines were not to be levied upon and compensation not to be extracted from those who caused damage to forests during "calamities."[104] There was a moratorium on recovery of debts with respect to the creditor "involved in

---

[94]*See* PRATAP CHANDRA RAY, MAHABHARATA, Book XII SANTI PARVA, CXXXVIII, 435 *et seq*, tells the story of a cat which was ensnared in a trap at the foot of a banyan tree. A mouse, who lived in a hole under the tree, one day found himself hunted by both a mongoose and an owl without any means of escape. "At such a season of great danger, when death itself was staring one in the face, when there is fear on every side" the mouse decided to befriend the trapped cat and hid under its belly on the condition that it (the mouse) would release the cat from the trap as soon as the danger to the mouse had passed away and before the hunter comes for the cat. The story ends by narrating how the mouse wisely refused to release the cat at any time prior to the arrival of the hunter; when released just as the hunter was approaching, the cat could only escape to safety without making a meal of the mouse.

[95]Manusmriti, X. 102.

[96]*Id.* at X. 113.

[97]*Id.* at X. 117.

[98]*Id.* at XI. 128.

[99]*See, inter alia*, PRATAP CHANDRA RAY, MAHABHARATA, Book XII SANTI PARVA, CXL, 461; Prasad [34, pp. 60–61].

[100]Manusmriti, supra note 4, X. 118.

[101]KAUTILYA, ARTHASASTRA, 341–42 (Rudrapatna Shamasastry ed., trans., 1915) (*circa* 300 B.C.).

[102]PRATAP CHANDRA RAY, MAHABHARATA, Book XII SANTI PARVA, LXXXVII, 23–24.

[103]KAUTILYA, ARTHASASTRA, 61 (Rudrapatna Shamasastry ed., trans., 1915) (*circa* 300 B.C.).

[104]KAUTILYA, ARTHASASTRA, 139 (Rudrapatna Shamasastry ed., trans., 1915) (*circa* 300 B.C.).

calamities" or affected by "disturbances in the kingdom."[105] Deposits of money or property lost due to destruction by enemies, invasion, fires, floods and similar calamitous causes would not be reclaimable.[106] Great stress was laid on the conservation and maintenance of well-stocked treasuries to meet emergencies.[107]

Finally, it is noteworthy that many of the contemporary constitutional effects of a state of exception, viz., enhanced centralization, unitary decision making, augmented executive and discretionary powers, and a summary trial procedure, were also reflected in ancient India. As a commentator on the *Arthasastra* puts it

> Vast discretionary powers were vested in the hands of the administrators and judges, to checkmate forces of disruption and tendencies to destroy the fabric of society.[108]

Indeed, the practice of "Kantaka Shodhana" (literally "removal of thorns") was well known, whereby special courts manned by "dandadharas," and actuated by the sole desire of preserving the integrity and unity of the state, relentlessly suppressed wickedness and conspiracy against the Janapada (i.e., the polity) by conducting summary trials without the civil procedure code or the assistance of jurists.[109] As the Roman dictator had summary jurisdiction extending to all criminal cases affecting the safety of the state, the Indian ruler,

> [I]n the interests of righteousness, (could) inflict punishment in secret on those courtiers or confederacy of chiefs who are dangerous to the safety of the kingdom and who cannot be put down in open daylight.[110]

Hindu rulers before the advent of Islamic conquests followed ancient precepts based on an admixture of textbooks conventions, practice and the demands of the situations, a combination of Shastrachar (code mandated or sanctioned by authoritative scriptures, codes or texts) and Lokachar (custom, usage and practice). Conquerors, on their own, brought their principles and tribal mores, which were molded by their interaction with political, religious and social forces encountered by them. Each invasion or overthrow of government precipitated the general sense of martial, warlike ambience. Each conquest widened the gap between the ruler and the ruled until the time of Akbar (1542–1605) who created a stable empire in which state of military exception was not the rule. Two generations later, Aurangzeb's rule (1659–1707), however, appears to have been one long military emergency which sought to rationalize every deceit, treachery, mayhem, oppression, diplomatic and military alliance, levy of imposts, and transgression of rights on the basis of the reasons of state. Later Moghuls who were denuded of their imperial prowess by

[105]Kautilya, Arthasastra, 251 (Rudrapatna Shamasastry ed., trans., 1915) (*circa* 300 B.C.).

[106]Kautilya, Arthasastra, 255 (Rudrapatna Shamasastry ed., trans., 1915) (*circa* 300 B.C.).

[107]*See, inter alia*, Pratap Chandra Ray, Mahabharata, Book XII Santi Parva, CXXXII 423; *id.* at CXXXIII, 425; Kautilya, Arthasastra, 522 (Rudrapatna Shamasastry ed., trans., 1915) (*circa* 300 B.C.).

[108]Rao [35, p. 132].

[109]*Id.* at 131.

[110]Kautilya, Arthasastra, 336 (Rudrapatna Shamasastry ed., trans., 1915) (*circa* 300 B.C.).

successive foreign attacks and intrusions and emaciated by internal challenges to their authority etched out a hand to mouth existence in their pathetic quest for survival in a state of perpetual political, military and economic siege, without any consistent criteria or set norms. Obviously, ad hoc expediency reigned supreme during the period of an endless emergency, interspersed by brief and uneasy spells of normalcy.

Though these ancient and medieval, historical and philosophical concepts are undoubtedly diverse, multifaceted and unique, coming as they do from unrelated cultures and climes, they have a strange and striking unity of thought and have, directly, indirectly, and subconsciously influenced the entire common law jurisprudence—statutory or judge-made—on the subject of emergency powers up-to-date.

References

1. D. O'Donnell, *States of Siege or Emergency and their Effects on Human Rights: Observations and Recommendations of the ICJ*. U.N. Doc E/CN 4/Sub 2/NGO 93, Aug 1981
2. M. Questiaux, *Study of the Implications for Human Rights of Recent Developments Concerning Situations Known as States of Siege or Emergency*. UN Document, E/CN. 4/sub 2/1982/15 (July 27, 1982)
3. A.S. Miller, *Democratic Dictatorship* (1981), p. xiii
4. I. Jenkins, Book review. Am. J. Juris. **27**, 177–83 (1982)
5. J.G. Nicolay, J. Hay, *Abraham Lincoln Complete Works* (1902), p. 508
6. N. Machiavelli, *Discourses on The First Decade of Titus Livius* (Ninian Thomson trans., 1883) (1531)
7. N. Machiavelli, *The Prince* (Adams trans., 1977), pp. 50–51
8. A. Gewrith, *Marsilius of Padua—Defender of Peace*, vol. 1 (1951), p. 106
9. T. Hobbes, *Leviathan* (Micahel Oakeshott ed., 1946) (1651)
10. J. Locke, *Second Treatise on Civil Government* (J.W. Gough ed., 1948) (1690)
11. J.-J. Rousseau, *Social Contract* (Ernest Rhys ed., G.D.H. Cole trans., 1923) (1762)
12. B.D. Spinoza, *Tractatus Theologico-Politicus* (R.H.M. Elwes trans., 1862) (1670), p. 204
13. T. Hobbes, *Leviathan* (W.G. Pogson Smith ed., Oxford at the Clarendon Press, 1909) (1651)
14. M.T. Cicero, *Pro T. Annio Milone*, ed. by J.S. Reid (1897), p. 29
15. J.S. Mill, *Essays on Politics and Society* (J.M. Robson ed., 1970) (1861), p. 403
16. N. Machiavelli, *Discourses on The First Decade of Titus Livius* (Max Lerner ed., Christian E. Detmold trans., 1940) (1531)
17. J.B. Bury, *A History of Greece to the Death of Alexander the Great* (1951)
18. N.C.L. Hammond, *A History of Greece to 322 B.C.* (1959)
19. J.W. Powler, *The City-State of Greeks and Romans* (1952)
20. A.H.J. Greenidge, *Roman Public Life* (1930)
21. C. Rossiter, *Constitutional Dictatorship* (1948)
22. T. Mommsen, *Römisches Staatsrecht*, vol. 2 (1887), p. 153
23. C.D. Montesquieu, *The Spirit of the Laws* (Thomas Nugent trans., 1949) (1748), p. 172
24. F. Watkins, *The Failure of Constitutional Emergency Powers Under the German Republic* (1930), p. 148
25. J.S. Mill, *Considerations on Representative Government in Essays on Politics and Society* (J. M. Robson ed., 1970) (1861), p. 371, 403
26. C. McIlwain, *Constitutionalism—Ancient and Modern* (1940)

27. C.J. Friedrich, M. Curtis, B. Barber, *Totalitarianism in Perspective: Three Views* (1969)
28. C.J. Friedrich, *Totalitarianism Dictatorship and Autocracy* (1956)
29. H.M. Seervai, *Constitutional Law of India*, vol. 3, 4th edn. (2015), pp. 3109–3172
30. N.A. Palkhivala, *Our Constitution: Defaced and Defiled* (1974)
31. D.D. Basu, *Shorter Constitution of India* (1984)
32. J.W. Spellman, *Political Theory of Ancient India* (1964), p. 4
33. K.P. Jayaswal, *Hindu Polity: A Constitutional History of India in Hindu Times* (1955)
34. B. Prasad, *Theory of Government in Ancient India* (1968)
35. M.V.K. Rao, *Studies of Kautilya* (1953)
36. I. Hassan, *The Central Structure of Mughal Empire* (1980), p. 58
37. H. Beveridge, *The Akbarnama of Abu-L-Fazl* (1907), pp. 107–08
38. T.N. Ramaswamy, *Essentials of Indian Statecraft* (1962), p. 143

Chapter 2
Martial Law: A Comparative Analysis of USA, UK and India

1 Introduction

It has been commonly acknowledged for a long time now that martial law and military law are not the same things.[1] The words of Chief Justice Beaumont, Chief Justice of the Bombay High Court, written in 1931 provide a very pragmatic justification for power to proclaim martial law. Reviewing a martial law proclamation made by the Governor-General of India on May 15, 1930 proclaimed as a result of the Sholapur riots that took place in the wake of the arrest of Gandhi, the Chief Justice said:

> It is, no doubt, for that reason that in the case of countries not free from the risk of foreign invasion or civil strife, it is found convenient to arm the executive in cases of emergency with a weapon more easy to control and more certain in its operation.[2]

Note the use of the words, "countries not free from the risk of foreign invasion or civil strife." The power to proclaim martial law is therefore by its very nature an incidence of necessity. Necessity is what justifies its existence, necessity is what brings it into operation, and therefore necessarily, when that necessity is gone, the power also ceases to exist.[3] But this is not an ordinary necessity, it is a necessity that comes out of emergency and therefore martial law is to be proclaimed only in

[1]*See, e.g.*, Clode [1]. For an early history (from 1300 to 1628) of martial law in England, *see* Capua [2].

[2]Chanappa Shantirappa v. Emperor, 1931 AIR 57 (Bom.) 58.

[3]*See, e.g.*, Chanappa Shantirappa v. Emperor, 1931 AIR 57 (Bom.) 67 (Blackwell, J.,) ("It is clear that the civil authorities are not entitled to abrogate their duties and to hand over the control to the military except in cases of emergency").

A. Singhvi and K. Gautam, *The Law of Emergency Powers*,
https://doi.org/10.1007/978-981-15-2997-9_2

extreme circumstances.[4] Another important point is the necessity to proclaim martial law in countries that are at risk of foreign invasion or civil strife. In countries like India, surrounded by neighboring nations that are hostile and organized groups within the territory of India working to destabilize the country by different types of terrorist activities, the existence of the power to declare martial law in a certain area cannot be denied. Even in countries like the United States, that have a geographical advantage of not being surrounded by hostile neighbors, the power to declare martial law has not been denied but its use has become less and less frequent. Even when martial law was proclaimed in the United States, it was almost always in conditions where there was a war or a warlike situation within the country (e.g., President Lincoln's proclamation of martial law) or when the territory of the United States was under attack from a foreign nation (e.g., the proclamation of martial law in Hawai'i in WWII). Absent US's geographical autonomy from hostile neighbors and the clear and present danger always operating on Indian borders from hostile neighbors, the legal concept of martial law appears to be far more relevant to the Indian context though ironically, the frequency of its use has been much more in the United States.

2 A Brief History of Martial Law

Expounding the nature of martial law, Sir Matthew Hale in 1713[5] observed that martial law, owing to circumstances that make it necessary, "…in Truth and Reality [is] not Law, but something indulged rather than allowed as Law."[6] Sir Matthew also observed that the exercise of martial law, owing to its nature, is not to be permitted when civilian courts are functioning, "…for martial law, which is rather indulg'd than allow'd, and that only in Cases of Necessity, in Time of Open War, *is not permitted in Time of Peace, when ordinary Courts of Justice are open*."[7] In 1731, Congressman John Rowan of Kentucky expressed similar views: "Society will never submit life to the discretion of a military court, except under the most

[4]*See, e.g.*, Chanappa Shantirappa v. Emperor, 1931 AIR 57 (Bom.) 67 (Blackwell, J.,)

> A declaration of martial law is thus a very serious matter affecting as it does the ordinary rights of citizens. It is therefore plainly the duty of the civil authorities, assisted by all loyal subjects, whether civil or military … to carry on the civil administration, and not to hand over control to the military, unless the necessity of the case demands it (Internal Citations Omitted).

[5]Prof. Neocleous records the date of publication of Sir Matthew Hale's book at 1713. *See* Neocleous [3].

[6]Sir Hale [4]. However, Prof. Dennison records the date of publication of Sir Matthew Hale's book at 1820. *See* Dennison [5].

[7]Sir Hale [6] (Emphasis added).

absolute and imperious necessity, *in which a civil court cannot interfere*, particularly during war."[8]

Confusion was caused by the 1792 opinion delivered by Lord Chief Justice Loughborough in *Grant v. Sir Charles Gould*[9] because in this case, the phrase martial law was understood by Lord Loughborough as akin to what we today would call "military law,"[10] i.e., laws that apply to members of the military and the armed forces. By 1870, though, it was clearly understood that "martial law" and "military law" are not the same things.[11] By 1902, this distinction became very clear, i.e., military law is statutory[12] and is applicable to members of the military and armed forces[13] and martial law is the law of necessity and exists for the protection of society when, and where, civilian authorities and courts are unable to function.[14] However, in 1915 Dicey revived this confusion by stating that martial law as properly understood (i.e., the suspension of civilian authority and courts and its substitution by military government), "... is unknown to the law of England."[15] Dicey's views are not really helpful because even though he denies the existence of martial law under English Law,[16] he does concede "the common law right of the Crown and its servants to repel force by force" that, he states, "is essential to the very existence of orderly government, and is most assuredly recognized in the most ample manner by the law of England."[17] Incidentally, we may note that the incorrectness of Dicey's position, at least to the extent it was to be of any comparative use, was demonstrated in 1812 by General Jackson when he declared martial law in New Orleans during the war with Dicey's countrymen. Jackson proclaimed, "Why is martial law ever declared? Is it to make the enlisted or drafted soldier subject to it? He was subject to it before."[18] Dicey's view gives the military,

---

[8]Dennison [7] (Emphasis added).

[9]Grant v. Sir Charles Gould, 2 H. Bla. Rep. 69, 98; 126 Eng. Rep. 434, 449.

[10]Grant v. Sir Charles Gould, 2 H. Bla. Rep. 69, 98–99; 126 Eng. Rep. 434, 449–51; Clode [8], Dennison [9].

[11]
> Where tribunals are established under martial law, in the strict sense of the term, as, for instance, where a colony is in a state of disaffection or open revolt, it by no means follows, as in the case of the administration of the law military, that the persons composing the Courts should be military persons, or that those over whom the jurisdiction is exercised should be soldiers. In truth, under martial law, the difference between a soldier and a civilian disappears, as we have said, before that overpowering necessity which calls such a state of things into existence.

Clode [10].

[12]Holdsworth [11].

[13]Pollock [12].

[14]*See, e.g.*, 1 Smith [13].

[15]Dicey [14].

[16]*Id.* at 283, 287–289.

[17]*Id.* at 284, 286.

[18]Rankin [15] (quoting the martial law proclamation made by General Jackson in New Orleans).

"… a mandate for extensive action in situations of emergency, without the need for parliamentary approval, and with questionable regard to the wishes of the elected government."[19] Willoughby, in 1929, compounded the difficulty by defining martial law as inclusive of military law and calling martial law, as understood in 1902, as "martial law *in* sensu *strictiore*."[20] In England, a similar description was provided by Chalmers and Asquith in 1936.[21] Willoughby did for US constitutional law what Dicey had done for English constitutional law almost a decade and a half earlier stressing on the circumstances that make proclamation of martial law *in* sensu *strictiore* necessary.[22] Even though the text of the US Constitution does not talk about martial law, Willoughby found this power located in the bigger concept of Police Powers.[23] He also found some equivalence between the power to proclaim martial law and the power to suspend the writ of *habeas corpus*, something explicitly allowed by the US Constitution.[24]

By the 1960s, it was generally agreed, at least in the United States, that martial law is distinct from military law.[25] Disagreement existed as to whether martial law is a "… replacement for an otherwise functioning civil government …",[26] or as a "…supplement only to those functions of civil government which have been

[19]Colm Campbell & Ita Connolly, *A Model for the 'War Against Terrorism'? Military Intervention in Northern Ireland and the 1970 Falls Curfew*, 30 J.L. & Soc'y 341, 349 (2003).

[20]Westel Woodbury Willoughby [16].

[21]Chalmers and Asquith [17].

[22]Westel Woodbury Willoughby [18]. *See also* United States v. Diekelman, 92 U.S. 520 (1875) where the Supreme Court defined martial law as the law of necessity in the actual presence of war.

[23]3 Westel Woodbury Willoughby [19]. *See also* Rankin [20].

[24]In time of war, or of domestic insurrection or disorder, when so-called martial law has been declared, the privilege of the writ of habeas corpus, together with all the other civil guarantees may, for the time being, be suspended; but, as we have learned in the preceding chapter, actual public necessity, and this alone, will furnish legal justification for this.

> The existence of civil war operates as regards the enemy *ipso facto*, that is, without formal declaration, as a suspension of the privilege of the writ of habeas corpus, together with, as said, the suspension of the other guarantees to the individual against arbitrary executive action. In the preceding chapter the principle is argued that the establishment of martial law may properly take place not only upon the theater of active hostilities, but elsewhere when the actual necessities of the case demand it.
>
> The suspension of the privilege of the writ of habeas corpus falls short of the establishment of martial law, but to justify it there is required the same public necessity as that required for the enforcement of martial law.

3 Westel Woodbury Willoughby [21] (Emphasis added).

[25]*See, e.g.*, Note, *martial law*, 42 S. Cal. L. Rev. 546, 549 (1969).

[26]For old US judicial authority on this point, *see* Westel Woodbury Willoughby [16], Note, *martial law*, 42 S. Cal. L. Rev. 546, 549 (1969).

disrupted by the disturbance."[27] If the position before 1960 is seen, we will see that the second view is consistent with the historically accepted position. Martial law cannot be proclaimed to replace an otherwise functioning civilian government, rather it is proclaimed if the civilian government is unable to effectively discharge its functions. In fact, the Bombay High Court's opinion, expressed in 1930, is relevant on the point. Justice Madgavkar, speaking in the context of the civil administration's call to invoke martial law by handing over the administration to the military, observed:

> It is not a sign of his strength and duty discharged to the end, but rather a confession of helplessness and complete impotence to suppress breaches of the peace and to maintain laws even with the aid of the military.[28]

Thus proclaimed, if the civilian government is allowed to function, it is so allowed only because such is the will of the military commander.

Whereas military law applies only to the members of the military and armed forces, is statutory and exists for the preservation of discipline and order in the military and armed forces, martial law puts the military in-charge of an area that is under distress and where calling out the military to preserve order is necessary makes martial law a part of the constitutional process.[29] Martial law, justified and continued only by necessity, is not statutory[30] and can be proclaimed, in the words of Sir John Mackintosh, "When foreign invasion or civil war *renders it impossible for the Courts of law to sit, or to enforce the execution of their judgments*, [and] it becomes necessary to find a rude substitute for them, and to employ for that purpose the military, which is the only remaining force in the community."[31] Those that govern a nation must decide, during times of peace as well as war,[32] whether or not to proclaim martial law and that decision depends on whether or not, in a given situation, it has become necessary to so proclaim[33] thus making the process and the

---

[27]For old US judicial authority on this point, *see* Chalmers and Asquith [17]; Note, *martial law*, 42 S. Cal. L. Rev. 546, 549 (1969).

[28]Chanappa Shantirappa v. Emperor, 1931 AIR 57 (Bom.) 65.

[29]Clode [22].

[30]Rankin [20].

[31]Clode [24] (citing Sir John Mackintosh) (Emphasis Added).

[32]Rankin [25].

[33]Clode [26]

> For the proclamation which, under circumstances of admitted necessity, calls martial law into existence is not to be considered as the legal creation of that law, but is merely a statement of facts, which of their own force have already rendered that law necessary.

authority to proclaim martial law a part of constitutional law or public law.[34] In fact, the proclamation of martial law by General Jackson during the war (with the British) of 1812 in New Orleans and its continued operation even after the British having been defeated and peace being restored was justified by General Jackson by a direct reference to the US Constitution that allows the suspension of the writ of *habeas corpus*.[35] Once proclaimed, the military takes complete control, and as the threat becomes bigger or necessity becomes graver and therefore discretion becomes more free.[36]

At least since 1713, and certainly since 1731, the inability of the civilian authorities and courts to properly or effectively discharge their functions is the hallmark of the necessity that makes a proclamation of martial law necessary. Thus if the civilian authorities and courts are open and able to effectively discharge their functions, martial law cannot be imposed for it is not necessary to do so.[37] In reverse, if martial law has been imposed, it stands to reason that civilian authorities and courts were not able to discharge their functions. **Though this is a valid legal definition of martial law (viz., non-functioning of civil courts/tribunals), and though this binary division is both logical and legally supported, the actual practice of martial law has violated this theoretical construct on many occasions. It would be surprising if this were not so, because public law, more than other branches, thrives on exceptions which are supposed to prove the rule.**

We can, therefore, potentially examine the genuineness of a proclamation of martial law by examining whether or not the civilian authorities and courts were able to carry out their functions.[38] General Jackson's continued proclamation of martial law in New Orleans in 1812 even after the war with the British had ended and peace restored was reviewed by the courts in a similar way.[39] In other words, the military

---

[34]Smith [27], Birkhimer [28], Dicey [29], Westel Woodbury Willoughby [30], Rankin [31].

[35]Rankin [32] (quoting the General Order of March 14, 1815 issued by General Jackson saying, "If [the US Constitution] authorizes the suspension of the habeas corpus in certain cases, *it thereby impliedly admits the operation of martial law*, when, in the event of rebellion or invasion, the public safety may require it.") (Emphasis added).

[36]Holdsworth [33].

[37]1 Baldwin [34], 3 Westel Woodbury Willoughby [35], 1 Chalmers and Asquith [36], Holdsworth [33], Rankin [20], *Ex parte* Milligan 71 US 2, 127 (1866) ("martial rule can never exist where the courts are open, and in the proper and unobstructed exercise of their jurisdiction. It is also confined to the locality of actual war.").

[38]The US Supreme Court in two classic expositions of law on the point viz. Duncan v. Kahanamoku, 372 US 304 (1946), and *Ex parte* Milligan, 71 US 2 (1886), did exactly that. A proclamation of martial law cannot be justified if civilian courts are "open and able to function as usual" and the threat that necessitates the proclamation of martial law had ceased. *See* James D. Barnett, *Martial law and Civil Courts*, 25 or. L. Rev. 135 (1946).

[39]*See, e.g.*, 1 Rankin [23] (quoting Martin, J., in Johnson v. Duncan, 3 Martin (La.) 530 (1815), "The proclamation of martial law, *if intended to suspend the functions of this Court or its members*, is an attempt to exercise powers thus exclusively vested in the legislature. I therefore cannot hesitate in saying that it is in this respect null and void.") (Internal citations omitted) (Emphasis added).

cannot be called out and allowed to exercise its authority independent of any control and supervision by the civilian authorities and courts in a given area, unless it can be shown that the civilian authorities and courts are unable to effectively discharge their functions.[40] For the military to be acting independent of civilian authorities and courts, the latter must not be able to effectively function[41] and when such a thing happens it necessitates, as an *ipso facto* and *ipso jure* last resort, calling out the military and putting the entire area under military administration. It is then that we are in a state of martial law, notwithstanding whatever nomenclature maybe attached to it.[42]

3 Martial Law in the United States

3.1 Military Law, Military Government and Martial Law

Several different phrases come into play in the United States in the broad context of "martial law." These are—martial law, Absolute and Qualified martial law, Punitive and Preventive martial law, Use of Military in Aid of Civil Authority (or Military Acting in Aid of Civilian Authority), State of War and State of Insurrection. However, a lack of clarity as to the exact meaning of these terms led an eminent US Attorney General (Caleb Cushing) to call it "a composite blunder," "a total misapprehension of the matter" and "pitiable confusion."[43] This semantic confusion was based on a simplistic conception reminiscent of early English formulations on the subject, as discussed in the introductory chapter. Thus, in *Egan*[44] where the legality of the trial of a citizen by a military commission after cessation of hostilities

---

[40]Military troops are sometimes used as an aid to the civil authorities when martial law is declared. The troops then act a role similar to deputy sheriffs, and do nothing under their own responsibility but act directly under the civil power. This use of troops is easily recognizable from the use of troops under martial law because there is no declaration of martial law, and the troops act in entire subordination to the civil authority.

Rankin [31].

[41]Davis [37], arguing that in the event of civilian agencies becoming "overwhelmed in an environment of chaos and panic" the President has the "obvious option" to declare martial law. This position has been accepted since the "close of 17th century England" where, "*...never in peacetime—that is, so long as the ordinary courts were open—was government to resort to its armed forces to quell civil disturbances; nor could it otherwise take recourse to martial law.*" *See* Engdahl [38].

[42]A state of martial law, given its nature, can proclaim itself and can exist with or without a formal declaration of the same. *See* 1 Birkhimer [39]; Note, *martial law*, 42 S. CAL. L. REV. 546, 548 (1969) (authorities cited in note 11).

[43]Caleb [40]. Referring to this opinion of Caleb Cushing in 1945, Black, J., of the US Supreme Court in Duncan v. Kahanamoku, 327 U.S. 304, 315 (1946) observed, "What was true in 1857 remains true today."

[44]*In Re* Egan, 8 F. Cas. 367 (1866) (C.C.D.N.Y.).

in the Civil War was in issue, the New York Circuit Court simply adopted the view of the Duke of Wellington[45]

> All respectable writers and publicists agree in the definition of martial law – that it is neither more nor less than the will of the general who commands the army. It overrides and suppresses all existing civil laws, civil officers and civil authorities, by the arbitrary exercise of military power; and every citizen or subject, in other words, the entire population of the country, within the confines of its power, is subjected to the mere will or caprice of the commander. He holds the lives, liberty and property of all in the palm of his hand.[46]

Similarly the Supreme Court of Virginia in *Jones*[47] upheld the detention and trial by military commission of various West Virginians, while equating the domestic violence arising from a miner's dispute in West Virginia to "war" in the international sense of the word. The scope of the State Governor's powers was judged on the basis of Supreme Court precedents like *Diekelman,*[48] *Johnson,*[49] *Steamship Company*[50] and *Dooley,*[51] all of which dealt with wide-ranging and virtually

---

[45]*Id.* at 367–68. Nelson, J., observed:

> Lord Wellington, in one of his dispatches from Portugal, in 1810, in speaking of martial law, observes, that, as applied to persons, excepting officers and soldiers and followers of the army, for whose government there are particular provisions of law in all well-regulated countries, *it is neither more nor less than the will of the general of the army*, and that he punishes either with or without trial, for crimes either declared to be so, or not so declared by any existing law, or by his own orders. Subsequently, in a speech in the house of lords, he expressed the same opinion, and added: 'In fact, martial law means no law at all. Therefore, the general who declares martial law, and commands that it shall be carried into execution, is bound to lay down distinctly the rules and regulations according to which his will is to be carried out'.
>
> *Cf.* MATTHEW HALE, THE HISTORY OF COMMON LAW IN ENGLAND 40 (1713) (observing that martial law is not law but something indulged rather than allowed as law).

[46]*In Re* Egan, 8 F. Cas. 367 (1866) (C.C.D.N.Y.).

[47]*Ex parte* Jones, 77 S.E. Rep. 1029 (1913) = 71 W. Va. 567 (1913) (W. Va.).

[48]United States v. Diekelman, 92 U.S. 520 (1875).

[49]Dow v. Johnson, 100 U.S. 158 (1879) (holding that an officer of the US Army, while serving in enemy country during civil war is not liable to civil courts of the enemy country for injuries resulting from acts of war ordered by him in his military capacity).

[50]New Orleans v. Steamship Company, 87 U.S. 387 (1874) (holding that contracts entered into between a company and a representative of occupying military force is valid because the occupying military force during civil war can treat subjugated territory as territory conquered during foreign war and can exercise all powers and functions of government therein).

[51]Dooley v. United States, 182 U.S. 222 (1901) (import duties levied by US military forces occupying Puerto Rico prior to its cession to US under treaty upheld on the ground that levy of such duties was a legitimate act of an invading military power; contra in respect of the duties levied after island ceded to US under treaty).

limitless powers of an invading army in occupation of foreign belligerent territory[52] echoing the Duke of Wellington's exposition of martial law.

Indeed, even American scholarly writing has tended to fall into this verbal-conceptual trap. Concluding a historical account of the use of martial law in the United States, Rankin says:

> The definition of martial law sanctioned by the Supreme Court is 'the law of military necessity in the actual presence of war. It is administered by the general of the army, and is in fact his will. Of necessity, it is arbitrary, but it must be obeyed'.[53]

The correct meaning of martial law and the distinctions between it and military law or military government have been discussed earlier and need not be repeated except to mention that the US Supreme Court has recognized them on more than one occasion.[54]

3.2 *Absolute and Qualified Martial Law, and Preventive and Punitive Martial Law*

American jurisprudence reflects a distinction between Absolute and Qualified martial law. Situations of grave disorder are often referred to as Qualified or (synonymously) Preventive martial law, and trial or punishment of offenders under military justice is referred to as Absolute or (synonymously) Punitive martial law.[55] For example, in *Moyer v. Peabody*,[56] the US Supreme Court used the phrase Preventive martial law in the sense in which it has been defined above. Dismissing an action by Moyer, a labor

---

[52]Other cases of military occupation by an invading army, some of which did not distinguish such a situation from "martial law" include, Cross v. Harrison, 57 U.S. 164 (1853), Leitensdorfer v. Webb, 61 U.S. 176 (1868), Mrs. Alexander's Cotton, 69 U.S. 404 (1864), Ford v. Surget, 97 U.S. 594 (1878) and The Grapeshot, 76 U.S. 129 (1869).

[53]Rankin [41].

[54]*See, e.g.*, Duncan v. Kahanamoku, 327 U.S. 304, 324 (1946), (Black, J.)

> The phrase 'martial law' as employed in that act, therefore, while intending to authorize the military to act vigorously for the maintenance of an orderly civil government and for the defence of the islands against actual or threatened rebellion or invasion was not intended to authorizing the supplanting of courts by military tribunals.

Eugene A. Gilmore, *War Power—Executive Power and the Constitution*, 29 Iowa L. Rev. 463, 467 (1944) ("Martial law … means no more than that in a grave emergency and in war when the usual agencies of government are unable to function because of force and violence beyond their control, such agency as can, shall act for the public safety."); Carbough [93].

[55]A good example is the Montana Supreme Court's dictum in *Ex parte* MacDonald, 49 Mont. 454 (1914). In this case the Court held that, "*martial law is of all gradations*." While the governor could use the militia to "*suppress the insurrection*" and could "*take such measures as might be necessary including the arrest and detention of the insurrectionists*," he could not "*lawfully punish for insurrection or for other violations of the law*."

[56]Moyer v. Peabody, 212 U.S. 78 (1909).

leader, against Governor Peabody of Colorado, wherein Moyer's alleged wrongful arrest and detention by the military was contended to be in violation of due process of law and the Fourteenth Amendment, Justice Holmes said,

> ...[T]he governor may use the milder measure of seizing the bodies of those whom he considers to stand in the way of restoring peace. Such arrests are not necessarily for punishment, but are by way of precaution to prevent the exercise of hostile power.[57]

Qualified or Preventive martial law simply means that troops can keep citizens in detention without regard to writs of habeas corpus or any interference from the civil forces and this detention can continue until the disturbance is over and the civil courts are again functioning in the proper manner.[58] Those who deny the existence of Punitive martial law in the United States have expressed similar views on the nature of Qualified or Preventive martial law.[59]

3.3 State of Insurrection and State of War

References to a State of War have generated additional confusion. In *Luther v. Borden*[60] the US Supreme Court (Justice Woodbury dissenting) observed that a declaration of martial law could not be made in peacetime.[61] It can only be made in a State of War to be used against a public enemy. The legal proposition whereby martial law could be declared only during a State of War seems to be an attempt to distinguish the situations where cases before the courts arose from war and to reject the view advanced by the State that mere disorder turned the inhabitants of the State into public enemies and belligerents. In other words, by holding that martial law could be declared only during wartime, the courts seem to be attempting to protect the citizens from the grave consequences that follow a declaration of martial law. This does not help in arriving at a clear legal definition of the concept of martial law. Both Federal and State judges have made the mistake of remarking in passing that martial law is a domestic incident of international war or armed conflict and

---

57 Moyer v. Peabody, 212 U.S. 78, 85 (1909).

58 Rankin [42].

59 *See, e.g.*, Glenn [44] ("It is the function of the military forces to hold the prisoner until order is restored and he can be safely turned over to the civil authorities for trial. Martial law prevents but it does not punish").

60 Luther v. Borden, 48 U.S. 1 (1849).

61 Luther v. Borden, 48 U.S. 1, 87 (1849) (Woodbury, J., dissenting)

> To conclude, it is manifest that another strong evidence of the control over military law in peace and over these belligerent rights in civil strife which is proper in a bold and independent judiciary, exists in this fact, that whenever they are carried beyond what the exigency demands even in cases where some may be lawful the sufferer is always allowed to resort, as here, to the judicial tribunals for redress.

have suggested that martial law can exist only in the "actual theatre of war" or the "locality of actual war."[62]

Such statements should not be read to mean that martial law exists *only* during (external) wartime. This definition of martial law, which recognizes domestic use of martial force only as an incident of actual international war or conflict, is evidently wrong because it mistakenly equates military government and martial law. Martial law can and does exist without any State of War in the international arena and without even civil war. The error of these remarks is the assumption which views everything which is not war in the international sense as a State of Peace and overlooks the basic fact that disorder and violence are "of all gradations."

On the other hand, judicial remarks distinguishing between a State of War and State of Insurrection, and asserting that domestic inhabitants cannot be treated as belligerents and public enemies during mere insurrection are correct as they emphasize the fundamental difference between a State of War and use of martial law. As a dissenting judge of the Supreme Court of West Virginia puts it:

> The failure in the majority opinion to observe the sharp distinction between public war and civil law disorder, between enmity against the state and individual enmity between citizens of the state, belligerent territory and territory retaining allegiance, accounts for the application of the decisions, legislative enactments and quotations relied on therein.[63]

The view of Justice Sanner, speaking for the Montana Supreme Court, is even more unequivocal,

> There is a very great distinction between insurrection and war. It is this: War is an act of sovereignty, real or assumed; insurrection is not. War makes enemies of the inhabitants of the contending states; but insurrection does not put beyond the pale of friendship the innocent in the affected district. War creates the rights and duties of the belligerency, which to a mere insurrection are unknown. Doubtless an insurrection may become war, as was the case with the Great Rebellion. But it does not become so in the legal sense until the rebellious party assumes political form … In internal wars, the object is to coerce the power opposed to the sovereign and so it is competent for the sovereign to exercise powers belonging to belligerents at international law … How inapplicable all this is to a formless insurrection, and how impossible to characterize such a movement as a state of war.[64]

Two other distinctions, between martial law and Military Action in Aid of Civil Authority and between martial law and suspension of habeas corpus, are discussed later in this book.

---

[62]*See Ex Parte* Milligan 71 U.S. 2, 127 (1866); Hussain [45], Birkheimer [46], Bowman [47], Sir Fredrick Pollock [48].

[63]*Ex parte* Jones, 77 S.E. 1029, 1051 (1913) (Robinson, J.) (W. Va.).

[64]*Ex parte* MacDonald, 49 Mont. 454 (1914) (Mont.).

3.4 Historical Instances of Use of Force

Although this work does not deal with the *history* of emergency powers or of martial law, a brief narration of the historical instances of use of martial law is necessary to delineate the matrix from which legal principles, discussed later, have evolved.

It has been estimated that in the first three decades after the American independence, federal and state governments dispatched troops on six occasions to aid in the enforcement of laws.[65] Early federal uses of force occurred during Shays' Rebellion and then in the Whiskey Rebellion in 1794 where President Washington sent some 13,000 troops, comprising militia from four states into Western Pennsylvania to restore order amongst farmers rebelling against imposition of the liquor tax, but no battle ensued and the few rebel trials were conducted in ordinary courts. Federal forces were also used in the Fries's Rebellion in 1798, the Burr conspiracy in 1806–07 (troops were used to arrest Aaron Burr, the mercurial US Vice President who had killed Alexander Hamilton in a duel, for conspiracy to form an empire on the Napoleonic model with New Orleans as its capital) and finally during Thomas Jefferson's efforts to enforce the embargo in 1808. However, in these cases, the state and federal law enforcement agencies administered the law with the aid of military power and the latter acted exclusively under civilian authority. Even in the Burr case, General Wilkinson used only qualified martial law, doing no more than arresting men and summarily transporting them to Washington D.C. for trial.

The most significant use of martial law before the US Civil War occurred in 1814 during the battle of New Orleans between the Americans, led by General Jackson, and the English.[66] The former proclaimed martial law immediately upon arrival and exercised rigid control over the populace, culminating in the well-known arrest and detention, under his orders, of Louaillier who had authored an article severely criticizing Jackson's rule by martial law. When Judge Hall of the federal district court issued a writ of habeas corpus ordering the detenu's release, Jackson had the judge transported beyond the city and detained. General Jackson's period of martial rule, which lasted three months, was nothing less than what we have characterized as Military Government. After martial law was lifted, Judge Hall held General Jackson in contempt and ordered him to pay $ 1,000 as fine (which he promptly paid). Jackson's defence that his actions were taken under necessity and in the prosecution of martial law was rejected by Judge Hall. Later, the then Secretary of State, Dallas, wrote to Jackson mildly reprimanding him for his conduct. Dallas told Jackson that only the severest crisis could justify Jackson's conduct and suggested that the available evidence did not bear out the existence of such a severe crisis.

---

[65]Wilson [44].

[66]Richards [49].

The so-called Dorr Rebellion in Rhode Island in 1842 arose because a group of persons, led by Thomas Dorr, who were dissatisfied with the existing Charter Government and its governing constitutional document restricting, inter alia, adult suffrage, adopted a new constitution and elected Dorr as Governor under it.[67] He sought to assert his authority against the existing Charter Government by force, whereupon the latter passed an Act declaring the State to be under martial law. However, no large-scale arrests or detentions ensued and no trial by military commission took place; martial law was used primarily to justify the use of force against Dorr and his followers, whose attempts to gain political control failed. The next occasion for the use of martial law by the Federal Government was the American Civil War which has been discussed later in detail.

The last major use of force during the nineteenth century occurred during the Pullman Strike in 1894, when, anticipating a major disruption of US mails and commerce due to the organized boycott of Pullman cars by all employees, President Cleveland's Attorney General (Mr. Olney) obtained an injunction from the circuit court in Illinois preventing any obstruction. Some force was used to enforce the injunction and labor leaders were found guilty of contempt of court. However, the civil agencies of law and order retained complete command throughout the episode.[68]

In the First World War, a bill proposing the institution of martial law for punishing spies (the so-called Chamberlain Bill) died an early death in the US Senate because of President Wilson's opposition to it. The Bill stated that on account of changed conditions of modern warfare the US mainland had become a war zone and that the establishment of martial law was essential to the winning of the war. President Wilson, in a letter to Senator Overman, rejected the bill saying,

> I am wholly and unalterably opposed to such legislation … I think that it is not only unconstitutional, but that in character it would put us upon the level of the very people we are fighting and affecting to despise. It would be altogether inconsistent with the spirit and practice of America … I think it unnecessary and uncalled for.[69]

Two infamous instances occurred during the Second World War. The first involved large numbers of Japanese Americans who were evacuated from the west coast under a Presidential Executive Order authorizing the Secretary of State, in his discretion, to establish military areas to which persons suspected of espionage and sabotage could be removed.[70] Of the 110,000 persons of Japanese ancestry evacuated, about 70,000 were American citizens. The second occurred when absolute and punitive martial law was vigorously and severely applied in Hawai'i between 1941 and 1944 with large-scale military arrests, detentions and trials by military commissions.[71]

---

[67] *See* Dennison [50].

[68] This episode lead to the decision in *In Re* Debs, 158 U.S. 564 (1894).

[69] Rankin [51].

[70] *See* Rostow [52].

[71] *See* Frank [53], Garner [55].

Finally, it may be mentioned that none of the instances of federal use of force internationally since the Second World War (e.g., in Korea in 1950, in Vietnam and Indo-China in the 1960s and 1970s and in the Middle East or the Caribbean in the 1980s) have involved an application of martial law in the domestic sphere.

The late nineteenth century and the twentieth century have, however, seen a number of instances of use of force in various American States following local disorders.[72] Thus martial law was proclaimed, inter alia, in Idaho (1892 and 1899),[73] Pennsylvania (1902),[74] Colorado (1903, 1904 and 1913–14),[75] West Virginia (1912–13 and 1921),[76] Montana (1914),[77] Louisiana (1915),[78] Texas (1920 and 1931),[79] Nebraska (1922),[80] Minnesota[81] (1934), Indiana (1935)[82] and South Carolina (1935).[83] An overwhelming majority of these instances involved industrial strife and most of them concerned the coal mining industry. The State Governor's proclamation did not always mention martial law; other terms used were "state of war" (West Virginia, 1912–13) or "disorder" (Pennsylvania, 1902) or "insurrection" (West Virginia, 1921). In only four of the aforesaid cases were military commissions set up for trial of civilians (West Virginia, 1912–13; Montana, 1914; Galveston, Texas, 1920; and Nebraska, 1922). Although the state militia sufficed in most cases, request for Presidential aid in the form of federal troops was also made and honored in some cases (Idaho, 1892 and 1899; Colorado, 1913–14; and West Virginia, 1921).

---

[72]Engdahl [54].

[73]*Report of the Investigation Committee of House of Representatives*, Vol. 7 H.R. Rep. No. 1999 at 2 (56th Congress, 1st Sess., 1899–1900); *In Re* Boyle, 57 P. 706 (1899) (Idaho).

[74]*See* Commonwealth v. Shortall, 98 Am. St. Rep. 759 (1903).

[75]*In Re* Moyer, 117 Am. St. Rep. 189 (1905) (Colo.); Moyer v. Peabody, 212 U.S. 78 (1905).

[76]*See* the famous (or rather infamous) trilogy of West Virginia Supreme Court judgements—State v. Brown, 77 S.E. 243 (1912), *Ex parte* Jones 77 S.E. 1029 (1913), Hatfield v. Graham, 81 S.E. 533 (1914); *see also* Matthews [57].

[77]*In Re* McDonald, *In Re* Gillis, 143 Pac. 947 (1914) (Mont.) (Both cases were disposed of by a single order).

[78]*In Re* State *ex rel.* Barataria Land Co., 70 So. 423 (1915) (La.).

[79]Smead [56]; Sterling v. Constantin, 287 U.S. 378 (1932); Fairman, *martial Rule in the Light of Sterling v. Constantin*, 19 Cornell L. Q. 20 (1933).

[80]United States *ex rel.* Seymour v. Fischer, 280 Fed. 208 (1922) (D. Neb.).

[81]Powers Mercantile Co. v. Olson, 7 Fed. Supp. 865 (1934) (D. Minn.).

[82]Cox v. McNutt, 12 Fed. Supp. 385 (1935) (Ind.).

[83]Hearon v. Calus, 183 S.E. 13 (1935) (S.C. Sup. Ct.).

3.5 *Is Martial Law Constitutional in United States?*

While some judicial decisions have simply assumed the existence of the power to declare and use martial law, without discussing its constitutional or legal basis,[84] others have rejected the power on a variety of grounds. Six main objections to the constitutionality and legality of martial law may be outlined:

1. Firstly, at the federal level (we may use the term federal martial law here), the US Constitution contains no affirmative grant of power to declare martial law. While it contains various clauses (notably the Bill of Rights) guaranteeing individual rights, some or all of which would be denied or diluted by the use of martial law. Even so, the Federal Government in the United States may become involved in the administration of martial law in two ways:

   (i) When there is a Presidential or Congressional declaration of martial law and troops are used at the initiative of the Federal Government. This is relatively rare: its most significant use was during the Civil War. Congress has rarely taken the initiative in these matters, although it has ratified, *post facto*, President Lincoln's use of martial law during the Civil War.
   (ii) When the State Governor proclaims or institutes martial law, but requests the President for aid from federal troops. This is much more common.

2. Secondly, at the state level, in cases where the state constitutions and statutes affirmatively grant the power to use martial law, such grants have to pass the test of the Fourteenth Amendment which guarantees individual rights and due process to state inhabitants.
3. Thirdly, few state constitutions do, in fact, authorize the use of martial law, while a large number of them categorically assert that the civil authority shall be supreme and that the military power shall always be subordinate to it.[85]
4. Fourthly, martial law became obsolete and illegal since the Petition of Right in 1628 in UK and has not been used in that country for many centuries; it is therefore argued that no such doctrine of martial law could have been imported into the United States from UK or from common law.
5. Fifthly, it is argued that if the suspension of the writ of habeas corpus requires Congressional action under the US Constitution, *a fortiori*, the use and the declaration of martial law, which could include denial of the writ and have other far-reaching consequences, would not be initiated either by the federal or the state executive, at least not without Congressional authorization.
6. Finally, there is the argument, discussed earlier, that martial law cannot be used or proclaimed except as a domestic incident of full-scale international war.

---

84 *See, e.g.*, Commonwealth v. Shortall, 98 Am. St. Rep. 759 (1903).

85 *See, e.g.*, The Civil Supremacy Clause in the Constitution of West Virginia, Art. 3, § 12.

A strong basis for upholding the constitutionality of martial law is provided by the constitutional mandate authorizing Congress to provide for "calling forth the militia, to execute the laws of the Union, suppress insurrections and repel invasions"[86] (the Calling Forth Clause). This power to call out the militia is, it is submitted, equivalent to the power to impose martial law. Various statutory enactments by Congress in pursuance of this constitutional power exist and some have also been constitutionally challenged and upheld by the Supreme Court.[87] Additionally, the Executive Powers Clause[88] vesting executive powers in the President, the Commander-in-Chief Clause[89] making him the commander-in-chief and the Taking Care Clause[90] obliging him to take care that the laws be faithfully executed may be taken to imply martial authority in the President.

At the state level, the paramount and supreme duty of the State Governor to preserve the State buttressed by the presence in most state constitutions, of provisions making him the chief executive of the state, the commander-in-chief of the state militia, vesting in him the power to call out the latter, and imposing on him a duty to see that the laws are executed are all collectively relied upon to justify use of martial law in the state. Martial law is justified as an exercise of inherent power by the State executive. Chief Justice Taney puts it thus in *Luther v. Borden*,[91]

> And unquestionably, a state may use its military power to put down an armed insurrection, too strong to be controlled by the civil authority. The power is essential to the existence of every government, essential to the preservation of order and free institutions, and is as necessary to the states of this union as to any other government.

As far as the Fourteenth Amendment is concerned, it is arguable that as the federal constitution itself contains affirmative authorization for the use of martial law (the Calling Forth Clause),[92] the other provisions of the federal constitution (including the Fourteenth Amendment) must be read subject to this power. It would be anomalous to say that those who inserted the Calling Forth Clause allowed federal martial law while those who added the Fourteenth Amendment intended to prohibit state martial law. This is particularly true in view of the absence of any explicit rejection of state martial law by the Fourteenth Amendment. On the

---

[86]U.S. Const. art. I, § 8, cl. 15.

[87]*See, e.g.*, 18 U.S.C.A. §1385 (Use of Army and Air Force as *posse comitatus*); *see also* U.S. v. Hitchcock, C.A. 9 (Hawai'i) 2001, 263 F.3d 878 (discussing the participation of military personnel in Drug Enforcement Administration's investigation of civilian defendant did not violate the Posse Comitatus Act); U.S. v. Allred, C.A. 5 (Tex.) 1989, 867 F.2d 856 (Posse Comitatus was intended as an attempt to end the use of federal troops to police state elections in ex-Confederate states). U. S. v. Hartley, C.A.5(La.) 1986, 796 F.2d 112 (Posse Comitatus Act was designed to limit direct active use of federal troops by civil law enforcement officers to enforce laws of nation).

[88]U.S. Const. art. II, § 1, cl. 1.

[89]U.S. Const. art. II, § 2, cl. 1.

[90]U.S. Const. art. II, § 3.

[91]Luther v. Borden, 48 U.S. 1 (1849).

[92]U.S. Const. art. I, § 8, cl. 15.

contrary, state constitutions, whether pre-existing the Fourteenth Amendment[93] or after it,[94] have recognized the power of martial law and used it.

It may be added that even assuming that the Fourteenth Amendment applies to State action implementing martial law, it prohibits only violation of due process. The latter itself is not an unchangeable yardstick but varies according to what is considered reasonable in the light of all the facts and circumstances. State action amidst domestic disorder, and pursuant to a reasoned opinion of the chief executive of the State that martial law is necessary, would usually be held to be reasonable and hence not violative of the Fourteenth Amendment.

The Civil Supremacy Clauses in state constitutions have been read as being subject to other provisions in the state constitutions dealing with executive power. Sometimes, martial law has been justified by saying that the State Governor acts as a chief civil executive even when instituting martial law and hence maintains civil supremacy[95]; at other times, the Civil Supremacy Clauses have simply been held to be inoperative during "invasion, insurrection, rebellion or riot."[96] The clause is thus said to operate only during normal times and not during emergencies. It is difficult to ignore the opposing view, articulated by Justice Steele in his dissent in *Moyer* that such an interpretation of the supremacy clauses would mean that the clause has no restraining effect and that it only requires that the military shall always be under the command of the Governor.[97] This, he says, would simply annul the Bill of Rights.

A partial reconciliation of these opposing views may be suggested. While the supremacy clauses cannot displace the power to use martial law, their presence in state constitutions must conclusively oust the use of military commissions for trial of civilian offenders. Thus supremacy clauses would permit only Qualified and Preventive martial law, but not Absolute or Punitive martial law because the latter truly makes the military supreme and violates the supremacy clauses. In any event, it has been argued later that judicial authority upholding the use of Absolute martial law is weak and sparse.

---

[93]The Constitutions of Arkansas and Mississippi prior to 1868 (when the Fourteenth Amendment) was adopted are two such examples.

[94]The current Constitutions of Arkansas (1874) and Mississippi (1980) would serve the purpose.

[95]*In Re* Moyer, 117 Am. St. Rep. 189, 195 (1905) (Colo.)

> The governor, in employing the militia to suppress an insurrection, is merely acting in his capacity as the chief civil magistrate of the state, and although exercising his authority conferred by the law through the aid of military under his command, he is but acting in a civil capacity. In other words, he is but exercising the civil power vested in him by law through a particular means which the state has provided for protection of its citizens.

[96]*See* State v. Brown, 77 S.E. Rep. 243, 245 (1912) (W. Va.).

[97]*In Re* Moyer, 117 Am. St. Rep. 189, 197 (1905) (Colo.).

The historical argument cannot, by itself, be conclusive. The probable illegality of martial rule within England at the time of American independence can hardly be a ground for its exclusion from US law, especially if the latter's institutional or statutory law impliedly or explicitly permits it. Nor can the tenuous and unsatisfactory remarks of Justice Sutherland in *Curtiss-Wright*,[98] suggesting that the US Federal Government inherited the incidents of sovereignty directly from the British Crown and therefore possesses extra constitutional powers in the sphere of foreign relations,[99] be relied upon to argue that denial of martial law powers to the British Crown after the Petition of Right meant a similar denial to the US President. Such an argument would not only be far-fetched and unreal, it would ignore the fact that *Curtiss-Wright* restricted itself to the "delicate...plenary (sphere of) international relations," that it was a grand obiter of Justice Sutherland and that serious doubts have been expressed by many writers about its validity and historical premises.[100]

The habeas corpus argument is not tenable, simply because the power to suspend the writ of habeas corpus and the power to proclaim martial law are separate and distinct and it is incorrect to suggest that martial law must be legislatively proclaimed because habeas corpus can only be legislatively suspended. Indeed, strong objections have been expressed to the view that habeas corpus may only be legislatively suspended. In fact, the writ has often been suspended or denied by the executive or even by a military commander.[101] More importantly, the constitution uses words suggesting that only Congress may suspend the writ but no such words occur in respect of martial law. Many states also possess constitutions or statutes impliedly authorizing use of martial law, which would satisfy the requirements, if any, of legislative authorization preceding use of martial law. It has been shown earlier, and it need not be repeated, that martial law need not exist only as an incident of international war or even civil war. This argument against the constitutionality of martial law is, therefore, also untenable.

Hence, it is submitted that martial law simpliciter is constitutional and legal in US law, albeit certain kinds of actions under it, notably trial of civilians by military commissions (so called Absolute martial law) may well not be. The latter issue is discussed later.

---

[98]United States v. Curtiss-Wright Export Co., 299 U.S. 309 (1936).

[99]United States v. Curtiss-Wright Export Co., 299 U.S. 309, 320 (1936).

[100]*See* Berger [58], Levitan [59], Lofgren [60].

[101]*See, e.g., Ex parte* Bollman and Swartout, 2 L. Ed. 554 (1807).

3.6 Proclamation of Martial Law

3.6.1 Identity of Proclaimer

There cannot be any doubt that the proclamation of martial law must be made by the chief executive of the federal or the state government, i.e., the President or the State Governor,[102] especially as it is the President who is empowered to call out the militia and it is the State Governor who is given similar power under state constitutions and statutes and it is the President and State Governors who are made commander-in-chief of the army and state militia, respectively. It appears unlikely that the power of proclaiming martial law is delegable by the chief executive. Courts have regarded such emergency powers as special and valuable, capable of abuse, and hence fit to be entrusted only to a high dignitary like the chief executive of the union or the state.[103] Indeed, this is one of the main reasons for judicial deference to executive opinion in respect of the proclamation of martial law.[104] Hence, it is submitted that while the actual exercise of power pursuant to a declaration of martial law and the manner of operation of the military is decentralized and delegable,[105] the power to proclaim or institute martial law is not.

Moreover, the power to proclaim martial law would be exclusive to the executive, unless there is an explicit denial of the power to use martial law in either the federal or a state constitution. In fact, however, no such denial exists. Mere implied statutory or constitutional denial would not suffice, for, such implied denials have been read as being subject to the executive power to repulse force with force. Even an explicit statutory denial of such power would, it is submitted, be found to conflict with the constitutional provisions conferring executive power, the power to execute the laws and inherent emergency power. Whenever martial law invoked by the Governor or the President is challenged before courts, they would inevitably have to rely on a legal or a constitutional provision from where the power to invoke martial law would flow. It would not be an empty guess to say that in such conditions they are most likely to cite a constitutional provision to support their authority to invoke martial law. Under such circumstances, if there is a law that

---

[102] *See, e.g.*, Corpus Juris Secundum, 93 C.J.S., *War & Nat'l Defense* § 40 ("The authority to institute or proclaim martial law within the United States, however, is vested in the legislative department of the federal and state governments, but may by them be delegated to executive officers.").

[103] Gross and Aolain [62].

[104] *Id.*

[105] After Presidential or gubernatorial proclamation, the actual application and administration of martial law can be left to a military general or commander. *See, e.g.*, the administration of martial law by the military in Hawaii during the Second World War (Duncan v. Kahanamoku, 327 U.S. 304 (1946)).

explicitly denies the Governor or the President the power to invoke martial law, it would clearly be in conflict with the constitutional provision so cited. The Governor or the President's case would become far stronger if the law only impliedly denies this power. Finally, mention may be made of the decision by the Michigan Supreme Court in *Walsh v. City of River Rouge*[106] where it was held that only the Governor, and not the city Mayor, could declare martial law during a riot.

3.6.2 Nature and Content of Proclamations

The characteristic features of martial law proclamations include:

i. A narration of facts which in the opinion of the proclaimer gave rise to the emergency[107];
ii. The finding of a state of insurrection, disorder, war, violence or rebellion, by whatever name called[108];
iii. The effect of the proclamation: calling out the militia, instituting martial law, ordering arrests, detentions or trials or other stated effects;
iv. (Usually) a recital of the source of his power (e.g., "by virtue of the constitution and laws of the state"[109] or "by virtue of the authority in me vested")[110] although the specific provisions of the state constitution or statutes need not be recited.

---

[106]Walsh v. City of River Rouge, 189 N.W. (2d.) 318.

[107]For example, President Lincoln's proclamation during the Civil War issued on September 24, 1862 had the following proclamation:

> … during the existing insurrection, and as a necessary means for suppressing the same, all rebels and insurgents, their aiders and abettors, within the United States, and all persons discouraging volunteer enlistments, resisting military drafts, or guilty of any disloyal practice affording aid or comfort to rebels against the authority of the United States, shall be subject to martial law and liable to trials and punishment by courts martial or military commissions; second, that the writ of habeas corpus is suspended in respect of all persons arrested or who now or hereafter during the rebellion, shall be imprisoned …

See 6 Richardson [63].

[108]Unlike President Lincoln who used the phrase "martial law," some other proclamations do not use this word. Idaho Governor's proclamation dated March 4, 1899 and Pennsylvania Governor's proclamation dated August 6, 1902 reproduced, respectively, *In Re* Boyle, 57 P. 706, 706 (1899) and Commonwealth v. Shortall, 98 Am. St. Rep. 759, 761 (1903) are examples of martial law proclamations where the said phrase isn't used.

[109]*See, e.g.*, the proclamation of West Virginia Governor Glascock in 1921, quoted in Rankin [63].

[110]*See, e.g.*, the proclamation of Texas Governor Hobby in 1929, quoted in Rankin [63, p. 87].

3.6.3 Necessity and Effect of Proclamations

President Lincoln's Attorney-General, Caleb Cushing stated with clarity the view that a proclamation is not a necessary prerequisite for the validity of the power to use martial law. He said:

> When martial law is proclaimed under circumstances of assumed necessity, the proclamation must be regarded as the statement of an existing fact, rather than the legal creation of that fact. In a beleaguered city, for instance, the state of siege lawfully exists because the city is beleaguered; and the proclamation of martial law, in such a case, is but notice and authentication of a fact, ... civil authority has become suspended, of itself, by the force of circumstances, and that by the same force of circumstances, the military power has had, devolved upon it, without having authoritatively assumed, the supreme control of affairs, in the care of the public safety and conservation.[111]

Similarly, Frazer Arnold, writing in 1929, accepted that martial law "proclaims itself." Arguing that after the existence of an insurrection is established, the Governor does two things: (a) sends troops to restore order and (b) simultaneously issues a proclamation of martial law. Frazer says,

> The first of these is necessary, as there can be no martial law unless a military force has been called out. The second is not necessary, although usual and advisable ...The commander's powers are limited by the orders and instructions given to him by the governor and by the extent and nature of the exigency, rather than by the phraseology of his own or the governor's proclamation.[112]

Similar views have been expressed by Ballantine,[113] and earlier by Finlason,[114] albeit the latter erroneously viewed martial law also as an inseparable incident of formal international war. Indeed, *Luther v. Borden*[115] was the first case to accept that the state could formally proclaim martial law and use it against its citizens; before this, the state was denied the power to do so. In fact, *Milligan*[116] reflects a strong inclination by the US Supreme Court to revert to the earlier view even despite the decision in *Luther v. Borden.*

It is thus clear that a proclamation of martial law is neither constitutive of an emergency, nor necessary for its legal validity. But it does act as a warning to the populace[117] and as "a notice and authentication of a fact."[118] Secondly, it acts as one of the factors to be weighed in concluding whether martial law is being used or

---

[111] Opinion of AG Caleb Cushing, 8 Op. Att'y Gen. 365, 374 (1857).

[112] Arnold [65].

[113] Ballantine [66].

[114] Finlason [64].

[115] Luther v. Borden, 48 U.S. 1 (1849).

[116] *Ex parte* Milligan, 71 U.S. 2 (1866).

[117] *See, e.g.,* Willis [67]. ("So called declarations of martial law are, indeed, often made, but their legal effect goes no further than to warn citizens that the military powers have been called upon by the executive to assist him, in the maintenance of law and order.").

[118] Opinion of AG Caleb Cushing 8 Op. Att'y Gen. 365, 374 (1857).

whether troops are merely being called out to aid the civil authority. For example, the absence of a proclamation of martial law was one of the factors which led the US Federal District Court to conclude in *Palmer v. Adams*[119] that no martial law existed in Colorado and that troops were therefore acting only in aid of civil authority. The case was, therefore, decided by principles applicable to the latter rather than to martial law.[120]

That the proclamation of martial law may occasionally be of crucial significance in distinguishing between martial law and use of military in aid of civil authority was emphasized by the Pennsylvania Supreme Court,

> If the Sheriff finds his power inadequate, he calls upon the larger power of the state to aid with the military. The sheriff may retain the command, for he is the highest executive officer of the county, and if he does so, ordinarily the military must act in subordination to him. But if the situation goes beyond county control, and requires the full power of the state, the Governor intervenes as the Supreme executive and he or his military representative becomes the superior and commanding officer.[121]

There is, therefore, need for greater clarity in the proclamation of martial law.

3.7 *Permissible Consequences of Martial Law*

3.7.1 Exercise of Powers in the Absence of Trial of Civilians by Military Tribunals

There appear to be hardly any limitations upon the actions of the federal and state government during martial law. A number of decisions have upheld the use of force by the military to repel force and restore order, to arrest individuals, to detain without trial and to deny due process safeguards.[122] The discretion of State authorities to use all necessary measures for the restoration of peace and order includes the regulation or destruction of property and effects upon first amendment

[119]United States *ex rel.* Palmer v. Adams, 26 Fed. Rep. (2d) 141 (D. Colo.).

[120]Thus, for example, the Supreme Court of Michigan in Bishop v. Vandercook, 200 N. W. 278 (Michigan Supreme Court) treated the case as one of military acting in aid of civil authority and not martial law, partly because of the absence of a proclamation of martial law. *See also* Cox v. McNutt, 12 Fed. Supp. 355 (1935) where a proclamation not using the phrase "martial law" was given effect as if it had been a proclamation of martial law.

[121]Commonwealth v. Shortall, 98 Am. St. Rep. 759, 765 (1903).

[122]*See, e.g.,* Luther v. Borden, 48 U.S. 1 (1849); *In Re* Boyle, 57 P. 706 (1899) (Idaho Supreme Court); Commonwealth v. Shortall, 98 Am. St. Rep. 759 (1903), State *ex rel.* Roberts v. Swope, 28 Pac. Rep. (2d) 4 (1933) (New Mexico Supreme Court). *See also* Charles Fairman, *Martial Rule and the Suppression of Insurrection*, 23 Ill. L. Rev. 766, 776–83 (1929).

rights.[123] The fact that arrest without charge or detention without trial by the military denies due process and a host of other procedural criminal safeguards does not invalidate state action because such arrests and detention are seen as an inseparable part of martial rule and must cease upon the restoration of order and suppression of insurrection. Thereupon, the detenus must be handed over to the civil authorities for appropriate action under (normal) civil law.

3.7.2 Trials of Civilians by Military Tribunals

Judicial opinion has been more equivocal on the issue of the legality of military trials of civilian offenders during martial law. On one hand, use of military tribunals during the grave troubles in West Virginia in 1912–13,[124] during the longshoremen's strike in Texas in 1920[125] and during the disturbances in Nebraska in 1922,[126] was emphatically upheld by the respective Supreme Courts of those states. These decisions removed virtually all fetters on State action during martial law: military arrests, detentions, trials, convictions and imprisonments by the military were all upheld. Indeed, as discussed earlier, the West Virginia cases equated martial law with war, the States' forces to an invading army and the States' inhabitants to belligerents in foreign occupied territory. On the other hand, the US Supreme Court has, equally emphatically, expressed a contrary opinion on the two occasions when it has been squarely presented with the issue. It is submitted that the true significance of the *Milligan* case[127] is its holding, which remains good law today, that martial law does not permit, except in the actual theatre of war when civil courts are unable to function, the trial of civilians by military commissions. Amidst numerous criticisms of the decision directed primarily at the unnecessarily

---

[123]Cox v. McNutt, 12 F. Supp. 355, 358–59, 360 (1935) (Ind.) ("If the Governor determines that an exigency requires the use of the military forces, then, in his discretion, he has authority to call out such forces, and the courts will not interfere therewith … The purpose of martial law is to restore law and order … If it becomes necessary to imprison a person, to deprive him of a right of trial by jury, to deny him the right of habeas corpus, or to deprive him of other rights, in order to restore law and order, the military authorities are given that power …"); State *ex rel.* Roberts v. Swope, 28 P.2d 4, 6–7 (1933) ("… the Governor might seize the bodies of those whom he considered to stand in the way of restoring peace and restrain them of their liberty until the disorders were quelled … The Governor and his officers have a wide discretion in the steps which they may take in suppressing insurrection.").

[124]State v. Brown 71 W. Va. 519 (1912) (W. Va.).

[125]United States v. Wolters 268 Fed. 69 (1920) (Tex.).

[126]United States v. Fischer 280 Fed. 208 (1922) (D. Neb.).

[127]*Ex parte* Milligan, 71 U.S. 2 (1866).

broad remarks of Justice Davis,[128] it is often forgotten as to what the Court really decided. This was simply that Milligan, a US citizen of Indiana, which was a state not in the actual "theatre of war," could not be tried or convicted by a military commission. The qualification with respect to "theatre of war" simply means that where war is actually raging (i.e., amidst the actual clash of arms), normal judicial process is physically impossible to apply and hence civil courts necessarily cannot function. Hence, trial by military tribunals may be permissible, on grounds of necessity.

But the qualification is itself heavily qualified and cannot be allowed to swallow the rule. The rule is that as long as civil courts *are* open or *can* function without any obstruction, they, and not military tribunals, should try civilian offenders arrested by the military. It is only if the area has not enough manpower available to permit a jury to function or the proceedings require a greater secrecy than even an impounded civil record will permit or the jury in an area, for reasons of disloyalty, will not convict the guilty and that a change of venue is impractical, that this rule can be derogated from. Frank concludes that "there are few, if any, incidents in American history which could justify the exclusion of civil court jurisdiction on any of these grounds."[129] It may be added that the aforesaid decisions of the Supreme Courts of West Virginia, Texas, Nebraska, upholding military trials of civilian offenders, do not qualify as such exceptions.

The *Milligan* rule against such military trials was categorically reiterated by the Supreme Court almost eighty years later in *Kahanamoku*.[130] Invalidating the trial, conviction and imprisonment of the petitioners by a military commission established in Hawai'i by the Governor who had declared martial law following the attack upon Pearl Harbour, Justice Black for the majority of the court, stated, in words deserving extensive quotation:

> We are not concerned with the recognized power of the military to try civilians in tribunals established as a part of a temporary military government over occupied enemy territory … Nor need we here consider the power of the military simply to arrest and detain the civilians … these petitioners were tired before tribunals set up under a military programme which took over all government and superseded all civil laws and courts … As we shall indicate later, military trials of civilians charged with crimes … are … obviously contrary to our political traditions and our institution of jury trials in courts of law … Indeed, prior to the Organic Act, the only time this court has ever discussed the supplanting of courts by military tribunals in a situation other than that involving the establishment of a military government over recently occupied enemy territory, it had emphatically declared that "civil

---

[128]*Ex parte* Milligan, 71 U.S. 2, 76, 127 (1866). Davis, J., observed that, "The Constitution of the United States is a law for rulers and people, equally in war and in peace, and covers with the shield of its protection all classes of men, at all times, and under all circumstances. No doctrine, involving more pernicious consequences, was ever invented by the wit of man than that any of its provisions can be suspended during any of the great exigencies of government." He further observed, "martial rule can never exist where the courts are open, and in their power and unobstructed exercise of their jurisdiction. It is also confined to the locality of actual war." *See also*, Carbaugh [69].

[129]Frank [68].

[130]Duncan v. Kahanamoku, 327 U.S. 304 (1946).

> liberty and this kind of martial law cannot endure together; the antagonism is irreconcilable; and in the conflict, one or the other must perish." … The phrase "martial law" as employed in that Act, (i.e. Organic Act of Hawai'i) therefore, while intending to authorize the military to act vigorously for the maintenance of an orderly civil government and for the defense of the islands against actual or threatened rebellion or invasion, was not intended to authorize the supplanting of courts by military tribunals."[131]

A striking application of this rule is provided by the decision of the Montana Supreme Court in *Ex parte MacDonald* where Justice Sanner upheld the arrest and detention of McDonald by the military during the martial law in the state but invalidated the trial of Gillis by a military commission.[132]

The *Milligan* rule against military trials was not an innovative creation of the US Supreme Court in 1866. It reflected a deep seated American abhorrence of military trials which was supported by respectable judicial authority going back to the early nineteenth century.[133] Prior to the creation of formal standing armies and the perception of a distinction between martial law and military law, a string of decisions existed invalidating trials by court martial of individuals who had proved themselves to the US citizens. Thus Clark, an American citizen who was tried and sentenced by court martial on charges of being a spy because he had ventured too near an army base in New York was acquitted on review by President Madison who ruled that since Clark had never renounced his citizenship he was not "liable to be tried by a court martial as a spy."[134] Similarly in *Smith v. Shaw*, the New York Supreme Court ruled that since Smith was an American citizen he might be amenable to the civil authority for treason, but could not be punished under martial law as a spy.[135] Indeed, *Quirin*[136] which established the inapplicability of the

---

[131] *Id.* at 317, 324.

[132] *Ex parte* MacDonald *In Re* Gillis, 143 P. 947, 954 (Mont.).

[133] For a history of this abhorrence, *see*, Engdahl [54].

[134] Dennison [70].

> For example, Elijah Clark's case joined due process with involuntary divestiture of citizenship. Clark, an American citizen, who had migrated to Canada and acquired property there before the war, was tried and sentenced by a court martial on charges of being a spy. His alleged crime constituted of venturing too near an army base in upstate New York. On review, President Madison ruled that since Clark had never renounced his citizenship he was not "liable to be tried by a Court martial as a spy." (Internal Citations Omitted).

[135] Smith v. Shaw, 12 Johns. 257, 265 (1815) (Supreme Court of New York)

> None of the offences charged against *Shaw* were cognizable by a court-martial, except that which related to his being a spy; and if he was an *American* citizen, he could not be charged with such an offence. He might be amenable to the civil authority for treason; but could not be punished, under martial law, as a spy (Emphasis in original).

[136] *Ex parte* Quirin, 317 U.S. 1 (1942).

Milligan rule to non-US citizens being tried for violations of the laws of war is itself premised upon the alien enemy character of the defendants.

These and other early decisions[137] are paralleled by judicial pronouncements to the same effect made later. Thus the Supreme Court has held that neither the President nor a military commander may establish a court in a conquered country and authorize it to decide upon the rights of the United States, or of individuals[138]; that an ex-serviceman charged with murder allegedly committed while he was an airman in Korea could not be tried by a court martial[139]; and that present threats to peace in an area of world tension were insufficient to justify the trials of serviceman's wives for murder by military courts.[140] The Supreme Court has not been prepared to go further than allowing the trial by military commission of a non-resident enemy alien captured and tried in China.[141] The general approach of the court to military trials, even in cases involving military law or military government, is exemplified by the following remarks of Justice Black, speaking for a majority, in *Reid v. Covert:*

> There have been a number of decisions in the lower federal courts which have upheld military trial of civilians performing services for the armed forces "in the field" during time of war … The government urges that the concept "in the field" should be broadened to reach dependents accompanying the military forces overseas under the conditions of world tension which exist at the present time. It points out how "war powers" include the authority to prepare defenses and to establish our military forces in defensive posture about the world. While we recognize that the "war powers" of the Congress and the Executive are broad, we reject the Government's argument that present threats to peace permit military trial of civilians accompanying the armed forces overseas in an area where no actual hostilities are under way.[142]

It is not wholly clear why arrests and detentions by the military are deemed unobjectionable while trials by military commission are invalidated. Three likely explanations may be submitted. Firstly, arrests and detentions are seen as preventive measures having no punitive effect. A man arrested and detained temporarily during a situation of emergency, to be handed over to normal civil process as soon as possible is not seen as suffering from the same disability or stigma as a man who

[137]A justice of the peace is exempt from militia duty under the militia law of the US as a judicial or executive officer of the US and cannot be subjected to a Court martial, *see* Wise v. Withers, 3 Cranch 351 (1806); Upholding the constitutionality of federal and state enactments prescribing penalties for disobeying calls to do militia duty but assuming, without discussion, that such penalties by court martial would apply only to those who serve in or eligible to serve in the militia, *see* Houston v. Moore, 5 Wheaton 1 (1820); Those in militia service or those who ought to be in it are subject to courts martial, relying on *Houston v. Moore*, *see* Martin v. Mott, 12 Wheat 19 (1827); Under Virginia law, no court martial can be called for the assessment of fines, or for the trials of privates not in actual service, *see* Meade v. Deputy Marshal, 16 Fed. Cas. 1291 (1815).

[138]Jecker v. Montgomery, 54 U.S. 498 (1851).

[139]United States *ex rel.* Toth v. Quarles, 350 U.S. 11 (1955).

[140]Reid v. Covert, 354 U.S. 1 (1955).

[141]Johnson v. Eisentrager, 339 U.S. 763 (1950).

[142]Reid v. Covert, 354 U.S. 1, 33–35 (1955).

is tried by a military commission. Secondly, military detention is seen as a temporary aberration, to be followed soon thereafter by a civil trial with its panoply of procedural and substantive safeguards. Military justice is entirely devoid of the latter. Finally, the prohibition of military trials is seen in some measure to avoid a wholescale supplanting of civil authority. This is in conformity with American democratic traditions and harmonizes well with the repeated assertions of civil supremacy found in various enactments. Indeed, this prohibition of absolute martial law remains, as submitted earlier, the best way of harmonizing the civil supremacy clauses of state constitutions with exercises of martial rule.

3.8 Suspension of the Writ of Habeas Corpus

The writ of habeas corpus, the greatest of all monuments of Anglo-American liberty[143] is inextricably intertwined with a discussion of emergency powers. Judicial authority in the United States tends to agree that the writ of habeas corpus under US law has its origins in English law.[144] The great writ[145] of habeas corpus, the fundamental instrument for safeguarding individual freedom against arbitrary and lawless state action,[146] can only be suspended, as per the Suspension Clause in the US Constitution, in cases of rebellion or invasion or where compelling considerations of public safety and necessity may require it.[147] The Suspension Clause has been called "one of the more extreme forms of war power in the Constitution" since it amounts to suspension of due process—a cornerstone of Anglo-American legal system for almost a millennium.[148]

---

[143]Duker [72].

[144]*See* Stidham v. Swope, 82 F. Supp. 931, 932–33 (1949) (D. Cal.) (Chief Judge Denman).

[145]*See, e.g.*, Gregory [74].

> The Great Writ, like all judicial writs, is a government power. It is a judicial order, issued by a government official, to compel another person, typically another government official, to bring forth the body of a person, usually a detainee, for the purpose of testing the legitimacy of that person's detention…

Scaggs v. Larsen, 369 U.S. 1206, 1208 (1969) (Douglas, J.) ("The Great Writ was designed to protect every person from being detained, restrained, or confined by any branch or agency of government").

[146]Harris v. Nelson, 394 U.S. 286, 290 (1969).

[147]US Const. art. I § 9, cl. 2. ("The Privilege of the Writ of Habeas Corpus shall not be suspended, unless when in Cases of Rebellion or Invasion the public Safety may require it.").

[148]Tor Ekeland, *Suspending Habeas Corpus: Article I, Sect. 9, Clause 2, Of The United States Constitution and the War On Terror*, 74 Fordham L. Rev. 1475, 1476 (2005).

Prior to the Civil War, the most significant occasion when the writ of habeas corpus was purportedly suspended arose during the so called "Burr conspiracy,"[149] when Wilkinson, the military commander, declared martial law and ignored a writ of habeas corpus issued by the Supreme Court of New Orleans in respect of two detainees. Although, at the request of the Administration, the Senate, with only one dissent (of Senator James Bayard of Delaware), passed a bill providing directly for the suspension of habeas corpus in specified circumstances without delegating authority to suspend to the President,[150] the bill was overwhelmingly rejected (113 votes to 19) by the House of Representatives on the first reading. The US Supreme Court later ordered the release of the detainees.[151] The most significant and controversial use of the suspension power occurred during the Civil War, when the writ was suspended seven times in 1861[152] and once in 1862,[153] all by executive orders. This was followed by the Habeas Corpus Act of 1863 which gave very broad powers of suspension to the President.[154] A number of later occasions when the writ was suspended (but always under specific and prior Congressional authorization) include Congressional empowerment of President Grant to suspend the writ in order to combat the activities of the Ku Klux Klan, which power was exercised by the

[149]Schachner [73].

[150]The Bill read—

> … That in all cases, where any person or persons, charged with treason, or other high crime or misdemeanor, endangering the peace, safety, or neutrality of the United States, having been or shall be arrested or imprisoned, by virtue of any warrant or authority of the President of the United States, or from the Chief Executive Magistrate of any State of Territorial Government, or from any person acting under the direction or authority of the President of the United States, the privilege of the writ of habeas corpus shall be, and the same hereby is suspended, for and during the term there months from and after the passage of this act, and no longer.

See 1 Annals of Cong. 44 (1805) (Gales & Seaton ed. 1852). [Bluebooked. But the text above is not present at the page mentioned].

[151]*Ex parte* Bollman and Swartout, 4 Cranch 75 (1807).

[152]April 27 (allowing General Scott to bomb rebel cities "if necessary" but to suspend the writ of habeas corpus only in the "extremest necessity"); April 27 (authorizing suspension at "any point or in the vicinity of the military line … between … Philadelphia and … Washington … where resistance occurs"); May 10 (authorized suspension on the Florida coast); June 20 (authorized suspension in the case of Major Chase allegedly guilty of treason because he had resigned from the US army and become a Major-General in the Confederate Army); July 2 (authorized suspension on the line between New York and Washington); October 14 (authorized suspension on line between Bangor, Maine and Washington and places in between); December 2 (authorized suspension in the military department of Missouri "to secure public safety and the authority of the United States"). *See* Halbert [71].

[153]Halbert [76]. The proclamation suspending habeas corpus issued on September 24, 1862 directed primarily at rebels and insurgents and (if literally read) not applying to civilians.

[154]The Habeas Corpus Act, 1863, 12 Stat. 755. (Section 1 provided, "That, during the present rebellion, the President of the United States, whenever, in his judgment, the public safety may require it, is authorized to suspend the privilege of the writ of habeas corpus in any case throughout the United States, or any part thereof").

President in 1871 in North Carolina; the suspension of the writ by Theodore Roosevelt in Philippines in 1905 under an Act of 1902; and suspension of the writ in Hawai'i during the Second World War pursuant to the Habeas Corpus Act.

3.8.1 Martial Law and Suspension of Writ of Habeas Corpus Differentiated

Martial law may conceivably be used during emergencies not amounting to "rebellion or invasion," which alone is specified in the Constitution as a ground for suspension of habeas corpus. Moreover, martial law may involve the application of a variety of measures, some of which (e.g., arrest and detention by the military) may be effectively circumscribed by grants of the writ, while others (e.g., search, seizure or destruction of property) may have nothing whatsoever to do with the writ. Martial law need not necessarily involve a suspension of the writ and a number of instances of martial law mentioned earlier, especially of Qualified martial law, did not involve suspension of the writ. The converse situation, suspension of the writ without the existence of martial law, has also been recognized,[155] and could theoretically occur when the military is called in aid of the civil authority. Suspension of the writ without martial law may also occur in the United States because the power of granting the writ derives from a statute.[156] Arguably, though this is an unlikely eventuality, Congress may simply repeal such statutory authority and deny *habeas corpus* even without the existence or use of martial law or even without the existence of any threat to public safety as required by the Suspension Clause. This view seems to be based on Chief Justice Marshall's dictum in *Bollman* (1807).[157] The contrary view, apparently based on the authority of *Carbo* (1961)[158] that

---

[155]Fairman [77] ("The suspension of the writ of habeas corpus does not of itself inaugurate martial rule. It would be quite possible for the executive to continue to act through civil magistrates.").

[156]*See, e.g.,* 28 U.S.C. § 2241(a). Power to Grant Writ. ("**(a)** Writs of habeas corpus may be granted by the Supreme Court, any justice thereof, the district courts and any circuit judge within their respective jurisdictions.").

[157]*Ex parte* Bollman and Swartout, 8 U.S. 75, 93–94 (1807). ("Courts which originate in the common law possess a jurisdiction which must be regulated by their common law, until some statute shall change their established principles; but courts which are created by written law, and whose jurisdiction is defined by written law, cannot transcend that jurisdiction. It is unnecessary to state the reasoning on which this opinion is founded, because it has been repeatedly given by this court; and with the decisions heretofore rendered on this point, no member of the bench has, even for an instant, been dissatisfied. The reasoning from the bar, in relation to it, may be answered by the single observation, that for the meaning of the term *habeas corpus*, resort may unquestionably be had to the common law; **but the power to award the writ by any of the courts of the United States, must be given by written law**.") (Emphasis added) It would therefore stand to reason that whereas the power of the US Supreme Court to grant a writ of habeas corpus may not be taken away by statute, the power of other courts to grant this writ may be taken away, since it has been granted by a statue (28 U.S.C. § 2241(a)) in the first place.

[158]Carbo v. United States, 364 U.S. 611, 618–620 (1961).

Congressional authorization is not a necessary predicate for the grant of habeas corpus and that the Suspension Clause constitutes a directive to all superior courts of record,[159] state as well as federal, to make the writ routinely available is one which, although forcefully argued, is contradicted by earlier precedent, and appears not to be widely accepted.[160] In any event, these distinctions between institution of martial rule and suspension of the writ indicate that the judicial dicta[161] and other writing[162] equating the two are erroneous.

However, the view that martial law and the writ of habeas corpus are incompatible with each other[163] is not wholly without basis and there are many instances of writs of habeas corpus being disregarded by military authorities during martial law.[164] But this does not mean that martial law must, *ipso facto*, lead to suspension of the writ, or vice versa. Habeas corpus is not a remedy available as of course but only upon showing of adequate cause by the petitioner.[165] Hence, it may be granted or denied, but after review and on the merits, even during martial law. There is a valid distinction between suspension of the writ and its denial after judicial review in view of the existence of martial law. Secondly, the distinction between martial law and suspension of the writ would also become important if military trials of civilians are resorted to. Such trials would be unconstitutional under American law

---

[159]*See, e.g.,* Griffin v. Wilcox, 21 Indiana 370, 383 (1863).

[160]*See* Marshall, C.J., in *Ex parte* Bollman and Swartout, 8 U.S. 75, 94, 95, 99 (1807), asserting unequivocally that the "power to award the writ by any of the courts of the United States, must be given by written law" and that Congress may deny the privilege, *inter alia*, to prisoners in state custody (reiterated in Carbo v. United States, 364 US 611, 614 (1961)); *Ex parte* McCardle 74 U. S. 506 (1869) (repeal by Congress of Act of 5/2/1867, providing appeal to Supreme Court from circuit courts, held to remove Supreme Court's jurisdiction to hear habeas corpus application of detainee McCardle challenging the constitutionality of Reconstruction legislation). For other authority regarding *McCardle* similarly, *see* National Mutual Insurance Co. v. Tidwater, 337 US 582, 655 (1948) (Frankfurther, J. dissenting); Herbert Wechsler, *The Courts and the Constitution*, 65 COLUM. L. REV. 1001, 1005 (1965); Sheldon D. Elliot, *Courts curbing proposals in Congress*, 33 NOTRE DAME LAWYER 597 (1958). But *see also contra*, *Ex parte* Yerger, 75 U.S. 85 (1869), State v. Fleming 26 Tenn. 152 (1846), De Chastellux v. Fairchild, 15 Pa. 18 (1871), and United States v. Klein, 80 U.S. 128 (1871). However, while these decisions clearly reject legislative attempts to alter, interfere with or even influence judicial decisions, they would arguably be of little assistance to a Congressional limitation of jurisdiction (e.g. by repeal of statue) in the absence of or unrelated to actual pending cases between litigants.

[161]Griffin v. Wilcox, 21 Indiana 370 (1863); Jones v. Seward, 40 Barbom 563 (New York).

[162]Theophilus Parsons, *Martial law—Habeas Corpus*, 3 WESTERN L. MONTHLY 329, 331 (June, 1861). ("It may indeed be said that, for all practical considerations, martial law and the suspension of the right to habeas corpus, are one and the same thing.").

[163]*Ex parte* Field, 9 F.Cas. 1, 8 (1862).

[164]*See, e.g., In Re* Boyle, 57 Pac. Rep. 706 (1899); *In Re* Moyer, 117 Am. St. Rep. 189 (1905); *Ex parte* MacDonald, 49 Mont. 454 (1914); Moyer v. Peabody, 212 US 78 (1909).

[165]*See, e.g., Ex parte* Terry, 128 US 289, 301 (1888) (Harlan, J.) ("... the writ need not be ... awarded, if it [appears] upon the showing made by the petitioner, that if brought into court, and the cause of his commitment inquired into, he would be remanded to prison.").

and in such a case, the writ ought to be available to secure the liberty of the undertrial prisoner. Indeed, this is what had happened in *Milligan*.[166]

3.8.2 Who May Suspend the Writ?

It is incontrovertible, and has been accepted by the Supreme Court in *Milligan*[167] that Congress can suspend the writ of *habeas corpus*. To deny this power to Congress would make the writ non-suspendable and this would be contrary to the Suspension Clause.[168] Thus three points are clear—(1) Congress can legislatively suspend the writ; (2) joint Presidential and Congressional action is not necessary and (3) the writ is not non-suspendable (in other words, the writ can be suspended). The question naturally arises—is Congress the *only* body which has powers of suspending the writ or does the President also possess a similar power? The controversy as to whether the President can suspend the writ without Congressional authorization had led to considerable judicial and non-judicial writing.

The principal arguments in favor of an exclusive Congressional suspension power have included the *Historical* argument that as Parliament and not the king was empowered to suspend the writ in England, the legislature and not the executive should be similarly empowered in the United States.[169] Then there is the *Precedential* argument that, prior to the Civil War judicial opinion,[170] academic writing,[171] and legislative practice[172] were virtually unanimously in favor of this view. There is also the *Textual* argument that as the Suspension Clause uses the word "suspend" and no law can be suspended except by the legislature, Congress

---

[166]*Ex parte* Milligan, 71 U.S. 2 (1866).

[167]*Ex parte* Milligan, 71 U.S. 2 (1866).

[168]US CONST. art. I § 9, cl. 2. ("The Privilege of the Writ of Habeas Corpus shall not be suspended, unless when in Cases of Rebellion or Invasion the public Safety may require it.").

[169]*See, e.g., Ex parte* Merryman, 17 Fed. Cas. 144, 152 (1861) (Taney, C.J.)

> If the President of the United States may suspend the writ, then the Constitution of the United States has conferred upon him more regal and absolute power over the liberty of the citizen than the people of England have thought it safe to entrust to the Crown; a power which the Queen of England cannot exercise at this day, and which could not have been lawfully exercised by the sovereign even in the reign of Charles the First.

See also Ex parte Benedict, 3 F. Cas. 159, 162–63 (1862).

[170]*See, e.g., Ex parte* Bollman and Swartout, 4 Cranch 75, 101 (1807), Johnson v. Duncan, 6 Am. Dec. 675 (1816) (La).

[171]*See, e.g.,* JOSEPH STORY, COMMENTARIES ON THE CONSTITUTION OF THE UNITED STATES, § 1342.

[172]For example, President Jefferson's request to the House of Representatives for suspension of habeas corpus during Burr Rebellion. Jefferson never claimed any right to suspend the writ himself.

alone may suspend a writ which is granted by it under statute.[173] There is the *Structural* argument emphasizing that the Suspension Clause occurs in an article devoted to Congress while the article devoted to the President is silent on the issue.[174] Finally, the *Constitutional Restriction* argument[175] (that may fairly be characterized as another *Structural* argument) which suggested that the constitutional power of Congress to regulate courts (under article 3) included the power to regulate and suspend the writ; that the suspension power could be implied from any of the congressional powers to declare war, raise and support armies, call out the militia and make all necessary laws[176]; that this meant that Congress had an independent and inherent power to suspend the writ outside the Suspension Clause, that the Suspension Clause was thus a restriction on Congressional power (to suspend only during rebellion or invasion) and not a grant of power and hence could not be applicable to the President.

The principal argument in favor of a concurrent Presidential suspension power was the *Constitutional Grant* argument.[177] It was emphasized that the Suspension Clause was elliptical and, upon supplying the ellipsis, would read as a grant of power rather than a restriction upon pre-existing power.[178] It was added that the grantee of this power was the President because all the conditions for the exercise of the suspending power—existence of rebellion or invasion and threat to public safety —are necessarily matters of executive cognizance.[179] Other arguments in favor of a Presidential power included the *Structural* argument (based on powers of the

---

[173]This argument is based on the authority of Johnson v. Duncan, 6 Am. Dec. 675, 677 (1816) (Louisiana Supreme Court). ("If therefore this suspending power exist in the executive, under whose authority it has been endeavored to exercise it, it exists without any limitation; then the President possesses without limitation a power which the legislature cannot exercise without a limitation; thus he possesses a greater power alone, than the House of Representatives, the Senate and himself, jointly. Again the power of repealing a law, and that of suspending it, which is a partial repeal, are legislative powers … every legislative power that may be exercised under the Constitution of the United States is exclusively vested in Congress …").

[174]Fisher [78].

[175]Nicholas [79].

[176]McCullough v. Maryland, 17 U.S. 316 (1819). In this case a technique of implication was used to imply a Congressional power to charter a bank from its powers to collect taxes, borrow money, regulate commerce, declare war and raise and support armies.

[177]This argument was espoused by the influential leader of the Philadelphia Bar, Horace Binney, in his eighty-second year in the three pamphlets (all with the same title) that he authored (titled 'The Privilege of the Writ of Habeas Corpus under the Constitution', the first two published in 1862, and the third published in 1865 in Philadelphia). *See* Fisher [80].

[178]*See* Fisher [81] (Fisher notes that the clause ought to read as—"The privilege of the writ of habeas corpus shall not be suspended, unless when in cases of rebellion or invasion the public safety may require it; *and then it may be suspended.*") (Emphasis added).

[179]Thus, in words of Horace Binney's 1862 pamphlet, the one who championed this argument, "The President being the properest and the safest depositary of the power, and being the only power which can exercise it under real and effective responsibilities to the people, it is both Constitutions has placed (the suspension power) … in him." *See* S. G. Fisher, *The Suspension of Habeas Corpus during the War of the Rebellion*, 3 Pol. Sci. Q. 454 (1888).

President) to the effect that as the President was empowered by a host of constitutional provisions to preserve and protect the nation and execute its laws (e.g., the oath of office, vesting of executive power, making him Commander in Chief, obliging him to faithfully execute the laws), the suppression of insurrection and the means to do so must be left entirely to his discretion.[180] There is the *martial law* argument that the suspension of the writ was an inseparable incident of martial law and as the power to use martial law was available to the President, the suspension power must flow from it.[181] The *Constitutional Intent* argument argues that the initial draft of the Suspension Clause at the Constitutional Convention of 1787 explicitly used the word "legislature" when referring to suspension of the writ[182] but that this initial proposal was altered to delete this reference.[183] The *Locational* argument emphasizes that the appearance of the Suspension Clause in an article dealing with the legislature (article 1) was not conclusive as that article contained

---

[180]*See* Opinion of AG Bates 10 Op. Att'y Gen. 74 [?]. ("… in the end, the suppression of the insurrection, is required of him; the means and instruments to suppress it are lawfully in his hands; but the manner in which he shall use them is not prescribed … [and] he is, therefore, necessarily, thrown upon his discretion as to the manner in which he will use his means to meet the varying exigencies as they arise.").

[181]Joel Parker, Habeas Corpus and Martial Law 27–29 (1861). ("The power [of suspension] exists as an incident to other powers expressly conferred … the existence of martial law, so far as the operation of that law extends, is ipso facto, a suspension of the writ." *See also Ex parte* Field, 9 Fed. Cas. 1 (1862) (Vt. Cir. Ct.); Jones v. Seward, 40 Barbour 563 (1863) (C.C.D.N.Y.); Griffin v. Wilcox, 21 Indiana 379 (1863) (Ind.).

[182]The initial draft of the Suspension Clause formulated by Pinckney read—

> The *legislature* of the United States shall pass no law on the subject of religion nor shall the privilege of the writ of habeas corpus ever be suspended except in case of rebellion or invasion. (Emphasis Added)

Three months after the preparation of this clause, Pinckney proposed the following draft to be sent to the Committee of Detail—

> The privileges and benefits of the writ of habeas corpus shall be enjoyed in this government in the most expeditious and ample manner; and shall not be suspended *by the legislature* except upon the most urgent and pressing occasions and for a limited time not exceeding __ months.
>
> (Emphasis Added, Blank-space provided in original)

3 Max Farrand, The Records of the Federal Convention of 1787, 595 (Appendix D).

[183]Pinckney's proposals, including that of legislative suspension, never saw the light of day but were replaced by Governeur Morris's formulation, which read—

> The privilege of the writ of habeas corpus shall not be suspended, unless where [when] in cases of rebellion or invasion the public safety may require it.

See S. G. Fisher, *The Suspension of Habeas Corpus during the War of the Rebellion*, 3 Pol. Sci. Q. 454, 463 (1888).

other sections and clauses not dealing with Congress.[184] The *Analogy* argument rejects comparisons with early British law and practice by stating that seventeenth century British jealousy and distrust of the Crown was not paralleled by American misgivings about their President and that the American position was totally different as certain conditions were specified in the Suspension Clause. The *Ratification* argument provides that Congressional silence in the face of numerous Presidential suspensions of the writ constituted implies Congressional ratification of the President's actions.

It is not easy to make a choice between these opposing viewpoints. There is merit in the view that a Congressional suspension power can, on the analogy of *McCullough v. Maryland*,[185] be implied from various clauses of section 8 of article 1 (and not section 9) and that the Suspension Clause in section 9 is merely a restriction on this power. Similarly, the *Constitutional* argument is circular and begins by assuming what is sought to be proved. The argument suggests that the President has the power to suspend because he has the power to arrest and imprison; but the right to arrest is derived, if at all, from the right to suspend and "it is impossible to reverse the order."[186] Finally, the recognition of the differences between martial rule and suspension of the writ provide an answer to the *martial law* argument. According to the authors, as per legal theory at least, the exclusive Congressional power argument appears more attractive.

These answers do not, however, rob the executive of its say in the exercise of the suspension power. Firstly, in the thick of war or battle, where "might" trumps "right," the writ may simply be ignored by the military commander. This has, in fact, occurred on more than one occasion. In such circumstances, the writ, as indeed other safeguards, becomes irrelevant and academic due to the immediate exigencies of the situation. Secondly, in situations of Absolute martial law, where courts become non-existent for practical purposes, the writ must necessarily be suspended *ipso facto*, as the existence of a functioning civil court is a necessary predicate for issuance of the writ. The constitutional invalidity of Absolute martial law would be largely irrelevant for this argument, as it would lead only to post facto judicial intervention. In any event, despite doubts about its constitutionality, Absolute martial law has been used in some states on a number of occasions.

But the numerous occasions on which Lincoln exercised this suspensions power during the Civil War constitute perhaps the strongest arguments in favor of the concurrent Presidential power to suspend. Faced today with an emergency, a US President would find rich precedential support in the Lincoln era for suspending the writ and it is arguable that denial of such power to an executive head of state during

[184]Thus, for example, one clause in that section restrains the executive department by prohibiting grant of nobility, and another restrains all those who hold office of trust or profit under the United States. US Const. art. 1, § 9, cl. 8. Another clause contains a prohibition on States to not to enter into treaty, alliance etc. and another clause gives power of veto to the President. US Const. art. 1, § 7, cl. 3.

[185]McCullough v. Maryland, 17 U.S. 316 (1819).

[186]Bishop [82].

an emergency as grave as the Civil War would denude American constitutional law of its pragmatic functional and dynamic content.

Fisher, writing in 1888, and having strongly argued that a Presidential suspension power would probably be violative of the Constitution in strict theory, best exemplified the moral dilemma:

> It might be well therefore if Binney's argument were the true one. It is the only one that, under the present wording of the constitution, can by any possibility give the power to the executive … The habeas corpus clause as now understood stands in the way of the government's protecting itself. In such a case we want something more than a claim of right. Violations of the Constitution demoralize the people and abate their reverence for the great charter; but violations will surely come if such provisions are to remain. Every man thinks he has a right to live. Ever man when driven to the wall by a murderous assailant will override all laws to protect himself and this is called the great right of self-defense. So every government, when driven to the wall by a rebellion, will tremble down a constitution before it will allow itself to be destroyed. This may not be constitutional law, but it is fact.[187]

4 Martial Law in England

Martial law may, for contemporary purposes, be defined as the use of extraordinary or abnormal force by the military or, less often, by individuals, against domestic inhabitants during a situation of serious domestic disorder (including war, insurrection, rebellion or other grave public violence) for one or all of the following purposes: to repel force by force, restore order, arrest and detain wrongdoers or try them by military commissions or similar special tribunals.[188] The distinction between martial law and other methods of preserving public order is, however, as much one of degree as of kind: the degree being dependent on the amount of force used, the seriousness of the situation of emergency, the extent to which normal civil agencies are superseded and the degree of intrusion into private rights.

In the most severe case, the paradigm situation for use of martial law occurs in actual war or battle, where, amidst the clash of arms, the will of the military is absolute, supreme and unchecked. In situations not amounting to actual war or battle, there may be arrests and detentions by the military during open insurrection and rebellion followed by trial of the detenus by military commissions under summary procedure. In a third case, however, there may be violent public disorder in particular areas of the country which the civil authorities are unable to quell; the military may then take charge, detaining individuals and using force to repel force but handing the detenus over to the civil authorities after restoration of order for

---

[187] S. G. Fisher, *The Suspension of Habeas Corpus during the War of the Rebellion*, 3 Pol. Sci. Q. 454, 463 (1888).

[188] For other definitions of martial law, *see inter alia*, Chase [83], Forsyth [84] quoting Serjeant Spankie in "Hough on Courts martial"; 2 Hallam, Constitutional History 326 (3rd ed.) (1897); Capua [85].

appropriate legal action under normal law. Fourthly, the civil authorities may be unable to control a large and riotous mob and call up additional manpower in the form of the military to restore order; all arrests, detentions and trials in this case being done by or under the direct supervision and control of civil authorities.

The first two situations outlined above would clearly be one of martial rule[189]; indeed, many of the principles and phrases relating to martial law as also some infirmities in the law on this subject arise from this first paradigm case of martial law. The last example above is clearly one of the military actions in aid of civil authority and not in substitution or supersession of it. In between lies the rather uncertain third situation, where the military authorities have arguably superseded civil authority but do not use military justice to punish wrongdoers. These four examples show how differences in degree make for differences of kind.[190] Trial by military commission is not a necessary concomitant of martial law,[191] though it seems to have been a feature of martial rule in UK and overseas colonies on most occasions. In contrast, in the United States, military trials even during martial law appear to be unconstitutional.[192]

The distinction is now well recognized between martial law, as defined above, and military law, which is the set of rules and regulations governing the conduct of soldiers serving in the army, at home or abroad, during war or peace and military government, i.e., the power exercised by the military and its officers over occupied foreign enemy territory during war or other international armed conflict.[193] This,

---

[189]This term was first used and popularized by CHARLES FAIRMAN, THE LAW OF MARTIAL RULE (1943).

[190]*See, e.g.*, Alexander Bickel, *Congress, the President and the Power to Wage War*, (1971) 48 CHI-KENT L. REV. 131, 134 (But there comes a point when a difference of degree achieves the magnitude of a difference in kind). Bickel was refuting the argument that Presidential commitment of troops to Vietnam was different only in degree from his earlier uses of force at home or abroad.

[191]For example, in the celebrated Marais case (*In Re* The Queen v. Marais [1902] A.C. 109 (JCPC)), the petitioner was arrested and kept in custody by the military during the Boer War in South Africa but was not tried under military regulations; in R v. Gildenhuys [1900] 17 SCR 266 (SC of Cape of Good Hope) where the applicant was detained by the military during the Boer War and an "inquiry" was held by the (Civil) Resident Magistrate; in R(O'Brien) v. Military Governor [1924] IR 32 (C.A.), Mrs. O'Brien was arrested and detained by the military at an internment camp in Dublin but not tried or punished; *In Re* De Silva [1915] NLR 2777 (SC, Ceylon), Mr. De Silva was arrested and detained without trial and his detention was sought to be justified by reference to the proclamation of martial law.

[192]The US Supreme Court has so held on the only two occasions when it has directly considered the question: *see Ex parte* Milligan (1866) 18 L.ed. 281 and Duncan v. Kahanamoku (1946) 327 U.S. 304. Only a few state courts and two federal district courts have held to the contrary: *see* State v. Brown (1912) 77 S.E. 243 (W. Va.); *Ex parte* Jones (1913) 77 S.E. 1029; Hatfield v. Graham (1914) 81 S.E. 533; United States *ex rel.* McMaster v. Wolters (1920) 268 F. 69 (D. Tex.); United States *ex rel.* Seymour v. Fischer (1922) 280 Fed. 208 (D. Neb.).

[193]W. FORSYTH, CASES AND OPINIONS ON CONSTITUTIONAL LAW 552–53 (1869). Early recognition of this distinction can be found in the Joint Opinion of Queens' Counsel James and Stephen, given in 1866, on the Jamaica Insurrection. Although Lord Loughborough's judgement in Grant v. Sir Charles Gould, [1792] 2 H. Bla. 69, 98 contains many remarks equating present day military law and martial law, he seems to be aware of the distinction when he says:

After the reign of the two Stuarts, martial law of a non-statutory character has never been used within mainland Great Britain.[218] It has, however, been resorted to on a number of occasions in British colonies and overseas territories, including Ireland in 1798,[219] 1916 and 1920–21; British Guiana in 1823–24.[220] Ceylon (as it then was) in 1848 by Lord Torrington[221]; Canada in 1837–38; South Africa in 1835–36, 1846–47, 1850–53 and during the Boer War between 1899 and 1902; Jamaica in 1865[222] and India on a number of occasions between 1857 and 1940.[223]

4.2 Martial Law: Prerogative or Common Law?

The use of martial law between 1550 and 1628 under royal commission, in the absence of war or serious disorder and against the general populace, was rationalized as the "prerogative view" of martial law, said to be a special power exclusive to the Crown and State.[224] Prerogative martial law was conceived as an

---

[218]Arguably, the Defense of the Realm Acts of 1914 established "martial law and something more" within England during World War I. *See* Baty & Morgan War, Its Conduct and Legal Results 112–13 (1915); Bowman *martial law and the English Constitution* 15 Mich. L. Rev. 93 (1916–17).

[219]Acts were passed giving statutory effect to proclamations of martial law by the Lord-Lieutenant. *See*, for example, 37 Geo 3, ch. 38 (1797); 39 Geo 3, c. 11 (1799).

[220]For a brief discussion, *see* Finlason, History of the Jamaica Case Iiii–iv (Chapman & Hall eds., 1869).

[221]*Id.* at Ivi-Ixxiii.

[222]For an exhaustive account of martial law in Jamaicà and other places upon official documents, *see* Finlason, History of the Jamaica Case (Chapman & Hall eds., 1869).

[223]*See, inter alia*, Minnatur, martial law in India, Pakistan and Ceylon (1962); Finlason, History of the Jamaica Case 1–3 (Chapman & Hall eds., 1869).

[224]Probably the strongest proponent of the prerogative view of martial law was W.F. Finlason. See his three works; Treatise upon martial law (1866); Commentaries upon martial law (1866); A Review of the Authorities as to the repression of Riot or Rebellion (1868). The other works of Finlason which may be referred to include *martial law* in Law Magazine and Review of May and June 1872 (reprinted as a monograph); *martial laws* (Thoronton Pres, Camb. Univ. Lib. No. J.gm. 9.M.3.).

The best judicial authority for this view is R v. Hampden [1637] 3 How. St Tr. 826. *See also* W. Forsyth, Cases and Opinions on Constitutional Law 189–90 (1869) (opinion of Mr. Hargrave on an Irish Case involving martial law); R v. Nelson & Brand [1867] F. Cockburn's Sp. Rep. 85, 101–03 (citing the views of the Judge Advocate General and Sir David Dundas); W. S. Holdsworth, *Martial law Historically Considered*, 18 L. Q. Rev. 117, 126–128 (1902).

additional source of power, distinct from the widely acknowledged common law power to repel force with force.[225]

The prerogative was not extinguished, as one might have expected, by the Petition of Right of 1628 but indeed received a boost by the decision of the Court of Exchequer Chamber in Hampden's Case (1637).[226] A majority of the court[227] upheld the levy of the ship-money[228] by King Charles I and rejected the defence of Hampden—who had refused to pay the levy and been asked to show cause in a writ of *scire facias*[229]—inter alia, on the ground that the levy was a part of the royal prerogative exercisable during war or apprehended danger of which the king was the sole judge. The judgments in favor of the king reflect a very expansive view of the prerogative during emergency and make it free from all fetters by ascribing to

---

[225]See the views of Cockburn, C.J., in R v. Nelson & Brand [1867] F. Cockburn's Sp. Rep. 72–74, 85, 86, who opined that martial law is merely the application of the common law principle "that life may be protected and crime prevented by the immediate application of any amount of force, which, under the circumstances may be necessary"; Fredrick Pollock, *What is martial law* 18 L. Q. Rev. 152, 153 (1902): Firstly, it is not a matter of prerogative, but appertains to all lawful men. Secondly, it is not specifically vested in military officers, though they may most often be the proper persons to exercise it. Thirdly, its exercise requires to be justified on every occasion by the necessity of the case; W. Forsyth, Cases and Opinions on Constitutional Law 188 (1869), (giving the opinions of the Crown's law officers (opinions of Henely and Yorke in 1757); opinion of Sir J.S. Copley in 1824 at 194; Opinions of Sir J. Campbell & Sir R.M. Rolfe in 1838 and 1839 at 198, 204; Lord Loughborough in Grant v. Sir Charles Gould [1792] 2 H. BL. 69, 98; Holdsworth, *Martial law Historically Considered* 18 L. Q. Rev. 127–28 (1902).

A point of distinction between the two is that prerogative martial law imposes no limitations of proportionality or judicial review over the action of military such as the common law power would suffer from. Under prerogative martial law, those using force would be liable, after the emergency if, and only, absence of good faith could be established, while under the common law view, civil and criminal liability could be established under ordinary principles of reasonableness unless protected by Acts of Indemnity. Recourse to numerous such Acts indicates an inclination for the common law view. *Cf.* Bowman *Martial law and the English Constitution* 15 Mich. L. Rev. 93, 108–09 (1916–17), who opines that the "practical consequences" of this distinction are "slight" because in either case, the power exercised is limited by the requirement that "reasonable necessity" must exist and be shown to exist.

[226][1637] 3 How. St. Tr. 826.

[227]Although seven judges held for king and five against him, it is noteworthy that of the twelve judges who heard the case, nine had no doubt that ship money was a legitimate charge on the subject, a tenth did not decide the issue and found in favor of Hamden on a technical point and the remaining two alone (Croke and Hutton, JJ.) held in favor of Hampden on substantive grounds. *See* Keir [94].

[228]*See* Holdsworth [95].

[229]Campbell notes that a writ of scire facias is "a warning given to the defendant to appear in court and plead in bar of the execution, or show any cause if he can by release of otherwise, why execution should not issue on the judgement or record against him." *See* Foster [96].

the king the sole power to judge the existence and extent of the emergency.[230] Further support for the prerogative view is found, inter alia, in three statutes during the first part of the nineteenth century, which mentioned the "prerogative" of "martial law."[231]

It is difficult to see how the classic prerogative view can have any validity today. Hampden's Case is, of course, of no more than historical significance: not only were earlier precedents adopting a much less expansive view of the prerogative[232] and the Petition of Right of 1628 not given due weight in Hampden's Case, but the decision itself, along with the levy of ship-money, was declared by an Act of Parliament to be retrospectively "contrary to the laws and statutes of this realm."[233] Although echoes of the majority judgments in Hampden's Case were heard in a decision of the King's Bench as late as 1915,[234] they were quickly silenced in later decisions progressively limiting the role of the prerogative by making it operable

---

[230]Indeed, the point about the King being the sole judge of dangers from abroad and the means requisite to avert them was partially conceded by St. John and not strongly disputed by Holborne, Hampden's two counsel ([1637] 3 How. St. Tr. 826). For expansive remarks on royal power to meet actual or apprehended danger, *see id.* at 1081 Crawley, J.; Crawley, J. at 1083; Trevor, J. at 1126; Davenport, J. at 1214; Bramston, J. at 1248; Berkeley, J. at 1097; Finch, J. at 1234.

[231]These statutes included 39 Geo. III, c. 11 (1799); 43 Geo. III, c. 117 (1803) and 3 & 4 Will. IV, s. 40 (1833–34), all passed by the Parliament of Ireland.

[232]The Case of the Kings Prerogative in Saltpetre [1606] 12 Co. Rep. 12 = 77 E.R. 1294 (Upholds limited power to invade private property to combat the enemy within the realm, but emphasizes that it is limited to actual war and must cease immediately "after the danger is over"); Prohibitions del Roy [1607] 12 Co. Rep. 63 (the King cannot judge cases except through his judges for "His Majesty" was not learned in the laws of his realm of England… (or in cases which are) to be decided (not) by natural reason but by the artificial reason and judgement of law, which law is an art which requires long study and experience, before that a man can attain to the cognizance of it…"); Case of Proclamations [1611] 12 Co. Rep. 74 (the King has no legislative authority without Parliament; hence, he cannot, by his proclamation, prohibit new buildings or the making of starch or wheat). *Cf.* Bate's Case [1601] 2 St. Tr. 371 (Levy of poundage of 5 shillings per owt. On imported currants by James I under letters patent, in addition to a statutory poundage, upheld, *inter alia*, on the ground that the King can impose duties for regulation of trade though not for raising revenue and the Court must accept the King's statement that the levy was only for regulation of trade); Darnel's Case for refusal to pay contributions to a forced loan imposed by the king, upheld; the king's power to detain by special command or proclamation accepted.

[233][1641] 17 Car. 1, c. 14.

[234]*See in Re* Petition of Right [1915] 3 K.B. 649 at 651–52 (Avory J. in the King's Bench Div.), although the Court of Appeal took a relatively more restrained view (*id.* 659–60). After some arguments in the House of Lords, the appeal was withdrawn by the claimants on consent terms which included the Crown's agreement to pay compensation for use of the suppliant's land. *See* Hazeltine [97].

only in areas unoccupied explicitly or impliedly by statute[235] and by reading into the prerogative a duty to pay compensation when used to destroy or appropriate property during war.[236] The decision of the House of Lords in the so-called *GCHQ Case* of 1984[237] arguably makes the distinction between "prerogative" and "common law" theories of martial law academic. It is arguable that this so-called "prerogative" martial law would not be a prerogative power since its exercise would essentially involve an attribute—the use of force—shared by any ordinary citizen.[238] On the other hand, there is merit in the view that the use of force by the Crown through its soldiers is different from use of force by ordinary citizens and, indeed, this view has recently been judicially articulated.[239] Perhaps the best approach would be to treat martial law as *sui generis* prerogative power, though not as an inherent and absolute power. It is a *sui generis* emergency constitutional power usable when civil authority is unable to function or has been superseded.

4.3 Proclamations of Martial Law

An additional reason why the classic prerogative view of martial law may be said to be of doubtful validity is the fact that proclamations of martial law are widely regarded to be declaratory and not constitutive of the facts stated therein. This view

---

[235]A-G v. De Keyser's Royal Hotel Ltd. [1920] AC 508 (HL), where the decision in *In Re* Petition of Right, *id.*, was disregarded (Lord Dunedin, *id.*, at 525–26; Lord Sumner, *id.*, at 564–65; Lord Parmoor, *id.*, at 573, 578) and may be considered to be overruled (Lord Dunedin, *id.*).

[236]Burmah Oil v. Lord Advocate [1964] 2 All ER 348 (HL). Lord Reid opined that this view was supported by, although not decided in, the Zamora Case [1916] 2 AC 77; De Keyser's Hotel, *id.*; Crown of Leon (Owners v. Admirality Commissioners) [1921] 1 KB 595. Further, in Universities of Oxford and Cambridge v. Eyre & Spottiswoode Ltd. [1964] Ch. 736, Plowman, J. held that the expropriation of a private copyright by means of the royal prerogative was illegal; compensation must be paid.

[237]Council of Civil Service Union v. Minister for Civil Service [1984] 3 All ER 935; [hereinafter *GCHQ Case*].

[238]*See* Wade, Constitutional Fundamentals 46–49 (1980); Wade, *Procedure and Prerogative in Public Law* 101 L. Q. Rev. 180, 191–94 (1985) has persistently and persuasively argued for the exclusion of numerous items usually cataloged as prerogative powers on the ground that they are either not "singular and eccentrical" to the Crown or because they have no effect in the domestic sphere.

[239][1976] 2 All ER 937, 946, [hereinafter referred to as *Reference of 1975*]. Reference under Sect. 48A of the Criminal Appeal (NI) Act 1968 (No. 1 of 1975).

is widely supported by judicial authority,[240] by the law officers of the Crown,[241] by eminent lawyers,[242] by legal writers[243] and in other works on law.[244] The position in the United States is similar.[245] This view is usually justified by the argument that martial law depends on the actual circumstances of grave emergency and necessity, which can neither be created nor altered by the proclamation. The prerogative view of martial law, premised upon the existence of inherent State powers would seem to

---

[240]Tilonko v. AG, Colony of Natal [1907] AC 93 (JCPC) at 94:

> The notion that "martial law" exists by reason of the proclamation… is an entire delusion. The right to administer force against forces in actual war does not depend upon the proclamation of martial law at all. It depends upon the question whether there is war or not;

In Re De Silva [1915] 18 NLR 277 (SC, Ceylon) at 280:

> The proclamation…is in no way necessary to give martial law its efficacy and validity, any more than it would constitute an ultimate justification for acts in excess of what the needs of the war require. It is merely what it purports in terms to be, a declaration to the whole community of the assumption by the executive Government of powers which it already possesses.

See also R (Ronayne & Mulchay) v. Striekland [1912] 2 Ir. R. 333 at 334.

[241]*See* the Jt. Op. of A-G Sir John Campbell and Sir R.M. Rolfe, given in 1838, in respect of the power of the Governor of Canada to proclaim martial law:

> We must, however, add that in our opinion such proclamation confers no power on the Governor which he would not have possessed without it. The object of it can only be to give notice to the inhabitants of the course which the Government is obliged to adopt, for the purpose of restoring tranquility…(the) Governor may, even without any proclamation, proceed to put down the rebellion by the force of arms…

W. Forsyth, Cases and Opinions on Constitutional Law 198 (1869); *See also* the 1849 opinion of Sir David Dundas, Judge Advocate General, which is to similar effect, (quoted by Mr. James QC and Mr. Stephen QC) *id.* at 558–559.

[242]*See* W. Forsyth, Cases and Opinions on Constitutional Law 559 (1869) (Joint Opinion of Queens Counsel Mr. James and Mr. Stephen, 1866).

[243]Frazer Arnold, *The Rationale of martial law* 15 Am. Bar Ass'n. J. 550 (1929); F.W. Maitland, The Constitutional History of England 491 (H.A.L. Fisher 1963 ed.) (1919); Pollock 18 L. Q. Rev. 152, 154 (1902); Richards 18 L. Q. Rev. 133, 139 (1902); Cyril Dodd 18 L. Q. Rev. 143, 145 (1902); Clinton Rossiter, Constitutional Dictatorship 146 (1963); McDermott, *Law & Order in Times of Emergency* 17 Jur. Rev. 1, 11–12 (1972); Robert Sharpe, The Law of Habeas Corpus 109 (1976).

[244]Manual of Military Law, para 11(b) at 6–7 [1907].

[245]*See* opinion of AG Caleb Cushing 8 Op. Att'y Gen. 365, 366–67 (1857).

be inconsistent with this emphasis on actual necessity.[246] Proclamations, however, are not wholly superfluous. They serve the important function of operating

> [A]s a warning that the government is about to resort, in a given district, to such forcible measures as may be necessary to repel invasion or suppress insurrection.[247]

In those dubious instances outside war or actual battle where the seriousness of the emergency is unclear,[248] or where the dividing line between martial law and military action in aid of civil authority is difficult to draw, proclamations of martial law may not be conclusive evidence of the recitals contained therein, but may well be a probative factor.

The identity of the proclaimers of martial law and the essential content of the proclamations has not greatly varied over the ages. It has invariably been the executive authority of the State which has issued or authorized the issuance of proclamations of martial law or the institution of martial rule.[249] The commissions of martial law issued during the Elizabethan period illustrate some of the important elements of a martial law proclamation, viz., the recital of the facts in a whereas clause, the entrustment of the power to institute martial law, the delineation of the ambit of martial law (usually restricted to a particular area) and a description of the classes of individuals and the kinds of acts which are to be the target of martial law.

---

[246]On necessity, *see* the early decisions in R. v. Stratton [1779] St. Tr. 1224 (Lord Mansfield's direction to the jury). *See also* Devlin v. Armstrong [1971] NICA (Crim.) 13, 35 (N. Ir); The Case of the Kings Prerogative in Saltpetre [1606] 12 Co. Rep. 12 = 77 E.R. 1294.

[247]Manual of Military Law, para. 11 (b) at 7 (1907).

[248]The existence of these "cases of difficulty" was recognized in the Marais Case [1902] AC 109, 115 and in Tilonko v. AG, Colony of Natal [1907] AC 93, 95.

[249]An early (and unusual) example of a commission by statute is found in 2 Rich. II, stat. 1, c. 6 (1379). Other commissions include those in 1551 (by Edward VI); in 1556 (by Queen Mary) to use martial law against "idle and masterless men," "rogues" and "vagabonds"; in 1557 (also by Queen Mary) for the arrest and trial of Robert Cockerell, who was later executed; in 1558 by Queen Elizabeth against leaders of a minor disturbance in Lincolnshire. In 1595, Queen Elizabeth issued a very broadly worded commission. The Stuarts issued numerous commissions: James I in 1617, 1620, 1624 and 1625; Charles I in 1625, 1626 and 1627. Some commissions of martial law are reproduced or quoted in W. Forsyth, Cases and Opinions on Constitutional Law 481–83 (1869). *See also* 1 Hallam [98], Capua [2], *passim*.

Whether used by the chief executive of an overseas British territory[250] or by a military commander,[251] non-statutory martial law has been instituted under explicit or implied authorization from the central executive power and generally reflects the elements of a proclamation discussed earlier.[252] While it is arguable that the power to decide whether to sue the military in aid of civil authority has, at different times during English constitutional history, vested variously in the central executive authority or the civil magistracy at the local level,[253] no such transfers of the proclaiming power have occurred at different historical stages in respect of martial law. This is not surprising, as martial law involves a much graver emergency necessitating central executive cognizance and intervention.

5 Martial Law in India

The Indian Constitution is an interesting case study in the emergency power of proclamation of martial law. In England, the executive's power to proclaim martial law is covered by the common law as well as certain Parliamentary legislation that we have discussed above. In United States, the Constitution is clearly silent on the issue but certain constitutional provisions are interpreted to mean that the executive has the power to proclaim martial law. The history of martial law in the United States as discussed above leaves no doubt as to the power and its several contours in the United States. The Indian Constitution, like its American counterpart, is silent on the issue of martial law to the extent that there is no express provision in the

---

[250] *See, e.g.*, by the Governor Eyre in Jamaica in October 1865. *See, inter alia*, R v. Eyre [1868] Finlason Sp. Rep; WILLIAM FRANCIS FINLASON, A REVIEW OF THE AUTHORITIES AS TO THE REPRESSION OF RIOT OR REBELLION 160 (1868).

[251] For example, in Ireland in 1920 and 1921. *See* R v. Allen [1921] 2 Ir. R 241; R (Garde & Ors.) v. Strickland [1921] 2 Ir. R 317; R (Johnstone) v. O'Sullivan [1923] 2 Ir. R 13; R (Childers) v. Adjutant General [1923] 1 Ir. R 5; R (O'Brien) v. Military Governor [1924] 1 Ir. R 32.

[252] For an example from the twentieth century, *see* the proclamation issued by the Commander-in-Chief, Sir Neville Macready, in Ireland on Dec. 12, 1920:

> [T]hat a state of armed insurrection exits, and that any person taking part therein, or harboring any person who has taken part therein, or procuring, inviting, aiding or abetting any person to take part therein, is guilty of levying war against His Majesty the King, and is liable, upon conviction by a military court, to suffer death.

Quoted in R (Garde & Ors.) v. Strickland [1921] 2 IR 317, 328 (Ir.).

[253] *See* Steven C. Greer, *Military Intervention in Disturbances: The Legal Basis Reconsidered*, PUB. L. 573 (1983).

Indian Constitution that authorizes the executive branch of either the Union or the State governments to proclaim martial law.[254] The closest the Indian Constitution comes to a direct reference to "martial law" is article 34.[255]

Article 34 inter alia allows the Indian Parliament to "indemnify any person in the service of the Union or the State … in respect of any acts done by him in connection with the maintenance or restoration of order in any area within the territory of India where martial law was in force." Article 34 therefore is only an enabling provision that enables the Parliament to indemnify and validate things done under a proclamation of martial law. But can it then safely be argued that unless the Indian Constitution allows for martial law to be proclaimed, there is no need for article 34 to be there?

When we search the Indian Constitution for a provision that specifically authorizes martial law, we would be at a loss. An argument can perhaps be made that both article 355[256] (which is rather similar to the Guarantee Clause of the US Constitution[257]), and article 352 are wide enough to include the power of the Union Parliament and/or Union Government to proclaim martial law. This presents a unique conundrum—is article 352 or article 355 the source of the power to proclaim

---

[254]Though it is arguable that a proclamation of emergency on any of the three grounds mentioned in article 352 could be taken to be a de facto proclamation of martial law, or in the alternative, is at least capable of being worked as if it was a proclamation of martial law. *See* India Const. art. 352, § 1. The point has been discussed and elaborated later in this part. One of us have elsewhere argued that issuance of a "disturbed area notification" under the Armed Forces Special Powers Act, 1958 is the practical equivalent (i.e., a de facto proclamation) of a proclamation of martial law. *See* Gautam [99, p. 117].

[255]India Const. art. 34.

> **Restriction on rights conferred by this Part while martial law is in force in any area.** Notwithstanding anything in the foregoing provisions of this Part, Parliament may by law indemnify any person in the service of the Union or of a State or any other person in respect of any act done by him in connection with the maintenance or restoration of order in any area within the territory of India where martial law was in force or validate any sentence passed, punishment inflicted, forfeiture ordered or other act done under martial law in such area. (Emphasis supplied).

[256]India Const. art. 355.

> **Duty of the Union to protect States against external aggression and internal disturbance.** It shall be the duty of the Union to protect every State against external aggression and internal disturbance and to ensure that the government of every State is carried on in accordance with the provisions of this Constitution (Emphasis supplied).

[257]U.S. Const. art. 4, § 4.

> The United States shall guarantee to every state in this union a republican form of government, and shall protect each of them against invasion; and on application of the legislature, or of the executive (when the legislature cannot be convened) against domestic violence.

martial law? Or is it article 34 that by implication is the source of the power to proclaim martial law or is it only an indemnifying and validating provision? But if it is so, what purpose does article 34 serve at all? What is the need to have an indemnifying provision in the Constitution when there is no corresponding power to proclaim martial law? The overarching question of course is, can martial law be proclaimed under the Indian Constitution, and if yes where is that power located? Let us first survey the pre- and post-independence Indian judicial opinion on martial law.

5.1 Pre-independence Judicial Opinion

Before the Indian Constitution, and before the establishment of the modern Indian Republic in 1949–50, the Government of India Act, 1915,[258] Government of India Act, 1919,[259] and later Government of India Act, 1935,[260] were the constitutional documents that were applicable to the territory known as British India.[261] The 1915 Act remained in force for about 21 years since its enactment.[262] Section 72 of the 1915 Act authorized the Governor-General of India, in cases of emergency, to promulgate ordinances that had the force and effect of law in British India.[263] Later, this power was retained when the 1935 Act was enacted[264] and all previous Government of India Acts were repealed.[265]

So far as the power to promulgate ordinances in cases of emergency is concerned, though, this power was vested in the Governor-General of India much before the enactment of the Government of India Act, 1915. For example, section 23 of the

---

[258]*See* Government of India Act, 1915 (5 & 6 Geo V, c. 61).

[259]*See* Government of India Act, 1919 (9 & 10 Geo 5, c. 101).

[260]*See* Government of India Act, 1935 (Ch. 2, 26 Geo 5).

[261]*See* Government of India Act, 1915, § 1; Government of India Act, 1953, § 2(1). For a detailed list all pre-1915 governing British legislations applicable to British India *see* Government of India Act 1935, Tenth Schedule.

[262]Dam [100, p. 43].

[263]Government of India Act, 1915, § 72—

> The Governor-General may, in cases of emergency, make and promulgate ordinance for the peace and good government of British India or any part thereof, and any ordinance so made shall, for the space of not more than six months from its promulgation, have the like force of law as an Act passed by the Indian legislature; but the power of making ordinances under this section is subject to the like restrictions as the power of the Indian legislature to make laws; and any ordinance made under this section is subject to the like disallowance as an Act passed by the Indian legislature, and may be controlled or superseded by any such Act.

See also Dam [100, p. 47] (noting the transformation of Governor-General's exceptional powers to become a rule rather than an exception).

[264]Government of India Act, 1935, Ninth Schedule (retaining Sect. 72 of the 1915 Act).

[265]Government of India Act, 1935, § 321, Tenth Schedule (for repeal).

Indian Councils Act, 1861 allowed the Governor-General to promulgate ordinances "in cases of emergency" and for "peace and good government" of the territories under the Governor-General's control.[266] In 1915, the 1861 Act was repealed and replaced with the Government of India Act, 1915. Section 72 of the 1915 Act retained the power of the Governor-General, "in cases of emergency," to "make and promulgate ordinances, for that peace and good government of British India."[267]

The Indian Constitution retained the power to promulgate ordinances and vested the executive branch to so promulgate when the Union Parliament or the State Legislature, as the case may be, is not in session.[268] For the purposes of promulgation of ordinances the 1915 Act did not actually define or specify the conditions that could be treated as "the cases of emergency," and the Indian Constitution, for the purposes of promulgation of ordinances, also does not so specify. A preliminary cautionary caveat may be advisable at this stage. The concept of "emergency" used in conjunction with ordinances is qualitatively different from the concept of "emergency" which is the principal focus of this work. Emergency in the context of ordinance making power is more to do with absence of time or facility to complete the various processes and stages of proper legislation or law making and it is in this respect of "executive law making" that the concept of emergency is used. The latter does not concern this study, *stricto sensu*, though all forms of actual physical exercise of emergency powers, their legal validity and scope and judicial control thereof, does.

Two additional points may be noted here. Firstly, the Indian Constitution provides for proclamation of emergency in pre-specified situations in a separate part of the Constitution.[269] And secondly, the promulgation of ordinances under the Indian Constitution is not contingent on an emergency and may be promulgated whenever the Parliament or the State Legislature is not in session. The traditionally accepted view seems to be that a declaration of emergency is a job entrusted with the executive branch of the government and the courts should not interfere, which the courts also seem to have accepted but it is also settled that while the courts cannot substitute their satisfaction with that of the executive, they can examine the

---

[266]Dam [100, p. 38–42].

[267]*Id.*

[268]*See* India Const. arts. 123, 213, and compare with Government of India Act, 1915, § 72 (later retained in Government of India Act, 1935, Ninth Schedule).

[269]Indian Const. Part XVIII (art. 352–360).

materials that the executive branch used to arrive at that satisfaction.[270] However, this was not always the case.

In 1916 Calcutta High Court opinion in *Jewa Nathoo*[271] the petitioner and a few others were arrested on the orders of the Commissioner of Police, Calcutta as they arrived in Calcutta from South Africa but the grounds on which they were arrested was not disclosed to them.[272] They moved a *habeas corpus* application before the Calcutta High Court. The Deputy Commissioner of Police resisted the petition on the ground that the petitioners were detained on the authority of a notification issued by the Governor of Bengal. The notification provided that any authorized officer could,

> ...[D]etain any person entering the Presidency of Bengal whether by sea or land after the 5th of September 1914 when it appeared to him that such person had entered the Presidency of Bengal, with intent to prosecute some purpose prejudicial to the safety, interest or tranquility of the State.[273]

It was stated before that court that "certain information" had been received and the petitioners were therefore arrested[274] and it was argued that *habeas corpus* had not been suspended by the ordinances whereunder the notification was issued.[275] The court found that the ordinance had been issued in "circumstances of emergency."[276] Under these circumstances the court held that,

> It is for the Governor-General in Council to be satisfied on the materials before him. The Court cannot call for the materials to examine him...It is asserted that even now the Government has no materials upon which they have purported to take action, but I have no power to enquire into that allegation, as the orders comply with the requirements of the Act.[277]

In *Jewa Nathoo* therefore the court refused to inquire into whether or not there existed any material before the police on the basis of which legality of the detention order could be reviewed. However, in *Jewa Nathoo* there was no martial law proclamation in force in Calcutta at the time of the petitioner's arrest.

---

[270] *See, e.g.*, Chanappa Shantirappa v. Emperor, 1931 AIR 57 (Bom.) 58. Chief Justice Beaumont:–

> Where martial law has been declared it is competent for the Courts—and is indeed the duty of the Courts if called upon—after the restoration of normal conditions to decide whether and to what extent martial law was justified.

[271] *In Re* Jewa Nathoo, (1916) ILR 46 (Cal.) 459.

[272] *Id.* at 465.

[273] *Id.* at 467.

[274] *Id.*

[275] *Id.* at 470.

[276] *Id.* at 474.

[277] *Id.* at 475–476.

In 1921, the Madras High Court, in *In Re Nair*[278] had the occasion to deal with the validity of actions taken in Ordinance No. II of 1921 that came into force on September 5, 1921.[279] The petitioner Nair was arrested by the police after he was questioned in relation to the "Moplah outbreak" at Mannarghat. He wasn't shown any warrant of arrest and he wasn't told anything about the offence(s) with which he was charged.[280] The petitioner approached the Madras High Court seeking *habeas* relief inter alia on the ground that, "…[he] could not be legally arrested for an offence committed inside the martial law area when he was at the time of arrest at a place outside it …."[281] Justice Spencer rejected this argument and held that, "I do not see anything in the Martial Law Ordinance which prohibits the arrest of persons who commit offences inside the martial law area but escape outside." An unsuccessful attempt therefore was made in *In Re Nair* to somehow restrict the scope of martial law powers to the geographical area that was put under the proclamation of martial law. Justice Spencer was clearly of the view that so long as the offence is actually committed inside the area that is under martial law, it does not matter from where the person is arrested. However, this does make one pause and examine the nature of martial law supposedly proclaimed by the Governor-General under Section 72 of the 1915 Act. The facts in *In Re Nair* do not disclose any warlike or such extreme situation where the civil administration has been rendered so helpless so as to be unable to discharge its duties. The facts also do not disclose that ordinary courts had ceased functioning and resumed their functions under military protection. It does seem that the September 5, 1921 proclamation of martial law was only so in name and was not truly supported by the facts as presented before the High Court. However, the petitioner had never challenged the validity of the proclamation itself and had only challenged the jurisdiction of the civilian officer acting under the proclamation. Thus there was never any occasion for the High Court to examine closely whether or not the proclamation was justified.

In 1922, the Madras High Court in *Erada*[282] once again had the occasion to examine acts done under the Ordinance V of 1921 promulgated on November 11, 1921, a proclamation of martial law proclaimed also in response to the "Moplah outbreak" but this time called the "Moplah rebellion."[283] The petitioners were found guilty of "assisting the rebels in destroying a bridge" and were awarded 18 months each in prison. The key grievance, raised in this case by the petitioners (by way of a *habeas* petition) was:

---

[278]*In Re* Kochunni Elaya Nair, 1922 AIR 215 (Mad.).

[279]*Id.* at 216.

[280]*Id.*

[281]*Id.*

[282]Erada v. Emperor, 1922 AIR 499 (Mad.).

[283]*Id.* at 500. There is nothing on record, however, to suggest that the incident in this case and that in *In Re* Kochunni Elaya Nair, 1922 AIR 215 (Mad.) are the same incidents.

> It was alleged that they had assisted the rebels in destroying a bridge. This they admitted but stated that they were compelled to do so under threat of death. They alleged, owing to the trial being summary and taking place away from the scene of action and far from their homes, they were not in a position to substantiate their defence by evidence which they could have called, if the trial had taken place under the ordinary law and in its proper place.[284]

They were summarily tried by a Magistrate appointed under the Ordinance, "… who held his Court at a place outside the area in which martial law was proclaimed, the alleged offence having been committed inside such area."[285] The Madras High Court was impressed by this argument[286] of the petitioners and held:

> Acting under the powers conferred by Section 72 of the Government of India Act, this Ordinance was made and promulgated by the Governor-General. By it martial law was put in force in certain areas called Administration areas, and by Section 6 Summary Courts of criminal jurisdiction might be constituted in any administration area with summary powers of trial of certain minor offences connected with rebellion. The Military Commander had power to direct cases to be tried by the Summary Courts and to distribute work among such Courts. By Section 7, no Summary Court can try any offence unless committed in the administration area in which such Court is established; except as so provided, the ordinary criminal Courts continued their functions.
>
> From the decision of such Summary Courts there is no appeal and further by section 16 of the Ordinance all powers of interference with such decision by writ of Habeas Corpus or otherwise is prohibited. It follows that if the Court that tried the petitioners was a properly constituted Court under the Ordinance we have no power to interfere. But in our judgment this was not a Court properly constituted under the Ordinance *for we can find no right at all to hold a Summary Court except in the martial law area*, and by the words of the Ordinance the jurisdiction of these Courts is local. Outside the area the ordinary rules of law prevail and there is nothing in the Ordinance to prevent this Court interfering with the decision of any Court outside the area purporting to exercise a criminal jurisdiction which it does not possess. That this is the proper construction of the Ordinance seems to have been recognized by the Government of India after these convictions by Section 10 of the Ordinance V of 1921 promulgated on November 11, 1921. By that section it was enacted: "Notwithstanding anything contained in any law for the time being in force, the Local Government may, by general or special order, appoint places, outside the area in which martial law is in force, at which any Summary Court, constituted under the Martial Law Ordinance, 1921, or Special Magistrate may sit for the trial of offences."

---

[284]Erada v. Emperor, 1922 AIR 499 (Mad.) 500.

[285]*Id.*

[286]*Id.* at 501–02. The High Court observed that,

> The law can be stated to be that in every part of the British Empire every person has a right to be protected from illegal imprisonment by the issue of the prerogative writ of *habeas corpus*. … In our judgment, this Court has the power to issue this writ and in this case it is its duty to do so.

It follows that the conviction of the petitioners was illegal and that there is no justification for their detention in prison.[287]

The 1931 opinion of the Bombay High Court delivered in *Chanappa*[288] is a comparatively detailed treatment of the subject by Chief Justice Beaumont. In this case Martial Law Ordinance No. 4 of 1930 promulgated on May 15, 1930 under Section 72 of the 1915 Act (proclaimed as a result of riots in Sholapur that took place following the arrest of Gandhi on May 6, 1930[289]) and withdrawn on June 30, 1930,[290] was under question. The facts are borne out by the opinion of the Chief Justice:

It is clear from the affidavit of Mr. Knight, the District Magistrate of Sholapur, whose evidence is not contradicted, that on 12th May a very serious state of civil insurrection existed in Sholapur; mobs had attacked the police on the 8th, and on several occasions the police had to open fire, and two unarmed constables had been murdered. The facts disclosed appear to show a deliberate intention on the part of the crowd to attack constituted authority, and the police were insufficient to deal with the situation. Accordingly, Mr. Knight, as the senior executive officer, decided to hand over the control of Sholapur to the military authorities, and this in my opinion, constituted a state of martial law in the strict sense. … On 15th May the Governor-General at Simla issued an ordinance under S. 72 of the [1915] Act reciting that an emergency had arisen in Sholapur which made it necessary to provide for the proclamation of martial law in the town of Sholapur …[291]

The Chief Justice observed that under English constitutional law, martial law can be proclaimed by the executive branch where a state of war or a state of insurrection amounting to war exists but the courts are competent, and indeed duty bound to review, "… after the restoration of normal conditions to decide whether and to what extent martial law was justified."[292] *Whether or not an emergency exists is a*

[287]*Id.* at 500. (Emphasis added). *But see* Jogendranath Ray v. Superintendent of Dum Dum Special Jail, (1933) ILR 60 (Cal) 742 (Holding that the Governor-General is competent to authorize the courts by means of an Ordinance to pass sentences of imprisonment for terms beyond the date of expiry of such Ordinance).

[288]Chanappa Shantirappa v. Emperor, 1931 AIR 57 (Bom.).

[289]The fact was noted in the judgment of Chief Justice Beaumont. *See* Chanappa Shantirappa v. Emperor, 1931 AIR 57 (Bom.) 61.

[290]*Id.*

[291]*Id.* at 59.

[292]*Id.* at 58 (Beaumont, C.J.)

Where martial law has been declared it is competent for the Courts—and is indeed the duty of the Courts if called upon—after the restoration of normal conditions to decide whether and to what extent martial law as justified.

question of fact that the courts can inquire into[293] but the extent to which they can inquire into this question is restricted.[294] The courts can only, "… inquire whether there is evidence upon which the Governor-General may reasonably conclude that an emergency exists. If that question be answered in the affirmative there is an end of the matter."[295]

We may note here that *Chanappa* is a far cry from *Jewa Nathoo* where the Calcutta High Court had plainly held that the court cannot examine the materials on the basis of which the Governor of Bengal had decided that there was emergency. But the notable difference between these two cases is that whereas in *Chanappa* it was a martial law proclamation that was in question, in *Jewa Nathoo* there was no martial law. This creates an inconsistency. A proclamation of martial law is in reality nothing but a proclamation of emergency imposing martial law under Section 72 of the 1915 Act. In other words, under Section 72 of the 1915 Act there is no express power granted to the Governor-General to proclaim martial law. But when judicially reviewing such a proclamation, as per *Chanappa* the court can "inquire whether there is evidence upon which the Governor-General may reasonably conclude that an emergency exists." But as per *Jewa Nathoo* if the emergency proclamation stops short of proclaiming martial law "the court cannot call for the materials" to examine whether such a proclamation is supported by any facts.

The petitioners in *Chanappa* were charged and convicted at Sholapur on May 12th and May 18th for offences against Martial Law Regulations by Military Tribunals acting under those Regulations.[296] They questioned the proclamation of martial law on the ground that, "… there was no state of war or armed insurrection against the Crown or public necessity to justify the civil authorities in abdicating and handing over charge to the military authorities …," and that, "… it was at most a case of riots which had ceased after [May 8th] …"[297] After a discussion of

---

[293]*Id.* at 58, 67–68 (Blackwell, J. concurring) (Emphasis added)

> It is undoubtedly the duty of the Courts if the necessity is challenged, to inquire into the matter, and if the necessity is not established, then any persons who have committed acts not sanctioned by the ordinary law are liable to be attacked in the Courts at the instance of those who have suffered from their lawless acts.

[294]*See, e.g.*, Chanappa Shantirappa v. Emperor, 1931 AIR 57 (Bom.) 62. Beaumont, C.J.,:

> Section 72, as a whole hardly empowers the Court to consider whether the Governor-General was right or wrong in his conclusion that an emergency existed, much less examine how far the provisions of the ordinance tend to the peace and good government of the country. That responsibility the statute has laid on the Governor-General and not on the Courts.

[295]*Id.* at 59.

[296]*Id.* at 58.

[297]*Id.* at 61 (Madgavkar, J., concurring).

English authority on the subject, the court concluded that for a valid proclamation of martial law, "Firstly, a state of war or armed rebellion or insurrection must exist and not merely a state of riot which could be put down with the aid of the military and other citizens."[298] On facts, it was found that it was no longer possible for the civil administration to function and thus handing over the administration of the district to military was justified.[299] *Chanappa* is thus important authority for judicial review of the very existence of a martial law emergency.

Nevertheless, the proposition that the Governor-General is the sole judge of whether an emergency, under Section 72 of the 1915 Act, exists or not was emphatically affirmed by the Privy Council in *Bhagat Singh.*[300] The Governor-General had promulgated the Lahore Conspiracy Case Ordinance, 1930 that transferred the trial of the famous Lahore Conspiracy Case (where the revered and highly respected freedom fighter and martyr Bhagat Singh and his associates were being tried) to a tribunal that was to be constituted by the Chief Justice of Lahore and to consist of three judges of the High Court.[301] The tribunal so constituted held Bhagat Singh and his associates guilty of waging war against the King, murder, conspiracy and offences under the Explosive Substances Act and sentenced three of them to death, seven to transportation for life and two to rigorous imprisonment. The petitioners applied for *habeas corpus* relief and argued that, "It was for the prosecution to show that an emergency existed, but they failed to do so. There was no emergency within the meaning of the section."[302] Viscount Dunedin, speaking for the Privy Council, rejected the argument and held:

> The petitioners ask this Board to find that a state of emergency did not exist. That raises directly the question who is to be the judge of whether a state of emergency exists. A state of emergency is something that does not permit of any exact definition:- It connotes a state of matters calling for drastic action which is to be judged as such by someone. It is more than obvious that that someone must be the Governor-General and he alone. Any other view would render utterly inept the whole provision. Emergency demands immediate

[298]Chanappa Shantirappa v. Emperor, 1931 AIR 57 (Bom.) 63.

[299]*See, e.g.*, Chanappa Shantirappa v. Emperor, 1931 AIR 57 (Bom.) 68. (Blackwell, J. concurring)

> There were only about 60 armed police available to deal with a disturbed city of 1,20,000 inhabitants and four other places in the District and most of them had been on duty from morning of 7th May, Mr. Knight having been informed by the Deputy Inspector-General of Police that no police assistance could be sent from other districts. It was in these circumstances that Mr. Knight considering that it was not possible to carry on the normal civil administration as stated by him in his affidavit, reported that the facts of the Local Government and with their approval handed over charge of the situation to the military authorities at 8:30 p.m. on 12th May.

[300]Bhagat Singh v. King Emperor, (1931) ILR 12 (Lah.) 280.

[301]*Id.* at 281.

[302]*Id.* at 282–283.

> action, and that action is prescribed to be taken by the Governor-General. It is he alone who can promulgate the ordinance.[303]

Bhagat Singh subsequently became an authority for the proposition first proposed by the Calcutta High Court in *Jewa Nathoo*, before Section 72 of the 1915 Act was even enacted. In every subsequent case where the authority of the Governor-General to proclaim emergency under Section 72 of the 1915 Act was questioned, *Bhagat Singh* was pressed into service and was cited favorably by the Indian courts. *Chanappa* unfortunately, and conveniently, was forgotten. For instance in *Pramila Gupta*[304] the Bengal Criminal Law Amendment Act, 1930 further amended by the Bengal Criminal Law Amendment Ordinance, 1932 provided that if,

> ...[I]*n the opinion of the Local Government* there are reasonable grounds for believing that any person (i) is a member of an association of which the objects and methods include the commission of any offence included in the first schedule, or the doing of any act with a view to interfere by violence or threat of violence with the administration of justice or (ii) has been or is being controlled by a member of any such association with a view to the commission or doing of any such offence or act or (iii) has done or is doing any act to assist the operations of any such association, the Local Government may, by order in writing, give directions that such person be committed to custody in jail.[305]

The petitioners were so arrested and brought action for *habeas corpus* before Calcutta High Court. The action failed and on the authority of *Bhagat Singh* it was held that:

> In our opinion, it was clearly the intention of legislature, as expressed in Section 2(1) of the Criminal Law Amendment Act, that in the opinion of the Local Government, whether or not there were reasonable grounds for making an order under the section, should be conclusive. ... [I]t is not possible to question the fact that, in the opinion of the Local Government, there were reasonable grounds for believing that Miss Gupta was a person in respect of whom an order might lawfully be made. It would be idle for the Court to examine those grounds, since, even if it is considered the grounds unreasonable, it would still have to pronounce the detention lawful because the Local Government took the opposite view. ... It will be observed that in the language of Section 72 there is nothing that directly or by implication makes the Governor-General the sole judge of those questions and it, therefore appears to us that the language of Section 2 of the Bengal Criminal Law Amendment Act, 1930 renders the position of the Local Government under that Act even more plain than the position of the Governor-General under the Government of India Act.[306]

In 1944 the Privy Council affirmed *Bhagat Singh* in *Sarma*.[307] By this time, the 1915 Act was replaced by the Government of India Act, 1935 but the power to declare a state of emergency as they were granted to the Governor-General under the 1915 Act were preserved as they were. Now the Governor-General could

[303] *Id.* at 284.

[304] Pramila Gupta v. W.S. Hopkyns, (1932) ILR 59 (Cal.) 1440.

[305] *Id.* at 1444.

[306] *Id.* at 1448–49.

[307] Emperor v. Benoari Lal Sarma, (1945) FCR 161 (IA).

proclaim emergency under Section 72 of Schedule 8 of the 1935 Act. The question again was as to whether or not the Governor-General's decision to declare a state of emergency under Section 72 could be reviewed by the courts. The question was again answered in favor of the Governor-General.[308] However, the fact that, "… Japan had declared war on previous December 7: Rangoon had been bombed by the enemy on December 23, and again on December 25 …,"[309] did not help the case of the petitioners. Speaking for the Privy Council, Viscount Simon L.C., on the authority of *Bhagat Singh* held that, "… the question whether an emergency existed at the time when an ordinance is made and promulgated is a matter of which the Governor-General is the sole judge."[310]

In all these decisions, *Chanappa* was conveniently ignored. However, *Chanappa* is not really an authority for the proposition that every proclamation of emergency could be reviewed by the courts. It is restricted to a proclamation of martial law. But as stated above, the fountainhead of a martial law proclamation or an emergency proclamation (being a non-martial law proclamation) is the same—Section 72 of the 1915 Act. Then why can the courts review one but not the other? This inconsistency is a constant feature of the pre-independence jurisprudence on emergency actions. Regrettably, the answer would have to be in the context of an imperial power trying to uphold its authority in, and occupation of the colonies and pressing to its aid all legal tools in support thereof.

5.2 *Post-independence Judicial Opinion*

There isn't much by way of post-independence judicial opinion on the issue of martial law. As noted above, the Constitution does speak about martial law but only in respect of indemnification of any government officials who might have taken any actions in order to maintain or restore order where martial law was in force.[311]

In *Subba Rao v. Supreme Commander*[312] the Andhra Pradesh High Court was presented with an unprecedented question. A writ petitioner sought a direction from the Court to issue a mandamus to the President to impose martial law in view of the alleged unstable political situation in the country. Normally, such a writ should have met the fate of a frivolous and vexatious writ. But since the Court examined the issue at (unnecessary) length, it may be worthwhile to legally analyze the decision where the Court formulated the issue thus: "Is the President of India

[308] *Id.* at 169.

[309] *Id.*

[310] *Id.* at 170.

[311] India Const. art. 34.

[312] Chinta Subba Rao v. Supreme Commander of Defense Forces, AIR 1980 (Andhra Pradesh) 172.

constitutionally competent to impose martial law on the country in the present circumstances? Has this Court got power and jurisdiction to issue this writ?"[313]

In dealing with this unusual petition, the High Court inter alia, said:

> [S]o long as Art. 21 is in full force, there is no legal way under our Constitution for the imposition of martial law. What follows is a constitutional anomaly. While Art. 34 read with Item II(A) of List I of the 7th Sch. clearly contemplates imposition of martial law, the scheme of fundamental rights and the device of remedial enforcement provided for by the Constitution makes the effectiveness of martial law regime legally impossible.[314]

While doing so the High Court quoted from *A.D.M. Jabalpur* as follows:

> It is, therefore, obvious that merely declaring Martial Law would not by itself, deprive the Courts of the power to issue the writ of habeas corpus or other process for the protection of the right of the individual to life and liberty. In our country, unlike England, the right to life and liberty is secured as a fundamental right and the right to move the Supreme Court for enforcement of this right is also guaranteed as a fundamental right....They could never have intended that the Government should have the power to declare Martial Law and yet it should be devoid of the legal effect which must inevitably follow when Martial Law is in force.[315]

Other portions of *A.D.M. Jabalpur* not quoted by the Andhra Pradesh High Court include the following:

> [M]erely declaring martial law would not, by itself, deprive the Courts of the power to issue the writ of habeas corpus. ... The only device therefore provided for the taking away of Art. 21 is to be found in Art. 359 read with Art. 352. Under Art. 352, the President can make a declaration of emergency, the President can by an order under Art. 359 suspend the right guaranteed by Art. 21 of the Constitution. ... [E]ven during the martial law or any emergency any order made by the executive or military affecting a citizen's right to life and liberty can be tested for its validity and legality in the ordinary Courts.[316]

The Andhra Pradesh High Court's conclusion in *Subba Rao* that martial law is an anathema to the Indian Constitution, based in turn on Justice Bhagwati's dictum above, yields several interesting ironies. Firstly, Justice Bhagwati in *A.D.M. Jabalpur* was discussing purely the suspension power under article 359 and the exegesis above on martial law is largely obiter. Secondly, it makes no reference and does not deal with article 34. Thirdly, it must be remembered that *A.D.M. Jabalpur* was decided prior to the 44th Amendment in 1978 whereas the High Court's decision specifically relies on the 44th Amendment, which, having rendered articles 20 and 21 non-suspendible even during an emergency, supports the view that martial law is anathema to the Indian Constitution post the 44th Amendment.

---

[313] *Id.* at 173.

[314] Chinta Subba Rao v. Supreme Commander of Defense Forces, AIR 1980 172 (Andhra Pradesh) 175.

[315] A.D.M. Jabalpur v. Shiv Kant Shukla, AIR 1976 SC 1207, 1369 (Bhagwati, J.).

[316] *Id.* at 1369 (Bhagwati, J.).

Fourthly, it is ironical that in the pre 44th Amendment era, the *A.D.M. Jabalpur* court, despite having made several pro-liberty observations as the one quoted above, four of the five judges in the *A.D.M. Jabalpur* bench (except Justice Khanna) in fact upheld the remedy-less status of a hapless citizen seeking redress qua his liberty during suspension of article 21 under article 359.[317] Fifthly, the *A.D. M. Jabalpur* nadir has been rectified by its comprehensive overruling by the nine-judge bench in *Puttaswamy v. Union of India*.[318] In the absence of the 44th Amendment the Andhra Pradesh High Court's decision in *Subba Rao* could hardly have been considered good law. Fifthly, for example, under the pre 44th Amendment position, *Subba Rao* would contradict *Chanappa* where it was held that even though the proclamation of martial law is strictly within the domain of the executive, the Courts are duty bound to review, "… after the restoration of normal

---

[317] *See* Chief Justice A.N.Ray's observation in A.D.M. Jabalpur v. Shiv Kant Shukla, AIR 1976 SC 1207, 2 SCC 521, 571–574,

> The safeguard of liberty is in the good sense of the people and in the system of representative and responsible government which has been evolved…where the Government believes the State to be threatened by traitorous conspiracies during times of grave emergencies the rights of individuals of ordinary times becomes subordinate to considerations of the State…In a period of public danger…the protective law which gives every man security and confidence in times of tranquility, has to give way to interests of the State…courts of law are…ill-equipped to determine whether a given configuration of events threatens the life of the community and thus constitutes an emergency.

A similar stance was adopted by the concurring opinion of Justice Chandrachud, who observed, *id.* at 654

> …[T]he object of Article 359 is to confer wider powers…than to merely suspend the right to file a writ of habeas corpus…[I]n order to achieve that object that Article 359 does not provide that the President may declare that the remedy by the way of habeas corpus shall be suspended during emergency.

[318] Justice K. S. Puttaswamy v. Union of India, (2017) 10 SCC 1, 414–420 (India) (Dr. Chandrachud, J.). *See also id.* at 419, where Dr. Chandrachud, J., notes,

> A constitutional democracy can survive hen citizens have an undiluted assurance that the Rule of Law will protect their rights and liberties against any invasion by the State and that judicial remedies would be available to ask searching questions and expect answers when a citizen has been deprived of these, most precision rights. The view taken by Khanna, J. must be accepted….

conditions to decide whether and to what extent martial law was justified,"[319] and further that the courts can, "… inquire whether there is evidence upon which the [executive] may reasonably conclude that an emergency exists."[320] Judicial review of actions taken under the color of martial law, and the proclamation of martial law itself are, as per *Chanappa*, thus not totally beyond judicial review. If the structural position in *Chanappa* is accepted as correct, then *Subba Rao* would have been incorrectly decided in the pre 44th Amendment era to the extent it holds that there is no power to proclaim martial law under the Indian Constitution. However, on facts, no other order could have been rendered by the Andhra Pradesh High Court in *Subba Rao* except that the outlandish prayer made by the petitioner in that case deserved emphatic rejection.

5.3 Can Martial Law Be Proclaimed Under Article 34?

While it is therefore clear that post 44th Amendment martial law cannot be proclaimed under the Indian Constitution at all, the more interesting question is, firstly, whether it, or a state resembling martial law (de facto martial law) could be so proclaimed prior to the 44th Amendment, and secondly, whether the source of power for such proclamation could legitimately be traced to article 34?

The answer to the first question, according to the authors, is in the affirmative; while the answer to the second is in the negative. The reasoning follows.

Prior to the 44th Amendment it would be absurd to deliberately posit a contradiction in the same Constitution which, on the one hand, contemplated the suspension of article 21[321] (which, though not identical to, could be considered a close analog of, or a de facto state of, martial law) and also specifically mentioned martial law in article 34 and, on the other hand, to deny the very existence of martial law under the Indian constitutional scheme.

As regards the second query posed above it would be conceptually erroneous to confuse the recognition of pre-existing or past martial law (as contemplated in article 34) with the location and source of power to declare martial law being

---

[319]*Id.* at 58. Beaumont, C.J.:

> Where martial law has been declared it is competent for the Courts—and is indeed the duty of the Courts if called upon—after the restoration of normal conditions to decide whether and to what extent martial law as justified.

[320]Chanappa Shantirappa v. Emperor, 1931 AIR 57 (Bom.) 59.

[321]The unamended article 359(1) as it stood prior to the 44th Amendment permitted the President to "by order declare that the right to move any court for the enforcement of such of the rights conferred by Part III" of the Constitution. The 44th Amendment replaced the phrase "rights conferred by Part III" with "the rights conferred by Part III (except Article 20 and 21)." *See* Constitution (Forty-fourth) Amendment Act, 1978, § 40; India Const. art. 359, § 1.

located in the same article 34. As elaborated earlier, martial law contemplates inter alia a suspension of civil liberties including, most importantly, redressal of grievances from civil courts in times of de facto extreme physical stress and exigencies. Consequently, if Part XVIII renders such judicial redress of matters of life and liberty non-derogable and non-suspendable, the source of power to declare martial law and its extinction by the 44th Amendment must both necessarily be found in Part XVIII.

Furthermore, no other provision of our Constitution uses the phrase "martial law" except article 34. The different proclamations of emergency that can be made under articles 352, 356 and 360 also do not expressly authorize the President to proclaim a state of "martial law." But articles 352, 356 and 360 being located in Part XVIII, and Part XVIII being a complete code in itself, it is not possible to argue that article 34, outside of and dehors the whole of Part XVIII, could be taken as the source of the constitutional authority to proclaim martial law. Nor would it constitute harmonious construction to treat article 34 as a vast standalone source of power, virtually decimating the letter and spirit of both Parts III and XVIII.

A significant clue of the true meaning and scope of article 34 is found in its text and especially in its opening words. It is placed rather curiously in Part III of the Constitution that deals with fundamental rights. Article 34 is indeed a peculiar provision. It provides:

> **Notwithstanding anything in the foregoing provisions of this Part**, Parliament may by law indemnify any person in the service of the Union or of a State or any other person in respect of any act done by him in connection with the maintenance or restoration of order in any areas within the territory of India **where martial law was in force** or validate any sentence passed, punishment inflicted, forfeiture ordered or other act done under martial law in such area.[322]

Before moving forward, a brief comment on the phrase "any person in the service of the Union or of a State or any other person" may be apposite. Article 34 enables Parliament to indemnify any person for acts done for maintenance or restoration of order in an area where martial law was in force, notwithstanding whether such a person was in the service of the Union or of a State. Dr. Ambedkar had himself stressed that it was necessary to indemnify not just members of the armed or other forces employed during martial law but any person who comes to help for restoring order during martial law.[323] Responding to the criticisms raised by several members of the Constituent Assembly against article 34 in its draft form, Dr. Ambedkar noted:

> [W]hen martial law is there it is not merely the duty of the Commander-in-Chief to punish people, *it is the duty of every individual citizen of the State to take the responsibility on his*

[322] INDIA CONST. art. 34 (Emphasis added).

[323] *See e.g.*, 5 B. SHIVA RAO, THE FRAMING OF INDIA'S CONSTITUTION: A STUDY 309 (Kashyap ed., 2012) (1968).

> *own shoulder and come to the help of the Commander-in-Chief.*[324] Consequently it was found that any person who was an ordinary person and did not belong to the Commander-in-Chief's entourage, so to say, does any act it is absolutely essential that he also ought to be indemnified because whatever act he does he does it in the maintenance of the peace of the State and there is a no reason why a distinction should be made for a military officer and a civilian who comes to the rescue of the State to establish peace.[325]

Clearly therefore the framers contemplated article 34—(a) as enabling Parliamentary law; (b) in the case of on-going or past martial law; (c) for the limited purpose of indemnifying the category of persons mentioned above in respect of acts done by them while martial law was in force; (d) for purposes of such indemnification alone, to override all the fundamental rights in Part III. All this drafting history would also support the proposition that article 34 was never contemplated to be an independent source provision enabling the proclamation of martial law in any way or form.

In the above view of the matter, another interesting conclusion follows and that is this. Post the 44th Amendment in view of the now permanently non-derogable and non-suspendable nature of articles 20 and 21, it is first clear that article 34 would be reduced to vanishing point because martial law as explained cannot be proclaimed post the 44th Amendment. Article 34 has, therefore, become a historical relic[326] and in view of the 44th Amendment, continues as a superfluity in the Constitution. Indeed, it may be treated as repealed by implication.

Another purely academic but interesting conceptual question arises—would the aforesaid conclusion hold good, despite the non-obstante clause in the opening words of article 34? Theoretically, a strong argument may be raised that the non-obstante clause in article 34 overrides article 21 and the 44th Amendment does not directly address this contradiction between the override of article 21 by the non-obstante clause of article 34 and the special non-derogable status given to the same article 21 by the 44th Amendment.

---

[324]For an authority on the duty of the citizen(s) to be called upon to keep public peace, *see*, R. v. Pinney, [1832] 5 Car. & P. 254, 273,

> …[T]he general rules of law require of magistrates: which are, that they should keep the peace and restrain rioters, and pursue and take them; and to enable them to do this, they may call on all the king's subjects to assist them; and the king's subjects are bound to do so. They are to call on the King's subjects who are bound to assist them upon reasonable warning.

See also Dicey [101].

[325]11 CONSTITUENT ASSEMBLY DEBATES, Book 5, 578 (Lok Sabha Secretariat, reprint 2014) (16th November, 1949).

[326]An "alternative view" of article 34 as presented in the next section would support the proposition that article 34 is indeed a historical relic and was always intended to apply to past events that happened between 1947 and 1950, and was never intended to have any application beyond those events.

This apparent paradox may be harmonized and resolved in the following manner. Firstly, one has to examine the anchor principle as to whether suspendability of article 21 and martial law are virtually synonymous. The authors have above argued that this is so,[327] despite the former being a legal process and the latter signifying a factual state of affairs. If this fundamental conclusion is correct, then it follows, secondly, that non-derogability of articles 20 and 21 cannot co-exist with a state of martial law, factual or legal. Thirdly, and candidly, while the 44th Amendment reflects an inadvertent *casus omissus* by non-addressing the non-obstante clause of article 34 (which it could easily have amended), the well-established principle of both a later and a specific amending act (in this case the 44th Constitution Amendment Act, 1978) will, on established principles of interpretation, reinforce the authors' view herein. The 44th Amendment is not only a later constitutional amendment but since the source of martial law is located not in article 34 but in article 352 and article 359 read with article 21, the 44th Amendment is also specific and not general. For these three reasons, article 34 would stand virtually obliterated in any practical sense, save and except the category of cases discussed below.

This exception which might give a role to article 34 even post the 44th Amendment would arise in the following hypothetical manner. It is possible to comprehend a declaration of emergency under article 352 which suspends various parts of Part III of the Constitution except articles 20 and 21. For example, an article 352 proclamation that suspends article 19(1)(a) and prejudicially affects the rights of freedom of speech and expression during the pendency of such a proclamation. Similarly, another example could involve the suspension of article 19(1)(g) and prejudicially affect the business, vocational and professional rights of Indian citizens. If either of these rights in aforesaid two examples are compromised by the class of persons intended to be covered by article 34, the alleged perpetrator, in case Parliament enacted an indemnity law post the article 352 proclamation, would get indemnity from prosecution, damages, or other civil, criminal or tortious claims to aggrieved citizens and provide an arch of immunity to the personnel contemplated by article 34. This is the narrow zone of operation in a hypothetical sense that might attract article 34 post 44th Amendment. Needless to add, these examples can be replicated for any other provision of Part III except for articles 20 and 21 (e.g., 19 (1) (g), etc.)

[327]For further authority and discussion on the subject, *see*, ROBERT STANLEY RANKIN, WHEN CIVIL LAW FAILS: MARTIAL LAW AND ITS LEGAL BASIS IN THE UNITED STATES 12 (Duke University Press 1939) (quoting General Order of March 14, 1815 issued by General Jackson) ("If [the US Constitution] authorizes the suspension of the habeas corpus in certain cases, *it thereby impliedly admits the operation of martial law*, when, in the event of rebellion or invasion, the public safety may require it.") (Emphasis added); Khagesh Gautam, *Martial Law in India: The Deployment of Military under the Armed Forces Special Powers Act, 1958*, 24 SW. J. INT'L L. 124 (2018).

5.4 An Alternative View: Historical Analysis of Article 34

A historical analysis suggests that article 34 was intended solely to indemnify pre-constitutional excesses and not intended for use in a post-constitutional setting.

At the outset, the authors would like to clarify that what follows is not necessarily supported by a textual analysis of article 34. Textually and based upon normal literal and reasonable interpretation, article 34 should be interpreted and applied as per the foregoing and preceding discussion. However, historical evidence from the drafting era offers considerable support to an alternative interpretation of article 34. As per this interpretation, article 34 was limited to the providing indemnity for potential and possible claims, arising, inter alia, from the Hyderabad action in 1948–49 and not as a continuing charter of indemnity in post-constitution independent India.

On November 3, 1949, when the Drafting Committee of the Constituent Assembly forwarded the revised draft of the Constitution to the Assembly, they made an important observation pertaining to article 34 in their letter that was sent with the draft.[328] The letter was signed by Dr. Ambedkar, N. Gopalaswami Ayyangar, A. Krishnaswami Ayyar, K. M. Munshi, Syed Mohd. Saadulla, and T. T. Krishnamachari.[329] In this letter, with regard to the newly inserted article 34, they said:

> It was pointed out to us that the fundamental rights in the Constitution might prevent validation by the Legislature of acts done during the period *when martial law is in force* and also prevent the indemnifying of persons in the service of the Union or of a State in respect of action taken by them during such period. This new article has been suggested by us to cover this contingency.[330]

The choice of the words in this comment and in the text of article 34 is very interesting. The comment was made in present tense ("when martial law ***is*** in force") whereas the provision is drafted in past tense ("when martial law ***was*** in force"). This use of present tense and past tense might ordinarily be of no avail, but when examined in the light of relevant historical circumstances prevalent during the drafting of the Constitution it throws considerable light on the true meaning and scope of this article. To appreciate this crucial choice of words, we have to go back to what we will call the "Hyderabad Crisis" in order to fully understand the argument.

The Indian Constitution came into force on January 26, 1950 (with some provisions coming into force on November 26, 1949). Between August 15, 1947 and January 26, 1950, the Government of India Act, 1935 was proclaimed as the interim

[328]Rao [102].

[329]*Id.* at 750.

[330]*Id.* at 747 (emphasis added).

constitution of independent India.[331] Note that India became a republic only upon the coming into force of the Constitution on January 26, 1950 (which of course we all proudly celebrate every year as our Republic Day). Between August 15, 1947 and January 26, 1950, India was independent but it was not yet a constitutionally proclaimed republic. One of the biggest challenges faced by the government of independent India, governed by the Government of India Act, 1935 as the interim constitution, was the integration of princely states into the Union of India which was to be a republic.[332] Republicanism of course meant abolition of sovereignty of princes. And the Nizam of Hyderabad, Mir Osman Ali Khan who was one of, if not the wealthiest of princes,[333] was not very pleased with this proposed arrangement.[334] Thus he declared not to commit Hyderabad to either Pakistan or India.[335] The problem was that geographical considerations made it practically impossible for Hyderabad to remain independent except in name.[336] Sunil Purushotham notes:

> Hyderabad signed a "Standstill Agreement" with India in November 1947 that essentially maintained the indeterminate constitutional relationship it had enjoyed with the Government of India under the British system known as "paramountcy." With neither side

---

[331]*See* Indian Independence Act, 1947, § 8 cl.2. Section 8, which falls under the heading of "Temporary provisions as to the government of each of the new Dominions." Section 8 reads as "(1) In the case of each of the new Dominions, the powers of the legislature of the Dominion shall, for the purpose of making provision as to the constitution of the Dominion, be exercisable in the first instance by the Constituent Assembly of the Dominion, and references in this Act to the Legislature of the Dominion shall be construed accordingly.

(2) Except in so far as other provision is made by or in accordance with a law made by the Constituent Assembly of the Dominion under subsection (i) of this section, each of the new Dominions and all Provinces and other parts thereof **shall be governed as nearly as may be in accordance with the Government of India Act, 1935**; and the provisions of that Act, and of the Orders in Council, rules and other instruments made thereunder, shall, so far as applicable, and subject to any express provisions of this Act, and with such, omissions, additions, adaptations and modifications as may be specified in orders of the Governor-General under the next succeeding section, have effect accordingly...." *See also* MAX PLANCK ENCYCLOPEDIA OF COMPARATIVE CONSTITUTIONAL LAW 770 (Rainer Grote et al. eds., 2013).

[332]For a comprehensive account of the difficulties associated with the integration of the princely states, *see generally* Menon [103].

[333]*See* Singh [104].

[334]*See* Talbot [105] (noting that "Lord Mountbatten, who had directed the transfer of power from Britain to the Governments of India and Pakistan, failed to resolve the Hyderabad impasse. A further contretemps occurred in June when the Nizam disavowed an agreement which provided the substance but not the form of accession and which had been initialed by his negotiators. This set the stage for the final act. By now India had raised its demands. It insisted that the Nizam not only accede but also establish responsible government, leaving himself only as constitutional head of state."

[335]Purushotham [106].

[336]*See* Sherman [107].

> willing to consider the question of sovereignty as a purely legal matter, further negotiations regarding accession to the Indian Union followed a torturous path until their ultimate collapse in June 1948. From the beginning of 1948, the Government of India instituted a blockade of Hyderabad that prevented nearly all goods from entering the state.[337]

The Standstill Agreement provided that the Union of India would handle Hyderabad's foreign affairs and the Indian troops stationed in Secunderabad would be removed.[338] Unfortunately, the Standstill Agreement was violated soon after it had been made. Taylor C. Sherman notes:

> India claimed that the government of Hyderabad was edging towards independence by divesting itself of Indian securities, banning the Indian currency, halting the export of ground nuts, organising illegal gun-running from Pakistan, and inviting new recruits to its army and to its irregular forces, the Razakars. ... In [July, 1948] Razakars killed six Indian Army troops in an ambush near enclave of Nanaj. Equally, there were allegations that Indian troops crossed Hyderabad borders as they gave chase to Razakars. The Government in Delhi concluded that the increasing influence and violence of these unruly volunteer paramilitaries proved that the Nizam had lost control over his territory.[339]

Under these circumstances, on September 13, 1948, martial law was proclaimed in Hyderabad.[340]

Under the Government of India Act, 1935 the government was legally empowered to proclaim martial law.[341] Accordingly, on September 13, 1948,

> ... [T]he Government of India declared a state of emergency, and sent its troops into Hyderabad State. During the 'police action', the Indian Army entered Hyderabad with the objective of forcing the Nizam to re-install Indian troops in Secunderabad to allow them to restore order in the state. The Nizam surrendered in four days, and the Government of India appointed Major-General J. N. Chaudhari as Military Governor. Delhi decided that the Nizam could retain his position as Rajpramukh, through law-making and enforcement power rested with the Military Governor.[342]

---

[337] Purushotham [108].

[338] *See* Sherman [99].

[339] *See* Sherman [106].

[340] *See* Emergency Proclamation by C. Rajagopalachari, Gazette of India, (Sep. 13, 1948) under the Government of India Act, 1935, 9 & 10 Geo. 5 c. 101, § 102. The said proclamation read—

> In pursuance of section 102 of the Government of India Act, 1935, I, Chakravarti Rajagopalachari, Governor-General of India, being satisfied that there is imminent danger of the security of India being threatened by internal disturbance, do by this Proclamation, declare that a grave emergency exists whereby the security of India is threatened by internal disturbance.

[341] The power to proclaim martial law under the Government of India Act, 1935 was exercised under a provision of the Government of India Act, 1915 that was carried over from the 1915 Act to the 1935 Act through its Ninth Schedule. *See supra* notes 259–266.

[342] *See* Sherman [108].

During this "police action" (what we have called the "Hyderabad Crisis") the Indian army made mass arrests and jailed thousands of suspects without any real knowledge of their activities.[343] It is submitted that the Indian army at that point was not concerned about effective prosecutions and were most probably working on either incomplete or defective intelligence. Special courts were instituted to deal with thousands who were incarcerated during this period. One estimate says that over 11,000 detainees were released for lack of evidence.[344]

In these circumstances it is understandable why the draftsmen of our Constitution might have thought it necessary to put an enabling provision in the Constitution that would allow Parliament to indemnify by legislation those who had acted for "maintenance or restoration of order" during the time proclamations of martial law were in force in independent but not yet republican India. Examined from this unique historical perspective, the use of the word *was* in the phrase "where martial law was in force" in article 34 and the use of the word *is* in the phrase "where martial law is in force" in the forwarding letter dated November 3, 1949 would make abundant sense. Not just that, an examination of the phrase "where martial law was in force" in final article 34 adopted, from this historical perspective, would also suggest that article 34 does, and was indeed always intended to, enable Parliament only to enact indemnificatory legislation that was to be limited to proclamations of martial law that were made under the interim constitution, the Government of India Act 1935.[345] In contrast, since the Hyderabad Crisis was an ongoing contemporary crisis, contemporaneous to the writing of the letter dated November 3, 1949, the latter had to use the present tense, though the intent was the same in both cases, viz., not to create an independent head or source of power to declare or initiate martial law, derogating and trumping all fundamental rights, but to regularize and indemnify past actions taken under the emergency known as martial law.

In fact, the objections of Prof. Shibban Lal Saxena to the introduction of the new article 34 that he made on the floor of the Constituent Assembly on November 14, 1949 would seem to indicate that the Parliament was empowered to proclaim martial law.[346] Saxena noted:

---

[343] *Id.* at 498.

[344] *Id.*

[345] *See* 5 Rao [102]. It is noted in this work that prominent members of the Constituent Assembly, like Shibban Lal Saxena, feared that article 34 'might encourage officers working in a martial law area to commit excesses in the hope of indemnification by an Act of Parliament'. *See also* 9 Constituent Assembly Debates, Book 5, 468 (Lok Sabha Secretariat, reprint 2014). (Nov. 14, 1949).

[346] 9 Constituent Assembly Debates, Book 5, 468 (Lok Sabha Secretariat, reprint 2014) (Nov. 14, 1949).

> Yes sir, this article 34 is a new article. It says that when martial law is declared, then Parliament will have the power to indemnify the officers. I think that this new article should be ruled out of order. It was never passed by the Assembly before. Secondly, I think the provisions of this article will encourage officers working in the martial law area to commit excesses and hope for indemnification by an act of Parliament. Therefore, I say it is not proper. Martial law whenever proclaimed, should be proclaimed according to the law about it. It should not be permitted to go beyond the law. So I think this article is not necessary and it should be removed from the constitution, and also as I said, it is out of order.[347]

Lastly, one must turn to a post-Constitution Indian law that has direct bearing on the issue of both martial law and article 34. One of us has elsewhere argued that a "disturbed area notification" under section 3 of the Armed Forces Special Powers Act, 1958 ("AFSPA") is a de facto proclamation of martial law.[348] As far as that article was concerned, the question whether martial law can indeed be proclaimed under our Constitution was left open.[349] This question has been answered in the negative in the present chapter. It is, of course, obvious that a "disturbed area notification" under AFSPA is not the same as an article 352 emergency proclamation. The more important question is whether, in practice, an AFSPA "disturbed area notification" amounts to martial law for a limited geographical area. Again, *stricto sensu*, this may not be the case for the simple reason that courts in that notified area and in all other areas of the same state are entitled to entertain writ petitions and other legal actions and there is no closure of access to civil courts.

The story, however, does not end here. In practice, even if not in theory, it appears that the residents within AFSPA notified area aggrieved by state action have virtually no real possibility of either assailing the very proclamation of AFSPA with even a minimal chance of success or of claiming any practical redress by way of damages, compensation, or punishment arising from alleged invasion of their civil rights. This is the closest statutory analog to martial law that one can think of, though it might not be martial law as understood in England or the United States. Though AFSPA does not provide a full indemnification to members of the armed forces acting under the color of a "disturbed area notification," Section 6 reads thus:

> No prosecution, suit or other legal proceeding shall be instituted, except with the previous sanction of the Central Government, against any person in respect of anything done or purported to be done in exercise of the powers conferred by this Act.[350]

---

[347] *Id.*

[348] Gautam [15].

[349] *Id.* at 145.

[350] Armed Forces (Special Powers) Act 1958, § 6.

The provision provides no blanket immunity/indemnification but, sadly, in practice, it provides hardly any practical redress to aggrieved citizens. It must also be noted that this provision was upheld by a five-judge bench of the Supreme Court in *Naga People's Movement of Human Rights v. Union of India.*[351] More importantly and more recently, in *Extra-Judicial Execution of Victim Families Association v. Union of India,*[352] a division bench of the Supreme Court while reasserting judicial review fully observed that section 6 of AFSPA, "... grants immunity, inter alia, from prosecution to any person in respect of anything done or purported to be done in exercise of power conferred [under section 4] of the AFSPA, except with the previous sanction of the Central Government."[353] It would be highly anomalous to enact a limited and circumscribed indemnity legislation like AFSPA on the one hand, subject it to full judicial review on the other and yet treat it as coexisting with untrammeled, uncircumscribed literal "martial law" as described in article 34.

Such a reading would also be highly incongruous with the constitutional arrangement that we have. All emergency powers are listed in Part XVIII that bears the heading "Emergency Provisions." In the light of a fully occupying Part XVIII, it is not possible to examine article 34 as a standalone provision. It has to be harmonized with other provisions in Part XVIII. It might be possible to argue that article 355 read with article 34 has enough structural as well as textual flexibility to say that a proclamation of martial law can be provided for by Parliament by enacting a special law and allowing the President to make a proclamation thereof, subject to such procedures and limitations as this special law might provide. It would be reasonable to speculate that such a special law would be enabled by a conjoint reading of articles 355 and 34. But ultimately it would boil down to mere semantics because every such law, by whatever name called, and whether relying on article 34 or any provision of Part XVIII or both, or indeed invoking common law, would have to meet the categorical textual tests and scheme of Part XVIII and would allow derogation from Part III only to the extent permitted by Part XVIII.

It is therefore concluded that for the several reasons elaborated above, no emergency power, by whatever name called, whether martial law or otherwise, can exist under the Indian Constitution, without conforming to the strict requirements of Part XVIII. Consequently, article 34 must necessarily be harmoniously construed and limited to, and only to, a constitutional recognition of the ex post facto power to provide indemnification to those, including the military, acting during emergency periods. It cannot and should not be treated as a standalone or separate source of power to declare martial law in addition to and distinct from the powers found in Part XVIII.

[351]Naga People's Movement of Human Rights v. Union of India, (1998) 2 SCC 109.

[352]Extra-Judicial Execution of Victim Families Association v. Union of India, (2016) 14 SCC 536.

[353]*Id.* at 602.

References

1. C.M. Clode, *The Law Military as distinct from martial law*, 29 Law Mag. & L. Rev. Quart. J. Juris. 3d Ser. 24 (1870)
2. J.V. Capua, *The Early History of martial law in England from the Fourteenth Century to the Petition of Right*, Cambridge L. J. (1977)
3. M. Neocleous, *From martial law to the War on Terror*, 10 New Crim. L. Rev. **489**, 491 (2007)
4. M. Hale, The History of Common Law of England 26 (Charles M. Gray ed., 1971)
5. G.M. Dennison, *Martial law: The Development of a Theory of Emergency Powers, 1776–1861*, 18 Am. J. Legal Hist. 52, 53 (1974)
6. M. Hale, The History of Common Law of England 27 (Charles M. Gray ed., 1971)
7. G.M. Dennison, *martial law: The Development of a Theory of Emergency Powers, 1776–1861*, 18 Am. J. Legal Hist. **52**, 57 (1974)
8. C.M. Clode, *The Law Military as distinct from martial law*, 29 Law Mag. & L. Rev. Quart. J. Juris. 3d Ser. 24, 25 (1870)
9. G.M. Dennison, *Martial law: The Development of a Theory of Emergency Powers, 1776–1861*, 18 Am. J. Legal Hist. 52, 54–55 (1974)
10. C.M. Clode, *The Law Military as distinct from martial law*, 29 Law Mag. & L. Rev. Quart. J. Juris. 3d Ser. 24, 27–28 (1870)
11. W.S. Holdsworth, *Martial law Historically Considered*, 18 L. Q. Rev. **117**, 122 (1902)
12. F. Pollock, *What is martial law?*, 18 L. Q. Rev. **152**, 153 (1902)
13. H.E. Smith, Studies in Juridicial Law 109–116 (1902)
14. A.V. Dicey, Introduction to the Study of the Constitution **283**, 289 (1915)
15. R.S. Rankin, When Civil Law Fails: martial law and its Legal Basis in the United States 14 (1939)
16. Westel Woodbury Willoughby, The Constitutional Law of the United States 1586 (1929)
17. D. Chalmers, C. Asquith, Outlines of Constitutional Law 363 (1936)
18. Westel Woodbury Willoughby, The Constitutional Law of the United States 1588, 1602 (1929)
19. Westel Woodbury Willoughby, The Constitutional Law of the United States 1590–92 (1929)
20. R.S. Rankin, *The Constitutional Basis of martial law*, 13 Const. Rev. **75**, 75 (1929)
21. Westel Woodbury Willoughby, The Constitutional Law of the United States 1612–13 (1929)
22. C.M. Clode, *The Law Military as distinct from martial law*, 29 Law Mag. & L. Rev. Quart. J. Juris. 3d Ser. **24**, 30–32 (1870)
23. R.S. Rankin, When Civil Law Fails: martial law and its Legal Basis in the United States 17 (1939)
24. C.M. Clode, *The Law Military as distinct from martial law*, 29 Law Mag. & L. Rev. Quart. J. Juris. 3d Ser. **24**, 29 (1870)
25. R.S.Rankin, *The Constitutional Basis of Martial Law*, 13 Const. Rev. **75**, 76, 77 (1929)
26. C.M. Clode, *The Law Military as distinct from martial law*, 29 Law Mag. & L. Rev. Quart. J. Juris. 3d Ser. **24**, 32 (1870)
27. H.E. Smith, Studies in Juridical Law 112–115 (1902)
28. W.E. Birkhimer, Military Government and martial law 481–489 (1914)
29. A.V. Dicey, Introduction to the Study of the Constitution 280–90 (1915)
30. Westel Woodbury Willoughby, The Constitutional Law of the United States 1587 (1929)
31. R.S. Rankin, *The Constitutional Basis of martial law*, 13 Const. Rev. 75 (1929)
32. R.S. Rankin, When Civil Law Fails: martial law and its Legal Basis in the United States 12 (1939)
33. W.S. Holdsworth, *Martial Law Historically Considered*, 18 L. Q. Rev. **117**, 129 (1902)
34. S.E. Baldwin, The American Judiciary **299**, 299 (1905)
35. Westel Woodbury Willoughby, The Constitutional Law of the United States 1599 (1929)
36. D. Chalmers and C. Asquith, Outlines of Constitutional Law 368 (1936)

37. M.K.L Davis, *The Imposition of martial law in the United States*, 49 Air Force L. Rev. **67**, 85 (2000)
38. D.E. Engdahl, *Soldiers, Riots, and Revolution: The Law and History of Military Troops in Civil Disorders*, 57 Iowa L. Rev. **1**, 16 (1971)
39. W.E. Birkhimer, Military Government and martial law 488 (1914)
40. A.G. Caleb Cushing 8 Op. Att'y Gen. **365**, 366–67 (1857)
41. R.S. Rankin, When Civil Law Fails: martial law and its Legal Basis in the United States 137 (1939)
42. R.S. Rankin, When Civil Law Fails: martial law and its Legal Basis in the United States 84 (1939)
43. G. Glenn, The Army and the Law, 182 (1918)
44. F.T. Wilson, Federal Aid in Domestic Disturbances 1787–1903 (1903) S. Doc. Series No. 7975 at 1–43 (67th Congress, 2nd Sess., 1921–22)
45. N. Hussain, The Jurisprudence of Emergency 116 (2003)
46. W.E. Birkheimer, Military Government and martial law 538–39 (3rd ed. 1914) (1892)
47. H.M Bowman, *Martial law and the English Constitution*, 15 Mich. L. Rev. 93, 113–14 (1916–17)
48. Sir Fredrick Pollock, *What is martial law?*, 18 L.Q. Rev. 152, 156 (1902)
49. Peter Judson Richards, Military Tribunals in Historical and International Context 16-18 (2007)
50. G.M. Dennison, *martial law: the Development of a Theory of Emergency Powers 1776–1861*, 18 Am. J. Legal History, 52 (1974)
51. R.S. Rankin, When Civil Law Fails: martial law and its Legal Basis in the United States 138–39 (1939)
52. Rostow, *The Japanese-American Cases—A Disaster*, 54 Yale L. J. 489 (1945); Dembitz, *Racial Discrimination and the Military Judgment*, 45 Colum. L. Rev. 175 (1945)
53. J.P. Frank, *Ex P. Milligan v. the Five Companies: martial law in Hawaii*, 44 Colum. L. Rev. 639 (1944); Anthony Garner, *martial law, military government and the writ of habeas corpus in Hawaii*, 31 Calif. L. Rev. 477 (1943)
54. D.E., Engdahl, *Soldiers, Riots and Revolution: The Law and History of Military Troops in Civil Disorders*, 57 Iowa L. Rev., 1 (1971)
55. A. Garner, *Martial law, military government and the writ of habeas corpus in Hawaii*, 31 Calif. L. Rev. 477 (1943)
56. E.S. Smead, *Martial law in the oilfields of Oklahoma and Texas*, 6 Okla State Bar J. 6; O'Brien, *Constitutional law – Due Process – martial law*, 31 Mich. L. Rev., 988 (1933)
57. W.G. Matthews, Martial law in West Virginia, S. Doc. No. 230 at 20 (63rd Congress, 1st Sess, 1913)
58. Berger, *Presidential Monopoly of Foreign Relations*, 71 Mich. L. Rev. 1 (1972)
59. Levitan, *The Foreign Relations Power: An analysis of Mr. Justice Sutherland's Theory*, 55 Yale L. J. 467 (1946)
60. C.A. Lofgren, *US v. Curtiss-Wright Export Corporation: An Historical Reassessment*, 83 Yale L. J. 1 (1978)
61. J.D. Richardson, A Compilation of Messages and Papers of the President 98 (1909)
62. Gross & Aolain, Law in Times of Emergency 178 (2006)
63. R.S. Rankin, When Civil Law Fails: martial law and its Legal Basis in the United States 87 (1939)
64. W.F. Finlason, Treatise on martial law (1866)
65. F. Arnold, *The Rationale of martial law*, 15 Am. Bar Assn. J. 550, 552 (1929)
66. H.W. Ballantine, *Unconstitutional Claims of Military Authority*, 24 Yale L. J. 189, 198–200 (1915)
67. H.E. Willis, US Constitutional Law 1591 (1929)
68. J.P. Frank, *Ex P. Milligan v. the Five Companies: martial law in Hawaii*, 44 Colum. L. Rev. **639**, 642 (1944)
69. H.C. Carbaugh, *Martial law*, 7 Ill. L. Rev. 479 (1913)

70. G.M. Dennison, *Martial law: The Development of a Theory of Emergency Powers 1776–1861*, 18 Am. J. Legal History, **52**, 59 (1974)
71. S. Halbert, *The Suspension of the Writ of Habeas Corpus by President Lincoln*, 2 Am. J. Legal History 95, 104 (1958)
72. W.F. Duker, A Constitutional History of Habeas Corpus (1980); R. Sharpe, Habeas Corpus (1976)
73. N. Schachner, Aaron Burr: A Biography (1937); C. Warren, The Supreme Court in United States History (1935)
74. Gregory, The Tissue of Structure: Habeas Corpus and the Great Writ's Paradox of Power and Liberty, 16 The Indep. Rev. **53**, 53–54 (2011)
75. S.G. Fisher, *The Suspension of Habeas Corpus during the War of the Rebellion*, 3 Pol. Sci. Q. 454, 458 (1888)
76. C. Fairman, The Law of martial Rule 44 (2nd ed. 1943)
77. Chase, C.J., dissenting in *Ex parte* Milligan 71 U.S. 2, 141–142 (1866)
78. S.S. Nicholas, Habeas Corpus: The Law of War and Confiscation (1862)
79. S.G. Fisher, *The Suspension of Habeas Corpus during the War of the Rebellion*, 3 Pol. Sci. Q. **454**, 463 (1888)
80. J.W. Bishop, Jr., *Law in Control of Terrorism & Insurrection: The British Laboratory Experience,* 42 L. & Contemp. Probs 140, 193–6 (1978)
81. S.G. Fisher, *The Suspension of Habeas Corpus during the War of the Rebellion*, 3 Pol. Sci. Q. 454 (1888)
82. J.V. Capua, *The Early History of martial law in England from the Fourteenth Century to the Petition of Right,* Cambridge L. J. **152**, 154–55 (1977)
83. W. Forsyth, Cases and Opinions on Constitutional Law 211 (1869)
84. J.V. Capua, *The Early History of martial law in England from the Fourteenth Century to the Petition of Right,* Cambridge L. J. 152, 153, 161, 173. (*passim*)
85. L. Boynton, *The Tudor Provost Marshall*, 77 Eng. Hist. L. Rev. 445 (1962) relying upon E. P. Cheney History of England 1585–1603, 247 (1948)
86. H. Singh, *The Indian States: A Study of Their Constitutional Position*, 64 Pol. Sci. Q. **95**, 95 (1949)
87. J.V. Capua, *The Early History of martial law in England from the Fourteenth Century to the Petition of Right,* Cambridge L. J. 152, 153 (1977)
88. L. Boynton, *The Tudor Provost Marshall*, 77 Eng. Hist. L. Rev. 437, 440 (1962)
89. L. Boynton, *The Tudor Provost Marshall*, 77 Eng. Hist. L. Rev. 437 (1962)
90. L. Boynton, *The Tudor Provost Marshall*, 77 Eng. Hist. L. Rev. 445 (1962)
91. H. Hallam, The Constitutional History of England 389–90 (1908 ed.) (1827)
92. R.S. Rankin, *The Constitutional Basis of martial law*, 13 Const. Rev. 75, 77 (1929)
93. H.C. Carbough, *Martial law*, 7 Ill. L. Rev. 479 (1913); H.D. Linscott, *Martial law & Executive Process*, 1 Geo. Wash. L. Rev. 102–05 (1932)
94. Keir, The Case of Ship Money 52 L. Q. Rev. 546, 546 (1936)
95. W.S. Holdsworth, The Power of the Crown to Requisition British Ships in a National Emergency 35 L. Q. Rev. 12, 26–27 (1919).
96. T.C. Foster, A Treatise on the Writ of Scire Facias, pp. 41–42 (1851)
97. H.D. Hazeltine, Thomas Madox as Constitutional and Legal Historian II, 32 L. Q. Rev. pp. 339–40 (1916)
98. S.G. Fisher, *The Suspension of Habeas Corpus during the War of the Rebellion*, 3 Pol. Sci. Q. 454, 465–66 (1888)
99. K. Gautam, *Martial Law in India: The Deployment of Military under the Armed Forces Special Powers Act, 1958*, 24 Sw. J. Int'l L. 117 (2018)
100. B.S. Rao, The Framing of India's Constitution: a study 308–09 (kashyap ed., 2012) (1968)
101. A.V. Dicey, Introduction to the Study of the Law of the Constitution, 271 (1897)
102. B.S. Rao, The Framing of India's Constitution: A Study 745 (Kashyap ed., 2012) (1968)
103. V.P.Menon, The Story of The Integration of Indian States 484–493 (1955)

104. S. Purushotham, *Internal Violence: The "Police Action" in Hyderabad*, 57 Comp. Stud.in Soc'y & Hist. **435**, 437 (2015)
105. Phillips Talbot, *Kashmir and Hyderabad*, 1 World Pol. 321, 325–26 (1949)
106. T.C. Sherman, *The Integration Of The Princely State Of Hyderabad And The Making Of Postcolonial State In India, 1948–56*, 44 Indian Econ. & Soc. Hist. Rev. 489, 491 (2007)
107. S. Purushotham, *Internal Violence: The "Police Action" in Hyderabad*, 57 Comp. Stud.in Soc'y & Hist. **435**, 438 (2015)
108. T.C. Sherman, *The integration of the princely state of Hyderabad and the making of postcolonial state in India, 1948-56*, 44 Indian Econ. & Soc. Hist. Rev. **489**, 495–96 (2007)

Chapter 3
Military Acting in Aid of Civilian Authority

1 Introduction

At the outset it may be clarified that India does not have jurisprudence liable to be analyzed in a comparative perspective on the subject of military acting in the aid of civil authority. That is why the overwhelming bulk of this chapter is devoted to the legal position in UK and United States alone. However, at the end, a short discussion of the Indian position is added for the sake of completeness.

Short of a proclamation of martial law, whereby the will of the military commander is supreme, there exists another concept—that of "military acting in aid of civilian authority." Traces of this concept can be found in the writings of William Birkhimer in 1914 when he observed that, "… in times of peace statutes authorizing the exercise of military power over civilians are to be construed strictly."[1] We should note the use of the phrase "*in times of peace*" here. A distinction between the use of the military (or "armed forces"—these two phrases are used synonymously here) during peacetime and during wartime is a fair distinction and has been made

[1]Birkhimer [1].

A. Singhvi and K. Gautam, *The Law of Emergency Powers*,
https://doi.org/10.1007/978-981-15-2997-9_3

often.[2] Furthermore, a declaration of war is a formal state of affairs between two sovereign states under international law.[3] But it cannot be anybody's case that hostilities can't exist between two sovereign states in the absence of a formal declaration of war.[4] In fact, Dicey in 1915, gave a precursor to this concept (having denied the existence of Martial Law under English law) when he spoke of the common law right of the Crown and its servants to "repel force by force."[5] However, in England the distinction between war and civil disorder had been accepted since fourteenth century.[6] Edward VI and Mary in 1549 and 1553 had created the institution of Lord-Lieutenants who were "chiefly of a military character" but were to be appointed "only in periods of stress."[7] As is usually the case with authorities of this kind, they were soon abused.[8] Later, in America in the late 1700s, British soldiers and not civilian authorities were used by the British "with increasing regularity" for suppression of civil disorders.[9]

In 1929, views expressed by two leading American scholars gave shape to this concept. First was Dicey's American counterpart, Willoughby, who defined martial law as, "... that law which has application when the military arm does not supersede civil authority but it is called upon *to aid it* in the execution of its civil function."[10] The other was Rankin who expressed the view much more clearly than

---

[2]*See, e.g.*, India Const. art. 352, § 1 (that talks about the President's power to proclaim an emergency on the ground, *inter alia*, of war), and art. 355 (that talks about the duty of the Union to ensure that there is no breakdown of constitutional machinery). Whereas art. 352(1) clearly authorizes the President to use the armed forces of the Union of India in the event of a war, art. 355 can potentially be argued to be authorizing the Union of India to use its armed forces in the event of an "internal disturbance" or "external aggression" in situations that are not warlike but yet grave enough to merit emergency action. *See also* Report of The Sarkaria Commission ¶ 7.7.02 (1988) (noting that the use of military to maintain day to day administration of law and order has been avoided for the past seventy five years, and recommended that the Army ought not to be deployed "except as a last resort when the para-military forces cannot by themselves handle an acute internal disturbance situation."); Extra-Judicial Execution Victim Families Association v. Union of India (2016) 14 SCC 536, 597–600 (using the observations of Justice Puncchi's report on center–state relations to draw a distinction between art. 352 and art. 355 and art. 356 and the role played by the Army to restore Public Order as envisaged in Naga People's case); Vladeck [2].

[3]*See, e.g.*, Green [3]; Ackerman [4].

[4]*See, e.g.*, Commonwealth of Massachusetts v. Laird 451 F.2d 26 (1971) (1st Cir.) (discussing whether the US involvement in Vietnam is unconstitutional since no war had been declared.); Drinan v. Nixon 364 F. Supp. 854 (1973) (D. Mass.); Kucinich v. Obama 821 F. Supp. 2d 110 (2011) (D.C.) (discussing the strikes ordered by President Obama in Libya without a formal declaration of war and whether they circumvented the Congress's power to declare war).

[5]Dicey [5].

[6]Engdahl [6]. *See also* Collins [7]; Head and Mann [8].

[7]Engdahl [6, p. 1, 9].

[8]*Id.* at 9–10.

[9]*Id.* at 26.

[10]Willoughby [9].

Willoughby by emphasizing the distinction between martial law and military acting in aid of civilian authority.[11] Rankin clarified that:

> Military troops are sometimes used as an *aid to the civil authorities* when martial law is not declared. The troops then act a role similar to deputy sheriffs, and do nothing under their own responsibility but *act directly under the civil power*. This use of troops is easily recognizable from the use of troops under martial law because there is no declaration of martial law, and the troops act in entire subordination to the civil authorities.[12]

Rankin provides the key distinction between martial law (which he called "Punitive martial law"[13]) and military acting in aid of civilian authority (which he calls "Preventive martial law"[14]) whereby under the former the military reigns supreme and the continued existence of civilian authority is only because the military commander allows it to exist[15] whereas under the latter the military is not independent of the civilian authority and acts subordinate to it. There is historical evidence to support this well-accepted[16] distinction from the America of mid 1800s.[17] The only criticism of Rankin's view is that he insists on a "declaration" of martial law whereas a state of martial law can potentially exist without a formal declaration.[18] In England, this concept of military acting in aid of civilian authority was stated as a part of English constitutional law by Chalmers and Asquith in 1936.[19] The responsibility for maintaining order being vested with the local civilian authorities, the assistance of military should be invoked as a "last expedient" and having invoked it the military, "... should act under the direction of civil authority ... [and] should not, in ordinary cases, fire without his orders, nor omit to fire when ordered by him."[20] Just like Rankin, Chalmers and Asquith also accepted the

---

[11]Rankin [10].

[12]*Id.* at 77 (Emphasis added).

[13]*Id.* at 84 ("Punitive when the courts are not functioning in the proper manner...").

[14]*Id.* at 84 ("... and preventive when it is desired that the troops *act as aid* to the civil authorities.") (Emphasis added).

[15]Birkhimer [1, p. 482, 488].

[16]This distinction has been drawn in the context of administration of criminal law during civil disorders. *See* Pye and Lowell [11].

[17]But far more common were the cases in which soldiers were called to aid civil officials in dispersing mobs or suppressing riots precipitated by hotly contested elections or other public issues, or in other ways to assist the civilian officers. It was well understood that when they were used under such circumstances the soldiers were not used in their military character, but merely as civilian assistants subject to the command of ordinary civil officers, and no more privileged in their use of force against citizens than the civil officers were themselves.

Engdahl [6, p. 1, 50] (Internal citations omitted).

[18]*See* Birkhimer [1, p. 488]; Note, *Martial Law*, 42 S. Cal. L. Rev. 546, 548 (1969) (authorities cited in note 11). In this context, it has been argued that the deployment of the armed forces by the Union of India under the Armed Forces Special Powers Act, 1958 amounts to a de facto proclamation of Martial Law. Gautam [12].

[19]Chalmers and Asquith [13].

[20]*Id.* at 362.

distinction between martial law and military acting in aid of civilian authority but they seem to allow much greater leeway to the military even when acting in aid of civilian authority.[21]

Military acting in aid of civilian authority is a dangerous concept, and unless close attention is paid to what it actually means and where its scope ends, it is a concept big enough to subsume within itself all the power and authority that the military commands under martial law and leave out the limitations imposed on the military under martial law.[22] Prof. Mark Neocleous notes, "... the explicit declaration of martial law in situations which were understood implicitly to be emergencies of some sort has been transformed into the explicit use of emergency powers involving the implicit use of martial law powers."[23] Preserving and maintaining peace and order is generally the responsibility of the local civil authorities and courts[24] presumably because local authorities are better aware of local problems[25] and the military is not designed for this purpose anyway.[26] It might happen that in order to maintain peace and order circumstances might worsen to a point where the local civil authorities become overwhelmed and distressed. In such a situation the local civil authorities might deem it necessary to call out the military (which is under the control of federal authorities) for help and assistance with law enforcement functions.[27] Calling out the military to aid the civilian authorities and courts at times when they are in distress however does not, and has never been accepted to, amount to a proclamation of martial law.[28] During these times, the military's assistance is generally requested by civilian authorities themselves and once called, the military acts under the command of the local civilian authorities.[29]

The danger arises as follows. If overwhelmed and under distress, the choice of calling out the military for assistance in law enforcement functions is a choice available to the local civil authorities. However, if the deployment of the military is authorized by a statute and in such a deployment the local civil authorities have no say, and once deployed the military and civil authorities both continue to function

---

[21]*Id.* at 362 ("Still, circumstances may exist which make it the duty of the troops to ignore or act in independence of the orders of the magistrate, or, indeed, of their own superior officers.").

[22]*See, e.g.*, Neocleous [14].

[23]Neocleous [14, p. 489, 508]. *See also* Note, *A Republic of Emergencies: Martial Law in American Jurisprudence*, 36 CONN. L. REV. 1397 (2004) (urging "... the US Supreme Court to narrowly interpret congressional authorization of emergency powers as a means to limit excessive emergency measures imposed by the executive.").

[24]*See, e.g.*, Krum [15].

[25]Note, *Riot Control and the use of Federal Troops*, 81 HARV. L. REV. 638, 640 (1968).

[26]Campbell and Connolly [16].

[27]*See, e.g.*, U.S. CONST. art. IV, § 4; 10 USC §§ 331, 334.

[28]Engdahl [6, p. 1, 71].

[29]Bishop v. Vandercook, 228 Mich. 299, 306 (1924) (Mich.); State v. McPhail, 182 Miss. 360, 390 (1938) (Miss.). However, for a slightly contrary position *see* Herlihy v. Donohue, 161 Pac. 164, 167 (1916) (Mont.); Engdahl [6, p. 1, 71].

but the military acts independent of the civilian authorities and courts, we are dangerously close to a situation where we have in fact, knowingly or unknowingly, proclaimed martial law but are (mistakenly) calling it military acting in aid of civilian authority.[30] Consequently, we are liable to make the error of reviewing the legality of this act by applying an incorrect and inapplicable judicial standard of review. In other words, we end up reviewing the legality of a *de facto* proclamation of martial law by analyzing whether or not it is a statutorily valid call out of the military to come and aid the civilian authorities. Meanwhile, the military, acting independent of the civilian authorities, continues to exercise its authority in complete disregard of the local civilian authorities, something that, in the past, it could only exercise once martial law was proclaimed.[31] It will be important to note that in the modern world the military and armed forces across the common law world have been granted "advanced statutory authority" to do pretty much whatever they would have, in the past, claimed to do under the authority of a proclamation of martial law.[32] Therefore the military can now do under the color of statutory authority what in the past they could do only under the color of a proclamation of martial law.

There is another problem. If the troops (as well as their officers) are not clear as to why they have been called out they will be unclear as to whether they are supposed to enforce the law (i.e., act strictly as assistants of the local civilian authorities and courts; in other words, take their orders from civilian authorities) or maintain peace and order (i.e., act independently and exercise discretion as to use of force), and the extent to which they are allowed to go in enforcing the law.[33] One proposed method to deal with this problem is to limit and clearly define the powers of the military when called out to act-in-aid of the civilian authorities.[34]

---

[30]This point is illuminated by a similar thing that was done in Canada. The military could be called for assisting in law enforcement functions by the provincial Attorney General, but in 1998 the Canadian Parliament amended the law and vested this authority in the federal authorities. This was criticized as, "Unlike the traditional aid of civil power, there is no requirement that the provinces be consulted before the troops are called out." *See, e.g.*, Editorial, *Calling out the Troops*, 48 CRIM. L.Q. 141 (2003). The Canadian Supreme Court also expressed its concerns as this move impinged the provincial jurisdiction over administration of justice. *See* R v. Nolan, [1987] 1 S.C.R. 1212 (Canada). These issues have been raised in Australia as well. *See, e.g.*, Head [17]. The definition of martial law in a 1967 Michigan statute also supports this point. Here martial law is defined as, "… exercise of partial or complete military control over domestic territory in time of emergency because of public necessity." *See* MICH. STAT. ANN. § 4.678(105)(j) (1968 Supp.).

[31]*See, e.g.*, Campbell and Connolly [16, p. 341, 349].

[32]Dyzenhaus [18].

[33]This point has been noted by Colonel Robin Evelegh (who was the Commanding Officer of an infantry battalion in Belfast, Ireland) in his book PEACE-KEEPING IN A DEMOCRATIC SOCIETY (1978) reviewed in, and quoted from, *Book Reviews*, 8 ANGLO-AM. L. REV. 65, 66 (1979).

[34]*See, e.g.*, Pye and Lowell [11, p. 581, 655, 690]; Wing Commander Jha [19].

2 Use of Military in Situations not Amounting to Martial Law in the United States

2.1 The National Guard

The National Guard comprises such organized forces of the State as may be created under law, regardless of the name they bear, and is a "hybrid federal-state creature."[35] Its most common use is as a State enforcement agency, under state direction.[36] The President, however, has the constitutional authority to "call out the militia" to enforce the law. Guard units are treated as a reserve component of the US army under certain statutes[37] and may thus be used to fight in wars (e.g., Vietnam).[38] The Federal Government primarily undertakes the training of the Guard; and, significantly ninety percent of the Guard's operating costs, virtually all its equipment and weapons and half the cost of its physical installations and facilities are supplied and supported federally.[39]

2.2 Some Instances of Use of the Military in Aid of Civil Authority

The circumstantial patterns surrounding the use of the National Guard are varied. Notable examples include its use by a mayor for preservation of order during the return of a Negro slave from Boston to Virginia in 1855[40]; by the State Governor to control a riotous mob threatening destruction of valuable property in a coal mine in King County in Washington State in 1891; by Mayor Hay of Dallas, Texas, to protect President Taft during his visit in 1909[41]; by the Governor of Kentucky in 1910 to put an end to certain raids made by a group of men called "nightriders"[42]; by the Governor of Oklahoma in 1912 to enforce the result of an election whereby it

---

[35]Waranoff [20].

[36]Warnoff [20, p. 1, 2] citing the Report of the National Advisory Commission on Civil Disorders 275 (1968) at note 9.

[37]*See, e.g.*, 10 U.S.C. § 261.

[38]*See, e.g.*, Johnson v. Powell, 414 F. 2d. 261 (1969) (5th Cir.) (10 U.S.C. § 261, which regulates individuals who are members of the US National Guard, and this body being a reserve component of the US Army, is supportable under constitutional clause giving the Congress the power to raise and support armies though not supportable under US Const. art. 1, § 8, cl. 15; hence habeas corpus applications by petitioner for release from active military duty in Vietnam rejected.).

[39]Warnoff [20, p. 1, 2] citing the Report of the National Advisory Commission on Civil Disorders 275 (1968) at note 9.

[40]Ela v. Smith, 71 Mass. (6 Gray) 121 (1855) (Supreme Judicial Court, Mass.).

[41]Manley v. State, 62 Tex. Crim. 392 (1911) (Tex.).

[42]Franks v. Smith, 134 S. W. Rep. 484 (1911) (Ky.).

had been decided to move the capital of Delaware County from Grove to Jay[43]; by the civil authorities and State Governor of Michigan in 1918 to enforce Prohibition in the state[44]; by the Governor of Alabama in 1922 to preserve order during a strike[45]; by the Governor of Colorado in 1927 for the same purpose[46] and by the Governor of Oklahoma in 1932 to enforce the conservation laws of the state.[47] These examples can be multiplied manifold.[48]

2.3 *Distinction Between Martial Law and Use of Military in Aid of Civil Authority*

The distinction was noticed and well stated by the Supreme Court of Mississippi in *McPhail* while upholding the use of the National Guard for the execution of search warrants.[49] Justice Griffith said:

> We are not here concerned with the powers and duties of the Governor, nor with the conduct of the militia, in respect to the suppression of insurrections or riots, or the repulsion of invasions or mobs, or the like. We deal solely with the constitutional and statutory powers of the Governor, and of the militia, in the execution of the laws. And that means also that we lay aside any consideration or discussion of martial law, or of the power of the Governor to declare martial law in any given area, or the reasons or exigencies which will authorize such a declaration.[50] … **[W]hatever the Governor does in the execution of the laws, or whatever members of the militia do, under such authority, must be as civil officers, and in strict subordination to the general law of the land**. … Thus and for the stated reason, the chief executive was given the authority and it was made his duty to act to enforce the laws, duly and constitutionally enacted, in every portion of the state, so that every citizen and all property would have the protection of the laws and that every criminal statute should be observed. … **The militia was established for the use of the civil power**, when necessary, and the Governor is a civil officer and the militia, under his control, are civil agencies, in the execution of laws.[51]

---

[43]Fluke v. Canton, 123 P. 1049 (1912) (Okla.).

[44]Bishop v. Vandercook, 228 Mich. 299 (1924) (Mich.).

[45]Orr v. Burleson, 214 Ala. 257 (1926) (Ala.).

[46]United States *ex rel.* Palmer v. Adams, 26 F.2d 141 (1927) (D. Colo.).

[47]Russell Petroleum Co. v. Walker, 162 Okla. 216 (1933) (Okla.).

[48]*See* Schlichter [21]; Pye and Lowell [11, p. 581, 661].

[49]State v. McPhail, 182 Miss. 360 (1938) (Miss.).

[50]State v. McPhail, 182 Miss. 360, 389 (1938) (Miss.).

[51]State v. McPhail, 182 Miss. 360, 390 (1938) (Miss.) (Emphasis added).

A similar view was echoed by the US District Court in Minnesota in *Wilson*[52] while invalidating the proclamation and use of martial law by the State Governor to close a plant during a strike:

> But obviously where there is actual war in a community, or where insurrection or revolt occurs so that the duly constituted government is usurped and overcome by the insurrectionists or mobs, the Governor is impliedly authorized to declare martial law. But where any disturbance caused by a strike or otherwise presents a situation with which the local police or other local law enforcement agencies are not able to cope, it does not follow that, without more, the drastic and oppressive rule of martial law can be imposed upon any community.[53]... **At the time the Governor declared martial law, the local government of the City of Albert Lea and the County of Freeborn was functioning. The courts were open, the citizens were moving freely in and about their daily pursuits without danger**, except those who desired to continue with their work for plaintiff. The District Court of Freeborn County had issued restraining orders against mass picketing and violence, and contempt citations by reason of the violation of such orders had been set for hearing before the court, but without any attempt to call out the National Guard in aid of the Civil authorities in maintaining peace and order in the suppression of mob violence, the Governor summarily declared martial law for the City of Albert Lea and the entire county of Freeborn. The rights of the courts to proceed against members of the mob by way of contempt were enjoined. The workers who desired to return to their work at the plant were forbidden to return, and plaintiff's right under the Federal Constitution to operate its plant was abrogated by the decree of the military.[54]

Another noteworthy distinction is that when the military is called in aid of civil authority, the phrase "martial law" rarely occurs.[55] Moreover, the proclamation or order of martial law, if made, must necessarily be made by the Governor, whereas the militia may be called in aid of the civil authorities either by an order or precept of a local civil officer (e.g., sheriff or mayor) or by the Governor at the request of a local civil officer[56] or on his own initiative.[57] However, if no units of the National

---

[52]Wilson & Co. v. Freeman, 179 F. Supp. 520 (1959) (D. Minn.).

[53]Wilson & Co. v. Freeman, 179 F. Supp. 520, 525 (1959) (D. Minn.).

[54]Wilson & Co. v. Freeman, 179 F. Supp. 520, 526 (1959) (D. Minn.) (Emphasis added).

[55]*See* §§ 130–31 The Criminal Procedure Code 1973, No. 2 of 1974, Code Crim. Proc. (India).

[56]In Ela v. Smith, 71 Mass. (6 Gray) 121 (1855) (Mass.), the Mayor called out the militia; and in Chaplin v. Ferry, 15 L.R.A. 116 (1891) (Wash.), the Iowa statutes allowed the sheriff to do so for his own county but the Governor had to be asked for other counties.

[57]Most cases accept this position. *See, e.g.*, Bishop v. Vandercook, 228 Mich. 299 (1924) (Mich.); Chaplin v. Ferry, 15 L.R.A. 116 (1891) (Wash.) and Franks v. Smith, 134 S.W. Rep. 484 (1911) (Ky.).

Guard are available in a particular county, the local civil officers must ask the Governor for aid from outside the county over which they exercise jurisdiction.[58]

The element of civilian control predominates and the military power is really subordinate to the civil authority when the military is used in aid of civil authority. In a characteristic situation of real civilian control and supremacy, military detentions, trials and punishments are non-existent. The military is merely an addition of manpower to aid the normal agencies of civil government, and their military uniforms of status are irrelevant in legal terms. They are purely civil agents for repulsion of force by force and for the restoration of peace and order; military arrests are permitted only because they are used to handing over alleged wrongdoers to the civil authorities for appropriate actions.[59]

2.4 Principles Governing Liability of Guardsman and Higher Officers

2.4.1 General Principles

Of the three options available to the courts in respect of liability of Guardsmen—(1) to treat soldiers as citizens with no more than the latter's authority to make arrests and prevent crimes; (2) to treat them as a special extra normal military force with special enhanced powers; or (3) to invest them with powers equal to and not more than those enjoyed by the police and other peace officers, the US Courts chose the last. The leading decision of the Kentucky Court of Appeals in *Franks v. Smith*[60]

---

[58]*See* Seaney v. State, 188 Miss. 367 (1940), 194 So. 913, 915 (Miss.) (upholding the power of the National Guard to execute search warrants, the Court held, "It is not necessary for the governor to await the request of the sheriff or the judge of the circuit court or any other local officer").

[59]To quote the Supreme Court of Montana in Herlihy v. Donohue, 161 P. 164, 166 (1916) (Mont.).

> When the organized militia was called into the service of the state in 1914, *it but performed the function of the strong arm of the executive by which he could aid in executing the law or in suppressing the insurrection. Independently of the executive, it had no power or authority*, except possibly with reference to its own internal affairs. *It acted as an executive agency*, subject to the orders of the Governor and bound by the authority which he might lawfully exercise. (Emphasis Added).

[60]Franks v. Smith, 135 S.W. 484 (1911) (Ky.). *See also* Flood [22].

rejected the first option on the ground that the powers of the private citizen to act for public peace or order were too restricted[61] and the second option on the ground that this would invest the military with extra constitutional and excessive powers.[62] Upholding the award of damages against Guardsmen who had halted, searched and detained overnight the plaintiff upon an "unfounded charge," while he was traveling on the highway, Justice Carroll expressed his preference for the third option.[63] The

---

[61]Franks v. Smith, 135 S.W. 484, 489–90 (1911) (Ky.).

[62]*Id.* at 490–91.

[63]*Id.* at 492–93.

> Upon this point, after mature consideration, *we have reached the conclusion that any military order, whether it be given by the Governor of the state or an officer of the militia or a civil officer of a city or county, that attempts to invest either officer or private with authority in excess of that which may be exercised by peace officers of the state is unreasonable and unlawful*; and if it is obeyed, the officer or private giving obedience subjects himself to such punishment and liability as the penal and civil laws of the state might inflict against a private individual guilty of similar transgression of the law or the rights of the citizen. We feel at liberty to thus define the limits within which soldiers may lawfully act, because all the authorities agree that the courts may at the instance of any person who has been aggrieved or on behalf of the commonwealth inquire into their acts and doings and determine whether or not they have been guilty of any conduct that would subject them to liability or punishment. The only difference between our ruling and that obtaining in the authorities cited is that we define more precisely than they do what orders a soldier is justifiable in executing, and hold as a matter of law that these orders are confined to such as a peace officer in the discharge of his duty might execute. In respect to these orders, the powers of the military and local civil officers of the state are identical. What one cannot do, neither can the other; what one may do, so may the other. The soldier has the same measure of protection and is subject to the same liability, whether he is acting under the orders of a military officer, independent of the local civil authorities, or is acting under immediate direction of these authorities. Neither has the right to give any orders or directions except those that a peace officer of the state might rightfully execute; and if the soldier does only what a peace officer may do, then he is entitled to the immunity afforded peace officers in the performance of their duty. This rule of conduct is of course not free from objection, but upon the whole we think it furnishes a reasonable guide for the militia, and describes with as much accuracy as conditions will permit the lines within which they may act with safety and beyond which they may not go without peril. Its observance will protect the quiet and orderly citizen from disturbance, and arrest and leave the lawbreaker to be dealt with as his conduct deserves. (Emphasis Added)

equation of the liabilities of Guardsmen and civilian peace officers is thus well established[64] and judicial dicta to the contrary[65] should be seen as somewhat inaccurate obiter.

2.4.2 False Arrest and Imprisonment

In respect of false arrest and imprisonment, the common law rule (stated in *Franks v. Smith*[66]) itself was that peace officers could arrest any person who had committed a felony, or was reasonably thought by them to have done so, or was committing one in their presence. This was summarized as an objective test of "reasonable good faith and probable good cause" by the Supreme Court of North Carolina[67] and was

---

[64]Ela v. Smith, 71 Mass. (6 Gray) 121, 140 (1855) (Mass.).

> But while thus recognizing the authority of civil officers to call out and use an armed force to aid in suppressing a riot or tumult actually existing, or preventing one which is threatened, *it must be borne in mind that no power is conferred on the troops, when so assembled, to act independently of the civil authority. On the contrary, they are called out, in the words of the statute, "to aid the civil authority," not to usurp its functions, or take its place. They are to act as an armed police only, subject to the absolute and exclusive control and direction of the magistrates and other civil officers designated in the statute, as to the specific duty or service which they are to perform.* The statute does not even enlarge the power of the civil officers by giving them any military authority; but only places at their disposal, in the exercise of their appropriate and legal functions, an organized, disciplined and equipped body of men, capable of more efficient action in an emergency, and among a multitude, than an ordinary police force. Nor can the magistrate delegate his authority to the military force which he summons to his aid, or vest in the military authorities any discretionary power to take any steps or do any act to prevent or suppress a mob or riot. They must perform only such service and render such aid as is required by the civil officers. This is not only essential to guard against the use of excessive force and the exercise of irresponsible power; but it is required by the fundamental principles of our constitution, which provides that "the military power shall always be held in an exact subordination to the civil authority, and be governed by it. (Emphasis Added)

See also Fluke v. Canton, 123 P. 1049 (1912) (Okla.) and Bishop v. Vandercook, 228 Mich. 299 (1924) (Mich.). These cases reiterate the remarks as made in Franks v. Smith, 135 S.W. 484 (1911) (Ky.). Similar remarks have been made in Orr v. Burleson, 214 Ala. 257 (1926) (Ala.), Seaney v. State, 188 Miss. 367 (1940), 194 So. 913 (Miss.) and Scheuer v. Rhodes, 416 U.S. 232 (1974).

[65]*See, e.g.*, Allen v. Gardner, 182 N.C. 425, 109 S.E. 260 (1921) (N.C.), where a soldier's power and liabilities are equated to that of a civilian. On the other hand, the decision in Manley v. State, 62 Tex. Crim. 392, 137 S.W. 1137 (1911) (Tex.) does not distinguish between the powers of a peace officer or a citizen.

[66]Franks v. Smith, 135 S.W. 484 (1911) (Ky.).

[67]Allen v. Gardner, 182 N.C. 425, 109 S.E. 260 (1921) (N.C.).

also accepted by the Alabama Supreme Court.[68] In *Moyer v. Peabody*, however, the U.S. Supreme Court upheld an arrest based on good faith alone and said, "So long as such arrest are made in good faith and in the honest belief that they are needed in order to head the insurrection off, the Governor is the final judge and cannot be subjected to an action after he is out of office on the ground that he has not reasonable grounds for his belief."[69]

Moyer v. Peabody has purportedly been applied by the US Court of Appeal (10th circuit) where on the question of probable cause it upheld a direction to the jury supposedly based on the *Moyer* doctrine of the sufficiency of good faith alone.[70] It is submitted that it would be erroneous to read *Moyer* as establishing that good faith may supplant the probable cause requirement. Consequently, the acceptance of the latter interpretation in *Valdez* is erroneous.[71] Firstly, *Moyer* dealt with the validity of an order of arrest issued by a state chief executive and not with the issue whether good faith arrests without probable cause by guardsmen are lawful. *Moyer* is confined to the Governor of Colorado and does not discuss the liability of guardsmen. Secondly, *Moyer* did not explicitly or impliedly attempt to modify the earlier views of the Supreme Court that guardsmen may make lawful arrest or lawfully expropriate property only if reasonable grounds exist.[72] Thirdly, the later Supreme Court decision in *Scheuer v. Rhodes*[73] shows that the liability for arrests by the Governor and by the guardsmen may well be different. *Scheuer* decided that claims for damages against the Governor of Ohio and others, by relatives of students killed on Kent State University campus by National Guardsmen were not barred by the Eleventh Amendment. Relying on an earlier Supreme Court decision[74] the court accepted that "when a court evaluates police conduct relating to arrest, its guideline is "good faith and probable cause",[75] and drew a sharp distinction between the liability of policemen (and, by implication, guardsmen) on the one hand, and the "higher officers of the executive branch" (e.g., the Governor) on the other.

---

[68]Orr v. Burleson, 214 Ala. 257, 259 (1926) (Ala.) ("The arrest was made without a warrant; but an officer may arrest any person at any time "when a felony has been committed"—in this case the dynamiting of the passenger train—"and he has reasonable cause to believe that the person arrested committed it; or when he has reasonable cause to believe that the person arrested has committed a felony, although it may afterwards appear that a felony had not in fact been committed; or on a charge made, upon reasonable cause, that the person arrested has committed a felony."... These questions were proper as going to show that Guice-or Burleson, if he was responsible in any way-had reasonable cause for believing that plaintiff had been party to a felony). In Luther v. Borden, 48 U.S. 1 (1849), and Mitchell v. Harmony, 54 U.S. 115 (1851), the US Supreme Court had stated that guardsmen could make lawful arrests or lawful expropriation of property only if reasonable grounds exist for such action.

[69]Moyer v. Peabody, 212 U.S. 78, 85 (1909).

[70]Valdez v. Black, 446 F.2d. 1071 (1971) (10th Cir.).

[71]Nicholas B. Waranoff (1972), 1, 14–15.

[72]*See* Luther v. Borden, 48 U.S. 1 (1849) and Mitchell v. Harmony, 54 U.S. 115 (1851).

[73]Scheuer v. Rhodes, 416 U.S. 232 (1974). *See also* Foster [23].

[74]Piersen v. Ray, 386 U.S. 547 (1967).

[75]Scheuer v. Rhodes, 416 U.S. 232, 245 (1974).

The latter were required to measure up to a less stringent test, in view of the fact that their inquiry is far more complex and the range of decisions and choices are virtually infinite.[76] Even this broader range of discretion is not, however, merely a test of good faith as supposedly suggested by *Moyer*. The Court in *Scheuer* formulated the test as follows (and relied on *Moyer* to reach its conclusion), "It is the existence of reasonable grounds for the belief formed at the time and in light of all the circumstances, coupled with good faith belief, that affords a basis for acts performed in the course of official conduct."[77] It is therefore submitted that guardsmen would incur similar tortious liability as peace officers, whether under statute[78] or otherwise, and that probable (or reasonable) cause, coupled with good faith, continues to be a valid test for liability for false arrest or imprisonments. The equation of peace officers and guardsmen for purposes of illegal action would further suggest that warrantless searches by guardsmen would be illegal,[79] unless done in hot pursuit,[80] or as an incident of the power of arrest.[81] Moreover, apart from the warrant requirement,

---

[76]Scheuer v. Rhodes, 416 U.S. 232, 247 (1974) ("In short, since the options which a chief executive and his principal subordinates must consider are far boarder and far more subtle than those made by officials with less responsibility, the range of discretion must be comparably broad").

[77]Scheuer v. Rhodes, 416 U.S. 232, 247–48 (1974).

[78]*See, e.g.*, 42 USC § 1983 which is titled Civil Action for Deprivation of Rights and reads as:

> Every person who, under color of any statute, ordinance, regulation, custom, or usage, of any State or Territory or the District of Columbia, subjects, or causes to be subjected, any citizen of the United States or other person within the jurisdiction thereof to the deprivation of any rights, privileges, or immunities secured by the Constitution and laws, shall be liable to the party injured in an action at law, suit in equity, or other proper proceeding for redress, except that in any action brought against a judicial officer for an act or omission taken in such officer's judicial capacity, injunctive relief shall not be granted unless a declaratory decree was violated or declaratory relief was unavailable. For the purposes of this section, any Act of Congress applicable exclusively to the District of Columbia shall be considered to be a statute of the District of Columbia.

[79]Coolidge v. Hampshire, 403 U.S. 443 (1971) (holding that search and seizure under illegal warrant not issued by a neutral and detached magistrate is invalid); Camara v. Municipal Court, 387 U.S. 523 (1967) (holding that refusal to permit building inspectors to inspect defendant's residence without warrant does not justify criminal prosecution under ordinance).

[80]Warden v. Hayden, 387 U.S. 294 (1967) (holding that entry without warrant to search for robber reported to have escaped in vicinity is not unconstitutional because the "exigencies of the situation made that course imperative").

[81]Chimel v. California, 395 U.S. 752 (1969) (upholding the power of search incident to arrest subject to qualifications, although applications of the test lead to invalidation of police action in the instant case).

there must be probable cause as to the specific items to be seized[82] and as to the premises to be searched.[83] It has been argued that these principles would make "dragnet, massive, house to house searches by guardsmen unlawful."[84]

On the other hand, the power of the guardsmen to execute search warrants (validly obtained from authorized civil officers) has been consistently upheld. In a leading decision the Mississippi Supreme Court upheld this power as a valid incident of the Governor's power to uphold and execute the laws, on which the power to call out the militia in aid of civil authority is itself premised.[85] This view has been repeatedly applied in various cases.[86] This does not mean that the guardsmen may invade property rights with impunity. The principle of reasonableness, essentially similar to the test of probable cause for arrests is used by courts to invalidate searches, seizures and destruction of property done in an arbitrary manner.[87]

None of the elements of the reasonableness test—necessity for the impugned acts, their effect on the aggrieved individual, the availability of less stringent but more efficacious alternatives, the nexus with the objects sought to be achieved are immune from examination. In adopting this approach, courts were repeating (albeit without acknowledgment) the test for invasion of property rights during emergencies which had been enunciated more than sixty years earlier by the US Supreme Court in *Mitchell v. Harmony*.[88] Upholding the award of damages to Harmony, an American trader accompanying the US army on their incursions into Mexican territory, for destruction of his goods, the Supreme Court had said:

---

[82]Marron v. US, 275 U.S. 192 (1927) (holding that to prevent the seizure of one thing under warrant describing another, the 4th Amendment requires particularization of items to be seized; thus, a warrant allowing seizure of intoxicating liquors does not allow seizure of a ledger and bills for service).

[83]United States v. Hinton, 219 F.2d. 324 (1938) (7th Cir.) (holding that a single search warrant may cover several different places or residences in a single building, but probable cause must be shown for searching each residence).

[84]Warnoff [20, p. 1, 16].

[85]State v. McPhail, 182 Miss. 360 (1938) (Miss.).

[86]Seaney v. State, 188 Miss. 367 (1940) (Miss.), McBride v. State, 221 Miss. 508 (1954) (Miss.); Brady v. State, 229 Miss. 677 (1957) (Miss.).

[87]Herlihy v. Donohue, 161 Pac. Rep. 164 (1916) (Mont.). The Governor of Monatana declared Silver Bow county to be in a state of insurrection, called out the militia to restore order but did not proclaim martial law. The commander of troops issued an order restricting the opening hours of places where intoxicating drinks could be purchased. Herlihy's saloon was entered by guardsmen and his liquor stock destroyed for allegedly violating the closure order. The Supreme Court of Montana, in an action for damages for trespass and destruction of property, treated the case as one involving the use of military in aid of the civil authority and found for the plaintiff. The Court examined the state of affairs existing in the area and concluded that there was no military necessity as there was no state of war; that the liquor was not needed for the use of troops; that its destruction was not necessary to prevent liquor falling into the hands of the rioters; that the latter were not threatening to break into saloons to obtain intoxicants and that the more efficacious alternative to temporary arrest and imprisonment of Herlihy by the civil authorities was not followed.

[88]Mitchell v. Harmony, 54 U.S. 115 (1851).

> But we are clearly of the opinion, that in all of these cases the danger must be immediate and impending; or the necessity urgent for the public service, such as will not admit of delay, … It is impossible to define the particular circumstances of danger or necessity in which this power may be exercised. Every case must depend on its own circumstances. It is the emergency that gives the right, and the emergency must be shown to exist before the taking can be justified.[89]

2.4.3 Use of Excessive Force

As regards the use of excessive force by the State or its servants during emergencies, the *Scheuer* test of "reasonable grounds for belief coupled with good faith"[90] that applies to the actions of higher executive officers including Governors, must, a fortiori, apply to Guardsmen. On the other hand, if the test for peace officers is applied, a showing of gross negligence is necessary.[91] The former test is probably less stringent as it involves some subjective elements, whereas the latter test is primarily objective in nature. This suggests that, at the very least, Guardsmen would be liable for use of excessive force if they are unable to show reasonable grounds for the belief that such force was necessary or if it could be shown that they acted with malice.[92]

2.4.4 Immunity, if Any?

Scheuer establishes that the Governor and higher executive officers do not possess any absolute immunity from tortious liability under 42 USC §1983.[93] Despite

---

[89]Mitchell v. Harmony, 54 U.S. 115, 134 (1851).

[90]Scheuer v. Rhodes, 416 U.S. 232 (1974).

[91]Jenkins v. Averett, 424 F.2d. 1228 (1970) (4th Cir.); Whirl v. Kern, 407 F.2d. 781 (1969) (US Court of Appeals, 5th Cir.); Joseph v. Rowlen, 402 F.2d. 367 (1968) (7th Cir.).

[92]*See, e.g.*, Bishop v. Vandercook, 200 N. W. 278, 283 (Mich.). An award of damages for injury to person and automobile were upheld on the ground of use of excessive force. The Court said:

> The use of the log to ditch automobiles, if drivers thereof should refuse or neglect to stop, was an unlawful and wanton and wilful disregard of human life, open to no justification, and no defense of contributory negligence. … It was intended and well calculated to inflict injury upon anyone not observing or not obeying its challenge to disaster, and placed across the roadway after it was apparent a driver might not stop on signal, and left there to ditch him for not stopping.

[93]42 U.S.C. § 1983 under the heading of Civil Action for Deprivation of Rights reads as:

> Every person who, under color of any statute, ordinance, regulation, custom, or usage, of any State or Territory or the District of Columbia, subjects, or causes to be subjected, any citizen of the United States or other person within the jurisdiction thereof to the deprivation of any rights, privileges, or immunities secured by the Constitution and laws, shall be liable

recognizing the twin underlying rationales of a doctrine of immunity from tortious liability—the injustice of subjecting to liability an officer required to exercise discretion by the legal obligations of his position and the danger that threat of such liability would deter his willingness to execute his office with the decisiveness and the judgment required for public good—*Scheuer* rejected the doctrine of absolute immunity from tortious liability for the Governor or other high officials, in the following words:

> It can hardly be argued, at this late date, that under no circumstances can the officers of the state government be subjected to liability under this statute ... government officials, as a class could not be totally exempt, by virtue of some absolute immunity, from liability under [42 USC § 1983's] terms ... under the criteria developed by precedents of this court [42 USC § 1983] would be drained of meaning were we to hold that the acts of a governor or other high executive officer have 'that quality of supreme and unchangeable edict, overriding all conflicting rights of property and unreviewable through the judicial power of the Federal Government'.[94]

2.5 *Judicial Review of Actions of the Guard in Other Situations*

Courts have repeatedly invalidated or injuncted the use of the militia by State officials for ulterior motives and especially if made to circumvent judicial orders. In doing so, they have had little regard to the actual words used by the executive and have treated alleged proclamations of martial laws as well as other mobilizations of the militia with equal disapproval. Thus the US Supreme Court invalidated the proclamation of martial law by the Governor of Texas and injuncted the use of troops to limit the production of oil from the complainant's wells, emphasizing the absence of any emergency, and noting that the impugned actions had occurred after the federal district court had prohibited the state Railroad Commission from

to the party injured in an action at law, suit in equity, or other proper proceeding for redress, except that in any action brought against a judicial officer for an act or omission taken in such officer's judicial capacity, injunctive relief shall not be granted unless a declaratory decree was violated or declaratory relief was unavailable. For the purposes of this section, any Act of Congress applicable exclusively to the District of Columbia shall be considered to be a statute of the District of Columbia.

[94]Scheuer v. Rhodes, 416 U.S. 232, 243, 248 (1974).

limiting the production of oil from the wells.[95] Similarly, the Oklahoma Supreme Court invalidated a detailed order of the State Governor creating a military zone around named oil wells and calling out the state militia to regulate and limit the oil production in the specified area, on the ground that a legislative enactment enacted for the same purpose had earlier been held to be invalid by the United States Supreme Court.[96] The Federal District Court of Oklahoma also injuncted the State Governor from sending troops to the site of the Grand River Dam Authority to stop construction of a dam because the Governor was found by the court to be attempting to defeat the financial interests of the Federal Government (which held coupons and bonds issued by the dam authority) by stopping construction of the dam.[97] In another decision, the 8th Circuit invalidated the Governor's attempt to use the National Guard to interfere with court ordered school integration in Arkansas.[98]

The converse principle—that the court will uphold the use of National Guard to enforce court orders, provided such use is not illegal for other reasons—has also been articulated and applied in at least one decision. The Oklahoma Supreme Court voided a restraining order prohibiting a State Governor from using guardsmen to move the seat of government of Delaware County from Grove to Jay.[99] The decision to do so had been taken by the Governor after local elections had decided that the seat should be at Jay and after the Oklahoma Supreme Court had itself declared the result of the election to be valid.

2.6 Use of Force by the Federal Government: The Debs Principle

In 1895, an unusual use of force by the federal executive was upheld by the US Supreme Court in unnecessarily broad terms. *In Re Debs*[100] President Cleveland, acting through a US attorney in Chicago, obtained an injunction from a US circuit court to keep the trains moving during the Pullman strike of 1895 and enjoined the strike itself on the ground that it threatened interference with inter-state commerce

[95]Sterling v. Constantin, 287 U.S. 378, 387–88 (1930). Chief Justice Hughes said:

> … Governor Sterling, learning that the orders made by the Railroad Commission could no longer be enforced, issued his oral and written orders to General Wolters to limit the production of oil … this was the limit fixed by the Railroad Commission's order of October 10th the enforcement of which was subject to the restraining order.

[96]Russell Petroleum Co. v. Walker, 19 P.2d. 582 (1933) (Okla.).

[97]United States v. Phillips, 33 F. Supp. 261 (1940) (D. Okla.).

[98]Fabus v. US, 254 F.2d. 797 (1958) (8th Cir.).

[99]Fluke v. Canton, 31 Okla. 718 (1912) (Okla.).

[100]*In Re* Debs 158 U.S. 564 (1895).

and with the free flow of mail. The Supreme Court sustained Debs' jailing for contempt of the circuit court's order on the ground that since the wrongs complained of by the President had inherent authority, he could seek judicial aid in enforcing them. It must be remembered that there was no statutory warrant for the injunction obtained by the President. During the course of the judgment, Justice Brewer said:

> ... [T]here is no such impotency in the national Government. The entire strength of the nation may be used to enforce in any part of the land the full and free exercise of all national powers and the security of all rights entrusted by the Constitution to its care. The strong arm of the national government may be put forth to brush away all obstructions to the freedom of interstate commerce or the transportation of the mails. If the emergency arises, the army of the nation, and all its militia, are at the service of the nation to compel obedience to its laws.[101]

It is submitted that *Debs* does not create any additional basis for the exercise of state power during domestic emergencies. It would be questionable to base a claim of inherent presidential authority to use force in the domestic sphere upon the *Debs* doctrine. The later decision of Supreme Court in the Steel Seizure cases[102] confirms that no such inherent presidential power exists, at least in the absence (as in Debs) of statutory authority. The Supreme Court decision in *US v. US District Court*[103] also unanimously rejects inherent executive authority to engage in warrantless electronic surveillance on grounds of domestic security. *Debs* does not decide more than this: that the federal government may obtain a (labor) injunction to prohibit strikes having a serious and crippling effect on interstate commerce and may enforce that injunction (as, indeed, any other) through contempt proceeding in a court of law. But the weight of *Debs* for even this limited proposition is of little practical value today in view of later detailed legislation which limits the use of labor injunctions to a clearly defined and narrow sphere. One must therefore agree with Tribe when he says:

> At least where a substantial personal interest in life, liberty or property is threatened by Presidential action, *Debs* should probably be regarded as more anachronism than authority.[104]

---

[101] *Id.* at 582.

[102] Youngstown Sheet & Tube Co. v. Sawyer (Steel Seizure), 343 U.S. 579 (1952).

[103] United States v. U.S. District Court (Keith), 407 U.S. 297 (1972).

[104] Tribe [24].

3 Military Acting in Aid of Civil Authority in UK

There are three main peacetime sources of authority for intervention of the military outside martial law[105]: the common law[106] power to use troops to maintain peace and order during emergencies; and the power to call out troops under the Emergency Powers Acts of 1920 and 1964, respectively.

3.1 Distinction Between Martial Law and Military Acting in Aid of Civil Authority

This distinction is implicit in the definition of martial law given earlier, each element of which would differ in degree when the military is used in aid of civil authority. By definition, when the military acts in aid of civil authority, the latter is, in law and in fact, not superseded or supplanted as in martial law but rather strengthened and supplemented by additional aid, usually in the form of troops. The military remains legally and factually subordinate to civil authority.[107] Most notably, no trials by military commission occur when the military acts in aid of the civil authority. Differences of degree continue to be important. Thus, when mere disorder turns to a serious riot, ordinary policing may have to be supplemented by additional manpower in the form of the military; when riots turn into rebellion, martial law may arise in place of military acting in aid of civil authority.[108] However, the distinction, though one of degree, cannot be ignored, as has occasionally been done.[109]

---

[105]Listed in the Queen's Regulations for the Army (1962; loose-leaf service) J1164–J1165.

[106]*Cf.* Whelan [25] (reference to the power as being "*under the royal prerogative*"). *See also*, Whelan [26], which is to the same effect.

[107]Finlason [27].

[108]*See* MacDermott [28]. *Cf.* Holdsworth [29] ("*…rebellion is but riot writ large.*").

[109]For example, at various points in his charge to the grand jury in R v. Eyre [1868] to consider a bill indicating Governor Edward Eyre for alleged misdemeanors during martial law in Jamaica in 1865, Blackburn, J. dealt with the law relating to military action in aid of civil authority. *See* FINLASON'S SP. REP. 56–59, 81 (1868).

3.2 *Historical Evolution and Current Status of the Civil Decision to Deploy Military in Aid of Civil Authority*[110]

There appear to be five significant historical stages in respect of the civil decision to call out troops or additional manpower in aid of civil authority.[111] During the first stage, which subsisted prior to the seventeenth century, law enforcement was in the hands of the posse comitatus.[112] The absence of effective communications and the absence of a strong central force in this first stage resulted in the local representatives of the King being invested with virtually complete autonomy and independence in respect of whether and when to call out the posse comitatus and other additional manpower to assist civil authority. The second stage may be dated from the creation of standing armies, by the Militia Act of 1661. This led, initially, to increasing control of the Crown over its soldiers and later, with the progressive growth of doctrines of Parliamentary sovereignty and ministerial responsibility, to increasing Parliamentary and executive control of the civil decision regarding the use of troops in aid of local civil authority. Although local civil magistrates invariably took the initiative in requesting military aid, this was subject to greater central control and supervision.[113]

The third stage, starting from the late eighteenth century, saw an increase in the frequency and scale of riots and disturbances. This led both to a relaxation of Parliamentary and executive control over the civil decision regarding use of troops in aid of civil authority and also to an increase in the number of judicial pronouncements in respect of the civil magistrate's duty "to opt for military pacification of civil unrest."[114]

With the creation of effective police forces in the nineteenth century, an improvement in communications, a general expansion of central government activity in every field and a decline in the frequency of riots and disturbances, the fourth stage saw a gradual decline in the role of local civil magistrates (e.g., justices of the peace) in respect of the decision to call out the military in aid of civil authority,[115] although it may be mentioned that the traditional dominant role of the

---

[110]*See generally*, Radzinowicz [30]; Jeffrey [31]; Jeffrey & Hennessey, States of Emergency (1983); Greer [32]; Hayter [33]; *Report of the Select Committee on Employment of Military in Cases of Disturbances*, H.C. 236 VII (1908); Wilcox [34].

[111]*See* Radzinowicz [30, pp. 106–07]; Greer [32, p. 581].

[112]That is a group of able-bodied free men, usually between 15 and 60 years old, who were pressed into service to assist in the maintenance of law and order and the preservation of the King's peace, by the King's local and civil representatives (e.g., the sheriff). *See* Radzinowicz [30].

[113]*Id* at 110–11; *see also* Hayter [33, p. 140].

[114]*See Report of the Select Committee on Employment of Military in Cases of Disturbances*, H.C. 236 VII ¶ 9 (1908); Greer [32, p. 581].

[115]Greer [32, pp. 586–87].

magistrates has been reasserted as late as 1893.[116] Finally, the fifth and the current stage differs only in degree from the fourth, with its outstanding feature being that the military has, with isolated exceptions,[117] not been used in this century without the initiative or approval of the Central Government.[118]

On the current legal status of the civil decision to deploy troops, it has been argued that the decision whether or not to deploy troops in aid of civil authority is an exclusive and unreviewable prerogative power of the Central Government, probably resting with the Home Secretary or Defense Secretary acting in consultation with the Prime Minister, and is akin to or part of prerogative powers in respect of the use and disposition of the army.[119] Although supported by political and legal practice the view that troops cannot be deployed without the concurrence or approval of the central government is not fully borne out by current instructions to the army as found in the Manual of Military Law or the Queen's Regulations,[120] both of which appear to be based on the traditional and contrary view that local civil authorities may directly request military aid during serious disturbance without reference to Whitehall.[121] Secondly, it is arguable that the inheritors of the power of the local magistracy were not the central government but the police forces, which during the nineteenth century, gradually replaced the magistracy as the primary

---

[116]That is during the Featherstone Riots. *See Report of the Committee Appointed to Inquire into the Circumstances Connected with the Disturbances at Featherstone on 7th of September 1893* (HMSO, 1893) (C.7234); *Report of the Interdepartmental Committee on Riots Appointed by the Home Secretary May 1894* (HMSO, 1895) (C. 7650).

[117]For example, during the miners' strike in South Wales in 1910, the Glamorganshire Chief Constable sought military assistance to combat the Tonypandy rioters and was immediately sent military forces by the competent military authority. *See* Wilcox [34, p. 405].

[118]*See generally* Jeffrey & Hennessey, States of Emergency (1983), which contains a historical discussion of the numerous occasions when the military has been used in Britain in aid of civil authority since 1919. The authors show, *inter alia*, that at least since that year, both policy planning and operational control in respect of use of military in aid of civil authority during industrial unrest of strikes has been in the hands of various organizations or departments established for this purpose within the central government. Starting with the transitional Industrial Unrest Committee (IUC) in 1919, such organizations have included the Supply and Transport Committee (STC), the Supply and Transport Organization (STO), the Organization for Maintenance of Supplies (OMS), the Industrial Emergencies Committee (IEC) and, now, the so called Civil Contingencies Unit (CCU), established in 1972 after the miners' strike and headed, since 1982, by Mr. Author Goodall. The existence of the CCU is not publicly acknowledged by the government. On the role of the central government in the use of military, especially in industrial disputes, *see* Mark [35].

[119]Greer [32, pp. 576–78, 588–90, 598–99].

[120]*See* Queen's Regulations for the Army J1164 (loose-leaf service) (1962). However, this does require, except in sudden emergencies, that the military "*inform the Ministry of Defense and his immediately superior authority.*" (Emphasis supplied).

[121]*See, Report of the Select Committee on Employment of Military in Cases of Disturbances,* H.C. 236 at 376, col. 2 (1908) (evidence of Sir Edward Troup).

preservers of peace and order within Britain.[122] Nor can the powers of the magistracy, and now the police be attenuated or extinguished by any doctrine of obsolescence or desuetude on the basis of its non-exercise. It must be remembered that the magistracy did not wield exclusive power to call out the army and the concurrent power of the central government to deploy troops is not in dispute. Thirdly, the oft-repeated and widely accepted view that police forces in Britain are autonomous and independent[123] and subject to no central government interference[124] would suggest that the local civilian decision to deploy troops in aid of civil authority by a chief constable may well be taken even in defiance of Whitehall and, a fortiori without reference to it. Fourthly, the view that the deployment power is exclusive to the central government would run counter to judicial and non-judicial statements imposing an obligation on soldier and citizen alike to intervene during disorder if requested by the civil authority and perhaps even if not so requested. Finally, even in practice, central government consultation and approval prior to deployment has not always proved beneficial, due to the inherent delays in such a process.[125]

The second argument that such deployment constitutes an unreviewable, high prerogative "ministerial" act is clearly untenable, especially after the decision of the House of Lords in the *GCHQ case*.[126] The "soldier is citizen" view is somewhat unreal.[127] There is a growing realization that the army cannot be permitted to operate at any time except under civilian control. Moreover, any immunity from judicial review in this sphere would sweep aside, as if by a side wind, the numerous judicial statements painstakingly detailing the powers and duties of local civil magistrates when suppressing disorder. Exclusion of judicial review of a "ministerial" decision would be inconsistent and indeed irreconcilable, with the established ambit of judicial review in respect of the much greater emergency represented by martial law. The use and the disposition of the army, even if it be in general a part of the prerogative cannot be treated as an unreviewable prerogative power when used domestically to intrude upon private rights.

---

[122] *See* Report of the Committee appointed to inquire into the circumstances with the Disturbances at Featherstone on September 7, 1893 (London, HMSO, 1893), (C.-7234) ¶ 24 which recommended that all requests for military aid by the magistracy must be routed through the Chief Constables. This led to a suitable change in the Queen's Regulations. The same point is made by the *Report of the Select Committee on Employment of Military in Cases of Disturbances*, H.C. 236 (1908) 9.

[123] *See, inter alia*, Miller v. Knox (1838) 574 132 Eng. Rep. 910; Fisher v. Oldham Corporation [1930] 2 KB 364; AG, NSW v. Perpetual Trustee Co. [1955] AC 457 (JCPC); R. v. Commissioner of Police of Metropolis *Ex parte* Blackburn [1968] 2 QB 118,135–37 (Salmon, L.J.).

[124] *Cf.* Evelegh [36] (quoting the remarks of Assistant Chief Constable of Thames Valley Police Force as published in *The Guardian* on 25/9/1975: "We do not act accordingly to Home Office instructions. Chief Constables are not subject to any form of political control.").

[125] *See* the 1969 incident in Northern Ireland?

[126] Council of Civil Service Unions v. Minister for Civil Service [1984] 3 All ER 935.

[127] *See* Lord Diplock's obiter in *In Re* Attorney-General for Northern Ireland Reference (No. 1 of 1975) [1976] 2 All ER 937, 946.

Chandler,[128] sometimes cited for the contrary proposition, related only to governmental decisions dealing with the movement of armed personnel and their posting at particular sites[129] and did not deal with intrusion into private rights as a result of such use of the army.[130] In any event, the recent decision in the *GCHQ case*, and not *Chandler*, articulates the contemporary perspective of judicial review, suggesting that both the decision to deploy troops as well as the steps taken to restore peace and order are judicially reviewable.

3.3 Judicial Review and Some Other Issues

Before the seventeenth century, soldiers coming to the aid of civil authority were treated as citizens and were subjected to the same powers and duties as citizens during times of disorder.[131] Citizens, in turn were under a legal duty to assist in the restoration of order if asked by the competent civil authority.[132] Additionally, soldiers and citizens had the power, and, indeed, the duty, to step in and quell serious disorder without being requested to assist.[133] These legal controls were imposed by the common law from the Middle Ages.[134]

---

[128]Chandler v. DPP [1964] AC 763, 791.

[129]*Id.* at 807–08, 810–811 (Lord Devlin).

[130]Nor was the issue decided in the earlier decision of the Court of Appeal in China Navigation Co. v. AG [1932] 2 KB 197 where an application by ship owners for a declaration that the Crown provide free armed protection for their vessels against pirates near Hong Kong was rejected. *See id* at 211, 213 (Scrutton, L.J.).

[131]Burdett v. Abbott (1811) 104 Eng. Rep. 501. Chief Justice Mansfield remarked in obiter:

> …I will correct a strange mistaken notion which has got abroad, that because men are soldiers, they cease to be citizen; a soldier is gifted with all the rights of other citizens, and is bound by all the duties of other citizens…

To similar effect *see* Report of the Committee appointed to inquire into the circumstances with the Disturbances at Featherstone on September 7, 1893 (London, HMSO, 1893), (C.7234). *See also* Manual of Military Law ¶ 3 (1968); *Report of the Select Committee on Employment of Military in Cases of Disturbances*, H.C. 236 at 376, col. 1 (1908) (evidence of Sir Edward Troup).

[132]Manual of Military Law ¶ 2 (1968); Report of the Committee appointed to inquire into the circumstances with the Disturbances at Featherstone on September 7, 1893 (London, HMSO, 1893) (C.7234).

[133]Report of the Interdepartmental Committee on Riots appointed by the Home Secretary, May 1894 (London, HMSO, 1895) (C. 7650) ¶ 23; Manual of Military Law ¶ 3 (1968); *Report of the Select Committee on Employment of Military in Cases of Disturbances*, H.C. 236 (1908) (evidence of Sir Edward Troup at 376, cols. 1–2). The current Queen's Regulations allow *suo moto* action by the military commander without request from civil authorities in cases which "*demand his immediate intervention to protect life and property*.".

[134]Radzinowicz [30, p. 107].

The local magistrate, a justice of the peace, was subjected to the most onerous duties. Under the Riot Act of 1714, he was required to read a proclamation to a disorderly crowd to disperse. If they did not do so within an hour, he was to use force to disperse or arrest and was legally excused for causing damage to life and property.[135] Nor did the Riot Act incapacitate the troops from acting prior to the expiry of one hour: their common law powers to prevent disorder subsisted in addition to those under the Riot Act.[136] The magistrate was the competent civil authority and was under a duty to summon sufficient force, whether military or civil or both, to quell disorder and restore peace. He was to "accompany the troops and remain as near the officer in command as he reasonably can."[137] He could be civilly or criminally indicted if he failed to "hit the exact line between excess and failure of duty."[138] Both the civil decision to deploy troops and actions done by the latter were treated as a justiciable issue which could be reviewed by a court and whose legality could be assessed by a jury.[139] The test applied to determine whether a public functionary as justice of the peace had neglected his duty to preserve law and order was an objective one.[140] It is exemplified by the following words used by Justice Littledale while charging a jury assembled to adjudge the guilt or innocence of the Mayor of Bristol, who was indicted for criminal neglect of his duty to preserve pace and order. The judge said:

> Has the defendant done all that he knew was in his power to suppress the riots that could reasonably be expected from a man of honesty and of ordinary prudence, firmness and activity under the circumstances in which he was placed?[141]

In applying this test, judges and Royal Commissioners made detailed examinations of the factual circumstances in which the disturbance occurred. For example, in *Redford v. Birley*[142] Chief Justice Abbott was of the view, with which his brother judges[143] agreed, that the issue could be decided, "... only by showing

---

[135] 1 Geo. 1, Stat. 2, c. 5. Earlier Riot Acts of similar nature include the 1411 Act (13 Hen. 4, c.7) and the 1414 Act (2 Hen. 5, stat 1). All these Acts were abolished by the Criminal Law Act 1967, c. 58 (UK) § 10 (2), Sch. 3, parts I & II.

[136] Report of the Committee appointed to inquire into the circumstances with the Disturbances at Featherstone on 7th of September 1893 (London, HMSO, 1893) (C.7234).

[137] Report of the Interdepartmental Committee on Riots appointed by the Home Secretary, May 1894 (London, HMSO, 1895) (C.7650) ¶ 16.

[138] R v. Pinney (1832) 172 Eng. Rep. 962.

[139] R v. Kennet (1781) 172 Eng. Rep. 976; Redford v. Birley (1822) 171 Eng. Rep. 773; R v. Pinney (1832) 172 Eng. Rep. 962; R v. Brown (1841) 174 Eng. Rep. 522; R v. Eyre (1868) Finlason Sp. Rep. 56–59, 81; Lynch v. Fitzgerald [1938] 1 IR. 382 (Ir.); Devlin v. Armstrong [1971] NI 13 (NICA).

[140] R v. Pinney (1832) 172 Eng. Rep. 962, 964.

[141] R v. Pinney (1832) 172 Eng. Rep. 962, 971.

[142] Redford v. Birley, (1822) 171 Eng. Rep. 773.

[143] *Id.* at 115 (Bayley, J.); *Id.* at 120–21 (Best, J.); *Id.* at 127 (Holroyd, J.).

what the antecedent state of alarm was, and what was previously done and said."[144] The jury was directed to, and did, examine and analyze in detail the feelings and statements of numerous inhabitants reflecting the state of alarm in the locality.[145] Although such remarks, whether by judges or others, were made in the context of civil actions or criminal prosecutions in the realm of private law, it must be remembered that they involved public officials (e.g., a mayor in *Pinney*; a justice of the peace in *Redford*) indicted for acts done (or not done) in the discharge (or non-discharge) of their official duties, having consequences for the general public.

Problems arise when some of the above rules are applied to contemporary times. These rules did not clarify whether the soldier acting in aid of civil authority is liable upon principles applicable to peace officers (e.g., police constables) or citizens; current statutory provisions confer somewhat different powers of arrest and use of force upon citizens and constables.[146] The posse comitatus "soldier in citizen" attitude might have been valid in a period when the citizenry was the primary instrument for preservation of law and order, but it became unrealistic when peace officers were made subject to new duties and liabilities and when soldiers constituted a distinct professional class of individual for protection of the nation against external threat and serious internal disorder. Indeed, the unrealism of the "soldier is citizen" view has been commented upon in a dictum by Lord Diplock in a decision of the House of Lords in 1976, where the Law Lord emphasizes that although in theory every citizen is under a duty to prevent commission of crime and take reasonable measures to restore order,

> [T]he duty is one of imperfect obligation and does not place him under any obligation to do anything by which he would expose himself to risk of personal injury, nor is he under any duty to search for criminals or seek out crime. In contrast to this, a soldier who is employed in aid of the civil power... is under a duty, enforceable under military law, to search for criminals if so ordered by his superior officer and to risk his own life should this be necessary in preventing terrorist acts.[147]

In the United States, the courts were presented with a similar list of options, i.e., whether soldiers be equated to citizens or to peace officers or to be put into separate class when acting in aid of civil authority and categorically chose the second.[148] This needs to be done unambiguously by English law. Further, if soldiers are to be treated as policemen when acting in aid of civil authority, the scope of their duties and the tests to adjudge their liability, especially for false arrest, use of excessive force and illegal search and seizure, all need to be clearly spelt out. It must also be

---

[144] *Id.* at 111.

[145] Similarly, the Royal Commission on the Featherstone Riots emphasized in 1893 that the necessity for the impugned acts established after due judicial scrutiny, could alone justify the action of individuals, whether civil peace offers, soldiers or civilians. *See* C.7234 (1893).

[146] *See* Criminal Law Act 1967, c. 58 § 2 (UK); Police and Criminal Evidence Act 1984, c. 60 §§ 24 & 25 (UK).

[147] *See* Lord Diplock's obiter in *In Re* Attorney-General for Northern Ireland Reference (No. 1 of 1975) [1976] 2 All ER 937, 946.

[148] Franks v. Smith, 134 S.W. 484 (1911) (Ky.).

clarified if they have any immunity from civil or criminal action, and if so, what is its ambit.

Another problem, and one which has caused some confusion in Northern Ireland, is the difficulty experienced by the military in identifying civil authority. In an interesting monograph published in 1978, a commanding officer of a battalion in the strife torn Upper Falls area of Belfast in Northern Ireland has lamented that the multiplicity of civil authorities in Belfast (e.g., the Police Commissioner or Inspector-General of the RUC, the Northern Ireland ministry in Whitehall, the Home office in London) has led to inordinate delays in the deployment of troops in aid of civil authority and has been responsible for some avoidable and tragic incidents in Belfast.[149] The problem in Northern Ireland in 1969 arose because the army had been instructed not to intervene at the request of the police forces in Belfast without prior consultation with and approval of the government in London. The latter could be obtained only after a long delay during which the law and order situation deteriorated with tragic results for life and property.[150] Modern practice vesting the civil decision to deploy troops in aid of civil authority exclusively with the central government may thus have deleterious consequences unless an alternative system is devised allowing quick and efficient decision making at the local level followed by its speedy implementation.

4 India: No Direct Comparative Jurisprudence Exists Though Some Principles Are Summarized

Strange though it may seem, the same Anglo-Saxon common law jurisprudence which spawned the rich diversity of case law in UK and United States, discussed in elaborate detail above, seems to have had hardly any progeny in the otherwise fertile Indian jurisprudential soil. The reason for this barrenness of case law and literature on this subject in India may well be not far to seek. Post 1950, India's status as a constitutional republic could hardly be consistent with multiple and diverse examples of either military acting in aid of civilian authority or for that matter martial law. Prior to 1950, most of the events and jurisprudence would stand merged with events related to the colonial power ruling India and is largely discussed in Chap. 2.

The authors believe, and have so argued in Chap. 2 that the Armed Forces Special Powers Act (AFSPA) is better characterized as an exercise of statutory emergency powers in peacetime. Whether and to what extent it amounts to *de facto* exercise of martial law as understood in English common law has also been

---

[149]Evelegh [36, pp. 6–8].

[150]*Id.*, with the repulsion and exhaustion of the police forces, and in the absence of the army, the Protestant mob invaded Bombay Street in the Falls Road area of Belfast and burnt it completely.

discussed in Chap. 2, and need not detain us here.[151] To suggest that AFSPA would be the Indian counterpart of the military acting in aid of civilian authority would, according to the authors, be a mischaracterization.

Military acting in aid of civilian authority presupposes that there is an extremely short and transient use of additional military power under total and complete civilian control with no denial or obstruction to access to courts.[152] These basic tests cannot be said to fulfill the AFSPA regime so as to characterize the latter as an example of military acting in aid of civilian authority. Though as discussed in Chap. 2, no denial of court access nor suspension of judicial remedies occurs during AFSPA, the writ of the army commander within an AFSPA notified area is not dependent on civilian control and command, which is why, if forced to characterize AFSPA, it is better treated as a closer cousin of martial law than the subject matter of the present chapter.[153] The latter is subject to the more detailed analysis in Chap. 2.

When the military may be called out to assist the civilian administration (e.g., during natural disasters or temporary rioting etc.) is chiefly the subject matter of "Instructions on Aid to the Civil Authorities by the Armed Forces, 1970."[154] What are the standard operating procedures during such joint operations and the limitations specified therein are equally the matter of nitty-gritty guidelines many of

---

[151] *See* Gautam [12, p. 117].

[152] Rankin [10, p. 75, 77] (observing that "Military troops are sometimes used as an aid to the civil authorities when martial law is not declared. The troops then act a role similar to deputy sheriffs, and do nothing under their own responsibility but act directly under the civil power. This use of troops is easily recognizable from the use of troops under martial law because there is no declaration of martial law, and the troops act in entire subordination to the civil authorities." A Government of India report, set up to review national security, seems to share this position. *See* Government of India, *Report of the Group of Ministers on National Security* 44 (2001) available at https://www.vifindia.org/sites/default/files/GoMReportonNationalSecurity.pdf (observing that, "The reins of Government must, of course, never be handed over to the Armed Forces. The civil face of the governance must remain visible at all levels, even in situations of militancy and terrorism. The Armed Forces of the Union can be used only in aid of civil power and not in suspension of it.").

[153] *See* Gautam [12, pp. 117, 140–143] (discussing the total or near-total breakdown of civilian administration as the key factor behind the issuance of successive "disturbed area notifications" under Sect. 3 of the Armed Forces Special Powers Act, 1958).

[154] *See* Government of India, *Report of the Group of Ministers on National Security* 44 (2001) available at https://www.vifindia.org/sites/default/files/GoMReportonNationalSecurity.pdf. The Report notes that, "The Union Government and the State Government have the constitutional responsibility for running the administration, in accordance with the Constitution. Although problems affecting public order are to be dealt with by the state police forces, the State may sometimes seek assistance from the Centre, and the Central Para-military Force/Army may be deployed in aid of civil power. The Standard Operating Procedure (SOPs) for doing this are laid down in the Instructions on Aid to Civil Authorities by the Armed Forces, 1970/SOP of CPMFs."

The Standard Operating Procedures of Ministry of Home Affairs, *Instructions on Aid to the Civil Authorities by the Armed Forces* (1970). These operational protocols envisage broad situations, such as internal disorders, natural calamities, maintenance of essential services etc., when the armed forces can be pressed into assistance.

which may even differ from state-to-state in their applications.[155] That is why, they cannot really be elevated to the status of substantive jurisprudence and hence have not merited any detailed treatment in the present chapter.

Finally it may not be out of place to mention certain well-known provisions of the Code of Criminal Procedure, 1973[156] (hereinafter "the Code") that adds further detail to such exercises. An executive magistrate may cause any unlawful assembly[157] to be dispersed by the armed forces if she thinks that it cannot be dispersed by any other means.[158] Of course, before the executive magistrate causes it to be dispersed by the armed forces, she is required to use civil force (i.e., the police) to disperse it.[159] Civil force is required to observe a statutory principle of proportionality while using force.[160] If civil force does not work or is not available, the executive magistrate is allowed to call in the armed forces. When so called the officer of the armed forces is legally obliged to "obey such requisition in such manner as he thinks fit, but in doing so use as little force, and do as little injury to person and property, as may be consistent with dispersing the assembly and arresting and detaining such persons."[161] Furthermore, if "public security is manifestly endangered" by an unlawful assembly and no civilian authority (i.e., an executive magistrate) is available the Code vests the power to cause dispersal of such an assembly in any "commissioned or gazette officer of the armed forces" (of course with the "help of armed forces under his command") who might be present.[162] As could be expected, the Code also provides immunity from prosecution to any person acting under the aforementioned provisions of the Code except with previous sanction of the Union or the State Government, as the case may be.[163]

---

[155]*Id. See also*, Commission on Centre-State Relations, Task Force Report V. 1 (annex.) at 83 (2010)

> When called out to quell civil disturbances or help during natural or man-made calamities the role of the defence forces is clearly defined, but when these forces are employed for long periods of counter insurgency or cross-border terrorism the laid down norms prove inadequate.

[156]*See* Code of Criminal Procedure, 1973, §§ 130, 131.

[157]*See* Indian Penal Code, § 141 (for the legal definition of an "unlawful assembly").

[158]Code of Criminal Procedure, 1973, § 130(1).

[159]*Id.* § 129(1).

[160]*Id.* § 129(2).

[161]*Id.* § 130(3).

[162]*Id.* § 131.

[163]*Id.* § 132.

In conclusion, however, it is necessary to refer to the guidelines issued by the Army Headquarters mandated by the constitution bench in *Naga People* case.[164] These certainly convey the flavor as if the case was adumbrating examples of and limitations on military acting in aid of civilian authority.[165] Such a conclusion would, however, be erroneous for the chief reason that the judgment assumes that the military acting even in an AFSPA notified area is fully subject to civilian control. Factually, operationally and legally this is not the case.[166] Section 4 of the AFSPA creates an extremely large zone of discretion vesting in the army commander in this regard with virtually no power or jurisdiction of the local administration.[167] Furthermore, the Army Headquarters' issued a list of "Dos and Don'ts" that comes in two parts—(a) a list of "Dos and Don'ts" applicable to the army personnel "while acting under" the AFSPA[168]; and (b) another list of "Dos and Don'ts" applicable "while providing aid to the civil authority."[169] There would be no need to have two separate lists if acting under AFSPA and acting to provide "aid" to the civilian administration were considered in practice as well as in theory to be one and the same.

References

1. W.E. Birkhimer, Mil Gov Martial Law **482**, 484 (1914)
2. S.I. Vladeck, Emergency power and the militia acts, Yale L. J. **114**, 149, 173 (2004)
3. L.C. Green, *The Contemporary Law of Armed Conflict*, 2nd ed. (2000), pp. 54–55
4. B. Ackerman, The emergency constitution. Yale L. J. **113**, 1029, 1032–34 (2004)
5. A.V. Dicey, *Introduction to the Study of the Constitution*, vol. 283 (1915), pp. 284–285
6. E.D. Engdahl, Soldiers, riots, and revolution: the law and history of military troops in civil disorders. Iowa L. Rev. **57**, 1, 7 (1971)
7. J.M. Collins, *Martial Law & English Laws: c.1500–c.1700* (2016), p. 5

[164]Naga People's Movement of Human Rights v. Union of India, (1998) 2 SCC 109, 147 (Agrawal, J., quoting with approval 'a list of "Dos and Don'ts" that are issued by the Army Headquarters from time to time).

[165]*Id.* at 147–50. The list of "Dos and Don'ts" issued by the Army Headquarters applicable to the armed forces included a detailed list of things pertaining to "Action before Operation", "Action during Operation", "Action after Operation", and "Dealing with Civil Court".

[166]*See* Gautam [12, pp. 140–143].

[167]*See, e.g.*, Armed Forces (Special Powers) Act § 4(a), ("Special Powers of the Armed Forces." If [any commissioned officer, warrant officer, non-commissioned officer or any other person of equivalent rank in the armed forces] is of opinion that it is necessary so to do for the maintenance of public order, fire upon or otherwise use force, even to the causing of death, against any person who is acting in contravention of any law or order for the time being in force in the disturbed area prohibiting the assembly of five or more persons or the carrying of weapons or things capable *of being used as weapons or of firearms, ammunition or explosive substances.*").

[168]Naga People's Movement of Human Rights v. Union of India, (1998) 2 SCC 109, 147.

[169]*Id.* at 149.

8. M. Head, S. Mann, *Domestic Deployment of The Armed Forces: Military Power, Law and Human Rights* (2008), pp. 19–20
9. W.W. Willoughby, *The Constitutional Law of the United States* (1929), p. 1586
10. R. S. Rankin, The constitutional basis of martial law. Const. Rev. **13**, 75 (1929)
11. A.K. Pye, C.H. Lowell, The criminal process during civil disorders. 1975 Duke L. J. **581**, 591–592, 596–597 (1975)
12. K. Gautam, Martial Law In India: The deployment of military under the armed forces special powers Act, 1958. SW J. Int'l L. **24**
13. D. Chalmers, C. Asquith, *Outlines of Constitutional Law* (1936)
14. M. Neocleous, From martial law to the war on terror. New Crim. L. Rev. **10**, 489 (2007)
15. L.J.C. Krum, The national guard and riot control: the need for revision. J. Urb. L. **45**, 863, 864–865 (1967)
16. C. Campbell, I. Connolly, a model for the 'war against terrorism'? Military intervention in northern Ireland and the 1970 falls curfew. J. L. & Soc'y **30**, 341, 346–347 (2003)
17. M. Head, Calling out the troops—disturbing trends and unanswered questions. U.N.S.W. L. J. **28**, 479 (2005)
18. D. Dyzenhaus, States of emergency, in *The Oxford Handbook of Comparative Constitutional Law*, vol. 442, ed. by M. Rosenfeld, A. Sajo (ed.) (2013), p. 447
19. U.C. Jha, Special laws and the armed forces in South Asia. ISIL Y.B. Int'l Human. & Refugee L. **10**, 134, 147 (2010)
20. B.N. Waranoff, Federal judicial control of the national guard. B. U. L. Rev. **52**, 1, 1 (1972)
21. K.A. Schlichter, Locked and loaded: taking aim at the growing use of the military in civilian law enforcement operations. Loy. L.A. L. Rev. **26**, 1291 (1993)
22. G.F. Flood, Martial Law and its effects upon the soldier's liability to the civilian. U. Penn. L. Rev. **73**, 380 (1925)
23. M.T. Foster, Executive military power: a path to American dictatorship. Nebraska L. Rev. **54**, 111 (1975)
24. L. Tribe, *American Constitutional Law* (1978), p. 184
25. C.J. Whelan, Military intervention in industrial disputes. Indus. L. J. **8**, 222, 223 (1979)
26. C. Whelan, The law and the use of troops in industrial disputes, in *Law, State and Society*, ed. by R. Fryer et al. (1981), pp. 160–76
27. W.F. Finlason, *Treatise Upon Martial Law*, XXV (1866)
28. Lord MacDermott, Law and order in times of emergency. Jurid. Rev. **17**, 1, 5–11 (1972)
29. W. Holdsworth, Martial law historically considered. L. Q. Rev. **18**, 117, 129 (1902)
30. L. Radzinowicz, *A History of English Criminal Law*, vol. 4 (1968), pp. 105–157
31. K. Jeffrey, Military aid to the civil power in UK—an historical perspective, in *The role of the military in society*, ed. by Rowe, Whelan (1982)
32. S. Greer, *Military intervention in disturbances: the legal basis reconsidered*. Pub. L. 573–99 (1983)
33. T. Hayter, *The Army and the Crowd in Mid Georgian England* (1978)
34. A.F. Wilcox, Military aid to the civil powers. NLJ **126**, 404 (1976)
35. S.R. Mark, *Policing a Perplexed Society* (1979), p. 30
36. R. Evelegh, *Peacekeeping in a Democratic Society* (1978), p. 10

Chapter 4
Judicial Independence and Economic Emergency in India

1 Introduction

Almost every constitutional order in the world grants the constitutional authorities power to take action to preserve itself in emergency situations.[1] Carl Schmitt famously described the sovereign as the "one who decides on the exception,"[2] the "state of exception" being a state of emergency as we understand the concept today.[3] The existence of this power has never been contingent on the text of the constitution expressly providing for such a power.[4] Scholars continue to debate as

---

[1]*See* Greene [1] (noting the presence of emergency powers in the constitutions around the world illustratively), Bjørnskov and Voigt [2] (relying upon the work of Elkins et al. to note that ninety percent of the Constitutions in the world contain emergency provisions written in their constitutions).

[2]Schmitt [3] [hereinafter 'Carl schmitt, political theology'].

[3]*Id.* at 6. Schmitt defines "the exception" as, "The exception, which is not codified in the existing legal order, can at best be characterized as *a case of extreme peril, a danger to the existence of the state*, or the like. But it cannot be circumscribed factually and made to conform to a preformed law." *See also*, Agamben [4] (noting that the etymology of "state of exception" has been referred to interchangeably, whereby the French referred to it as "state of siege," the Italians as "emergency decrees" and the Anglo-Saxon as "martial law" and "emergency powers").

[4]*See generally*, Scheppele [5], Issacharoff and Pildes [6], Gilbert [7] (noting that the constitutions of Canada and Australia derive their emergency powers through legislation rather than the constitution itself). *See also* Greene [1, pp. 19–21].

A. Singhvi and K. Gautam, *The Law of Emergency Powers*,
https://doi.org/10.1007/978-981-15-2997-9_4

to whether it is better to have express constitutional provisions providing for emergency powers or not,[5] but the existence and exercise of emergency powers has never been a derivative of constitutional text.[6] For instance, even though the phrase "emergency" does not actually appear in the text of the US Constitution,[7] during its drafting Alexander Hamilton spoke for the grant of all such constitutional powers as necessary to deal with any, "...emergencies which may confront the nation."[8] Though speaking in completely different historical contexts, but at least from a rather neutral constitutional design perspective, Schmitt and Hamilton both ended up making the same point, i.e., that since the content of an emergency cannot be anticipated, the powers required to deal with the emergency cannot be circumscribed.[9] That the US Constitution gives the power to deal with emergency situations, even though the word "emergency" or any acceptable synonym is absent in its text, is also clear from Justice Davis's 1866 opinion in *Ex parte Milligan* where he observed that the government, "... within the Constitution, has all the powers granted to it which are necessary to preserve its existence ...."[10] Several decades later, in 1934, in *Blaisdell*,[11] a case that eminently dealt with economic emergencies,[12] Chief Justice Hughes observed,

---

[5]*See, e.g.*, Lee [8], Vladeck [9], Keith and Poe [10].

[6]*See, e.g.*, *Ex parte* Milligan 71 U.S. (4 Wall.) 2, 125–26 (1866) (noting that the safety of the government is "essential" in a crisis, and therefore, justified the use of Suspension Clause); Youngstown Sheet & Tube Co. v. Sawyer (Steel Seizure), 343 U.S. 579, 650 (1952) (Jackson, J., concurring) (noting that the Suspension Clause is in fact the express provision for exercising emergency powers resultant of a crisis). In other words, the justification for the exercise of emergency powers has most commonly been "necessity" and its cognate. *See also*, Note, *Development in the Law: The National Security Interest and Civil Liberties*, 85 Harv. L. Rev. 1130, 1288–91 (1972), Issacharoff and Pildes [6, pp. 296, 296–97], Tyler [11], Greene [12], Davidson [13] (relying on *Lucas v. South Carolina Coastal Council* 505 U.S. 1003, 1029 (1992) to assert that doctrine of emergency provides a clear exemption from liability to avert imminent harm).

[7]*See* Us CONST.; Fisch [14] (observing that, "Neither the term 'emergency' nor any cognate of comparable generality appears in the text of the United States Constitution.").

[8]Fisch [14, p. 389, 391]. *See also* Fatovic [15].

[9]CARL SCHMITT, POLITICAL THEOLOGY 6; THE FEDERALIST No. 23, at 147 (Alexander Hamilton) (Jacob E. Cooke ed., 1961). Whereas Schmitt argued that the power to deal with emergencies, "...cannot be circumscribed factually and made to conform to a preformed law.," arguing for grant of emergency powers, Hamilton argued, "These powers ought to exist without limitation: *Because it is impossible to foresee or define the extent and variety of national exigencies, or the correspondent extent & variety of the means which may be necessary to satisfy them.*" (Emphasis in Original). *See also*, Fatovic [15, p. 257] (noting that the impossibility to ascertain the varying degrees of emergencies served as a major justification of unilateral use of executive powers for Hamilton and others.); Miller v. United States, 78 U.S. 268, 305 (1871) (observing that there can be no restrictions on the power to declare and prosecute war).

[10]*Ex parte* Milligan, 71 U.S. 2, 121 (1866).

[11]Home Building & Loan Ass'n v. Blaisdell, 290 U.S. 398 (1934).

[12]*See, e.g.*, Currie [16], Meyler [17].

> While emergency does not create power, emergency may furnish the occasion for the exercise of power … Thus, the war power of the federal government is not created by the emergency of war, but it is a power given to meet that emergency.[13]

Whereas some constitutions of the world do not expressly use the word "emergency" or any comparable phrase or expression,[14] several other constitutions of the world specifically provide for emergency provisions.[15] For example, in the Indian sub-continent, the constitutions of Bhutan, Bangladesh, Sri Lanka, Pakistan and India specifically provide for emergency provisions in their respective written constitutions.[16] The constitutions of Thailand, Malaysia (and other countries in this

---

[13]Home Building & Loan Ass'n v. Blaisdell, 290 U.S. 398, 426 (1934).

[14]Fisch [14] (observing that, "Neither the term "emergency" nor any cognate of comparable generality appears in the text of the United States Constitution."), Issacharoff and Pildes [6, pp. 296, 296–97], Martin [18], Gilbert [7, pp. 308–12], Lee [19].

[15]Bjørnskov and Voigt [2] (relying upon the work of Elkins et al., to note that 90% of the Constitutions in the world contain emergency provisions written in their constitutions).

[16]Bhutan const., art. 33 (2008) *translation at* http://www.nationalcouncil.bt/assets/uploads/files/Constitution%20%20of%20Bhutan%20English.pdf.

> The Druk Gyalpo may, on the written advice of the Prime Minister, proclaim an emergency if the sovereignty, security, and territorial integrity of Bhutan or any part thereof is threatened by an act of external aggression or armed rebellion.

Bangl. const. art. 141A (1972) *translation at* http://bdlaws.minlaw.gov.bd/sections_detail.php?id=367&sections_id=24703.

> If the President is satisfied that a grave emergency exists in which the security or economic life of Bangladesh, or any part thereof, is threatened by war or external aggression or internal disturbance, he may issue a Proclamation of Emergency for one hundred twenty days.

Sri lanka const. art. 154 J §1 (1978) *translated at* https://www.parliament.lk/files/pdf/constitution.pdf.

> Upon the making of a proclamation under the Public Security Ordinance or the law for the time being in force relating to public security, bringing the provisions of such Ordinance or law into operation on the ground that the maintenance of essential supplies and services is, threatened or that the security of Sri Lanka is threatened by war or external aggression or armed rebellion, the President may give directions to any Governor as to the manner in which the executive power exercisable by the Governor is to be exercised. The directions so given shall be in relation to the grounds specified in such Proclamation for the making thereof.

Pakistan const. art. 232 § 1 (1973)

> If the President is satisfied that a grave emergency exists in which the security of Pakistan, or any part thereof, is threatened by war or external aggression, or by internal disturbance beyond the power of a Provincial Government to control, he may issue a Proclamation of Emergency.

India Const. art. 352, § 1

region) also provide for emergency provisions in their constitutions.[17] Taking the specific, and perhaps a fairly representative example,[18] of the Indian Constitution, it not only uses the word "emergency" on more than one occasion, it actually devotes an entire chapter to the same. Part XVIII of the Indian Constitution is titled "Emergency Provisions."[19] It envisages three types of emergencies—(1) an emergency arising out of a "war, external aggression or armed rebellion" that threatens the "security of India or any part or territory thereof"[20] ("External Emergency"); (2) failure of constitutional machinery in a State[21] ("Internal Emergency"); and (3) a financial emergency that threatens the "financial stability or credit of India" ("Economic Emergency").[22] In any of the three situations, the President of India is empowered to proclaim an emergency, and such a proclamation is subjected to periodic review by the Indian Parliament that must approve of the Presidential proclamation within a fixed time-span in absence whereof the proclamation automatically lapses.[23] Short of proclaiming emergency, Part XVIII also lays down that it shall be duty of the Union government, "… to protect every State against external

---

> If the President is satisfied that a grave emergency exists whereby the security of India or of any part of the territory thereof is threatened, whether by war or external aggression or armed rebellion, he may, by proclamation, make a declaration to that effect in respect of the whole of India or of such part of the territory thereof as may be specified in the proclamation.

[17]THAI. CONST. § 21 (2014).

> In case of emergency and necessary urgency in order to maintain national security, public safety, national economic security or to avert public calamity or there is necessary to have a law on taxes, duties or currency which requires an urgent and confidential deliberation, the King has the prerogative to issue an Emergency Decree which shall have the force as an Act.

MALAY. CONST. art. 150 §1 (1957)

> If the Yang di-Pertuan Agong is satisfied that a grave emergency exists whereby the security, or the economic life, or public order in the Federation or any part thereof is threatened, he may issue a Proclamation of Emergency making therein a declaration to that effect.

[18]*See, e.g.*, Iyer [20], Omer [21], *See also*, Rosenn [22], Beloff [23], Bari [24].

[19]*See* INDIA CONST. Part XVIII.

[20]INDIA CONST. art. 352, § 1.

[21]*Id.* at art. 356, § 1.

[22]*Id.* at art. 360, § 1.

[23]*See* INDIA CONST. art. 352, § 4; art. 356, §§ 3, 4; art. 360, § 2.

aggression and internal disturbance and to ensure that the Government of every State is carried on in accordance with the provisions of this Constitution."[24] This chapter deals with the third category of emergency listed above and focuses on the Indian context and that of the Indian judiciary.

Two notable provisions of Part XVIII of the Indian Constitution are the Fundamental Rights Suspension Clause[25] and the Enforcement Suspension Clause.[26] The Fundamental Rights Suspension Clause provides that in the event of an External Emergency being proclaimed all fundamental rights[27] under article 19[28] of the Constitution shall remain suspended for the duration of the emergency.[29] The Enforcement Suspension Clause provides that when an emergency has been proclaimed, the President may by an order suspend the right to move any court for enforcement of fundamental rights (except articles 20 and 21).[30] Not just that, the President may by an order suspend ongoing proceedings for enforcement of

---

[24]INDIA CONST. art. 355.

[25]*Id.* at art. 358.

[26]*Id.* at art. 359.

[27]*See* INDIA CONST. Part III. Part III of the Indian Constitution provides for several fundamental rights, including the right to equality, freedom of speech and expression, life and personal liberty and other such civil and political rights, including the right to approach the Supreme Court of India directly, in writ proceedings, for the enforcement of these fundamental rights.

[28]INDIA CONST. art. 19. Article 19 provides the following rights to all citizens of India—freedom of speech and expression, the right to assemble peaceably without arms, the right to form associations or unions or cooperative societies, the right to move freely throughout the territory of India, the right to reside and settle in any part of the territory of India, and the right to practice any profession, or to carry on any occupation, trade or business. All these rights are subject to reasonable restrictions on grounds listed in article 19(2) to 19(6).

[29]INDIA CONST. art. 358, § 1—

> While a Proclamation of Emergency declaring that the security of India or any part of the territory thereof is threatened by war or by external aggression is in operation, *nothing in article 19 shall restrict the power of the State as defined in Part III* to make any law or take any executive action which the State would but for the provisions contained in that Part be competent to make or to take, but any law so made shall, to the extent of the incompetency, cease to have effect as soon as the Proclamation ceases to operate, except as respects things done or omitted to be done before the law so ceases to have effect… (Emphasis Added).

[30]INDIA CONST. art. 359, § 1—

> Where a proclamation of Emergency is in operation, the President may by order declare that the right to move any court for the enforcement of such of the rights conferred by Part III (except Articles 20 and 21) as may be mentioned in the order and all proceedings pending in any court for the enforcement of the rights so mentioned shall remain suspended for the period during which the Proclamation is in force or for such shorter period as may be specified in the order.

fundamental rights in any court, and the proceedings shall remain suspended for the duration of the emergency proclamation or any other shorter time period provided in the Presidential Order.[31] The Indian Constitution provides the right to move the Supreme Court directly or the State High Court(s) for enforcement of fundamental or any constitutional rights.[32] The right to move the Supreme Court directly for enforcement of fundamental rights is itself a fundamental right,[33] and was called by Dr. Ambedkar as the "the very soul of the Constitution and the very heart" of the Constitution.[34] It is also the foundation of the Supreme Court's view that the court is protector and enforcer of the fundamental rights—a "sentinel on qui vive."[35]

---

[31]INDIA CONST. art. 359, § 1.

[32]*See*, INDIA CONST. art. 32; art. 226.

[33]CONSTITUENT ASSEMBLY DEBATES, VOL. VII, 951–953 (Dec. 9, 1948). Clarifying the scope of Article 32, Dr. Ambedkar noted that the purpose of the article was 'to give general power' as well as to 'propose particular remedies'. Further, he reiterated that "*the right to move the Supreme Court by appropriate proceedings for the enforcement of the rights conferred by this Part is guaranteed.*" *See also* Prem Chand Garg v. Excise Commissioner, AIR 1963 SC 996, 998–99 (Gajendragadkar, J.) (discussing the right to move the Supreme Court for the enforcement of fundamental rights)

> It is in the light of this position that the Constitution makers thought it advisable to treat the citizen's right to move this court for the enforcement of their fundamental rights as being a fundamental right by itself. The fundamental right to move this court can, therefore, be appropriately described as the corner-stone of the democratic edifice raised by the Constitution.

[34]CONSTITUENT ASSEMBLY DEBATES, VOL. VII, 953 (Dec. 9, 1948). Speaking in context of Art. 32 of the Indian Constitution, Dr. Ambedkar remarked:

> If I was asked to name any particular article in this Constitution as the most important—an article without which this Constitution would be a nullity—I could not refer to any other article except this one. It is the very soul of the Constitution and the very heart of it and I am glad that the House has realized its importance.

See also, L. Chandra Kumar v. Union of India (1997) 3 SCC 261, 299–302 (Ahmadi, C.J.) (noting that Dr. Ambedkar's words regarding the importance of Art. 32 and 226 have been 'reiterated in several judgements' and they hold 'unique significance' in the constitutional scheme and that the power to review is a part of the basic structure).

[35]*See* State of Madras v. V. G. Row AIR 1952 SC 196, 199 (Patanjali Shastri J.)

> ...[O]ur Constitution contains express provisions for judicial review of legislation as to its conformity with the Constitution...the courts in this country face up to such important and none too easy task, it is not out of any desire to tilt at legislative authority in a crusader's spirit, but in discharge of a duty plainly laid upon them by the Constitution. This is especially true as regards the "fundamental rights," as to which this Court has been assigned the role of a sentinel on the qui vive.

High Court of Bombay v. Shirishkumar Rangrao Patil (1997) 6 SCC 339, 335 (Ramaswamy, J.)

> In a democracy governed by rule of law, under a written constitution, judiciary is the sentinel on the qui vive to protect the fundamental rights and posed to keep even scales of justice between the citizens and the state or the states inter se. Rule of law and judicial review are basic features of the Constitution. As its integral constitutional structure,

But there are crucial distinctions between the two in that while the Fundamental Rights Suspension Clause is mandatory, the Enforcement Suspension Clause is not. The Fundamental Rights Suspension Clause becomes operative automatically the moment a proclamation of External Emergency is made and only suspends article 19. It does not, however, suspend any ongoing judicial proceedings in any court for enforcement of fundamental rights. The Enforcement Suspension Clause, on the other hand, requires a Presidential order for it to become operative, and even after the order is made, articles 20[36] and 21[37] cannot be suspended. The Enforcement Suspension Clause further provides the President the authority to suspend any ongoing judicial proceeding in any court for the enforcement of fundamental rights. It is arguable whether the text of this clause authorizes the President to suspend an

---

independence of the judiciary is an essential attribute of rule of law. Judiciary must, therefore, be free from pressure or influence from any quarter. The Constitution has secured to them, the independence.

[36]*See* INDIA CONST. art. 20, §§ 1, 2, 3. Article 20 provides for three key rights to defendants in criminal proceedings, and the right is available to all 'persons' as against article 19 the rights whereunder are available only to "citizens"—(1) protection from *ex post facto* laws; (2) protection against double jeopardy; and (3) protection against self-incrimination.

[37]*See* INDIA CONST. art. 21. Article 21 provides that, "No person shall be deprived of his life or personal liberty except according to procedure established by law." Even though article 21 differs from the text of the 5th and 14th Amendments to the US Constitution significantly in that it does not use the phrase "due process," it has been held by the Supreme Court of India that the phrase "procedure established by law" means a just, fair and reasonable procedure. *See, e.g.*, Maneka Gandhi v. Union of India, (1978) 1 SCC 248. The position in India, after *Maneka Gandhi* is that the phrase "procedure established by law" is read as analogous to "due process of law." *See* State of Punjab v. Dalbir Singh, (2012) 3 SCC 346, 375, holding that, "... in our Constitution the concept of "due process" was incorporated in view of the judgment of this Court in *Maneka Gandhi.*" (Internal Citations Omitted); Selvi v. State of Karnataka, (2010) 7 SCC 263, 315, where the Supreme Court interpreted "right against self-incrimination" through the ethos of "substantive due process" and "right to fair" trial; Sunil Batra v. Delhi Admin., (1978) 4 SCC 494, 518, holding that, "True, our Constitution has no 'due process' clause ...; but, in this branch of law, after [R.C. Cooper v. Union of India, (1970) 1 SCC 248] and *Maneka Gandhi*, the consequence is the same."; *See also* Ramraj [25], Sripati [26], Mohapatra [27], Chandrachud [28].

ongoing judicial proceeding for enforcement of articles 20 and 21, the rights that cannot be suspended by the President under the Fundamental Rights Suspension Clause.[38]

This preliminary discussion was necessary in order to engage with the core question that this chapter will examine—the conflict between the principle of judicial independence and the Presidential power to reduce judicial salaries during an Economic Emergency. As we have noted above, the Indian Constitution gives the President emergency powers to deal with three kinds of emergencies—External Emergency, Internal Emergency and Economic Emergency. We are concerned in this chapter only with Economic Emergency.

Before we move forward, we may want to make a preliminary observation. Whereas fundamental rights under article 19 are automatically suspended in the case of an External Emergency, in case of an Economic Emergency they can be suspended only by a Presidential Order to that effect that must follow the proclamation of Economic Emergency. Furthermore, any ongoing judicial proceeding to enforce any right under article 19 may also be suspended by a Presidential Order to that effect that must follow the proclamation of Economic Emergency. In the context of the US Constitution it has been said that in case of an emergency, economic rights are not as important as civil and political liberties.[39] However, we must remember that the US Constitution does not explicitly provide for emergency powers.[40] The Indian Constitution on the other hand specifically provides for, not just the abstract idea of emergency powers, but several nitty-gritty facets of emergency powers. It also provides which rights may or may not be suspended during an emergency. Therefore, we should be careful before we reach the same conclusion in the context of economic rights under the Indian Constitution as has been reached in the United States.

[38]It is beyond the brief of this chapter to examine this question in detail. The point, however, made here is purely on the basis of the text of article 358. Article 358(1) provides that,

> When a Proclamation of Emergency is in operation, the President may by order declare that the right to move any court for the enforcement of such of the rights conferred by Part III (except Articles 20 and 21) as may be mentioned in the order and all proceedings pending in any court for the enforcement of the *rights so mentioned* shall remain suspended for the period during which the Proclamation is in force or for such shorter period as may be specified in the order. (Emphasis Supplied).

See India Const. art. 358. The phrase "rights so mentioned" is liable to be interpreted so as to attract the same limitations to the power to suspend judicial proceedings as they attach to the power to suspending the rights. However, it is arguable that the phrase "rights so mentioned" is used in the context of the Presidential order suspending judicial proceedings and not the Presidential power suspending the rights, and thus the power to suspend judicial proceedings does not attract the same restrictions as are attached to the power to suspend rights.

[39]*See* Meyler [17, p. 539].

[40]*See generally* Vladeck [9, p. 149, 184] (noting that *Neagle* and *Debs* cases are often cited to support the concept that the President by virtue of Take Care Clause, has emergency powers nowhere explicit in the Constitution); Ackerman [29] (emphasizing the need for a supplementary constitution which becomes enforceable in the times of emergencies).

Economic Emergency generally has not received the scholarly attention that it deserves, and in the context of the Indian Constitution, despite the specific provision for economic emergency powers, it has received no scholarly attention at all.[41] This chapter also intends to fill this crucial gap in emergency powers scholarship in general and economic emergency scholarship in particular.

The chapter closely examines the extent of the President's power (read union government) to act under the Economic Emergency Clause of the Indian Constitution in the specific context of independence of judiciary, a principle globally recognized as one of fundamental constitutional importance, as well as one so central to Indian constitutional law that it has been held by the Supreme Court to be a part of the basic structure of the Indian Constitution[42] and has been held in esteem so high so as to lead an eminent scholar to conclude that, "[a]ny interpretation of the Indian Constitution which comes in the way of the independence of judiciary is … not consistent with the constitution as is also not justifiable."[43] This chapter argues that the executive branch's power to reduce judicial salaries during an economic emergency under the Indian Constitution is subject to judicial review in order to protect and preserve judicial independence.

2 Economic Emergency Under the Indian Constitution

The use of emergency powers to handle an economic crisis is far more common than assumed in general impression.[44] The economic emergency that arose in the United States during the Great Economic Depression after the First World War

---

[41]Out of the several widely available commentaries on the Indian Constitution none deal with the question of economic emergency in any detail except perhaps for providing some basic textual analysis. *See* Jain [30] (highlights the procedure for declaring financial emergency and its implication on centre–state relations), Datar [31] (delineating the legislative history of Article 360), Basu [32] (making only a rudimentary interpretation of the text of Article 360 to ascertain a broad procedure for proclaiming financial emergency), Shukla [33] (simply makes a textual analysis of the actual text of Article 360). The Supreme Court of India has not yet been presented with any petition that involved a substantial question of law where article 360 was required to be interpreted. Furthermore, whereas article 352 has been invoked thrice and 356 has been invoked more than a 100 times, article 360 has never been invoked in more than 70 years of the Indian republic. *See* Austin [34], Tope [35], Sorabjee [36], Dam [37].

[42]*See, e.g.*, L. Chandra Kumar v. Union of India (1997) 3 SCC 261, 299–302 (Ahmadi, C.J.).

[43]Singh [38].

[44]Clinton Rossiter in his magisterial study of emergency powers under the US Constitution divided emergency powers into three categories, i.e., war, rebellion and economic depression. But he also acknowledged the existence of emergency powers in situations of natural disasters, riots and strikes. *See* Rossiter [39]. More recently Oren Gross and Fionnauala Ni Aolain in their study of emergency powers also accept that emergency powers have been used during economic depressions and in natural disasters. *See* Gross and Aolain [40]. *See also* Scheuerman [41].

prompted President Roosevelt to invoke emergency powers on a scale equivalent to what other presidents before him had invoked in the event of a wartime emergency. President Harry S. Truman also relied on broad emergency powers in order to take control of the steel mills during the Korean crisis that was later found unconstitutional by the US Supreme Court.[45] Successive US Presidents have relied on broadly worded Congressional legislations in order to invoke emergency powers to deal with mostly domestic and peacetime emergencies and sometimes international crisis that did not escalate to a state of wartime emergency.[46] Luckily in India such interpretative gymnastics are not necessary in order to claim constitutional powers to proclaim an Economic Emergency.

Very broad powers are granted to the Indian President to tackle an economic emergency. Though there is no clarity on the content of those powers in the constitutional text itself, the nature of the power is such that one cannot search for certainty or clarity for nobody knows what may or may not be required to deal with an emergency once it has arisen.[47] During the drafting stage, Dr. Ambedkar, who moved the amendment to insert this article into the Constitution, did make a comparative reference to the National Recovery Act of the United States and that,

> …[T]his article more or less follows the pattern of what is called the National Recovery Act of the United States passed in the year 1930 or thereabouts, which gave the power to the President to make similar provisions in order to remove the difficulties, both economic and financial, that had overtaken the American People as a result of the great depression from which they were suffering.[48]

---

[45]Youngstown Sheet & Tube Co. v. Sawyer (Steel Seizure), 343 U.S. 579 (1952).

[46]*See, e.g.*, Lobel [42]. Lobel notes that,

> In response to the post-war situation… Congress enacted hundreds of statutes providing for broad emergency power. By the 1970s, some 470 such statutes existed, delegating power to the executive over virtually every facet of American life. Some of the legislation contained positively draconian provisions. For example, the Internal Security Act of 1950 authorized the President to detain all persons whom the government had a "reasonable ground" to believe "probably" would commit or conspire to commit acts of espionage or sabotage… Moreover, in most of the emergency legislation, vague terms triggered executive power for unspecified lengths of time. State legislatures followed the federal example, delegating broad emergency power to governors.

[47]*See, e.g.*, Carl Schmitt, Political Theology 6; The Federalist No. 23, at 147 (Alexander Hamilton) (Jacob E. Cooke ed., 1961), Fatovic [15, p. 257] (noting that the impossibility to ascertain the varying degrees of emergencies served as a major justification of unilateral use of executive powers for Hamilton and others.); Miller v. United States, 78 U.S. 268, 305 (1871) (observing that there can be no restrictions on the power to declare and prosecute war), Vermeule [43].

[48]Constituent Assembly Debates, Vol. X–XII, 361 (Oct. 16th, 1949).

The Economic Emergency Clause of the Indian Constitution is a detailed provision providing for the powers of the President to act in times of an economic emergency and uses the following words—

> If the President is satisfied that a situation has arisen whereby the financial stability or credit of India or of any part of the territory thereof is threatened, he may by a Proclamation make a declaration to that effect.[49]

It could be said that "Credit of India" is in a position to be threatened only when the Reserve Bank of India has failed or is about to fail, or when there is a situation of hyperinflation that the government is not able to contain and the value of the currency is in freefall. "Financial stability" of India, on the other hand, can easily be threatened, and perhaps even to the point of making a proclamation of emergency, by the failure of non-governmental actors. In other words, a situation where "financial stability" of India is threatened could easily, and in current times will most probably, be caused by market failure. The term "market failure" does not always mean the same thing to everyone. Some economists would contend that skyrocketing prices in an emergency show that market is working and not failing. But these skyrocketing prices might be socially or politically unacceptable, and therefore the term "market failure" will most probably be used in a social or political sense and not in a purely economic sense.[50] The Economic Emergency Clause therefore provides for two different situations where an economic emergency can arise. One is a situation where we have a market failure that results in "financial stability" of India being threatened and the other is a government failure that results in "credit of India" being threatened. In both of these situations the President is authorized to proclaim a state of Economic Emergency and to do whatever is necessary to deal with the situation including the express grant of power to reduce governmental salaries, including judicial salaries.[51] It is also important to note that a situation whereby "credit of India" is threatened would certainly amount to a situation where "financial stability" of India would also be under threat, but a situation where only "financial stability" of India is under threat might not necessarily be so severe so as to threaten the "credit of India." In the event of a market failure, one scholar notes, the government has the following four options available—(1) don't do anything and let the markets correct themselves; (2) use price controls to stop price gouging so as to keep goods affordable; (3) purchase goods and distribute them; and (4) take the needed goods and distribute them.[52] All four of these choices have economic impacts that the government must carefully examine before they select any one of these options. Using price controls is usually the most attractive choice for politicians because it gives the impression of forceful action without actually costing the

---

[49] India Const. art. 360, § 1.

[50] Kirsch [44] ("When a disaster strikes, markets may fail to provide needed goods at prices that are socially and politically acceptable.").

[51] India Const. art. 360, § 4.

[52] Kirsch [44, pp. 1235, 1258].

government anything[53] but is not the most effective because it is likely to result in shortages and black markets.[54]

The emergency proclamation under the Economic Emergency Clause can be—(i) revoked or varied by a subsequent Proclamation[55]; (ii) has to be laid before both Houses of the Indian Parliament[56]; and (iii) automatically ceases to expire after two months of it being made unless approved by both Houses of the Parliament.[57] The requirement of having the emergency proclamation approved by both Houses of the Parliament and the automatic expiration of the proclamation in a time-bound fashion in absence of such approval is a great safety-valve in the Indian Constitution that was designed to prevent any possible misuse or abuse of this power.[58]

Once the Economic Emergency proclamation is in place, the following general power is granted to tackle the emergency situation—

> During the period any such Proclamation as is mentioned in clause (1) is in operation, the executive authority of the Union shall extend to the giving of directions to any State to observe such canons of financial propriety as may be specified in the directions, and to the giving of such other directions as the President may deem necessary and adequate for the purpose.[59]

In addition to this, and protected by a non-obstante clause, the following specific powers are granted, viz., (i) the power to reduce salaries and allowances of all or any class of persons serving in connection with the affairs of the State[60]; (ii) reserving for Presidential consideration all Money Bills or other Bills passed by the State Legislatures[61]; and (iii) the power to reduce salaries and allowances of all or any class of persons serving in connection with the affairs of the Union including Supreme Court and High Court judges.[62] It is with this power to reduce the salaries and allowances of the Supreme Court and High Court judges that we are specifically concerned with in this chapter. At the outset we may observe that there is a slight anomaly here. On the one hand, the Economic Emergency proclamation is subject to Parliamentary review and automatically lapses if not approved by the Parliament in two months, while on the other hand the extraordinary power to reduce the salaries and allowances of the Supreme Court and High Court judges is

---

[53]Kirsch [44, pp. 1235, 1258–1259].

[54]Posner [45].

[55]INDIA CONST. art. 360, § 2, cl. a.

[56]*Id.* at art. 360, § 2, cl. b.

[57]*Id.* at art. 360, § 2, cl. c. It is important, for clarify, to note the entire text of this clause—"shall cease to operate at the expiration of two months unless before the expiration of that period it has been approved by resolutions of both Houses of Parliament."

[58]*See, e.g.*, Tope [35], Sorabjee [36].

[59]INDIA CONST. art. 360, § 3.

[60]*Id.* at art. 360, § 4, cl. a(i).

[61]*Id.* at art. 360, § 4, cl a(ii).

[62]*Id.* at art. 360, § 4, cl. b.

not subject to any Parliamentary review. Parliamentary review is therefore limited to the actual proclamation of emergency, but not the actions taken by the President once the proclamation is made. By suggesting that this power to reduce judicial salaries during an economic emergency is subject to judicial review, this chapter also attempts to address this anomaly. But this thesis herein is only consequential, as the arguments presented in this chapter are not contingent on, and are presented notwithstanding this anomaly. In other words, even if the power to reduce judicial salaries was subjected to the same safety-valve of periodic parliamentary review, the view presented in this chapter (viz., of availability of judicial review in this regard) would still apply.

3 Financial Independence of the Judiciary

In any written constitution based on the principle of rule of law, like the Indian Constitution,[63] protecting and preserving independence of judiciary is a crucial requirement. Protecting independence of judiciary is also a well-recognized international principle of fundamental constitutional importance.[64] In one of the earliest such exercises at the international level, the United Nations commissioned a special rapporteur to study the independence of judges, lawyers, jurors and assessors and,

[63]That the Indian Constitution is a based on the principle of rule of law does not require any elaborate exposition. However, for a general reflective statement, *see* S. P. Gupta v. Union of India, (1981) Supp. SCC 87, 223–24, stating that:

> The concept of independence of the judiciary is a noble concept which inspires the constitutional scheme and constitutes the foundation on which rests the edifice of our democratic polity. If there is one principle which runs through the entire fabric of the Constitution, it is the principle of the rule of law and under the Constitution, it is the judiciary which is entrusted with the task of keeping every organ of the State within the limits of the law and thereby making the rule of law meaningful and effective.

[64]Several international documents like the "Bangalore Principles," the "New Delhi Declaration," the "Montreal Principles," the "United Nations Basic Principles" etc. all endorse and uphold the principles of judicial independence as a fundamental constitutional principle. *See, e.g.*, 7th U.N. Congress on the Prevention of Crime and the Treatment of Offenders, *Basic Principles on the Independence of the Judiciary*, 60 U.N. Doc. A/CONF.121/22/Rev.1 (Aug. 26–Sep. 6, 1985) art. 1, which states that "*the independence of the judiciary shall be guaranteed by the State and enshrined in the Constitution or the law of the country. It is the duty of all governmental and other institutions to respect and observe the independence of the judiciary.*"; Judicial Integrity Group, *Bangalore Principles of Judicial Conduct*, ESC Res. 2006/23 (July 27, 2006); U.N. ESCOR, *Strengthening Basic Principles of Judicial Conduct*, UN Doc E/RES/2006/23 (July 27, 2006), Value 1 "Independence"; International Bar Association, *Minimum Standards for Judicial Independence* (1982) ("New Delhi Declaration"); First World Conference on the Independence of Justice, *Universal Declaration on the Independence of Justice* (June 10, 1983) ("Montreal Declaration").

upon submission of a comprehensive report in Quebec in 1987, adopted the seminal principles therein as the "Singhvi Principles."[65]

The Supreme Court of India and the State High Courts have a very important place in the Indian constitutional scheme—they have the power of judicial review and can declare administrative, executive and legislative actions unconstitutional.[66] The institutional importance of the Supreme Court and the State High Courts was impressed upon during the drafting of the Constitution[67] and has been stressed upon ever since.[68] The Supreme Court of India has a vast jurisdiction[69] and has often been called the most powerful Supreme Court in the world.[70] Given the structural importance of the Supreme Court and the High Courts under the Indian system, it is essential that the independence of these courts be maintained at all costs.[71]

Several protections are provided in the Constitution itself. Stressing the importance of a fixed and secure judicial tenure, it was famously noted by Alexander Hamilton,

---

[65] Singhvi [46].

[66] India Const. art. 32; art. 226.

[67] Constituent Assembly Debates, Vol. VII, 953 (Dec. 9, 1948) (speech of Dr. B.R. Ambedkar).

[68] *See, e.g.*, State of Madras v. V.G. Row AIR 1952 SC 196 (Patanjali Shastri J.); High Court of Bombay v. Shirishkumar Rangrao Patil (1997) 6 SCC 339, 335 (Ramaswamy, J.).

[69] India Const. art. 32, 129, 131, 132, 133, 134, 136, 142 and 143; Jain [30]. By art. 129, the Supreme Court has the power to commit a person for its contempt; by art. 131, the Supreme Court has original jurisdiction to decide inter-governmental disputes; by arts. 132–134 and 136, the Supreme Court has appellate jurisdiction in all civil or criminal matters of the country; by art. 32, the Supreme Court has power to enforce the fundamental rights; by art. 137, the Supreme Court has the power to review its own decisions; by art. 142, the Supreme Court has the power to make any order for doing complete justice in any case; by art. 143, the Supreme Court has advisory jurisdiction by which on consultation of the President, the Court may render advisory opinions on questions referred by the President.

[70] Jain [30] ("The Supreme Court is a multi-jurisdictional Court and may be regarded as the most powerful Apex Court in the World."), Sinha [47].

[71] *See, e.g.*, High Court of Bombay v. Shirishkumar Rangrao Patil (1997) 6 SCC 339, 335 (Ramaswamy, J.)

> In a democracy governed by rule of law, under a written constitution, judiciary is the sentinel on the qui vive to protect the fundamental rights and posed to keep even scales of justice between the citizens and the state or the states inter se. Rule of law and judicial review are basic features of the Constitution. As its integral constitutional structure, independence of the judiciary is an essential attribute of rule of law. Judiciary must, therefore, be free from pressure or influence from any quarter. The Constitution has secured to them, the independence.

> [T]hat inflexible and uniform adherence to the rights of the constitution and of individuals, which we perceive to be indispensable in the courts of justice, can certainly not be expected from judges who hold their offices by a temporary commission.[72]

Hamilton's concerns about protecting and preserving judicial independence were chiefly motivated by the colonial experience that manifested itself in the American Declaration of Independence as well.[73] Hamilton's concerns were not lost on the framers of the Indian Constitution[74] who provided security of tenure to the Supreme Court and High Court judges in the Constitution.[75] The Constitution also provides for removal only by impeachment and on the ground of "proved misbehavior or incapacity."[76] The Salary Clause, with which we are concerned in this chapter, authorizes the Parliament to determine salaries and allowances of Supreme Court judges by law[77] and protects judicial salaries and allowance from being varied to their disadvantage after their appointment.[78] Similar protections are available to the

---

[72] THE FEDERALIST No. 78, at 529 (Alexander Hamilton) (Jacob E. Cooke ed., 1961).

[73] THE DECLARATION OF INDEPENDENCE, para. 11 (U.S. 1776). The Declaration, "...condemned King George because he had 'made Judges dependent on his Will alone, for the Tenure of their Offices, and *the Amount and Payment of their Salaries*'." *See* Entin and Jensen [48].

[74] *See, e.g.*, CONSTITUENT ASSEMBLY DEBATES, Book 3, Vol. VIII, 253 (May 24, 1949) (Speech of M. A. Ayyangar).

> The Supreme Court is the watchdog of democracy. It is the eye and the guardian of the citizens' rights. Therefore, at every stage, from the stage of appointment of the judges, their salaries and tenure of office, all these have to be regulated now so that the executive may have little or nothing to do with their functioning.

[75] *See* INDIA CONST. art. 124, § 2 (Supreme Court); INDIA CONST. art. 217 § 1 & art. 224 § 3 (High Court). The tenure of a Supreme Court judge is till the age of 65 years, and the tenure of a High Court judge is till the age of 62 years. In fact, in Canada, Prof. Colvin opines that tenure and financial security are equally important and put both at same footing. *See also*, Colvin [49].

[76] A Supreme Court judge can be removed by the President only after,

> ...[A]n address by each House of Parliament supported by a majority of the total membership of that House and by a majority of not less than two-thirds of the members of the House present and voting [and] presented to the President in the same session for such removal on the ground of proved misbehavior or incapacity.

See INDIA CONST. art. 124, § 4. Similarly, a judge of the High Court may be removed if the two Houses of Parliament pass a resolution for his removal, by a special majority, for proved misbehaviour or incapacity. *Id.* at art. 217 § 1 (b).

[77] INDIA CONST. art. 125, § 1.

[78] Written in the form of a proviso, the relevant clause provides that the salaries and allowances of Supreme Court judges cannot be varied to their disadvantage after their appointment. *See* INDIA CONST. art. 125, § 2 proviso—"Provided that neither the privileges nor the allowances of a Judge nor his rights in respect of leave of absence or pension shall be varied to his disadvantage after his appointment."

High Court judges.[79] All these protections were provided by the Constituent Assembly with an eye towards securing judicial independence.[80]

3.1 Judicial Salaries and Judicial Independence

Judicial salaries and allowances have been identified as one of the key indicators[81] and an important component[82] of judicial independence. Control over judicial salaries and allowances can potentially jeopardize judicial independence, thus making it imperative that they be given special protections.[83] Public perception plays an important part in protecting judicial independence—if people don't perceive the judiciary to be independent, public confidence in judiciary is going to be jeopardized, thus causing grave harm to judicial independence.[84] The Indian Salary Clause, and its US counterpart the Compensation Clause, are examples of these protections.[85] The protections mentioned in the Salary Clause in the Indian Constitution are similar to those mentioned in the Compensation Clause in the US

---

[79]A High Court Judge may only be removed if the two Houses of Parliament pass a resolution for his removal, by a special majority, for proved misbehaviour or incapacity. *See* India Const. art. 217 § 1 (b).

[80]Constituent Assembly Debates, Book 1, Vol. I—VI, 897 (July 29, 1947) (Speech of M. Ayyangar).

> It ought not to be left to the discretion of the President as to what the salary [of the judges] should be…[T]he salary ought not to be varied by the Legislature as long as a person who has occupied the post continued there.

[81]The key indicators of judicial independence are—(1) appointment; (2) tenure and remuneration; (3) operational independence; (4) decisional independence; and (5) personal independence. *See* Ananian-Welsh and Williams [50].

[82]Entin [51], The Queen v. Marc Beauregard, [1986] 2 S.C.R. 56, 74 (Canada).

[83]Colvin [49].

[84]*See* Ananian-Welsh and Williams [50, p. 593, 597], Colquitt [52], Wheeler [53]. The Supreme Court of India seems also to have accepted that public perception is very important in maintaining public confidence in judiciary which in turn is important to maintain judicial independence. *See, e. g.*, K. Veeraswami v. Union of India, (1991) 3 SCC 655, 705 (Justice Shetty for himself and Justice Venkatachaliah, Justice Ray & Justice Sharma concurring, Justice Verma dissenting),

> The judiciary has no power of the purse or the sword. *It survives only by public confidence and it is important to the stability of the society that the confidence of the public is not shaken*. The Judge whose character is clouded and whose standards of morality and rectitude are in doubt may not have the judicial independence and may not command confidence of the public. He must voluntarily withdraw from the judicial work and administration. (Emphasis added).

[85]Other constitutions also provide similar protections to judicial salaries and allowances. *See* Australia Constitution s 72 cl. (iii) which provides that Australian Parliament can fix judicial salaries but these salaries cannot be reduced during the continuation of the office. However, the Pennsylvania Constitution provides that judicial salaries cannot be reduced during the term of office, "…unless by law applying generally to all salaried officers of the Commonwealth." Pa. Const. art. V, § 16(a).

Constitution[86] and other comparable constitutions.[87] Alexander Hamilton's famous quote in the Federalist No. 79—"In the general course of human nature, *a power over a man's subsistence amounts to a power over his will*"[88]—is the bedrock for these constitutional provisions prohibiting reduction of judicial salaries. Interestingly, whereas the Compensation Clause has generated quite a bit of litigation in the United States, in India the Salary Clause has so far generated no litigation at all. Some of the judicial principles that emerge out of the litigation in the United States are instructive for this chapter and merit brief discussion here.

Before that, a brief exegesis on the international focus given by the United Nations to independence of justice would be in order. In a seminal report, and the first and most comprehensive such exercise by the UN, on independence of judges, lawyers, assessors and jurors, adopted at Quebec in 1987, also known as the "Singhvi Declaration" or the "Singhvi Principles," the UN Special Rapporteur, Dr. L.M. Singhvi, highlighted the important role which the security of tenure and guarantee of remuneration plays in ensuring the independence of the judiciary. The tenure of the judges and their remuneration cannot be "altered to their disadvantage."[89] More pertinently, it was noted that,

> The salaries and pensions of judges shall be adequate, commensurate with the status, dignity and responsibility of their office, and shall be periodically reviewed to *overcome or minimize the effect of inflation.*[90]

3.2 *Judicial Salaries and the Question of Independence in the United States*

The Compensation Clause in the US Constitution intended to preserve and protect judicial independence[91] provides that the salaries of judges of the Supreme Court

---

[86]US CONST. art. III, § 1; THE FEDERALIST NO. 79, at 531 (Alexander Hamilton) (Jacob E. Cooke ed., 1961) where Hamilton said, "Next to permanency in office, nothing can contribute more to the independence of the judges than *a fixed provision for their support.*" (Emphasis added).

[87]For example, the Canadian Constitution provides that judicial salaries "shall be fixed." *See* CANADA CONST. art. 100—"The Salaries, Allowances and Pensions of the Judges of the Superior, District, and County Courts (except the Courts of Probate in Nova Scotia and New Brunswick), and of the Admiralty Courts in Cases where the Judges therefore are for the Time being paid by Salary, shall be fixed and provided by the Parliament of Canada".

[88]THE FEDERALIST NO. 79, at 531 (Alexander Hamilton) (Jacob E. Cooke ed., 1961) (Emphasis provided).

[89]Singhvi [46]. *Cf.* European Commission v. Poland Case No. C-619/18 (2018) (noting that the reduction of the retirement age of judges from 70 to 65 violated the principles of judicial independence), Kelly [54] (highlighting the reduction in the salaries of the judges in Ireland to their disadvantage).

[90]Singhvi [46].

[91]Kaufman [55].

shall not be diminished during judges' continuation of office.[92] In the first case[93] that involved a substantial question regarding the interpretation of the Compensation Clause, *Evans*,[94] the US Supreme Court had the occasion to examine the underlying purpose behind this provision. In *Evans*, the plaintiff, a United States District Court judge for the Western District of Kentucky, had questioned the constitutionality of an income tax imposed on the salaries that would be paid to article III judges.[95] The main question before the Court was whether or not an income tax can be imposed on the salary of judges, and for the purpose of this chapter this question is not relevant. What is important however are the observations made by the majority with respect to the nature and purpose of the Compensation Clause.[96] Speaking for the Court, Justice Van Devanter observed the primary purpose of the Compensation Clause,

> ...was not to benefit the judges, but, like the clause in respect of tenure, to attract good and competent men to the bench and to promote that independence of action and judgment which is essential to the maintenance of the guarantees, limitations and pervading principles of the Constitution and to the administration of justice without respect to persons and with equal concern for the poor and the rich. Such being its purpose, the limitation is to be construed, not as a private grant, but as a limitation imposed in the public interest; in other words, not restrictively, but in accord with its spirit and the principle on which it proceeds.[97]

On facts, the Court held that the income tax in question was violative of the Compensation Clause, and declared the tax to be unconstitutional.[98] Justice Holmes, in his dissent, did not agree with the majority and upheld the tax as constitutional. However, on the important question of the underlying purpose that the Compensation Clause serves, Justice Holmes, with whom Justice Brandeis concurred, did not disagree with the majority opinion.[99] Even though Justice Holmes agreed on the underlying purpose of the Compensation Clause, he was of the opinion that the immunity provided to judicial salaries had to stop at a certain

---

[92]US Const., art. III, § 1.

[93]In the third reported case on the point, O'Malley v. Woodrough, 307 U.S. 277 (1939), Justice Frankfurter, writing for the Court, noted that Evans v. Gore, 253 U.S. 245 (1920) was the first case that raised a question pertaining to the Compensation Clause. *See* O'Malley v. Woodrough, 307 U. S. 277, 280 (1939).

[94]Evans v. Gore, 253 U.S. 245 (1920).

[95]*Id.* at 246–47.

[96]*Id.* at 248 (1920) (Van Devanter, J.) ("With what purpose does the Constitution provide that the compensation of the judges 'shall not be diminished during their continuance in office'?").

[97]*Id.* at 253–54. The original intent behind the Compensation Clause was also to, "...protect federal judges from external pressures that might keep the judges from acting impartially." On this basic purpose there was never any disagreement amount the founding fathers of the US Constitution. *See* Entin and Jensen [48, pp. 965, 969–70, 974].

[98]Evans v. Gore, 253 U.S. 245, 263–64 (1920).

[99]*Id.* at 265 (Holmes, J. dissenting, Brandeis, J. concurring). ("The exemption of salaries from diminution is intended to secure the independence of judges, on the ground, as it was put by [Alexander Hamilton] in [The Federalist No. 79] that 'a power over a man's subsistence amounts to a power over his will'.").

point, and a general non-discriminatory tax that was payable by everyone was such a point.[100]

The legal position regarding the unconstitutionality of the income tax levied on the judges as laid down in *Evans* did not remain good law for too long and was overturned in *Woodrough.*[101] The minority view taken by Justice Holmes was adopted by the majority opinion in *Woodrough*, and the majority view in *Evans* now found itself in minority. The facts of this case were almost identical to *Evans.*[102] In order to levy an income tax on judicial salaries, the US Congress had enacted a new law designed specifically to overcome the law laid down in *Evans*. Speaking for the Court, Justice Frankfurter adopted a comparative approach in order to reverse the legal position that had been laid down in *Evans.*[103] Thus having rejected the legal position in *Evans*, Justice Frankfurter adopted the position taken by Justice Holmes in *Evans* and laid down the standard of review in almost identical terms. Upon a careful examination of Justice Frankfurter's majority opinion in *Woodrough*, it is not difficult to conclude that the key issue in Compensation Clause cases was not to ascertain the core purpose that was served by this clause. In *Woodrough*, for example, the key question was whether or not the income tax that was imposed by the US Congress was permissible in light of the restrictions imposed by the Compensation Clause.[104] To that extent it might not be out of place to suggest that the observations of the US Supreme Court in *Evans*, as they relate to the core purpose that is served by the Compensation Clause are still relevant and the disagreement expressed by the Court in *Woodrough* is only to the extent of the limited question of law that was presented before the court, i.e., on the question of legislative competence of the US Congress to enact a law that imposed an income tax on judicial salaries.

---

[100] *Id.* at 265–66.

[101] O'Malley v. Woodrough, 307 U.S. 277 (1939).

[102] *Id.* at 278–79.

[103] Justice Frankfurter cited Canadian, Australian and South African decisions to support his point that the decision in *Evans v. Gore* did not lay down good law. *See* O'Malley v. Woodrough, 307 U.S. 277, 281 (1939) (Frankfurter, J.)

> However, the meaning which *Evans v. Gore* imputed to the history which explains Article III, § 1, was contrary to the way in which it was read by other English speaking courts. The decision met wide and steadily growing disfavour from legal scholarship and professional opinion. *Evans v. Gore* itself was rejected by most of the courts before whom the matter came after that decision. (Internal Citations Omitted).

[104] *Id.* at 281–82

> Having regard to these circumstances, the question immediately before us is whether Congress exceeded its constitutional power in providing that United States judges appointed after the Revenue Act of 1932 shall not enjoy immunity from the incidences of taxation to which every-one else within the defined class of income in subjected.

The dissenting opinion of Justice Butler in *Woodrough* deserves careful examination. In his dissent, Justice Butler laid great emphasis on the core purpose of the Compensation Clause and closely examined all the relevant historical authorities that were examined by Justice Van Devanter in *Evans*.[105] Whereas on the question of the legislative competence of the US Congress, Justice Butler took a very textual position, an interpretative technique with which his colleagues on the bench did not agree; but on the question of the core purpose served by the Compensation Clause, he followed the same method of interpretation that was earlier followed by Justice Van Devanter in *Evans*. It must be very carefully noted that the majority opinion in *Woodrough* expresses no disagreement with either the core purpose of the Compensation Clause that is exposited by the minority opinion, or with the method of interpretation that was followed by the minority. Furthermore, the majority opinion in *Woodrough* does no more than to convert the minority opinion in *Evans* into a majority opinion and therefore makes it good law. The minority opinion in *Evans* that was accepted as the correct legal position in *Woodrough* also never expressed any disagreement with the core purpose of the Compensation Clause or with the interpretive method that was followed to arrive at that core purpose in *Evans*. It is therefore fair to say that even though there has been judicial disagreement, in the US Supreme Court, on the extent of legislative powers of the US Congress with respect to subjecting judicial salaries to an income tax, there has been no disagreement on the core or the underlying purpose that is served by the Compensation Clause in the US Constitution.

Four decades after *Woodrough*, the US Supreme Court had to deal with another case that raised a question regarding the interpretation of the Compensation Clause. In *Will*,[106] the question was very different from what the Court had dealt with before. Whereas earlier the question before the Court was dealing with the legislative competence of the US Congress in subjecting judicial salaries to an income tax, this time the question was directly regarding a decrease in judicial salaries.[107] For the purpose of this chapter, this is an extremely important point to note. There is an extremely important distinction to be made between reduction of judicial salaries as a result of a tax which is imposed on the same, compared to a direct reduction of judicial salaries as a result of an executive proclamation, whether the proclamation is made in the context of an economic emergency or otherwise.[108] The doctrine of non-discriminatory tax as laid down by the Court in *Will* is restricted to examining the legislative competence of the US Congress with respect to its power to tax judicial salaries. This doctrine does not, and cannot extend to examining reduction of judicial salaries as a result of an executive proclamation or a legislative act.

---

[105]*Id.* at 283–294.

[106]United States v. Will, 449 U.S. 200 (1980).

[107]*See* the narration of facts and state of the question of law raised in the case, respectively, in United States v. Will, 449 U.S. 200, 205–210, 221 (1980).

[108]This distinction was noted by the US Supreme Court in United States v. Hatter, 532 U.S. 557 (2001).

To the extent whether a generally applicable non-discriminatory income tax amounts to a violation of the Salary Clause of the Indian Constitution, the question has never been raised in India, and for the purpose of this chapter is not relevant. The key question under inquiry in this chapter is whether the reduction of judicial salaries as a result of an executive (i.e., Presidential) or, for that matter, a legislative proclamation made in the context of an economic emergency, violates the protections and prohibitions provided for in the Salary Clause of the Indian Constitution. To that extent, given the textual and structural similarities between the Salary Clause and the Compensation Clause, the relevant observations of the US Supreme Court have considerable persuasive value for our analysis.

For the purpose of this chapter another important point that comes out of *Will* is the detailed exposition by the Court of the core or the underlying purpose that is served by the Compensation Clause.[109] Chief Justice Berger, speaking for a unanimous Court, observed that the underlying purpose of the Compensation Clause is to protect independence of judiciary and to make it free from control by the executive and the legislative branches of the government.[110] In order to arrive at this conclusion, Chief Justice Berger relied on the same authorities that were relied upon by Justice Van Devanter in *Evans*.[111] In fact, Chief Justice Berger relied on *Evans* to support his conclusion that promoting judicial independence is one of the core purposes that is served by the Compensation Clause.[112] This strong reliance on *Evans* by Chief Justice Berger lends considerable support to the proposition that there has never been any disagreement in the US Supreme Court on the observations originally made by Justice Van Devanter regarding the purpose that is served by the Compensation Clause.[113] It would therefore not be out of place to conclude that even though decisions subsequent to *Evans* have expressed different opinions on the extent of and the restrictions imposed on the legislative competence of the US Congress, those subsequent decisions have not expressed any disagreement on the scope and ambit of the Compensation Clause as it was first interpreted in *Evans*. As regards the key holding of the Court in *Will* is concerned, the unanimous Court held that,

---

[109]*See* United States v. Will, 449 U.S. 200, 217–221 (1980).

[110]*Id.* at 217–18 (1980) (Berger, C.J.).

> The Compensation Clause has its roots in the long standing Anglo-American tradition of an independent Judiciary. A Judiciary free from control by the executive and the legislature is essential if there is a right to have claims decided by judges who are free from potential domination by other branches of government. Our constitution promotes that independence specifically by providing [for the Compensation Clause].

[111]*See* United States v. Will, 449 U.S. 200, 217–221 (1980); *Cf.* Evans v. Gore, 253 U.S. 245, 249–253 (1920).

[112]*Id.* at 221.

[113]In United States v. Will, 449 U.S. 200 (1980), "...the Court emphasized the framers' concern with protecting judicial independence." Entin and Jensen [48, p. 965, 977].

> To say that the Congress could not alter a method of calculating salaries before it was executed would mean the Judicial Branch could command Congress to carry out an announced future intent as to a decision the constitution vests exclusively in the Congress. We therefore conclude that a salary increase "vests" for the purpose of Compensation Clause only when it takes effect as part of the compensation due and payable to Article III judges.[114]

Applying this standard of review, the Supreme Court found that certain reduction in salaries of federal judges was unconstitutional as it violated the protections and prohibitions laid down in the Compensation Clause.[115]

The last case that we must examine is *Hatter*.[116] The dispute in this case also arose in the context of certain (medicare and social security) taxes that were levied on federal judges who argued that these taxes were levied in violation of the Compensation Clause.[117] The distinction between reduction of judicial salaries as a result of a tax versus the reduction that is the result of a non-tax-related executive or legislative act was highlighted in *Hatter* and is directly relevant here.[118] Even though the taxes, the validity of which was questioned in this case, were upheld on the ground that the Compensation Clause does not prohibit the US Congress from in acting in a non-discriminatory tax that applies to judges in the same way as all of the citizens,[119] the Court went to great lengths to explain this distinction.[120] The following observations of the Court deserve to be quoted at length—

> We concede that this Court has held that the Legislature cannot *directly* reduce judicial salaries even as a part of an equitable effort to reduce *all* government salaries. ... But a tax law, unlike a law mandating a salary reduction, affects compensation indirectly, not directly. ... And those prophylactic considerations that may justify an absolute rule forbidding direct salary reductions are absent here, where indirect taxation is at issue. In practice, the likelihood that a nondiscriminatory tax represents disguised legislative effort to influence the judicial will is virtually nonexistent. Hence, the potential threats to judicial independence that underlie the Constitution's compensation guarantee cannot justify a special judicial examination from a commonly shared tax, not even as a preventive measure to counter those threats.[121]

---

[114]United States v. Will, 449 U.S. 200, 229 (1980).

[115]*Id.* at 226, 230.

[116]United States v. Hatter, 532 U.S. 557 (2001).

[117]*Id.* at 564 (Breyer, J.)

> We also agree with *Evans* insofar as it holds that the Compensation Clause offers protections that extend beyond a legislative effort directly to diminish of judge's pay, say, by ordering a lower salary...otherwise a legislature could circumvent even the most basic compensation close protection by enacting a discriminatory tax law, for example, that precisely but indirectly achieved the forbidden effect. (Internal Citations Omitted).

[118]*Id.* at 569.

[119]*Id.* at 571.

[120]*Id.*

[121]*Id.*

Two important points arise from *Hatter* and are relevant to this chapter. Firstly, even though *Hatter* specifically overruled *Evans*, the overruling was restricted to the tax-related restrictions that were laid down in *Evans*.[122] Secondly, even though *Evans* was specifically overruled to the extent as stated above, the observations of the Court stating the core or the underlying purpose of the Compensation Clause were accepted. Justice Breyer in *Hatter* cited with approval Justice Van Devanter's exposition of the Compensation Clause in *Evans*.[123] The Court's acceptance of *Evans'* purposive interpretation of the Compensation Clause, in the face of its direct overruling of one of the key holdings of that case, lends strong support to the proposition that the exposition of the core or the underlying purpose of the Compensation Clause as laid down by the Supreme Court in *Evans* remains the most authoritative statement of law on the point. Subsequent questioning of *Evans* does not affect the strength or the persuasive value of that case qua interpretation of the Compensation Clause. Rather, every subsequent questioning of *Evans* actually solidifies that case's interpretation of the Compensation Clause as authoritative.[124]

The above discussion supports the conclusion that in the United States the protections afforded by the Compensation Clause have always been understood to have been provided to protect and safeguard the independence of judiciary and to insulate it from any political influence.[125] The US Supreme Court, on more than one occasion, has gone to the extent of declaring legislation unconstitutional because it violated the protections afforded by the Compensation Clause. And in interpreting the Compensation Clause, the US Supreme Court has always been informed by a purposive approach rather than a purely textual one. Given the textual similarity between the Salary Clause in the Indian Constitution and the Compensation Clause in the US Constitution, as well as the remarkable similarity between the reasons why the framers of both these Constitutions provided for these protections in their respective Constitutions, it may fairly be concluded that the observations of the US Supreme Court, the evolution and content of which has been traced above, underling the core and underlying purpose served by the

---

[122]*Id.* at 567 (Breyer, J.) ("We now overrule *Evans* insofar as it holds that the Compensation Clause forbids Congress to apply generally applicable, nondiscriminatory tax to the salaries of federal judges, whether or not they were appointed before the enactment of the tax.").

[123]*Id.*

> The Court's opinion in *Evans* began by explaining why the Compensation Clause is constitutionally important, and we begin by reaffirming that explanation. As *Evans* Points out … the Compensation Clause, along with the Clause securing federal judges appointments "during good behavior" …helps to guarantee what Alexander Hamilton called the "complete Independence of the courts of Justice."

[124]*See, e.g.*, United States v. Hatter, 532 U.S. 557, 569 (2001), Entin [51, p. 25, 31] (noting that, "[Compensation Clause] cases establish a baseline principle: constitutional prohibitions against diminishing judicial compensation mean that the other branches may not reduce the salaries paid to judges once those salaries have vested.").

[125]*See, e.g.*, Entin [51, p. 25, 31].

Compensation Clause in US Constitution, apply with equal vigor and force to the Salary Clause in the Indian Constitution.

4 Financial Independence of Judiciary Under the Indian Constitution

The principle of independence of judiciary has been observed to be the cardinal principle of the Indian Constitution, so crucial that without it a free society would not exist[126] and so fundamental that, "[A]ny interpretation of the Indian Constitution which comes in the way of the independence of judiciary is, … not consistent with the Constitution and is also not justifiable."[127] The Supreme Court of India has held that the power of judicial review is a part of the basic structure of the Constitution[128]; that the Constitution guarantees an independent judiciary[129] and independence of the judiciary is itself a part of the basic structure.[130] This constitutional guarantee of an independent judiciary is provided, "… [N]ot for promoting personal prestige of the [judiciary] but for preserving and protecting the rights of the citizens …" thus making, "[F]reedom from control and potential domination of the executive [as] necessary conditions for the independence and impartiality of Judges."[131]

The Supreme Court of India has had many occasions to examine how this principle of independence of judiciary informs the interpretation of other provisions of the Constitution as well as that of ordinary legislation.[132] For example, in *Veeraswami*, speaking in the context of the Prevention of Corruption Act of 1947, the Supreme Court has held that the judges of the High Court as well as that of the Supreme Court are covered by the phrase "public

[126]Supreme Court Advocates-on-Record Association v. Union of India, (1993) 4 SCC 441, 522 (Pandian, J. concurring), "[I]t is the cardinal principle of the Constitution that an independent judiciary is the most essential characteristic of a free society like ours.."

[127]Singh [56].

[128]*See, e.g.*, L. Chandra Kumar v. Union of India, (1997) 3 SCC 261.

[129]*See, e.g.*, Pareena Swarup v. Union of India, (2008) 14 SCC 107.

[130]*See, e.g.*, Supreme Court Advocates-on-Record Association v. Union of India, (1993) 4 SCC 441; All India Judges Association (3) v. Union of India, (2002) 4 SCC 247; Madras Bar Association v. Union of India, (2010) 11 SCC 1.

[131]Pareena Swarup v. Union of India, (2008) 14 SCC 107, 111.

[132]Jain [30]

> The members of the Constituent Assembly were very much concerned with the question of independence of the Judiciary and, accordingly, made several provisions to ensure this end.41 The Supreme Court has itself laid emphasis on the independence of the judiciary from time to time. As the Court has observed recently in *Thalwal* "The constitutional scheme aims at securing an independent judiciary which is the bulwark of democracy." (Internal citations omitted.)

servant,"[133] and thus could be prosecuted for possessing assets disproportionate to their known sources of income.[134] However, in order to protect the judges from frivolous litigation and in order to protect their judicial independence, the Court also held that the prior requirement of obtaining sanction for prosecution[135] under the Prevention of Corruption Act of 1947 must be obtained from the Chief Justice of India.[136] In the event that it is the Chief Justice of India himself who is the subject of the prosecution, the government is required to consult, "...any other Judge Judges of the Supreme Court of India."[137] These protections regarding the sanction for prosecution in cases where sitting judges of the High Courts or the Supreme Court are involved were given on the basis of upholding judicial independence.[138] Even though the Supreme Court held that the judges of the High Courts and the Supreme Court are not immune from prosecution under ordinary criminal laws, the court stressed that the relationship between these judges and the government is not one of master and servant.[139] These judges discharge a high constitutional office and derive their authority from the Constitution and not from the warrant of their appointment.[140] Having thus declared that the judiciary is a

---

[133]K. Veeraswami v. Union of India, (1991) 3 SCC 655, 697.

[134]The Prevention of Corruption Act, No. 49 of 1988, India Code (1988) vol. 4 § 13(1)(e). Sub-clause (e) to §13(1) states that a public officer has committed the offence of criminal misconduct if he, or any person on his behalf, is or has been, at any time during his office tenure, been in the possession of resources or property disproportionate to his known sources of income. The explanation to sub-clause (e) clarifies that the term "known sources of income" to mean income received from a lawful source.

[135]*See* K. Veeraswami v. Union of India, (1991) 3 SCC 655. The majority opinion of the Supreme Court in this case rejected the contention of the appellant to interpret Section 6 *ejusdem generis*. Section 6 stipulated that previous sanction of the appointing authority was necessary for the cognizance of an offence. The majority held that clause (c) of Section 6 reading "in case of any other person..." the words any other person was applicable to the judges. In other words, the roles of judges were essentially brought under the ambit of the Prevention of Corruption Act, and now fall under the category of "public servant." A public servant can now be prosecuted for offences specified in the Prevention of Corruption Act with the prior sanction "of the authority competent to remove him from his office." Section 6 providing for prior sanction from the competent authority and its direction that no court shall take cognizance of the offence under Section 5(1) without such prior sanction is a protection for Judges from frivolous and malicious prosecution.

[136]*Id.* at 709.

[137]*Id.*

[138]*Id.* at 708–09.

[139]*Id.* at 695.

[140]*See generally* Union of India v. Sankalchand Himatlal Sheth, (1977) 4. SCC 193, 224 (Chandrachud, J.)

> Judges of the High Court owe their appointment to the Constitution and hold a position of privilege under it. They are required to "uphold the Constitution and the laws", "without fear" that is without fear of the executive; and "without favour" that is without expecting a favour from the executive. There is thus a fundamental distinction between the master and servant relationship between the government and the Judges of High Courts and the Supreme Court.

co-equal branch of the government and must be independent of the executive and legislature, but at the same time being sensitive to the fact that public perception plays an important role in maintaining judicial independence,[141] the Court declared that judges are not immune from ordinary criminal laws of the republic. On other occasions, the Supreme Court has been more directly confronted with executive and legislative actions that came in direct conflict with this principle and on all these occasions, the Court has constantly upheld this principle.[142] One of us has examined the historical reasons that require the complete insulation of the judiciary in India from political influences especially in the context of judicial appointments elsewhere.[143] Those historical considerations are relevant for this chapter as well because controlling the process of judicial appointments is not the only way by which judicial behavior can be influenced.

5 Judicial Review of Reduction of Judicial Salaries During an Economic Emergency

Before proceeding further, a potential preliminary objection may be disposed of. It can be argued that there is an obvious conflict in the proposition that the Supreme Court can judicially review an Economic Emergency proclamation by the President whereby judicial salaries have been decreased. After all, in the end, do we not have a position wherein judges are deciding the question of their own salaries?[144] There are three independent responses to this objection. Firstly, the judges are not deciding the question of their salaries to the extent that they are not deciding how much their salaries and emoluments would be. That question is reserved only for

---

[141]K. Veeraswami v. Union of India, (1991) 3 SCC 655, 705.

[142]*See, e.g.*, All India Judges Association v. Union of India, (1993) 4 SCC 288; C. Ravichandran Iyer v. Justice A. M. Bhattacharjee, (1995) 5 SCC 457; Union of India v. Sankalchand Himatlal Sheth, (1977) 4 SCC 193.

[143]Gautam [57].

[144]*See, e.g.*, Vermeule [58], arguing that,

> [The] current doctrine ignores half of the Compensation Clause conundrum, precisely the half that the judges are most likely to ignore. The conundrum of the Clause is that enforcement of a rule protecting judicial independence is committed to judges who, by virtue of the rule's subject matter, have a financial interest in maximizing their compensation, whether or not that is the legally accurate outcome.

the Parliament.[145] The question that they are really deciding is about the constitutionality of the proclamation reducing judicial salaries during the time a proclamation declaring economic emergency is in force.[146] Secondly, in the first US Supreme Court case that came out of the Compensation Clause, *Evans v. Gore*,[147] the Court examined and rejected this argument on the ground that the peculiar structural position afforded to the court under the US Constitution required the court to decide the constitutional question that arises out of the Compensation Clause.[148] Even though there was a strong dissenting opinion in *Evans*, the dissent was restricted to decision of the Court on merits.[149] There was no dissent on the question of jurisdiction. The logic applies to the Indian Constitution as well. The Supreme Court of India has specific powers of judicial review, and has regularly dealt with many cases that raise questions of independence of judiciary. If the peculiar structural position of the US Supreme Court allows that apex court to examine questions of constitutional law arising out of the Compensation Clause, then most certainly the peculiar structural position of the Supreme Court of India allows that apex court to examine questions of constitutional law arising out of the Salary Clause, especially when those questions pertain to the fundamental principle of independence of judiciary.[150] And thirdly, it is exactly during an emergency that we should be on high alert in order to ensure that constitutional powers are not

[145]*See* India Const. art. 125 § 1, which states that the salaries of the judges of the Supreme Court will be paid, as determined by the Parliament by law, and until such provision is made, such salaries as are specified by the Second Schedule. In the USA, "Although budget allocations are dependent on Congress, budget estimates are prepared by the Judiciary's own officials and transmitted by the Executive to Congress without revision." *See* Colvin [49, p. 229, 245].

[146]On this issue, the High Court of Australia (which is the Australian apex court) has also expressed similar views. In Austin v. Commonwealth, 215 CLR 185 (2003) (High Court of Australia), the Court held that, "…by regulating an aspect of judicial remuneration, the superannuation tax scheme impermissibly interfered with a state's freedom to determine the remuneration of its judges." *See* Ananian-Welsh and Williams [50, p. 593, 610].

[147]Evans v. Gore, 253 U.S. 245 (1920).

[148]*Id.* at 247.

[149]*Id.* at 264–267.

[150]To this extent, the observations of Prof. Irving R. Kaufman are extremely important. Prof. Kaufman, speaking in the context judicial independence in the United States very aptly observed,

> The essence of judicial independence, therefore, is the preservation of a separate institution of government that can adjudicate cases or controversies with impartiality. This principle is embodied in the doctrine of separation of powers, which elevates the judiciary to the status of a co-equal branch. Cases defining the separation of powers suggest that article III's protection to judicial independence extends beyond the specific prohibitions of the salary and tenure provisions to embrace all significant intrusions upon the exercise of judicial power.

See Kaufman [55, p. 671, 688]. *See also* Entin [51, p. 25].

exploited and used for colorable purposes.[151] In specific context of this chapter, any effort by the executive or legislative branches of the government that could result in jeopardizing judicial resources would have a real effect on the judicial functioning and such an interference would further jeopardize judicial independence.[152]

Established jurisprudence of the Supreme Court of India, especially in the context of emergency clauses, also shows that all the other coordinate branches of the government have accepted the jurisdiction of the Supreme Court over any questions that might arise out of the Constitution. In the past, the Supreme Court has determined the question of the extent of the amending powers of the Indian Parliament under the Constitution.[153] The Supreme Court has also determined the question of the reviewability of the President's satisfaction under the Internal Emergency Clause.[154] So far, a constitutional question arising out of either the External Emergency Clause or the Economic Emergency Clause has not been presented to the Supreme Court directly. If the Court's jurisprudence is considered a reliable guide, the question of jurisdiction will certainly be decided in the favor of the Court, notwithstanding the decision on merits.

Furthermore, long-standing jurisprudence of the Supreme Court of India discloses three independent grounds that can be used to justify judicial review of a Presidential proclamation to reduce judicial salaries during an economic emergency. These three are discussed in detail below.

5.1 Colorable Exercise of Power

All members of the judiciary, whether they are justices of the High Courts or the Supreme Court or judges of the District Courts, fall into one single category, and this category is not the same as the administrative executive (that includes all administrative officers).[155] Even though judicial salaries are to be paid by the executive branch of the government and can be modified by the Parliament[156] the

[151]*See generally* Reichman [59].

[152]Ananian-Welsh and Williams [50, pp. 593, 611–13].

[153]Kesavananda Bharati v. State of Kerala, (1973) 4 SCC 225.

[154]S.R. Bommai v. Union of India, (1994) 3 SCC 1; Nicholas Aroney & Khagesh Gautam, *Federalism—A Selected Comparison*, in India and Australia—A Comparative Overview of the Law and Legal Practice (Shaun Star ed., 2015).

[155]*See generally* All India Judges Association v. Union of India, (1993) 4 SCC 288.

[156]*See* India Const. art. 125 § 1 stating that the judges of the Supreme Court may be paid such salaries as may be determined by the Parliament by law, and until such provision is made, such salaries as are specified by the Second Schedule. *See also*, Jain [30].

> By the way of the 54th Amendment, the parliament has been given the power to determine the salary payable to a Supreme Court Judge. It should also be noted that the parliament can decide from time to time the questions of privileges, allowances and pensions etc. for these judges. None of these can be varied to the disadvantage of the judge. All these matters are

relationship between the judicial branch and other branches of the government is not that of a master and a servant.[157] The Supreme Court, and much before the Court, the Law Commission of India,[158] has stressed that the service conditions of the judiciary cannot be the same as that of the "administrative executive," and to the extent they are, it is only a "historical accident."[159] The "administrative executive" is not and cannot be taken to be equivalent of judiciary, and after the inauguration of the Constitution in 1950, the equivalence is between the judiciary and the "political executive."[160] The principles of separation of powers and independence of judiciary as envisaged in the Indian Constitution require that the "political executive's" power to control the service conditions of the judges be subject to, "… some desirable checks and balances."[161] To this extent, it would be important to examine the following observations of the Supreme Court—

> The judges, at whatever level they may be, represent the State and its authority unlike the administrative executive or the members of the other services. The members of the other services, therefore, cannot be placed on a par with the members of the judiciary, either constitutionally or functionally. It is true that under Article 309 of the Constitution, recruitment and conditions of service of the members of the subordinate judiciary are to be regulated by the acts of the appropriate legislature and pending such legislation, the President and the Governor or their nominees, as the case may be, are empowered to make rules regulating their recruitment and conditions of service. It is also true that after the Council of States makes the necessary declaration under article 312, it is the Parliament which is empowered to create an All India Judicial Service which will include posts not inferior to the post of a district judge as defined under article 236. However, this does not mean that while determining the service conditions of the members of the judiciary, a distinction should not be made between them and the members of other services or that the service conditions of the members of all the services should be the same.[162]

now regulated by the Supreme Court Judges (Salaries and Conditions of Service) Act, 1958. This act was recently amended by the High Court and Supreme Court Judges (Salaries and Conditions of Services) Amendment Act, 2009.

[157]Union of India v. Sankalchand Himatlal Sheth, (1977) 4 SCC 193.

[158]LAW COMMISSION OF INDIA, REPORT NO. 14, REFORM OF JUDICIAL ADMINISTRATION 163 (1958).

[159]All India Judges Association v. Union of India, (1993) 4 SCC 288, 296.

[160]*Id.* at 295–96, 297. *See also*, Glidden Co. v. Zdanok, 307 U.S. 530 (1962), holding that extra-judicial revisory authority is incompatible with the limitations placed upon drawn from article III of the US Constitution; and Chandler v. Judicial Council, 398 U.S. 74 (1970), holding that the power to direct trial judges in the execution of their decision-making duties is a judicial power entrusted only to a judicial body; Kaufman [55, p. 671, 693].

[161]All India Judges Association v. Union of India, (1993) 4 SCC 288, 297.

[162]*Id.* at 295–96.

This observation of the Court makes it abundantly clear that the judicial branch of the government, starting from a District Court judge and going all the way up to the Chief Justice of India, under the Indian Constitution is a co-equal branch of the government. All "significant intrusions upon the exercise of judicial powers" are therefore prohibited by the Constitution.[163] It stands to reason that if the judiciary as a whole is a co-equal branch of the government that exercises sovereign judicial power of the State whose service conditions are constitutionally protected, and if this protection is necessary in order to preserve independence of judiciary which itself is a fundamental feature of modern constitutionalism,[164] then any interference with judicial salaries that might be to the detriment of judiciary as a constitutional institution is subject to judicial review. To this extent the observations of the Supreme Court of Canada are extremely important and deserve to be quoted at length—

> The power of Parliament to fix the salaries and pensions of superior court judges is not unlimited. If there were any hint that a federal law dealing with these matters was enacted for an improper or colorable purpose, or if there was a discriminatory treatment of judges *vis-à-vis* other citizens, then serious issues relating to judicial Independence would arise and the law might well be held to be *ultra vires* s. 100 of the Constitution Act 1867.[165]

Colorable exercise of constitutional powers, by both the executive and legislature, has been the subject matter of litigation before the Supreme Court of India. The Court has declared that colorable exercise of constitutional powers is not immune from judicial review and if the Court is convinced that the powers were exercised in a colorable way the executive action will be, and in fact has been, struck down as unconstitutional.[166] Some might argue that reduction of judicial salaries during an economic emergency (or even otherwise), with the colorable objective of influencing judicial behavior is, in the current day and age, a practical and/or political impossibility in India.[167] This potential objection however does not

[163]Kaufman [55, p. 671, 688].

[164]Judicial independence is now universally accepted as a key feature of modern constitutionalism. *See, e.g.*, Rankin [60], noting that, "With its roots in the doctrine of the separation of powers, the need for an independent judiciary is increasingly considered a *sine qua non* of democratic constitutionalism." *See also* Vyas [61].

[165]The Queen v. Marc Beauregard, [1986] 2 S.C.R. 56, 77 (Canada).

[166]*See* Dr. D. C. Wadhwa v. State of Bihar (1987) 1 SCC 378, 393 (Bhagwati, C.J) (the Court emphasizing that it would amount to a colorable exercise of power on the part of the executive to re-promulgate an ordinance, the provisions of which are substantially the same as the lapsed one. In other words, the constitutional authority something cannot do indirectly, when it was not permitted to do it directly), and more recently Krishna Kumar Singh v. State of Bihar, (2017) 3 SCC 1.

[167]In the US context, it has been so argued. *See* Entin and Jensen [48, p. 965, 967], Entin [51, p. 25, 34].

detract from the fact that the possibility of abuse is there, and also the fact that identical executive powers have been abused in the past.[168] So long as the potential of executive powers being abused is there, the practical and/or political impossibility of such a power being actually abused (for reasons political or otherwise) cannot afford any ground to argue that such powers should not be suitably limited or that they should not be subjected to judicial review to check abuse.[169]

The increasingly important role of the idea of judicial independence in Indian constitutional law and the interpretation of the Indian Constitution[170] has now reached a level where executive powers granted in the constitution have to be balanced against this idea. Ever since the infamous supersession of judges for

---

[168]Under the Indian Constitution, the Governor of a State, if he feels that the urgency of the circumstances so require, has the power to promulgate ordinances during the time the Parliament is not in session. These ordinances are temporary in nature but have the force and effect of a legislation. The Supreme Court has declared unconstitutional the practice of re-promulgation of ordinances on the ground that such re-promulgation amounts to colorable exercise of executive power. *See* Dr. D.C. Wadhwa v. State of Bihar (1987) 1 SCC 378. Even though in the US context the practical/political possibility of a straight-forward attack of judicial independence by means of a colorable legislation intended to reduce judicial salaries to influence judicial behavior is conceded to be negligible, the possibility is not entirely denied and it has been said that such a measure will be unconstitutional. *See* Entin and Jensen [48, p. 965, 967], arguing that,

> And a facially neutral statute motivated by a congressional desire to influence the judicial (if that bad motive could be demonstrated) would probably fail constitutional requirements as well …it is almost impossible to imagine Congress's mounting a straightforward economic attack on the judiciary. With or without a Compensation Clause, a tax clearly directed at the judiciary is just not going to happen – or so one hopes.

[169]*See* Jennings [62]. Speaking in the context of exercise of governmental powers in a non-arbitrary manner, Ivor Jennings, stresses the point that it is not enough to hope that the power that is granted will be exercised in an honest and non-arbitrary manner. A grant of power must come with those necessary restrictions that are required in order to check the abuse of power. This, he argues, is the fundamental requirement in a system that is based on the idea of "rule of law." Commonwealth v. Stilp, 905 A.2d 918 (Pa. 2006) is a good example of such powers being abused for political reasons in the face of clear constitutional prohibitions. *See* Nomi Claire Lazar, States of Emergency in Liberal Democracies 3 (2009) (arguing that "in a real crisis, emergency powers do not violate rights and the rule of law because these rules are simply not in effect at such exceptional times."), Entin [51, pp. 25, 29–30]. Furthermore, the powers might be abused without it even being realized that they are being abused. In an emergency situation,

> …[I]f a state agency [is] created in order to promote a certain important public interest, it is likely to overvalue the importance of protecting this public interest and undervalue the harm to individual liberties which may occur in the course of achieving this end. …Judicial review [would be] therefore crucial to balance this tendency and protect the liberty of the individual.

See also, Reichman [59, pp. 63, 64–65].

[170]Singh [56].

political reasons during the Prime-Ministership of Indira Gandhi,[171] the Supreme Court has been on constant guard and has continuously stressed the need to maintain independence of judiciary by insulating it from the political pulls and pressures of the day, including but not limited to the political executive.[172] Speaking in the context of the Bar Council,[173] the Supreme Court observed—

> The judiciary stands between the citizen and the state as a bulwark against executive excesses and misuse or abuse of power by the executive. It is, therefore, absolutely essential that the judiciary must be free from executive pressure or influence which has been secured by making elaborate provisions in the Constitution with details. *The independence of judiciary is not limited only to the independence from the executive pressure or influence; it is a wider concept which takes within its sweep independence from any other pressure and prejudices.* It has many dimensions, viz., fearlessness of other power centres, economic or political, and freedom from prejudices acquired and nourished by the class to which the judges belong.[174]

This observation of the Supreme Court, given in the context of a sitting judge being forced to resign by external pressure created by a Bar Council resolution, is equally applicable to the hypothetical situation that is at the heart of this chapter. Highlighting the importance of judicial individualism and the fact that judges primarily work on their own and are therefore insulated to a large extent from the

---

[171] *See, e.g.*, Elkins et al. [63], Kamath [64] (Kamath notes supersession started after the Supreme Court delivered its opinion in the landmark case of *Kesavananda Bharati v. State of Kerala*, (1973) 4 SCC 225 and by a narrow majority ruled that any amendment to the Constitution that infringes the basic structure of the Constitution is void. After this opinion was delivered, the unwritten principle that the senior-most judge of the Supreme Court shall be appointed as the Chief Justice was broken, and Justice A. N. Ray was appointed as the Chief Justice. Kamath notes that this action of the government evoked "sharp reactions" from the Bar and that there was "a near unanimous vote condemning the government's actions."), Khanna [65] (Justice Khanna in his memoirs discusses the supersession of three judges after the decision in *Kesavananda Bharati* case and later his talks about his own supersession that came after his world famous dissent in *A.D.M. Jabalpur v. Shiv Kant Shukla*, AIR 1976 SC 1207, 2 SCC 521 which led him to resign from the Supreme Court.).

[172] A similar note of warning has been struck in the United States as well. Prof. Kaufman argued for insulating the judiciary from the other two branches in order to ensure its independence as, "… the political departments may attempt to enlist the judiciary in a campaign to subvert the Constitution …." *See* Kaufman [55, p. 671, 693].

[173] The case arose in rather unusual circumstances where certain Bar Councils had passed resolutions against the sitting Chief Justice of the Bombay High Court. The petitioner, who was a lawyer, approached the Supreme Court seeking an appropriate writ to permanently restrain these Bar Councils from, "…coercing Justice A. M. Bhattacharjee [the] Chief Justice of Bombay High Court, to resign from the office as Judge." The petitioner argued that these actions by these Bar councils, i.e., "removal by forced resignation," was unknown to law, and unconstitutional as it seriously jeopardized judicial independence. The then Attorney General supporting the petitioner's contentions argued that, "…any resolution passed by any Bar Association tantamounts to scandalising the court entailing contempt of the court. [The bar association] cannot coerce the judge to resign." *See* C. Ravichandran Iyer v. Justice A. M. Bhattacharjee, (1995) 5 SCC 457, 464–467, 468.

[174] C. Ravichandran Iyer v. Justice A. M. Bhattacharjee, (1995) 5 SCC 457, 469 (Emphasis added).

political pulls and pressures of the day, the Supreme Court in the same case noted that independence of judiciary would be seriously jeopardized if the supervision or control over the exercise of purely judicial functions is vested in executive branch.[175] In another case that involved the executive's, "…misguided desire to take over bit by bit and (*sic*) judicial functions and powers of the state exercised by the duly constituted courts …," the Court emphasized that, "Freedom from control and potential domination of the executive are necessary preconditions for the independence and impartiality of Judges."[176] It has been understood since the British Act of Settlement (1701) that protecting judicial salaries is an important component of protecting judicial independence.[177] Several years later Alexander Hamilton memorably declared that, "*…a power over a man's subsistence amounts to a power over his will*"[178] that has been relied upon by the US Supreme Court on every single occasion where the question of judicial salaries and the protections of Compensation Clause of the US Constitution were in question.[179] Hamilton's declaration when read in conjunction with the relevant observations of the Supreme Court of India clearly emphasizes the importance of preserving, protecting and

---

[175] *Id.* at 469–471.

[176] Pareena Swarup v. Union of India, (2008) 14 SCC 107, 111.

[177] *See* Michael Nash, *The Removal of Judges under the Act of Settlement (1701)*, Address at 18th British Legal History Conference: Judges and Judging Oxford (2–5 July 2007), Epstein [66], Kirby [67].

[178] The Federalist No. 79, at 531 (Alexander Hamilton) (Jacob E. Cooke ed., 1961).

[179] Evans v. Gore, 253 U.S. 245, 253–54 (1920), Justice Van Devanter (for the Court) holding that, "The original intent behind the Compensation Clause was also to, "…protect federal judges from external pressures that might keep the judges from acting impartially." *See also* United States v. Will, 449 U.S. 200, 217–18 (1980), (Berger, C.J., for the Court) noting that,

> The compensation clause has its roots in the long standing Anglo-American tradition of an independent judiciary. A Judiciary free from control by the executive and the legislature is essential if there is a right to have claims decided by judges who are free from potential domination by other branches of government. Our constitution promotes that independence specifically by providing [for the Compensation Clause].

On a similar vein, *see* United States v. Hatter, 449 U.S. 229 (1980), Justice Berger (for the Court), noting that,

> We also agree with *Evans* insofar as it holds that the Compensation Clause offers protections that extend beyond a legislative effort directly to diminish of judge's pay, say, by ordering a lower salary…otherwise a legislature could circumvent even the most basic compensation close protection by enacting a discriminatory tax law, for example, that precisely but indirectly achieved the forbidden effect. (Internal Citations Omitted).

On this basic purpose there was never any disagreement among the founding fathers of the US Constitution. *See* Entin and Jensen [48, pp. 965, 969–70, 974], Entin [51, p. 25, 31], noting that, "[Compensation Clause] cases establish a baseline principle: constitutional prohibitions against diminishing judicial compensation mean that the other branches may not reduce the salaries paid to judges once those salaries have vested."

defending the idea of judicial independence if the very idea of modern constitutionalism and all that it represents is to be preserved. We all know that emergency powers, whether or not explicitly granted by a constitution, have all been abused at one point of time or another.[180] In such circumstances it would clearly fall upon the judiciary to ensure that constitutional powers are not abused and to declare unconstitutional any colorable exercise of constitutional powers.[181]

---

[180]The most famous (or rather infamous) case study in the abuse of constitutional powers remains that of Adolf Hitler who abused the powers under article 48 of the Weimar Constitution in order to establish and then maintain his dictatorial regime in Nazi Germany. *See, e.g.*, Scheppele [68]. In USA, President Truman during the Korean War in 1950 claimed emergency powers that did not find favor with the US Supreme Court that declared the same as unconstitutional in the famous Steel Seizure Case. *See* Youngstown Sheet & Tube Co. v. Sawyer (Steel Seizure), 343 U.S. 579 (1952). President Lincoln's suspension of *habeas corpus* during the Civil War also had at its foundation a claim to emergency powers. Lincoln's famous rhetorical question in today's date is capable of being used as the ultimate justification for the invocation of emergency powers. He asked, "[A]re all the laws but one to go unexecuted, and the government itself go to pieces, lest that one be violated?" *See* Abraham Lincoln, Message to Congress in Special Session (July 4, 1861), in 4 The Collected Works of Abraham Lincoln 421, 429–30 (Roy P. Basler ed., 1953). The abuse of emergency powers by successive military regimes under the Pakistani constitution has been well documented. *See, e.g.*, Akhtar [69]. And lastly we may note the proclamation of emergency by Prime Minister Indira Gandhi in India during the early 1970s. Even though the Supreme Court of India never had a chance to judicially review the constitutionality of proclamations of emergency by Indira Gandhi, it was, and is widely regarded as an abuse and colorable exercise of constitutional powers. *See* Malhotra [70]. In a recent speech given in the Parliament, former Finance Minister of India, the late, Padma Vibhushan Shri. Arun Jaitley equated the proclamation of emergency by Prime Minister Indira Gandhi with the proclamation of emergency by Adolf Hitler. Manoj [71].

[181]*See* Kaufman [55, p. 671, 685]. Prof. Kaufman discusses a rather important incident where:

> …[T]he Rhode Island General Assembly summoned the Court to explain the grounds upon which it had adjudged a legislative act unconstitutional, and therefore void. When three of the court's five judges protested that they were not obliged to explain the basis for their decisions to the legislature, a resolution was introduced to remove them from office. Dismissal of judges was averted only after the Assembly was persuaded that it could not remove them except upon trial for criminal misconduct. (Internal Citations Omitted).

Such an exercise of constitutional powers quite clearly falls into the colorable category. Judicial review is one of the most effective remedies against such a potential misuse of constitutional powers. The point has been stressed by the Supreme Court of India. *See* L. Chandra Kumar v. Union of India, (1997) 3 SCC 261, 301, (Ahmadi, C.J., for the Court):

> The Judges of superior courts have been entrusted with the task of upholding the constitution and to this end, have been conferred the power to interpret it. *It is they who have to ensure that the balance of power envisaged by the constitution is maintained and that the legislature and executive do not, in the discharge of their functions transgress constitutional limitations*. (Emphasis Supplied).

In a 2006 case, *Commonwealth v. Stilp*, 905 A.2d 918 (Pa. 2006), arising from art. V, § 16(a) of the Pennsylvania Constitution (that provides protections similar to the Compensation Clause and the Salary Clause), the Pennsylvania Supreme Court, "…rebuffed an effort to roll back a pay raise four months after it had gone into effect." The Pennsylvania Constitution's Compensation Clause is the closest to the Indian Economic Emergency Clause in the sense that they both provide for

Furthermore, the protection of judicial independence is most urgently needed during the time an emergency has been formally proclaimed.[182] Independence of judiciary can be jeopardized by reducing judicial salaries.[183] One of the most obvious methods of compromising the independence of judiciary is to reduce or to use the threat of reducing judicial salaries.[184] Economic emergency presents a particularly peculiar situation because on the one hand it might be genuinely necessary to reduce the salaries of all government servants including those of the judges of the High Courts and the Supreme Court,[185] but on the other hand it is a power that can potentially be used by the executive branch to ensure that the judiciary becomes sufficiently compliant with the executive branch.[186] A compliant or a committed judiciary cannot be reasonably expected to discharge its constitutional responsibilities even during normal times, but during an emergency, a compliant or a committed judiciary is tantamount to having no judiciary at all.[187] Therefore, the power of the executive branch to reduce judicial salaries during the proclamation of an economic emergency has to be subjected to judicial review to ensure that the power is not exercised in a colorable manner. The extent of judicial review over this power, however, should be limited to an examination of the circumstances that required the executive branch to exercise this power so as to ensure that the power is exercised in a constitutional manner and consistent with

---

reduction of judicial salaries during an economic crisis. The Court in *Stilp* noted that the provision providing for reduction of judicial salaries applies only during a state-wide economic crisis and not as a reaction to a political backlash. Anything else would be an open invitation to attacks on judicial independence. Commonwealth v. Stilp, 905 A.2d 918, 944–48 (Pa. 2006). *See also* Entin [51, p. 25, 29–30].

[182] *See* Elkins et al. [63].

[183] *See* Beloff [23, pp. 1, 25–26], NOTE, *Legislative Reduction of Judicial Compensation during the Depression*, 43 YALE L. J. 1175, 1176–77 (1934), Anderson and Helland [72].

[184] *See* Topf [73] (the author notes Justice Joseph Story's efforts to stave of attack from democratic extremes, which sought to amend the Massachusetts State constitution to enable a reduction of the salary of the judges of the Massachusetts courts). *See also* Kelly [54].

[185] *See In Re*: Provincial Court Judges case, [1997] 3 S.C.R 3, 128; NOTE, *Legislative Reduction of Judicial Compensation during the Depression*, 43 YALE L. J. 1175, 1176–77 (1934), Anderson and Helland [72], Kelly [54].

[186] *See* Anderson and Helland [72, pp. 1277, 1303–04].

[187] *See* Seervai [74]; *id* at 2708–11 (noting that an abuse of power to transfer a judge would impair judicial independence); *id* at 2721 (asserting that Justice Vohra, who was an additional judge, was not given a permanent tenure, on account of a perverse judgement against the Prime Minister's son). *See also* Austin [34] (noting the repeated attempts made by the Indira Gandhi government to attack the independence of the judiciary in the 1970s), Sengupta [75]. For an account of executive's abuse of power to make the judiciary compliant in India, *see generally* Robinson [76], Rajagopalan [77], Ramnath [78]. For a comparison with the situation in the United States, *see* Fisher [79] (noting that the aftermath of 9/11 produced a complaint judiciary, and culminated in the abuse of presidential powers), Pfander [80].

constitutional principles.[188] In other words, there has to be an independent examination of whether or not the circumstances were so severe so as to require a reduction of judicial salaries.[189] The judiciary should not sit over the executive branch to examine how much reduction in judicial salaries is required in the particular economic emergency that has arisen—that question has to be left to the President. But the Supreme Court can certainly examine whether or not the particular economic emergency that arose required a reduction of judicial salaries as a necessary response to that emergency.[190]

5.2 Fundamental Rights Violation

So far in India the question of judicial independence has mostly,[191] but not exclusively,[192] been raised in the context of appointment procedures. However, the concerns, even when expressed in a context different from appointment procedures, have been almost identical. The jurisprudence developed by the Supreme Court in these contexts, appointment procedures or otherwise, is extremely useful and instructive for the purposes of this chapter. In fact, it is the jurisprudence that is developed outside of the context of appointments procedure and yet pertaining to the constitutional value of independence of judiciary that is particularly instructive for our purposes.

In the first *Madras Bar Association* case[193] that was subsequently followed in the second[194] and third *Madras Bar Association*[195] cases, the Supreme Court emphasized the connection between financial independence and judicial independence in the context of increasing "tribunalization of justice"[196] in India. In this case the petitioner Bar Association challenged the constitution of National Company Law Tribunal and the National Company Law Appellate Tribunal inter alia on the ground that, "Parliament does not have the legislative competence to vest intrinsic judicial functions that have been traditionally performed by High

[188]*See, e.g.*, Greene [12, p. 594, 620] (noting that deference to the executive during an economic crisis should be treated skeptically), Jethmalani [81] (noting that during an emergency, the role of judicial review is limited only to the scope of enforcement of *fundamental rights*), Vermule [43, pp. 163, 200–01]. *See also*, Bickel [82].

[189]*See* NOTE, *Legislative Reduction of Judicial Compensation during the Depression*, 43 YALE L. J. 1175, 1176–77 (1934) (noting the legislative reduction of judicial salaries in Oklahoma).

[190]U.S. v. Will, 535 U.S. 911 (2002) (Breyer, J. dissenting), NOTE, *Legislative Reduction of Judicial Compensation during the Depression*, 43 YALE L. J. 1175, 1176–77 (1934).

[191]*See* Gautam [83], Abeyratne [84], Singh [56]. *See also* Jain [30].

[192]*See, e.g.*, Gautam [85].

[193]Madras Bar Association v. Union of India, (2010) 11 SCC 1.

[194]Madras Bar Association v. Union of India, (2014) 18 SCC 1.

[195]Madras Bar Association v. Union of India, (2015) 8 SCC 583.

[196]*See* Datar [86], Ramesh [87], Padmanabhan [88], Gautam [85].

Courts for nearly a century in any Tribunal outside the judiciary,"[197] and since the constitution of these tribunals amounted to, "…transferring the entire company jurisdiction of the High Court to the Tribunal which is not under the control of the judiciary, [the same] is violative of the doctrine of separation of powers and independence of the Judiciary which are parts of the basic structure of the constitution."[198] One of the questions before the Supreme Court was whether or not this "wholesale transfer of power" offended, "… the constitutional scheme of separation of powers and independence of judiciary so as to aggrandize one branch over the other."[199] The Court was quick to stress the importance of the principle of independence of judiciary[200] and noted that this independence includes, "…security in tenure, freedom from ordinary monetary worries, freedom from influences and pressures within (from others in the judiciary) and without (from the executive)."[201] The Court held that, "…[T]he dependence of tribunals on the sponsoring or parent department for infrastructural facilities or personnel may undermine the independence of the Tribunal,"[202] and the only way to ensure the judicial independence of these tribunals is to completely sever their link with the parent department, especially the financial independence of the tribunal from the parent department.[203] Even though Alexander Hamilton was neither cited by counsel nor referred to by the Court, the similarity of the underlying logic captures the attention quite immediately. We may now carefully examine the "rule of law" holding in this case which is most important for this chapter—

> Independent judicial tribunals for determination of the rights of citizens, and for adjudication of the disputes and complaints of the citizens, is a necessary concomitant of the rule of law. The rule of law has several facets, one of which is that disputes of citizens will be decided by Judges who are independent and impartial; and that disputes as to legality of acts of the Government will be decided by Judges who are independent of the executive. Another facet of the rule of law is equality before law. The essence of the equality is that it must be capable of being enforced and adjudicated by an independent judicial forum.

[197] Madras Bar Association v. Union of India, (2010) 11 SCC 1, 18.

[198] *Id.* at 19, 54.

[199] *Id.* at 26.

[200] *Id.* at 35. Justice Raveendran, speaking for the Court, observed that:

> Impartiality, independence, fairness and reasonableness in decision making are the hallmarks of judiciary. If "Impartiality" is the soul of the judiciary, "Independence" is the lifeblood of the judiciary. Without independence, impartiality cannot thrive. Independence is not the freedom for judges to do what they like. It is the independence of judicial thought. It is the freedom from interference and pressures which provides the judicial atmosphere where he can work with absolute commitment to the cause of justice and constitutional values.

[201] *Id.* at 36.

[202] *Id.* at 42.

[203] *Id.* at 43.

> Judicial independence and separation of judicial power from the executive are part of common law traditions implicit in a constitution like ours which is based on the Westminster model.[204]

> The fundamental right to equality before law and equal protection of laws guaranteed by article 14 of the Constitution, clearly includes a right to have the person's rights, adjudicated by a forum which exercises judicial power in an impartial and independent manner, consistent with the recognised principles of adjudication. *Therefore wherever access to court to enforce such rights is sought to be abridged, altered, modified or substituted by directing him to approach and alternative forum, such legislative Act is open to challenge if it violates the right to adjudication by an independent forum.*[205]

The Equality Clause of the Indian Constitution guarantees to all persons the fundamental right of equality before law and equal protection of the laws.[206] The holding of the Court reproduced above makes it clear that having one's case heard by an impartial and independent judicial tribunal is itself a fundamental right protected by the Equality Clause. Any "abridgement, alteration, modification or substitution" of this right is subject to judicial review.[207] It has been elaborately argued above that financial independence is an essential and a very crucial component of judicial independence. This is a principle that is globally accepted and has been enforced by the United States, Canadian, and the Indian Supreme Courts. It stands to reason that if the independence of judiciary is jeopardized by a Presidential proclamation that reduces judicial salaries during the time an economic emergency is in force, every Indian citizen has the fundamental right to question the constitutional validity of such a proclamation (i.e., the proclamation that reduces judicial salaries) before the Supreme Court of India on the ground that their fundamental right to have their cases heard and decided by impartial and independent judicial tribunal is itself being violated.[208] Under these circumstances, the Supreme

---

[204] *Id.* at 56.

[205] *Id.* at 56 (Emphasis added).

[206] India Const. art. 14.

[207] In the Canadian context, but well applicable to India, as any administrative lawyer in India would intuitively know, Prof. Colvin notes:

> The independence of the Judiciary is further compromised if adjudicative work can be selectively advanced or impeded through decisions about the allocation of resources and support services, or if judges themselves perceive the quality of their occupational environment to be subject to the discretion of an Executive which is sometimes a party to litigation.

Colvin [49, p. 229, 234].

[208] *See* India Const. art. 32 (The right to approach the Supreme Court for enforcement of fundamental rights is a fundamental right); *See also* A.K. Gopalan v. State of Madras AIR 1950 SC 27 (emphasizing that the right to move the Supreme Court for the enforcement of fundamental rights through issuance of writ remedies); Romesh Thapar v. State of Madras AIR 1950 SC 124 (reiterating the court's stance as a 'protector and guarantor of fundamental rights); Prem Chand Garg v. Excise Commissioner AIR 1963 SC 996 (stating that the fundamental right to move the court for the enforcement of fundamental right is the "corner-stone of the democratic edifice" of the constitution).

Court cannot summarily dismiss the petition and shall have to examine the case on its merits. Article 50, constitutionally guaranteeing a separation of judicial versus executive powers, is another juristic source of this principle.[209]

5.3 Judicial Review and Basic Structure Constitutionalism

In *Kesavananda Bharati v. State of Kerala*,[210] a much celebrated and internationally studied decision of the Supreme Court of India,[211] the Court laid down the basic structure doctrine and held that even though the power of the Indian Parliament to amend the Indian Constitution under the Amendment Clause[212] could be exercised over any part of the Constitution, the Parliament could not disturb the basic structure of the Constitution.[213] In *Kesavananda Bharati* itself,[214] and then in perhaps one of, if not the, most important post-*Kesavananda Bharati* decisions—*Minerva Mills v. Union of India*[215]—Justice Bhagwati (later Chief Justice), inter

---

[209]INDIA CONST. art. 50 (The State shall take steps to separate the judiciary from the executive in the public services of the State). The importance of judicial independence and need for separation of the judiciary from the control executive have reiterated time and time again, and has been followed in a catena of cases, most recently in Supreme Court Advocates-on-Record Association v. Union of India, (2016) 5 SCC 1. *See, e.g.*, Chandra Mohan v. State of U.P. AIR 1966 1 SC 1987, 1993 (Subba Rao, C.J.) (noting that there "shall be a separate judicial service free from executive control."); Union of India v. Sankalchand Himatlal Sheth (1977) 4 SCC 193, 238 (Bhagwati, J.) (noting that the intent of the framers of the Indian Constitution in including Art. 50 was to immunize the judiciary from any form of executive control or interference.); S.P. Gupta V. Union of India (1987) Supp. SCC 87, 223 (Bhagwati, J.) (noting that the concept of "independence of the judiciary is a basic feature of the Constitution…which is essential for the establishment of real participatory democracy.); Supreme Court Advocates-on-Record Association v. Union of India (1993) 4 SCC 441, 680 (Verma, J.) (observing that the independence of the judiciary is a part of the basic structure of the Constitution and the "broad scheme of separation of powers" provides some "insight to the true meaning of the relevant provisions in the Constitution relating to the composition of the judiciary."); Registrar (Admn.) High Court of Orissa v. Sisir Kanta Satapathy (1999) 7 SCC 725, 728 (Venkataswami, J.) (reiterating that independence of the judiciary is a basic feature of the Indian Constitution to note that executive *control* over the retirement of judges would be violative of the fabric of the Constitution).

[210]Kesavananda Bharati v. State of Kerala, (1973) 4 SCC 225.

[211]*See, e.g.*, Mate [89–91].

[212]INDIA CONST. art. 368.

[213]For a discussion of the line of Supreme Court decisions leading up to the finale in the *Kesavananda Bharati*, *see* Mate [89, pp. 175, 179–191], Mate [90, pp. 441, 464–489].

[214]*See, e.g.*, Kesavananda Bharati v. State of Kerala, (1973) 4 SCC 225, 430, Shelat, J. (Grover, J., concurring), holding that, "Our constitution is federal in character and not unitary. In a federal structure the existence of both the Union and States is indispensable and so is the power of judicial review."; Robinson [92, p. 1, 31], noting that in *Kesavananda Bharati* the majority, "…described the basic structure as containing such principles as judicial review, democracy, federalism, secularism, and many of the fundamental rights."

[215]Minerva Mills v. Union of India, (1980) 3 SCC 625.

alia, held that judicial review was a part of the basic structure of the Constitution.[216] The remarkable thing about Justice Bhagwati's holding in *Minerva Mills* is that he held judicial review to be a part of basic structure review in the context of an External Emergency (that can only be declared in the event of a war, external aggression, or an armed rebellion).[217] In another extremely important post-*Kesavananda Bharati* decision, *I. R. Coelho v. State of Tamil Nadu*[218] a unanimous nine-judge bench of the Court reiterated that judicial review is a part of basic structure of the Constitution.[219] Several subsequent cases have also held that judicial review is a part of the basic structure of the Indian Constitution.[220]

---

[216]*Id.* at 694, Bhagwati, J. (partly dissenting) holding that,

> It is true that by reason of [article 352(5)(a)], the satisfaction of the President is made final and conclusive, and cannot be assailed on any ground, but, as I shall presently point out, the power of judicial review is a part of the basic structure of the Constitution and hence this provision debarring judicial review would be open to attack on the ground that it is unconstitutional and void as damaging or destroying the basic structure. This attack against constitutionality can, however, be averted by reading the provision to mean – and that is how I think it must be read – that the immunity from challenge granted by it does not apply where the challenge is not that the satisfaction is improper or unjustified but that there is no satisfaction at all.

The majority opinion by Chandrachud, C.J., also held judicial review to be a part of basic structure but in the context of reviewing constitutional amendments. Chandrachud, C.J. (for himself, Gupta, Untwalia, and Kailasam, JJ.), declaring the newly inserted article 31-C unconstitutional on the ground that it takes away the power of judicial review. *See id.* at 660. *See also* Seervai [74], Jain [30], Datar [31], Mate [89, p. 175, 210] noting that, "The Court's basic structure decisions in Kesavananda and later cases illustrate how courts may assert limits on governments to prevent them from amending the Constitution in a way that violates certain entrenched constitutional norms or principles."; Mate [90, p. 441, 477], Mate [91, p. 361, 375].

[217]Minerva Mills v. Union of India, (1980) 3 SCC 625, 694.

[218]I. R. Coelho v. State of Tamil Nadu, (2007) 2 SCC 1.

[219]*See id.* at 100, 105, Sabharwal, C.J. (for the Court), holding that, "After enunciation of the basic structure doctrine, full judicial review is an integral part of the constitutional scheme … Judicial review is an essential feature of the Constitution…."

[220]*See, e.g.*, N. Kannadasan v. Ajoy Khose, (2009) 7 SCC 1, 50, (Sinha, J. for the Court) holding that, "Judicial review in our constitutional scheme itself is a part of its basic structure."; Subhash Sharma v. Union of India, (1991) Supp. 1 SCC 574, 597, holding that, "Judicial review is a part of the basic constitutional structure and one of the basic features of the essential Indian constitutional policy."; Government of India v. Alka Subhash Gadia, (1992) Supp. 1 SCC 496, 515, Sawant, J. (for the Court) holding that judicial review of legislation or of any order passed by the administrative authorities is a part of the basic structure of the Constitution. *See also* Robinson [92].

Recently, judicial independence, being inextricably linked with judicial review,[221] has also been held to be a part of the basic structure of the Constitution.[222] The Indian basic structure doctrine that finds its roots in Germany[223] is, however, not unique to the Supreme Court of India.[224] The Turkish Constitutional Court annulled some of the Turkish Parliament's amendments to its Constitution on the ground that they violated the "protected and non-amendable principle of secularism."[225] Similarly the Colombian Constitutional Court struck down as invalid a

---

[221]*See, e.g.*, Supreme Court Advocates-on-Record Association v. Union of India, (2016) 5 SCC 1, 708, Justice Goel (for himself, Justice Khehar, Justice Lokur, and Justice Josepsh, concurring),

> The judiciary has an apolitical commitment in its functioning. Once the independence of the judiciary is acknowledged as a basic feature of the Constitution, the question is whether the power of appointing Judges can be delinked from the concept of independence of the judiciary or is an integral part of it.

Answering this question Justice Goel, "… concluded that "primacy of the Judiciary" and the "limited role of the Executive" in judicial appointments was a part of the basic structure of the Indian Constitution." (Internal Citations Omitted). *See also* Gautam [83, pp. 653, 661–69].

[222]Supreme Court Advocates-on-Record Association v. Union of India, (2016) 5 SCC 1. Justice Lokur, relying primarily on historical materials, held that that the opinion of the Chief Justice of India [should] be given primacy in judicial appointments in order to maintain the independence of judiciary, located the importance to preserve independence of judiciary within the broad structure of judicial review which is a part of the basic structure. Justice Joseph concurred with Justice Lokur completely but relied on a structural analysis, rather than a historical one. Justice Khehar and Justice Goel, both using a textual-doctrinal method of analysis arrived at similar conclusions. *See* Gautam [83, pp. 653, 661–669].

[223]Conrad [93, 94], Roznai [95].

[224]Albert [96], noting that,

> In countries far and near – from Argentina to Austria, Belize to Brazil, Greece to Hungary, India to Italy, Peru to Portugal, South Africa to Switzerland, Taiwan to Turkey – high courts have with accelerating frequency adopted the doctrine of unconstitutional constitutional amendment, authorizing themselves (sometimes in defiance of the constitutional text) to strike down an amendment for violating their reading of the constitution, whether or procedural or substantive grounds. (Internal Citations Omitted);

See also Landau [97], noting that,

> A series of countries have developed the so-called "unconstitutional-constitutional amendment doctrine," which holds that a constitutional amendment can itself be substantively unconstitutional under certain conditions. The doctrine has been espoused by courts such as the German, Indian, Turkish, and the Colombian Constitutional Courts.

[225]As noted by Yaniv Roznai in [95, p. 657, 659]. Other constitutional orders that provide for an unamendable core of their constitutions are the Mexican Constitution of 1824, the Venezuelan Constitution of 1830, the Peruvian Constitution of 1839, the Ecuadorian Constitution of 1843, the Honduran Constitution of 1848, the Dominican Republic's Constitution of 1865, and the El Salvadorian Constitution of 1886. *See id.* at 667–68.

constitutional amendment that allowed President Alvaro Uribe Velez to run for a third term, inter alia, on the ground that the amendment, "...would have deep repercussions on the institutional design adopted by the Constituent Assembly."[226] President Uribe complied and did not run for a third term.[227]

The basic structure doctrine is based on the well-founded distinction between "constituent" and "constituted power." Since the power to amend a constitution (viz., the constituted power) is normatively inferior to the power to establish a constitutional order (viz., the constituent power), the two cannot be equated.[228] Upon the adoption of the constitution, the constituent power having "irrevocably transformed itself into the amending power," it cannot have a separate existence side by side with the constituent power.[229] The correctness of the basic structure doctrine has never been seriously contested in India.[230] Post its decision in *Kesavananda Bharati* a half-hearted attempt to have the decision over-turned resulted in the bench being dissolved without even a written opinion being issued.[231] Since then, the Supreme Court of India has developed a rich basic structure jurisprudence, which has not been seriously contested. The doctrine of

---

[226]Landau [97, pp. 189, 201–03].

[227]*Id.* at 203.

[228]Roznai [95, p. 657, 664]. After an exhaustive study, Roznai notes—

> Constituent power is the extraordinary power to establish the constitutional order of a nation. It is the immediate expression of the nation and thus its representative. Constituted power is the power created by the constitution, an ordinary power that the nation grants through positive law. *These two powers exist on different planes: constituted power exists only in the state, inseparable from a pre-established constitutional order, while constituent power is situated outside the state and exists without it.* (Emphasis Added) (Internal Citations Omitted).

See generally, Roznai [98].

[229]Conrad [94, pp. 1, 13–15].

[230]But *see* Cassels [99] for a critical account of the Doctrine of Basic Structure; Coan [100] criticizing the Doctrine as lacking any basis in original understanding.

[231]Khanna [65]. Justice Khanna, who was the swing vote in *Kesavananda Bharati*, after his retirement wrote his memoirs in which he narrates the attempt to have the decision in *Kesavananda Bharati* reconsidered. At the height of Prime Minister Indira Gandhi's emergency, Khanna narrates,

> The main argument to oppose reconsideration was advanced by Nani Palkhiwala. ...[T]he height of eloquence to which Palkhiwala rose on that day had seldom been equaled and never surpassed in this history of the Supreme Court. Palkhiwala was still on his feet when the court rose for the day. Next day when we assembled in the Chief Justice's chamber he told us that he had decided to dissolve the bench and not to proceed with the matter. ...So ended the attempt to reconsider the correctness of the Kesavananda decision.

basic structure works because it allows the judges to protect core features of a democratic republican constitution[232] without being bound by its textual limitations.[233]

Judicial review and independence of judiciary have been held to be a part of the basic structure of the Indian Constitution.[234] It has earlier been argued in this chapter that the key idea underlying the Salary Clause, like its US counterpart the Compensation Clause, is that reduction of judicial salaries is prejudicial to independence of judiciary. It is not, and cannot be, the case that whereas in ordinary times reduction of judicial salaries is prejudicial to independence of judiciary, somehow during an emergency the same thing will not be equally, if not more, prejudicial. Preserving independence of judiciary is important during normal times,[235] but it is even more important during an emergency.[236] An independent judiciary is an indispensable part of a democratic society[237] and is often the key distinguishing factor between a free people governed by a written democratic republican constitution and unstable and authoritarian governments.[238] The International Lawyers Association and the International Commission of Jurists have proposed that emergency provisions should work in tandem with other

---

232 Issacharoff [101], noting that,

> …[W]hat is distinct about a basic-structure approach to constitutional adjudication is that it protects the core features of contested democratic governance, even if it is not apparent from the outset of a democracy which provisions may prove to be central.

233 Landau [97, p. 189, 233], noting that, "… it allows judges to defend the constitutional order without being constrained by the limits of constitutional text."

234 *See* S. P. Gupta v. Union of India, (1981) Supp. SCC 87, 225, where Justice Bhagwati in his lead opinion stressed that, "… the concept of independence of judiciary is not limited only to independence from executive pressure or influence but it is much wider concept which takes within its sweep independence from many other pressures and prejudices."; Gautam [83, p. 653], Mate [102].

235 Ely [103].

236 *See, e.g.*, Reichman [59], Note, *The Pakistani Lawyers' Movement and the popular currency of Judicial Power*, 123 Harv. L. Rev. 1705 (2010), Qureshi [104].

237 United States v. Will, 449 U.S. 200, 217–18 (1980), Chief Justice Berger (for the Court)

> The compensation clause has its roots in the long standing Anglo-American tradition of an independent judiciary. A Judiciary free from control by the executive and the legislature is essential if there is a right to have claims decided by judges who are free from potential domination by other branches of government. Our constitution promotes that independence specifically by providing [for the Compensation Clause].

See also Carlton, Jr. [105].

238 *See* Kline [106] (citing a former president of the American Bar Association who asserted that "[w]hat marks our nation from so many unstable or authoritarian governments is, to a substantial measure, the independence of our judges as preservers of our constitutional rights."), Keith [107, p. 195].

constitutional provisions that provide for judicial independence.[239] And for this reason alone judicial review of reduction of judicial salaries cannot be ousted during the proclamation of an Economic Emergency, for that would, inter alia, also directly violate the basic structure doctrine, (prohibiting) even a constitutional amendment seeking to do so.

6 Conclusion

The idea of judicial independence entails independence of the judiciary from outside interference especially in the area of judicial decision making. In order to protect judicial independence, the Indian Constitution, as do several others, provides for security of tenure, special procedures for removal and financial independence of the judges. But the Indian Constitution also provides emergency powers to the President of India. These emergency powers extend to taking drastic measures in the event of an economic or a financial emergency. Nobody questions the desirability of emergency powers to be granted in order to deal with an economic or a financial emergency and everybody equally agrees that independence of judiciary is an increasingly important feature of modern constitutionalism that must be preserved at all costs. This conflict of constitutional idealism creates a situation that can potentially result in a constitutional crisis. On the one hand, we might have a situation where the government might be required to act decisively and swiftly in order to deal with a potential economic crisis that might be in the making and might even threaten national security or the stability of the entire economic system. On the other hand, we might, simultaneously, have a situation where the actions of the government

---

[239] *See* Lillich [108] (reporting on the Paris Minimum Standards of Human Rights Norms in a State of Emergency). *See id.* at section B, sub-clause 3, which reads as follows—

> The guarantees of the independence of the judiciary and of the legal profession shall remain intact. In particular, *the use of emergency powers to remove judges* or to *alter the structure* of the judicial branch or otherwise to *restrict the independence* of the judiciary shall be prohibited by the constitution. (Emphasis Added)

See also, id. at sub-clause 5 of section B, which reads—

> The judiciary shall have the power and jurisdiction to decide: firstly, whether or not an emergency legislation is in *conformity* with the constitution of the state; secondly, whether or not any particular exercise of emergency power is in conformity with the emergency legislation …A court of law shall have full powers to declare null and void any emergency measure (legislative or executive) or any act of application of any emergency measure which does not satisfy the aforesaid tests.
>
> (Emphasis Added)

Lastly, *see* Keith [107].

taken in order to deal with this potential economic crisis might result in a potential and perhaps permanent harm, notwithstanding whether it is intended to or not, to constitutional institutions, including the judiciary and especially the independence of judiciary. Howsoever limited this danger might seem, it is not impossible that political pulls and pressures may call for ensuring that an obedient and compliant judiciary be secured.

A grant of constitutional powers cannot be questioned alone on the ground that the powers are liable to be abused.[240] A constitutional court, while judicially reviewing a grant of constitutional powers, cannot declare such a grant unconstitutional solely on the ground that the power is liable to be abused.[241] However, this does not mean that the potential of abuse of such a grant is completely irrelevant while judicial decision-making.[242] When judicially reviewing the extent of executive power of the government to take discretionary decisions,[243] for instance

[240]*See, e.g.*, Providence Bank v. Alpheus Billings 29 U.S. 514, 563 (1830) (Marshall, C.J., writing for the Court) ("This vital power may be abused; but the constitution of the United States was not intended to furnish the corrective for every abuse of power which may be committed by the state governments."); Raja Ram Pal v. Speaker, Lok Sabha, (2007) 3 SCC 184, 443–4, where C.K. Thakker, J., writing the majority judgement, placed reliance on Justice Marshall's words to conclude that it was a well-established principle of Constitution Law, that possibility of abuse of power does not make provision ultra vires or bad law; Govt. of A.P. v. P. Laxmi Devi (2008) 4 SCC 720, wherein a two judge bench of the Supreme Court held that the mere likelihood of abuse of discretionary power would not render a statute unconstitutional.

[241]*See, e.g.*, Dr. Khare v. State of Delhi, SCR 1950 SC 519, 524 ("Abuse of the power given by a law sometimes occurs; but the validity of the law cannot be contested because of such an apprehension"); Raja Ram Pal v. Speaker, Lok Sabha, (2007) 3 SCC 184, 443 ("Again, it is well-established principle of law that the mere possibility or likelihood of abuse of power does not make the provision ultra vires or bad in law").

[242]*See, e.g.*, Associated Provincial Picture Houses v. Wednesbury Corporation [1947] 2 All ER 680 (CA).

[243]*See, e.g.*, R.K. Garg v. Union of India (1981) 4 SCC 675, 691 (Bhagwati, J., writing for the majority)

> Every legislation particularly in economic matters is essentially empiric and it is based on experimentation or what one may call trial and error method and therefore it cannot provide for all possible situations or anticipate all possible abuses. There, may be crudities and inequities in complicated experimental economic legislation but on that account alone it cannot be struck down as invalid… There may even be possibilities of abuse, but that too cannot of itself be a ground for invalidating the legislation, because it is not possible for any legislature to anticipate as if by some divine prescience, distortions and abuses of its legislation which may be made by those subject to its provisions and to provide against such distortions and abuses. Indeed, howsoever great may be the care bestowed on its framing, it is difficult to conceive of a legislation which is not capable of being abused by perverted human ingenuity.

during the proclamation of an Economic Emergency, it is not sufficient to say that the power will be exercised in an honest and a transparent manner.[244] It might be the case that during the tenure of one particular officeholder the powers might be exercised in a completely honest and transparent manner. But the bigger question always is—whether the grant of the constitutional power comes with attendant restrictions that are necessary to prevent the abuse of that power? Historical experience shows that the grant of constitutional powers that come without the necessary restrictions that are required to prevent the abuse of such powers are often abused.[245] Political circumstances or personal ambitions of political leaders can cause these powers to be abused.[246] Once abused, these powers (that have been granted without any way of checking their abuse) become an instrument of perpetuation of arbitrariness.[247] Judicial review of these powers is the most effective non-political remedy against their abuse.[248] In the Indian context, the importance of preserving judicial independence is widely understood. This internationally accepted principle is a central tenet of the Indian Constitution, and has been declared a part of Indian Constitution's basic structure. It was in order to preserve the independence of judiciary that the Supreme Court of India first insulated the procedure of judicial appointments from political and executive interference, and later declared the creation of a new constitutional body for judicial appointments as unconstitutional on the same grounds.[249] It is also widely accepted and understood that preserving financial independence of sitting judges is a cornerstone of preserving judicial independence. Financial independence of sitting judges is preserved

---

[244]*Id. See also, Ex parte* Milligan 71 US 2, 125 (1866), where Justice Davis, writing for the court, noted in his inimitable manner that:

> Wicked then, ambitious of power, with hatred of liberty and contempt of law, may fill the place once occupied by Washington and Lincoln; and if this right is conceded, and the calamities of war again befall us, the, dangers to human liberty are frightful to contemplate.

[245]*See Ex parte* Milligan 71 US 2, 125 (1866); R v. Halliday [1917] AC 260, 271 (Lord Atkinson) However precious the personal liberty of the subject may be, there is something for which it may well be, to some extent, sacrificed by legal enactment, namely, national success in the war, or escape from national plunder or enslavement. It is not contended in this case that the personal liberty of the subject can be invaded arbitrarily at the mere whim of the Executive. A.D.M. Jabalpur v. Shiv Kant Shukla, AIR 1976 SC 1207, 2 SCC 521, 722

> It impossible that when past powers are vested in the executive, the exercise of which is immune from judicial scrutiny, they may sometimes be abused and innocent persons may be consigned to temporary detention. But merely because power may sometimes be abused, it is no ground for denying the existence of the power. All power is likely to be abused. That is inseparable from the nature of human institutions.

[246]*See* Elkins et al. [63, p. 155].

[247]*Id.* at 155–56.

[248]*See, e.g.*, Schechter Poultry Corp. v. United States 295 U.S. 495, 528 (1935) wherein the US Supreme Court, relying on its decisions *Ex parte* Milligan 71 US 2 (1866), and Home Building & Loan Ass'n v. Blaisdell 290 U.S. 398 (1934), opined that "extraordinary conditions do not create or enlarge constitutional power."

[249]Gautam [83].

in the US Constitution as well as the Canadian Constitution. The US Supreme Court and the Canadian Supreme Court have declared these constitutional provisions to be of paramount importance. The US Supreme Court has also declared legislation invalid, on more than one occasion, on the ground that it jeopardizes the protections and violates the protections of the Compensation Clause. The Salary Clause of the Indian Constitution provides the same protections to judges in India as are provided to judges holding high constitutional office in the US as well as in Canada. Under the circumstances, the power of the President of India to reduce judicial salaries in these event of an economic emergency is a power that requires to be squared with the protections against reduction of judicial salaries extended to the judges of the Supreme Court and the High Courts. Any interpretation of the Presidential power to reduce judicial salaries during an economic emergency that ousts the jurisdiction of the Supreme Court to judicially review such executive actions is incompatible with the paramount principle of judicial independence.

Since the possibility of abuse of this constitutional grant of power cannot be ruled out, and also the fact that this power is not subject to any independent review by another co-equal branch of the government, the only effective protection against checking such an abuse is judicial review. This chapter contends that the power of the President to reduce judicial salaries under the Economic Emergency Clause of the Indian Constitution is subject to judicial review. Assuming without admitting that the Supreme Court cannot review whether or not circumstances existed that made it necessary for the President to proclaim an economic emergency, in the event the President chooses to reduce judicial salaries, acting under the color of the proclamation of an economic emergency, the Supreme Court can certainly review, on grounds described in this chapter, whether or not such a reduction of judicial salaries was necessary in order to deal with the economic emergency that the President has proclaimed.

References

1. A. Greene, *Permanent States of Emergency and the Rule of Law* (2018), pp. 15–19
2. C. Bjørnskov, S. Voigt, The architecture of emergency constitutions. Int. J. Const. L. **16**, 101 (2018)
3. C. Schmitt, *Political Theology: Four Chapters on the Concept of Sovereignty*, vol. 5 (G. Schwab trans., MIT Press, 1985) (1922)
4. G. Agamben, *State of Exception*, vol. 4 (K. Attell trans., University of Chicago Press, 2005) (2003)
5. K.L. Scheppele, North American emergencies: the use of emergency powers in Canada and United States. Int. J. Const. L. **4**, 213 (2006)
6. S. Issacharoff, R. Pildes, Emergency contexts without emergency powers: the United States' constitutional approach to rights during war time. Int. J. Const. L. **2**, 296, 296 (2004)
7. C.D. Gilbert, There will be wars & rumors of wars: a comparison of the treatment of defence and emergency powers in the federal constitutions of Australia and Canada. Osgoode Hall L. J. **18**, 307 (1980)

8. H.P. Lee, Constitutionalised emergency powers: a plague on Asian constitutionalism, in *Emergency Powers in Asia: Exploring the Limits of Legality*, ed. by V.V. Ramraj, A.K. Thiruvengadam (2010), pp. 393, 393–411
9. S. Vladeck, Emergency power and the Militia acts. Yale L. J. **114**, 149, 190–92 (2004)
10. L. Keith, S. Poe, Are constitutional state of emergency clauses effective- an empirical exploration. Hum. Rts. Q. **26**, 1071–1096–1097 (2004)
11. A.L. Tyler, Suspension as an emergency power. Yale L. J. **118**, 600, 600–01 (2009)
12. A. Greene, Questioning the executive supremacy in an economic state of emergency. Legal Stud. **35**, 594, 597–98 (2015)
13. N. Davidson, Nationalization and necessity: takings and a doctrine of economic emergency. Brigham-Kanner Prop Rts. Conf. J. **3**, 187–203 (2014)
14. W.B. Fisch, Emergency in the constitutional law of the United States. Am. J. Comp. L. Supp. 389, 389 (1990)
15. Clement Fatovic, Outside the Law 193 (2009
16. D.P. Currie, The constitution in the Supreme Court: the new deal, 1931–1940. U. Chi. L. Rev. **54**, 504–512 (1987)
17. B. Meyler, Economic emergency and the rule of law. DePaul L. Rev. **56**, 539–542 (2007)
18. R. Martin, Notes on emergency powers in Canada U.N.B.L.J. **54**, 161, 162 (2005)
19. H.P. Lee, Emergency Powers (1984)
20. V. Iyer, *States of Emergency: The Indian Experience* (2000), pp. 67–75
21. I. Omer, *Emergency Powers and the Courts in India and Pakistan* (2002), pp. 13–14
22. K. Rosenn, The constitutional guaranty against diminution of judicial compensation. UCLA L. Rev. **24**, 308, 308–310 (1976)
23. M.J. Beloff, Paying judges: why, who, whom, how much? Neil lecture. The Denning L. J. **18**, 1, 3–6 (2006)
24. M.E. Bari, The unjust exercise of emergency powers in Bangladesh and their consequent impact on the fundamental rights: a critical appraisal. Juris **21**, 578, 581–82 (2014)
25. V.V. Ramraj, Four models of due process. Int. J. Const. L. **2**, 492–494–499 (2004)
26. V. Sripati, Towards fifty years of constitutionalism and fundamental rights in India: looking back to see ahead (1950–2000). Am. U. Int. L. Rev. **14**, 413–439 (1998)
27. M. Mohapatra, Learning lessons from India: the recent history of antiterrorist legislation on the subcontinent. J. Crim. L. Criminol. **95**, 315–325 (2004)
28. Abhinav Chandrachud, Due Process of Law (2012)
29. B. Ackerman, The emergency constitution. Yale L. J. **113**, 1029 (2004)
30. M.P. Jain, *The Indian Constitution Law* (R. Pal and S. Pal eds., 2010), pp. 535–36
31. A.P. Datar, *Commentary on The Constitution of India* (2nd edn, Wadhwa and Nagpur, 2007), pp. 2027
32. D.D. Basu, *Commentary on the Constitution of India* (8th edn, 2011), pp. 11054–55
33. V.N. Shukla, *Constitution of India* (M.P. Singh ed., Eastern Book Company, 2008) (1950), pp. 978–70
34. G. Austin, *Working of a Democratic Constitution* (1999), pp. 534–45
35. T.K. Tope, Dr. Ambedkar and article 356 of the constitution. SCC (Journal) **4**, 1, 6 (1993)
36. S.J. Sorabjee, Decision of the Supreme Court in S.R Bommai v. Union of India: a critique. SCC (Journal) **3**, 1, 2 (1994)
37. S. Dam, Constitutional fiat: presidential legislation in India's parliamentary democracy. Colum. J. Asian L. **24**, 1–42 (2010)
38. M.P. Singh, Securing the independence of the judiciary—the Indian experience. Ind Int. Comp. L. Rev. **245**, 287 (2000)
39. C. Rossiter, *Constitutional Dictatorship: Crisis Government in the Modern Democracies* (1948)
40. O. Gross, F.N. Aolain, *Law in Times of Crisis: Emergency Powers in Theory and Practice* (2006)
41. W.E. Scheuerman, The economic state of emergency. Cardozo L. Rev. **21**, 1869–1870 (2000)
42. J. Lobel, Emergency power and the decline of liberalism. Yale L. J. **98**, 1385, 1408–1409 (1989)
43. A. Vermuele, Holmes on emergencies. Stan. L. Rev. **61**, 163, 173 (2008)

44. G.R. Kirsch, Hurricanes and windfalls: taking and price controls in emergencies. Va. L. Rev. **79**, 1235, 1267 (1993)
45. R.A. Posner, *Economic Analysis of Law* (1992), pp. 151–52
46. L.M. Singhvi, *Draft Universal Declaration on the Independence of Justice* ("Singhvi Declaration") E/CN.4/Sub.2/1985/18/Add.5/Rev.1, at arts. 16, 17, 18, 18(b), 19 (August 24 1987)
47. S.B. Sinha, Constitutional challenges in the 21st century. Nat. L. Sch. India Rev. **21**, 117, 118 (2009)
48. J.L. Entin, E.M. Jensen, Taxation, compensation, and judicial independence. Case W. Res. L. Rev. **56**, 965, 970 (2006)
49. E. Colvin, The executive and the independence of the judiciary. Sask. L. Rev. **51**, 229 (1987)
50. R. Ananian-Welsh, G. Williams, Judicial independence from the executive: a first principles review of the Australian cases. Monash U. L. Rev. **40**, 593, 611–613 (2014)
51. J.L. Entin, Getting what you pay for: judicial compensation and judicial independence. Utah L. Rev. **2011**, 25, 44 (2011)
52. J. Colquitt, Rethinking judicial nominating commissions: independence, accountability, and public support. Fordham Urb. L. J. **34**, 73, 78 (2007)
53. R. Wheeler, Federal judicial independence. Hum. Rts. **36**, 10, 11 (2009)
54. C.E. Kelly, Ireland and judicial (in)dependence in light of the twenty-ninth amendment to the constitution. Trinity C. L. Rev. **18**, 15, 38–39 (2015)
55. I.R. Kaufman, The essence of judicial independence. Colum. L. Rev. **80**, 671, 686 (1980)
56. M.P. Singh, Securing the independence of the judiciary—the Indian experience. Ind Int. Comp. L. Rev. **10**, 245, 287 (2010)
57. K. Gautam, Political patronage and judicial appointments in India: a comment on the fourth judges appointment (NJAC) case. Indo. J. Int. Comp. L. **4**, 652 (2017)
58. A. Vermuele, The constitutional law of official compensation. Colum. L. Rev. **102**, 501, 522 (2002)
59. A. Reichman, Judicial independence in times of war: prolonged armed conflict and judicial review of military action in Israel. Utah L. Rev. **2011**, 63 (2011)
60. M.B. Rankin, Mapping judicial independence: toward a comparative taxonomy. Global J. Comp. L. **2**, 1, 2 (2013)
61. Y. Vyas, The independence of the judiciary: a third world perspective. Third World Leg. Stud. **11**, 127 (1992)
62. W. I. Jennings, The rule of law in total war. Yale L. J. **50,** 356, 371 (1941)
63. Z. Elkins et al., *The Endurance of National Constitutions* (2009), pp. 154–56
64. M.V. Kamath, *Nani A. Palkhivala: A Life* (2012), pp. 325–344
65. H.R. Khanna, *Neither Roses Nor Thorns* (2010), pp. 63–82
66. L. Epstein, Some thoughts on the study of judicial behavior. Wm. Mary L. Rev. **57**, 2017, 2074 (2016)
67. M.D. Kirby, Judicial independence in Australia reaches a moment of truth. U. N. S. W. L. J. **13**, 187, 300–301 (1990)
68. K.L. Scheppele, Law in the times of emergency: states of exception and the temptations of 9/11. U. Pa. J. Const. L. **6**, 1001, 1008–1009 (2004)
69. Z. Akhtar, A legal paradox: Pakistan's constitution, martial law and state necessity. Sri Lanka J. Int. Law **21**, 153, 161–65 (2009)
70. I. Malhotra, A Hammerblow to democracy: June 25, 1975: a lookback. The Hindu (25 June 2000). http://www.thehindu.com/2000/06/25/stories/13250831.htm
71. C.G. Manoj, Constitution Day debate: Arun Jaitley cites Hitler's Germany to target Congress over emergency. Indian Express (28 Nov 2015). http://indianexpress.com/article/india/india-news-india/arun-jaitley-cites-hitlers-actions-to-target-congress-over-emergency/
72. J.M. Anderson, E. Helland, How much should judges be paid? An empirical study on the effect of judicial pay on the state bench. Stan. L. Rev. **64**, 1277, 1300, 01 (2012)
73. M.A. Topf, *A Dangerous and Perilous Experiment* (2011), p. 31
74. H.M. Seervai, *Constitutional Law of India*, vol. 3 (4th ed., 2015), pp. 2705–15

75. A. Sengupta, Judicial independence and the appointment of judges to the higher judiciary: a conceptual enquiry. Indian J. Const. L **5**, 99, 117 (2011–12)
76. N. Robinson, Structure matters: the impact of court structures on the Indian and US Supreme Court. Am. J. Comp. L. **61**, 173, 181 (2013)
77. S. Rajagopalan, Incompatible institutions: socialism versus constitutionalism. Const. Pol. Econ. **26**, 328 (2015)
78. K. Ramnath, ADM Jabalpur's antecedents: political emergencies, civil liberties, and arguments from colonial continuities in India. Am. U. Int. Rev. **31**, 209 (2016)
79. L. Fisher, Judicial review of the war power. Presidential Res. Q. **466**, 492 (2005)
80. J. Pfander, Judicial compensation and the definition of judicial power in the early republic. Mich. L. Rev. **107**, 1, 27 (2008)
81. R. Jethmalani, The Indian crisis. Wayne L. Rev. **23**, 247, 250 (1976)
82. Alexander M. Bickel, The Least Dangerous Branch, 29–33 (1986)
83. K. Gautam, Political patronage and judicial appointments in India: a comment on the fourth judges appointment (NJAC) case. Indo. J. Int. Comp. L. **4**, 653 (2017)
84. R. Abeyratne, Upholding judicial supremacy in India: the NJAC judgement in comparative perspective. Geo. Wash. Int. L. Rev. **49**, 569 (2017)
85. K. Gautam, The curious case of tribunalization. VAT and Service Tax Cases (Journal) **47**, 17 (2012)
86. A.P. Datar, The tribunalisation of justice in India. Acta Juridica **288**, 301 (2006)
87. A. Ramesh, Tribunalisation of India's competition regime. NUJS L. Rev. **9**, 259, 286 (2016)
88. A. Padmanabhan, Copyright board and constitutional infirmities: failure of the copyright (amendment) act, 2012 and suggestions for reforms. NUJS L Rev. **5**, 703, 717 (2012)
89. M. Mate, Two paths to judicial power: the basic structure doctrine and public interest litigation in comparative perspective. San Diego Int. L. J. **12**, 175 (2010)
90. M. Mate, State constitutions and the basic structure doctrine. Colum. Hum. Rights L. Rev. **45**, 441 (2014)
91. M. Mate, Elite institutionalism and judicial assertiveness in the Supreme court of India. Temp. Int. Comp. L. J. **28**, 361 (2014)
92. N. Robinson, Expanding judiciaries: India and the rise of the good governance court. Wash. U. Global Stud. L. Rev. **8**, 1, 31 (2009)
93. D. Conrad, Limitation of amendment procedures and the constituent power. Indian Y.B. Int. Aff. **15–16**, 380 (1966–67)
94. D. Conrad, Constituent power, amendment and basic structure of the constitution: a critical reconsideration. Delhi L. Rev. **6–7**, 1 (1977–78)
95. Y. Roznai, Unconstitutional constitutional amendments—the migration and success of a constitutional idea. Am. J. Comp. L. **61**, 657, 692–94 (2013)
96. R. Albert, How a court becomes supreme: defending the constitution from unconstitutional amendments. Md. L. Rev. 181, 183 (2017)
97. D. Landau, Abusive constitutionalism. U.C. Davis L. Rev. **47**, 189, 231 (2013)
98. Y. Roznai, *Unconstitutional Constitutional Amendments—The Limits of Amending Powers* (2017)
99. J. Cassels, Judicial activism and public interest litigation in India: attempting the impossible? Am. J. Comp. L. **37**, 495 (1989)
100. A.B. Coan, The irrelevance of writtenness in constitutional interpretation. U. Pa. L. Rev. **158**, 1025 (2010)
101. S. Issacharoff, Constitutional courts and democratic hedging. Geo. L. J. **99**, 961, 1002 (2011)
102. M. Mate, Judicial supremacy in comparative constitutional law. Tul. L. Rev. **92**, 393 (2017)
103. John Hart Ely, Democracy and Distrust 75–101 (1980)
104. T.A. Qureshi, State of emergency: general Pervez Musharraf's executive assault on judicial independence in Pakistan. N.C. J. Int. L. Com. Reg. **35**, 485 (2010)
105. A.P. Carlton, Jr., Preserving judicial independence—an exegesis. Fordham Urb. L. J. **29**, 835, 835 (2002)
106. S.O. Kline, Judicial independence: rebuffing congressional attacks on the third branch. Ky. L. J. **87**, 679, 682 (1999)

Chapter 5
Emergency Powers in India

1 Historical Overview of Emergency Powers in Pre-independent India

1.1 Pre-British India

As in the West, the main idea underlying the concept of emergency powers in ancient Indian history and political thought is the idea of the preservation of the State. All the six juristic principles of Hindu state-craft deal with the preservation of the State.[1] The great Indian epic *Mahabharata* emphasizes the end of all activity "as the preservation of life itself."[2] The *Manusmriti* lists the preservation of self, wife and wealth in that descending order of priority.[3] Kautilya's idealization of the State

---

[1]Singh [1].

[2]Pratap Chandra Ray, Mahabharata, Book XII Santi Parva, Apaddharmanusasana Parva CXXX Viii, 447. The *Mahabharata* is dated by some to around 1500–1000 B.C. and runs to seven times the combined length of the Iliad and the Odyssey.

[3]The *Manusmriti* or Manava-Dharmashastra is a detailed legal code dated to around first century B.C. *See* English translation in 25 Georg Buhler, Sacred Books of the East, Viii, 213. (Max Mueller ed., Georg Buhler trans., 1886).

> ...[F]or times of need, let him preserve his wealth; at the expense of his wealth; let him preserve his wife; let him at all evens preserve even himself even by giving up his wife and his wealth.

A. Singhvi and K. Gautam, *The Law of Emergency Powers*,
https://doi.org/10.1007/978-981-15-2997-9_5

as a living organism, with spirit, body and matter[4] recurs in the consistent emphasis in Hindu political thought on the firmness, strength and power of the ruler.

Often, the supremacy of the king was considered synonymous with the supremacy of the State, partly because of an "almost pathological fear of anarchy"[5] which characterizes the ancient Indian literature in the composite field of political science, statecraft, public administration and diplomacy. A king was created or appointed "to hold the state" and was expected to remain firm without faltering.[6] Kautilya likened the king to the hub and axle of a wheel.[7] Republics were faulted and berated because of their lack of unity and strength and their inability to cope with situations of war, rebellion and natural calamities. The supremacy of the king was synonymous with the supremacy of the State.[8]

---

[4]KAUTILYA, ARTHASASTRA (R. Shamasastry trans. ed., 1951) (*circa* 300 B.C.). Kautilya, also called Chanakya, is most famous for his classic treatise on polity, *Arthasastra*, which is a compilation of "artha": property, economics, diplomacy, statecraft, politics, law and other secular affairs. The work is dated to about 300 B.C. and deals with central control by a king of a medium-sized realm. It speaks, *inter alia*, of the way the state's economy is organized and how ministries should be arranged and distributed. Great emphasis is placed on the importance of a network of runners, informers and spies which functioned as a surveillance corps for the king, particularly focusing on external threats and internal dissidence.

[5]Compared by many to Machiavelli and by others to Aristotle and Plato, Kautilya is alternately praised for his sound political wisdom and knowledge of human nature and condemned for his ruthlessness and trickery. All, however, agree that it was because of Kautilya that the Mauryan Empire under Chandragupta, (reign c. 321 B.C. to 297 B.C.), to whom Kautilya was advisor and counselor, and later under Ashoka… a model of efficient government. The best translation of Kautilya's book is to be found in the book by Shamasastry, who discovered the lost treatise. This author has referred to the 1951 edition.

[6]Spellman [2]

> The fear of anarchy was almost pathological. Underlying every concept of kingship was the doctrine of Matsya Nyaya, the analogy of the big fish eating up the little fish

[7]Atharva Veda VI. 87–88. Also Rig Veda X. 173 (slightly codified).

> [R]emain firmly without faltering… be you firm like the mountain and may you not come down. Be you firm here like India; remain you here and hold the state… firm as the heaven, firm as the earth, firm as the universe, firm as the mountains, let this raja of the people be firm … Vanquish you firmly, without failing, the enemies …. And for firmness the Assembly here creates (appoints) you.

See also Jayaswal [3, pp. 186–187], Prasad [4, p. 16]. The Vedas are the sacred hymns and oblational verses of Indo-European peoples on a pre-Sanskrit language and are widely regarded as the oldest literature in the history of mankind.

[8]Krishna Rao [5, pp. 165–166]. *See also* Hasan [6].

> The existence of the people, their happiness, the institutions of society and the rules of morality and religion depended upon the king's office. Hence there is no wonder that the king's importance is emphasized. He becomes supreme in his sphere.

There was a strikingly Lockean-Hobbesian emphasis on the duty of protection as the supreme function of government and the payment of taxes as a "quid pro quo" for the discharge of this duty.[9] Finally, the doctrine of necessity, justifying normally unsupportable actions in times of adversity, finds repeated articulation in early Indian texts. As a writer on the *Mahabharata* says:

> When face to face with dire adversity, government could do anything. The justification of it all is that abnormal times have an ethics of their own, Apaddharma as it is called. It must be clearly understood, that in days of distress, all the ordinary rules of morality and custom are suspended . . . The whole chapter of Apaddharma reminds one of Machiavelli. There are sentences written with the point of a stiletto (sic)? Which may pass for the Prince...The section as a whole may be styled... 'The circumstances under which it is right for a prince to be a scoundrel.' In both, the purpose is the same... the secular state, supreme self-interest and self-regard, avowed as the single principle of state action...here is the salvation of states...[10]

The kinds of emergencies faced by early and medieval Indian rulers were of a pattern and included wars with neighbors and foreign powers, attacks on the life of the rulers[11]; subversion, sabotage, intrigues, conspiracies and rebellion by princes or army commanders or provincial governors and disturbances of the peace; and providential visitations, like "fire, floods, pestilential diseases, famine, rats, tigers, serpents and demons."[12] There are also references to a large-scale decline in pro-

---

[9]*See, inter alia*, Prasad [4, pp. 51–52] ("The ... idea of protection as embodying the supreme function of royalty or government runs through the whole of Indian political speculation"). *See also* Jayaswal [3, p. 321]

> The theory that taxes were wages to the king for protection were wages to the king for protection was so ingrained in the constitution that even partial failure of protection was deemed to entitle the subject to claim refund of wages in proportion to loss.

The king has been described as "*preeminently the protector of this people...*," i.e., "gopa-janasya" (Rig Veda III. 43.) and as "Dharampravartaka" *See* Krishna Rao [5, p. 123]. *See also*, Pratap Chandra Ray, Mahabharata, Book XII Santi Parva, CXXXIX, 459 which states that according to Manu, one of the seven attributes of a king include "protection," the other six being "mother, father, preceptor, fire, vaicravana and Yama." It sanctions abandonment of a king who fails to protect, as a leaky ship is dangerous and ought to be abandoned. To the same effect is Hobbes (Leviathan, XXI).

[10]Prasad [4, p. 16].

[11]2 Beveridge [7, pp. 107–108]. There is the example of Akbar who, in 1564, wanted the slave Fulad put to death immediately for firing an arrow at him.

[12]Kautilya, Arthasastra, V. 3 (R. Shamasastry trans. ed., 1951) (*circa* 300 B.C.).

bity, morality and righteousness[13] and "extreme, frightful... drought,"[14] "fire, floods, pestilential diseases" and "famine and hunger." These hotchpot reasons illustrate the lack of fine distinctions and elaborate juristic formulations relating to states of exception,[15] which were regarded as "seasons of distress" and were governed by pragmatic expediency within the framework of a modified moral code and astute administration. Responses to seasons of distress varied also according to the form of government. Within monarchical systems, there were differences of style and approach.

Internal problems and dangers were often accorded prime importance in ancient India. In the *Mahabharata*, Bhishma puts his finger on "internal dissentions" as the besetting malady of republics.[16] The *Arthasastra* sees internal troubles as more serious than external ones, and amongst the internal troubles, those of internal origin with internal abetment as more serious and dangerous than those of external origin with external abetment. In Kautilya's hierarchy of internal troubles, those of

---

[13]Yudhishtir uses graphic language in *Mahabharata* to describe seasons of distress:

> When high righteousness suffers decay and is transgressed by all, when unrighteousness assumes the form of its reverse; when all wholesome restraints disappear, and all truths in respect of righteousness are disturbed and confounded; when people are oppressed by kings and robbers when men of all the four modes of life become stupefied in respect of their duties, and all acts lose their consequence of lust and covetousness and folly, when one another in their mutual dealings, when houses are burnt down throughout the country, when the Brahmanas become exceedingly afflicted, when the clouds do not pour a drop of rain, when every one's hand is turned against every one's neighbor, when all the necessaries of life fall under the power of robbers, when, indeed such a season of terrible distress sets in, by what means should a Brahmin live who is unwilling to cast off compassion and his children?
>
> How, indeed, should a Brahmin maintain himself at such a time? Tell me this, O grandsire? How also should the king live at such a time when sinfulness overtakes the world? How, O scorcher of foes, should the king live so that he might not fall away, from both righteousness and profit?

See PRATAP CHANDRA RAY, MAHABHARATA, Book XII SANTI PARVA, CXLI, 467–68.

[14]*Id.* at 468. Described in the *Mahabharata* as follows:

> [E]xtending for twelve years.... (when) the thousand eyed deity of heaven poured no rain... (when) agriculture and keep of cattle were abandoned, stakes for teethering sarcrifical animals disappeared, ... festivals and amusements perished... the cities and towns ... became empty of inhabitants.... Brahmins began to die on all sides, protection was at an end; herbs and plants were dried up; the earth became shorn of all her beauty and exceedingly awful like trees in a crematorium; ... when righteousness was nowhere... men in hunger lost their senses and began to eat one another...

[15]Indeed, the *Arthasastra* deals with "*alasya*" (laziness and inertia in the body politic) and "*premada*" (hedonism) as factors which undermine and subvert the foundation of the social and political order and must be combated. *See* Krishna Rao [5, p. 155].

[16]Prasad [4, p. 66].

internal origin with external abetment come third and troubles of external origin with internal abetment take the last place.[17]

Examples of non-derogable principles during "seasons of distress" spanned the material, spiritual and religious spheres of life. Thus, while the strict rule of caste duty and function could be modified substantially in an emergency, no Brahmin could ever "form a connection either through the Vedas or by marriage" with the people of the other three castes who had not been initiated and had not received the sacrament at the proper time.[18] "Even at the time of dire distress a teacher of Vedas should rather die with his knowledge than sow it in barren soil,"[19] i.e., should not disseminate knowledge where there is neither merit nor wealth nor obedience. A shudra woman (of the lowest caste) could not be taken as the first wife of a Brahmin or a Kshatriya, though they lived in the greatest distress.[20] No Brahmin, "even in the times of distress," must cause an injury to any creature which is not sanctioned by the Vedas[21] and no king, "though fallen into the deepest distress," should provoke Brahmins to anger.[22] The *Mahabharata* had the same conception of non-derogable rights: while the king may practice the laws for emergency situations and while he may expropriate and levy extraordinary taxes at such times,[23] he could not oppress Ritwijas, Purohitas, preceptors and Brahmins.[24] Nor could such expropriations be directed against "persons who are given to the performance of sacrifices, as also the wealth dedicated to the deities…."[25]

The effects of an emergency could be wide-ranging. In the ancient Indian context, few things could be more far-reaching than a substantial modification of the laws regulating professions, caste duties and caste functions, which embraced the entire spectrum of life. The *Mahabharata*[26] narrates the episode involving the eminent sage Vishwamitra, a great Brahmin, who, "urged by pangs of hunger"[27] and driven from pillar to post in search of food during a "frightful drought"[28] was forced to eat dog's meat illegally taken from a "Chandala."[29] Indeed the great rishi (sage) Agastya, sent to the south of India by Lord Shiva himself, is said to have

---

[17]Kautilya, Arthasastra, VIII. 2, IX. 5 (R. Shamasastry trans. ed., 1951) (*circa* 300 B.C.). *See also*, Ramaswamy [8, p. 143]. Indeed, Lord Buddha is said to have remarked that Republicans die of internal dissatisfaction, dissension and civil insurrection.

[18]Manusmriti, supra note 4, II. 40.

[19]*Id.* at II. 13.

[20]*Id.* at III. 14.

[21]*Id.* at V. 43.

[22]*Id.* at IX. 313.

[23]Pratap Chandra Ray, Mahabharata, Book XII Santi Parva, CXXXIT, 425.

[24]*Id.* at CXXXII, 423; CXXXII, 460; CLXVI, 531.

[25]*Id.* at CXXXVI, 431.

[26]Pratap Chandra Ray, Mahabharata, Book XII Santi Parva, CXLI, 468 *et. seq.*

[27]*Id.* at 470.

[28]*Id.* at 468.

[29]*Id. See also* Manusmriti X. 106 & 107, which tell of Vandeva and Bharadwaj, the former trying to eat dog's flesh to save his life.

devoured the asura (demon) Vatapi to survive a great famine,[30] while the sage Agigarta, suffering from hunger, attempted to slay his own son and "was not tainted by sin since he only sought a remedy against famishing (sic)."[31] These stories are perhaps meant to dramatize the underlying point of the law of the state of exception and emergency (Apaddharma). Bhishma justifies such actions by saying that "theft is allowable in a season of distress even by an eminent person."[32] The moral of the story is summed up by him thus:

> Even thus, when the end in view is the preservation of life itself, should a high souled person possessed of learning and acquainted with means rescue his own cheerless self when fallen into distress, by all means in his power. By having recourse to such understanding, one should always preserve one's life.[33]

The whole morality of adversity was different. Expediency tempered by wisdom was the call of the hour; foes could temporarily become friends when confronted by bigger and more dangerous enemies.[34] Further, "a Brahmin who has fallen into distress may accept (gifts) from anybody"[35]; he may beg food from the king[36] and practice usury by lending "to a very sinful man at a small interest."[37] But no one could "perform his duties according to the law for times of distress… 'without

---

[30]Pratap Chandra Ray, Mahabharata, Book XII Santi Parva, CXLI, 473.

[31]Manusmriti X. 105.

[32]Pratap Chandra Ray, Mahabharata, Book XII Santi Parva, CXLI, 471. *Cf.* Hobbes, Leviathan, XXVII

> If a man, by terror of present death, be compelled to an act against the law, he is totally excused; because no law can oblige a man to abandon his own preservation … When a man is destitute of food, or other thing necessary for his life, and cannot preserve himself in any other way but by some act against the law; as if in a great famine, he takes away the food by force or steals … or in defense of his life snatch away another man's sword, he is totally excused.

[33]Pratap Chandra Ray, Mahabharata, Book XII Santi Parva, CXLI, 477.

[34]*See* Pratap Chandra Ray, Mahabharata, Book XII Santi Parva, CXXXVIII, 435 *et seq*, tells the story of a cat which was ensnared in a trap at the foot of a banyan tree. A mouse, who lived in a hole under the tree, one day found himself hunted by both a mongoose and an owl without any means of escape. "At such a season of great danger, when death itself was staring one in the face, when there is fear on every side" the mouse decided to befriend the trapped cat and hid under its belly on the condition that it (the mouse) would release the cat from the trap as soon as the danger to the mouse had passed away and before the comes for the cat. The story ends by narrating how the mouse wisely refused to release the cat at any time prior to the arrival of the hunter; when released just as the hunter was approaching, the cat could only escape to safety without making a meal of the mouse.

[35]Manusmriti, X. 102.

[36]*Id.* at X. 113.

[37]*Id.* at X. 117.

being in distress'."[38] In short, the individual and the king may deviate from the path of righteousness, but only in times of distress.[39]

Extraordinary situations justified extraordinary taxation. The *Manusmriti* permitted expropriation of up to a fourth of the crops produced by citizens, "in times of distress … if he (i.e. the king) protects his subjects to the best of his ability."[40] The *Arthasastra* put this figure between one-third and one-fourth.[41] Sometimes kings became supplicants before "Paura Janapada," i.e., the general assembly of the cities and the countryside for such exceptional taxes in seasons of distress. The *Mahabharata* provides a graphic account of how this was done:

> Here a danger has arisen. A large enemy army. They forebode our end . . . In this serious difficulty, and in the nearness of this grim danger, I beg of you money gentlemen, for your safety. When the crisis is over, I will repay, gentlemen in full . . . Money is desired only for the sake of the citizens, the children and wives. In crisis, this honourable assembly should bear the burden. You should not value money very much in a crisis.[42]

Financial relief was equally common during natural calamities. During such "emergent occasions," Kautilya directed that "remissions of taxes shall be made."[43] "Similarly fines were not to be levied upon and compensation not to be extracted from those who caused damage to forests during 'calamities.'[44] There was a moratorium on recovery of debts with respect to the creditor" "involved in calamities" or affected by "disturbances in the kingdom."[45] Deposits of money or property lost due to destruction by enemies, invasion, fires, floods and similar calamitous causes would not be reclaimable.[46] Great stress was laid on the conservation and maintenance of well-stocked treasuries to meet emergencies.[47]

Finally, it is noteworthy that many of the contemporary constitutional effects of a state of exception, viz., enhanced centralization, unitary decision making, augmented executive and discretionary powers, and a summary trial procedure, were also reflected in ancient India. As a commentator on the *Arthasastra* puts it:

> Vast discretionary powers were vested in the hands of the administrators and judges, to checkmate forces of disruption and tendencies to destroy the fabric of society.[48]

---

[38]*Id.* at XI. 128.

[39]*See, inter alia*, Pratap Chandra Ray, Mahabharata, Book XII Santi Parva, CXL, 461; [4, pp. 60–61].

[40]Manusmriti, supra note 4, X. 118

[41]Kautilya, Arthasastra, V. 2 (R. Shamasastry trans. ed., 1951) (*circa* 300 B.C.).

[42]Pratap Chandra Ray, Mahabharata, Book XII Santi Parva, LXXXVII, 23–24.

[43]Kautilya, Arthasastra, II. 1 (R. Shamasastry trans. ed., 1951) (*circa* 300 B.C.).

[44]*Id.* at II 17.

[45]*Id.* at III. 11.

[46]*Id.* at III. 12.

[47]*See, inter alia*, Pratap Chandra Ray, Mahabharata, Book XII Santi Parva, CXXXII 423; *id.* at CXXXIII, 425; Kautilya, Arthasastra, II. 5 (R. Shamasastry trans. ed., 1951) (*circa* 300 B. C.).

[48]Krishna Rao [5, p. 132].

Indeed, the practice of "Kantaka Shodhana" (literally "removal of thorns") was well known, whereby special courts manned by "*dandadharas*," and actuated by the sole desire of preserving the integrity and unity of the state, relentlessly suppressed wickedness and conspiracy against the Janapada (i.e., the polity) by conducting summary trials without the civil procedure code or the assistance of jurists.[49] As the Roman dictator had summary jurisdiction extending to all criminal cases affecting the safety of the State, the Indian ruler,

> [I]n the interests of righteousness, (could) inflict punishment in secret on those courtiers or confederacy of chiefs who are dangerous to the safety of the kingdom and who cannot be put down in open daylight.[50]

Hindu rulers before the advent of Islamic conquests followed ancient precepts based on an admixture of textbooks, conventions, practices and the demands of the situations, a combination of *Shastrachar* (code mandated or sanctioned by authoritative scriptures, codes or texts) and *Lokachar* (custom, usage and practice). Conquerors, on their own, brought their principles and tribal mores, which were molded by their interaction with political, religious and social forces encountered by them. Each invasion or overthrow of government precipitated the general sense of martial, warlike ambience. Each conquest widened the gap between the ruler and the ruled until the time of Akbar (1542–1605) who created a stable empire in which state of military exception was not the rule. Two generations later, Aurangzeb's rule (1659–1707), however, appears to have been one long military emergency which sought to rationalize every deceit, treachery, mayhem, oppression, diplomatic and military alliance, levy of imposts and transgression of rights on the basis of supposed reasons of State and supposed emergent exigencies. Later Moghuls who were denuded of their imperial prowess by successive foreign attacks and intrusions and emaciated by internal challenges to their authority etched out a hand to mouth existence in their pathetic quest for survival in a state of perpetual political, military and economic siege, without any consistent criteria or set norms. Obviously, ad hoc expediency reigned supreme during the period of an endless emergency, interspread by brief and uneasy spells of normalcy.

1.2 Company Rule: 1600–1857[51]

After the grant of a royal charter by Queen Elizabeth I to some London merchants on the last day of the year 1600 for trading with the East Indies, including India, a

---

[49]*Id.* at 131.

[50]KAUTILYA, ARTHASASTRA, V. 1 (R. Shamasastry trans. ed., 1951) (*circa* 300 B.C.).

[51]*See generally*, Kaye [9], Ilbert [10], Keith [11], Patia [12], Pylee [13], Jain [14], Jois [15], Mittal [16]. Three good primary source books are Allen & Co [17], Eyre and Strahan [18], Banerjee [19] which contain a collection of statutes of that period and a detailed description of many charters issued to the East India Company.

multiplicity of sources of public law continued to apply within India: the terms of the successive charters issued to the Company; additional instructions occasionally issued by the British Crown to the Company; the inherent, though nominal authority of the Mughal Emperor within his realm and the de facto authority of local rulers under the ultimate or ostensible sovereignty of the Mughal Emperor. The terms of the Charters were of overriding importance as far as the company was concerned. For many years, however, the authority of the company and of its officers did not extend beyond its servants.[52] A succession of royal charters (and commissions under them) were issued in the seventeenth century,[53] and although some of them authorized the use of "martial law,"[54] it is clear that this term was understood as the synonym of military law and was to be applied primarily for the maintenance of discipline during voyages by the company's ships.[55]

By 1628, the power of the company to itself issue commissions to punish errant employees was established and was applied to the company's settlements on land, thus making it sovereign *vis-à-vis* its employees and investing it even with the power of imposing capital punishment upon them. With the growth of trading centers and communities at Surat (in 1612), Madras (1639) and Bombay (1665), and the construction of forts and factories at these places, the writ of the company soon began to extend not only to its servants but also to the other inhabitants of that area and in its hinterland.[56] It is noteworthy that while other British companies trading in other parts of the world (e.g., in United States) had been empowered to "make laws and ordinances for the good and welfare of the saide company and for the Government and ordering of the saide lands and Plantation and the people inhabiting the same…" this plenary power was not initially conferred upon the EIC.[57] But by the Charter of 1668, Charles II authorized the company to exercise powers of "good government" in respect of the island of Bombay which had been obtained by the British from the Portuguese as the dowry of Catherine of Braganza.[58] Statutory provisions dealing with "peace, order and good government" have been used as sources of the exercise of emergency power in some

[52]Keith [11, pp. 5–6].

[53]*See, inter alia*, the commission on 24.1.1601; the charters of 1609, 1615, 1657, 1661, 1668, 1676, 1683, 1686 and 1693. Perhaps the only existing collection of charters of the East-India Company is in the not easily available book Shaw [20].

[54]*See, e.g.*, Queen's Comm'n of 24/1/1601.

[55]Keith [11, p. 6]. *Cf.* Kaye [9] where an account is given of the execution of Gregory Lellington under martial law, for having killed another Englishman Barton in the town of Surat in February 1616. Both the accused and the victim were, however, members of the ships anchored near Surat and Lellington was convicted and executed by the Captain of his ship. Kaye considers thus "*the earliest account of our judicial proceedings in India with which I am acquainted.*" (*id.*).

[56]Jois [15, p. 247].

[57]Keith [11, p. 5].

[58]The princely sum of ten pounds was paid as annual rent by the company to the Crown (until 1730) for the transfer of Bombay by the latter to the company. *See* Keith [11, p. 9].

jurisdictions[59] and hence the words used in the charter of 1668 are significant. Similarly, the Charter of 1683 gave full powers to the company to raise and train an adequate army, to declare and make both peace and war with any other power and to use the law called "martial law for defence of the port" against "foreign invasion or domestic insurrection or rebellion." By now, the term "martial law" was being used in contradistinction to "military law" and "military occupation." The reference to martial law was again repeated in the Charter of 1686.

The Regulating Act of 1773, which marked the end of the era of Charters and the beginning of parliamentary enactments providing the constitutional framework for the Government of the Company, authorized the Governor-General and Council to make rules, regulations and ordinances for the good government of the English settlement. A number of enactments followed,[60] of which the East India Company Act 1784 deserves mention. It prohibited the British Presidents or Governors of Madras or Bombay or other subordinate settlements from "commencing Hostilities or levying war" with any Indian Prince or State except with the express permission of the Governor-General and Council at Calcutta.[61] This prohibition would not, however, apply "in cases of sudden emergency or imminent danger, when it shall appear dangerous to postpone such hostilities or treaty…".[62] It also authorized the Governor-General to arrest persons suspected of plotting against the peace or safety of the country.[63] A later amendment empowered the Governor-General to override the decision of the Council on his own responsibility.[64]

The consolidating Charter Act of 1793[65] reflected a strong intention to keep military and civil offices and functions separate.[66] The Governor-General was also prohibited from declaring war "without the express command and authority of the … Court of Directors" of the company "except where hostilities have actually been commenced or preparations actually made for the commencement of hostilities against the British in India" or against princes dependent upon them.[67]

---

[59]*See, e.g.*, The British North American Act, 1857, 30 Vict. c. 3, §§ 91 & 92, which was applicable to Canada until the recent introduction of the Canadian Charter of Freedom in 1982.

[60]*See, e.g.*, Act of Settlement of 1781, 21 Geo. 3, c. 70, which sought, *inter alia*, to remove doubts and difficulties regarding some clauses in the Regulating Act 1773, to support the lawful governance of Bengal, Bihar and Orissa and to maintain and protect the inhabitants in that enjoyment of laws, usages, rights and customs.

[61]§ 35. *See* Banerjee [19, p. 88].

[62]*Id.*

[63]*See* Banerjee [19, p. 91] (§ 53).

[64]*See* Act of 1786, 26 Geo III, c. 16.

[65]33 Geo III, c 52.

[66]*Id.* at § 30. *See also* Banerjee [19, pp. 139–141] (§§ 31–33).

[67]Banerjee [19, p. 146] (§ 42).

The three Charter Acts of 1813,[68] 1833[69] and 1853,[70] although ushering in far-reaching changes in the structure and administration of the Government of India under the East India Company, did not deal explicitly with emergency powers which were seen as inherent powers to be used on an ad hoc basis whenever necessary. However, the 1833 Act provided for a special legislative procedure to be followed whenever the safety or peace of India may be essentially affected.[71]

The actual use of emergency powers during company rule, which ended in 1858, occurred through the use of martial law on a number of occasions to combat the disorder.[72] The administration of martial law during company rule in India was given a statutory basis by the Bengal State Offences Regulation of 1804.[73] In essence, it provided that during the existence of any war or open rebellion against the authority of Government, the Governor-General in Council may suspend the ordinary courts, may establish martial law and may direct the immediate trial by court martial of all persons owing allegiance to the British Government who have been taken in arms in open hostility to the government or in the act of opposing its authority by force of arms or in the actual commission of any overt act of rebellion against the state or in the act of openly aiding and abetting the exercise of the British Government.[74]

The Regulation was supplemented in 1818 to provide for preventive detention of individuals against whom there might not be sufficient grounds to institute any judicial proceeding or when such proceeding would be "inadvisable or improper." The preamble of the supplementary regulation emphasized reasons of state, including foreign relations of the British Government and the preservation of tranquility and prevention of internal commotion in territories of native princes. The use of such emergency powers and the Regulation itself was judicially upheld on the ground that a "relaxation of the rules securing private rights in terms of public distress or danger" is permitted "*ne quid detrimenticapiatrespublica.*"[75] The Calcutta Supreme Court puts it thus in 1870:

> The Regulation differs from Acts passed for the suspension of the Habeas Corpus Act in this-that it is not a tempory Act; but if the danger to be apprehended from the conspiracies of people of such a character as those I have mentioned is not temporary; but from the condition of the country must be permanent, it seems to me that the principles which justify

[68]53 Geo III, c 155.

[69]3 & 4 Will IV, c 85.

[70]16 & 17 Vict., c 95.

[71]The 1833 Act provided that if there was a difference of opinion between the Governor-General and a majority of the Council over a measure thought by the Governor-General to "essentially affect" the "safety, tranquility or interests of the British possessions in India", and if such difference persisted after each group had recorded and exchanged their views in writing, then the Governor-General shall be entitled to either reject or accept such measure in whole or in part as he shall deem "fit and expedient" (§ 49).

[72]For a brief and pithy account of martial law during company rule, *see* Minattur [21, pp. 15–17].

[73]This difficulty to find regulation is reproduced in Clarke [23].

[74]Minattur [21, p. 15].

[75]*In Re* Amir Khan (1870) 6 Bengal LR 392, 454 (SC Calcutta) (Norman, J.).

> the temporary suspension of the Habeas Corpus Act in England justify the Indian Legislature in entrusting to the Governor-General in Council an exceptional power of placing individuals under personal restraint when, for the security of the British dominions from foreign hostility, and from internal commotion, such a course might appear necessary to the Governor-General in Council.[76]

Martial law was used on a number of occasions during the first half of the nineteenth century[77] and was also the subject of discussion by the Privy Council, hearing an appeal from the Supreme Court of Bombay, in the famous case of *Elphinstone v. Bedreechund*.[78] During what the British preferred to call Sepoy Mutiny of 1857, all civil courts were suspended for a considerable time over a large territory in Northern India. The only authority in existence in these areas was the military, acting in an ad hoc manner for self-preservation. The Varanasi and Allahabad divisions were also later put under martial law and everyone who appeared to belong to or to be siding with the rebels was treated as an enemy. Although a large number of arrests, detentions, killings and trials were conducted exclusively by the military acting in a summary fashion, some civilians were attached to the army after the end of hostilities for determining the guilt of some detenus.[79] The State Offences Act 1857 (XI of 1857) is noteworthy as it empowered the executive to notify any area or district which had been or was in a state of rebellion and to thereafter issue a commission for trial of rebels for any offence against the state or for murder, arson, robbery or any other serious crime against person or property. The proceedings were to be summary and without appeal but the sentence was to be such as provided for by law.

1.3 Direct British Rule Prior to First World War: 1858–1914

The 1857 disturbances convinced the British Government of the impossibility and impropriety of governing India from Whitehall through the instrumentality of a commercial and trading company yoked to the imperial chariot. Despite protestations from the Company, direct rule was imposed through the Government of India (GOI) Act 1858.[80] While making fundamental and far-reaching changes in the structure of Indian Government and administration, the Act required that orders to India directing commencement of hostilities in that country must be communicated within specified periods to Parliament.[81] It also required that the revenues of India

---

[76] *Id.* at 455.

[77] It was used, *inter alia*, in Cuttack (1817–18); Vizagapatnam and Palkonda (1832); Kimedi (1833); Gumsur (1835); Savantwadi (1844). Large parts of Northern India, including Meerut and other areas in U.P. were put under Martial Law during 1857 war of independence.

[78] Elphinstone v. Bedreechund (1830) Knapp PC 316 (Privy Council).

[79] Minnatur [21, p. 19].

[80] Full text in Basu [24].

[81] The Government of India Act, 1858, 21 & 22 Vict. c. 106, § 54.

shall not, without the consent of both Houses of Parliament, be applicable to defray the expenses of any military operation except "for preventing or repelling actual invasion of Her Majesty's Indian possessions."[82]

The Indian Council Act of 1861,[83] for the first time, ushered into Indian law the power of making ordinances having the status of law for a limited period in cases of emergency. This marked the formal introduction of powers of executive legislation or legislation by decree and the primary methods of use of emergency power till the Government of India Act, 1935, remained either the use of force under inherent powers at common law or the passage of martial law ordinances. Section 23 of the 1861 Act, quoted in full below,[84] was undoubtedly conceived as an emergency power to be used only on the rarest of rare occasions[85] in cases of real urgency when delay for want of legislation would be disastrous.[86] This conception of

[82]The Government of India Act, 1858, 21 & 22 Vict. c. 106, § 55.

[83]*See, inter alia*, Ilbert [10, pp. 338–344].

[84]The Indian Council Act, 1861, 24 & 25 Vict. c. 67, § 23 reads as follows:

> Notwithstanding anything in this Act contained, it shall be lawful for the Governor-General, in cases of emergency, to make and promulgate, from time to time, ordinances for the peace and good government of the laid territories or of any part thereof, subject, however, to the restrictions contained in the last preceding section, and every such ordinance shall have force of law with a law or regulation made by the Governor-General in Council, as by this Act provided, for the space of not more than six months from its promulgation, unless the disallowance of such ordinance by Her Majesty shall be earlier signified to the Governor-General by the secretary of state for India in Council, or unless some ordinance shall be controlled or superseded by some law a regulation made by the Governor-General in Council at a meeting for the purpose of making laws and regulations as by this Act provided.

[85]*See* despatch of SOS Wood to G-G in 1861 as mentioned in Minattur [21, pp. 19–19].

> By § 23 the Governor-General of India is vested with a new and extraordinary power of making his own authority. It is due to the supreme authority of India, who is responsible for the peace, security and good government of that vast territory, that he should be armed with this power, but it is to be called into action only on urgent occasions, the reasons for a resort to it should always be recorded, and these together with the ordinance should be submitted loss of time, for the consideration of Her Majesty's government.

[86]*See* speech of Secretary of State Wood, in House of Commons, June 6, 1861 as quoted in Minattur, *Id.* at 17–18.

> The Bill also gives power to the Governor-General in cases of emergency to pass an ordinance having the force of law for a limited period. Questions might arise about the arms Act or the press, as to which it would be very injudicious that delay should occur; and we, therefore, propose to empower the Governor General on his own authority to pass an ordinance having the force of law, to continue for a period of six months, unless disallowed by the secretary of state superseded by an Act of the legislature.

sparing exercise of an ordinance-making power appears to have been realized only during the period prior to the First World War during which, it is edifying to note, it was used only seven times over 53 years[87] and led a writer to remark:

> The power given by this section has rarely been exercised and should be called into action only on urgent occasions.[88]

The ordinances issued prior to the First World War covered a variety of subjects, including prohibitions upon the export of saltpetre from India[89] and prohibitions upon dramas thought to be scandalous, defamatory and prejudicial to public interest.[90] It may be noted that during that period there was no ordinance instituting martial law and no recourse to the latter from 1861 till the outbreak of the First World War.

1.4 First World War: 1914–18

The frugality in the exercise of ordinance-making power ended in 1914 when it was exercised many times. In the next year itself, it was exercised three times.[91] Between 1914 and 1918, twenty seven ordinances were issued.[92] The ordinance-making power became a permanent feature of India's various Constitution Acts and is found in every one of them since 1861, including the present democratic republican Constitution.[93]

A large variety of ordinances … whose subject matter ranged from shipping vessels[94] to visitors to India[95] to commercial intercourse with the enemy[96] to

---

[87]Minattur [21, p. 19]. *Cf.* Srivastava [22] where the figure of 5 is mentioned for the same period.

[88]Ilbert [10, p. 240].

[89]*See* Export of Saltpetre Ordinance, Ordinance 1 of 1861, (Dec. 27, 1861). The ground of urgency stated was that information had been received by the Governor-General by telegraph that export of saltpeter from UK had been interdicted by royal proclamation. *See also* Export of Saltpetre Ordinance, Ordinance 1 of 1862, (Jan. 3, 1862) also dealing with export of saltpeter.

[90]Ordinance of 24/2/1876. It is doubtful if any emergency existed to promulgate this ordinance. Other ordinances include those removing Angar Valley from the jurisdiction of the civil and criminal courts of Punjab (4/10/1869) and regulating meetings in various places including Bengal and Assam under the Regulation of meeting Ordinance 1907.

[91]*See* Srivastava [22].

[92]Minattur [21, p. 19].

[93]*See* The Indian Council Act, 1861, 24 & 25 Vict. c. 67, § 23; The Government of India Act, 1915, 5 & 6 Geo. 5 c. 61, § 72; Government of India Act, 1935, 9 & 10 Geo. 5 c. 101, § 72, and 9th Sch; India (Provisional) Constitution Order 1947, § 62; INDIA CONST. art. 123 & 213.

[94]The Impressment of Vessels Ordinance, Ordinance 2 of 1914 (Aug. 14, 1914).

[95]The Ingress into India Ordinance, Ordinance 5 of 1914 (Sep. 5, 1914).

[96]The Commercial Intercourse with Enemies Ordinance, Ordinance 6 of 1914 (Oct. 14, 1914).

military and naval news,[97] to name only a few,[98] passed during the pendency of the War and were given statutory effect for the duration of the war and for six months thereafter, by the Emergency Legislation Continuance Act 1915.[99] There was hardly any judicial interference with the legislative or executive use of emergency powers. Arrests and internments were upheld on the ground that the ordinances and enactments under which they were made were emergency measures. As the Governor-General was satisfied with the existence of a serious crisis and as the enactments and ordinances were not ultra vires the 1861 and 1915 Acts, the courts declined to interfere.[100] Special Tribunals constituted under a special enactment[101] to try cases of rioting and dacoity were upheld as intra vires the 1861 Act by emphasizing their emergency and temporary nature.[102] Even the exclusion of powers of superintendence of the High Courts over these Special Tribunals was upheld.[103] Finally, a whole host of other decisions adjudicated various economic claims arising from the altered legal regime during the war.[104]

---

[97]The Indian Naval and Military News (Emergency) Ordinance, Ordinance 1 of 1914 (Aug. 7, 1914).

[98]*See also* The Foreigners Ordinance, Ordinance 3 of 1914 (Aug. 20, 1914).; Defense of India Ordinance, Ordinance 3 of 1915 (Nov. 10, 1915); The Enemy Trading Ordinance, Ordinance 5 of 1916 (June 27, 1916); Indian Paper Currency (Amendment) Ordinance, Ordinance 1 of 1915 (Jan. 1, 1915); Indian Paper Currency (Amendment) Ordinance, Ordinance 1 of 1916 (Jan. 11, 1916); Indian Paper Currency (Amendment) Ordinance, Ordinance 6 of 1916 (Nov. 11, 1916); Indian Paper Currency (Amendment) Ordinance, Ordinance 7 of 1916 (Dec. 13, 1916); Indian Paper Currency (Amendment) Ordinance, Ordinance 2 of 1917 (Apr. 18, 1917); Indian Paper Currency (Amendment) Ordinance, Ordinance 1 of 1918 (Apr. 15, 1918); Indian Paper Currency (Amendment) Ordinance, Ordinance 3 of 1918 (Dec. 7, 1918); The Registration Ordinance, Ordinance 1 1917 (Feb. 2, 1917); The Foreigners (Trial by Court Martial) Ordinance, Ordinance 3 of 1916 (Jan. 26, 1916); The Gold Import Ordinance, Ordinance 3 of 1917 (June 29, 1917); The Silver Import Ordinance, Ordinance 4 of 1917 (July 11, 1917).

[99]Act 1 of 1915. Other statutes included the Enemy Trading Act 1916; Indian Defence Force Act 1917; Transfer of ships Restriction Act 1917; Indian Companies (Foreign Interest) Act 1918; Cotton Cloth Act 1918; Excess Profits duty Act 1919.

[100]*In Re* Jewa Nathoo & Ors, ILR 44 (Cal.) 459 (1917).

[101]The Defence of India (Criminal Law Amendment) Act, No. 4 of 1915.

[102]Parmeshwar Ahir v. Emperor, 1918 AIR 155 (Pat).

[103]Sheo Nandan Prasad Singh v. Emperor 1918 AIR 103 (Pat).

[104]*See, e.g.*, Textile Manufacturing Co. Ltd v. Saloman Bros. ILR 40 (Bom) 570 (1915) (defendants were entitled to return their deposits under § 65, Indian Contract Act as it became impossible for them to perform their part of the contract owing to the state of war; Hooper v. King Emperor ILR 40 (Mad) 34 (1916) (accused acquitted of trading with the enemy but convicted of attempting to trade with the enemy); Padgett v. Chottia ILR 41 (Bom.) 390 (1916) (the existence of a state of war between respective countries of the debtor and the creditor suspends the accrual of interest when it would ordinarily be recoverable as damages and not as a substantive part of the debt).

1.5 Inter War Years: 1919–39

This period saw the passage of more than fifty eight ordinances in the aftermath of the war from 1919 until 1935[105] when the Government of India Act 1935 was passed. Most of the ordinances dealt with law and order and some related to martial law in Malabar, Sholapur and Peshawar.

The immediate aftermath of the War saw the passage of the infamous Rowlatt Act, 1919,[106] which sought to supplement the ordinary criminal law by providing emergency powers to deal with anarchical and revolutionary movements. Part I authorized the Governor-General, if satisfied about the existence and promotion of anarchical or revolutionary movements, to make a declaration, pursuant to which special tribunals could be set up for speedy trial of scheduled offences.[107] It went on to specify detailed rules for appointment of members of the special tribunal,[108] the procedure to be adopted to initiate proceedings before it, the situs of hearings, the disclosure of information[109] and leading of evidence by and cross-examination of the accused.[110] In-camera trials were not specifically dealt with and no appeal lay from the tribunal's decision.[111] Part II of the Act authorized the imposition of a number of Provisional restrictions upon the movement and residence of a person suspected to be involved in revolutionary or anarchical movements,[112] which could be made final after the submission of an advisory report by an investigating authority appointed by the Government.[113] The absence of safeguards in respect of the independence and impartiality of the investigating authority, the executive nature of the whole proceeding, the meager procedural rights are given in respect of the proceedings before the authority and the omission of time limits were all too evident in the Act.

---

[105]Minattur [21, p. 19].

[106]That is, the Anarchial and Revolutionary Crimes Act, No. 11 of 1919. Mr. Rowlatt was a judge of the Queen's Bench Division of the High Court of England, who was appointed Chairman of the Committee to investigate into the extent of revolutionary crimes in the country and to recommend legislation to deal with it.

[107]*Id.* at § 3. of the 1919 Act.

[108]*Id.* at § 5. However, if the total number of judges of a High Court did not exceed three, the Chief Justice could nominate two of them and could co-opt either retired permanent judges of the High Court or sitting judges of another High Court. (*Id.*).

[109]*Id.* at §11.

[110]*Id.* at § 12.

[111]*Id.* at § 17. The Special Court's order was to be final and conclusive, although death sentence could be imposed only upon unanimity amongst all trial judges. (*Id.* at § 16, provision.).

[112]*Id.* at §§ 21, 22 & 25.

[113]*Id.* at §§ 25–27 & 30.

Finally, Part III of the Act conferred special powers of warrantless arrests,[114] searches[115] and confinement,[116] although the latter was limited to a maximum of fifteen days.[117] The scheduled offences included a variety of serious offences against the State, murder, rape and kidnapping and offences under statutes dealing with arms and explosives. However, no definition of an open-ended expression-like "anarchical and revolutionary movement," was provided.[118]

Ironically, enough, the Rowlatt Act, providing as it did extensive and exceptional emergency powers in respect of trial of certain offences, arrest, detention, search, seizure and the imposition of wide-ranging conditions and limitations affecting the life, liberty, property and general welfare of individuals, provoked and precipitated precisely what it was designed to prevent and combat. The reaction and resentment against what was widely regarded as a repressive measure led to riots in a large number of cities, including Bombay, Delhi, Calcutta and Lahore. This, in turn, led to a plethora of martial law ordinances during 1919. They were similar to the Rowlatt Act in providing for a special and altered trial procedure but were different in as much as they were of greater severity, brought in the military and authorized a procedure more summary than that under the 1919 Act. On the ground that the Governor-General was satisfied with the existence of an open rebellion in certain parts of the country,[119] the Bengal Regulation of 1804 was applied, although commissions of three persons appointed by the local government were substituted in place of courts martial.[120] The procedure of general courts martial under the Army Act 1911 was made applicable and the martial law ordinance was given limited retrospective effect.[121] The area subject to martial law was increased by a subsequent amendment[122] and the military authorities were empowered to inflict serve punishments upon those convicted[123] of an offence. Other legislative measures provided for continuance and completion of trials even after the end of martial

[114]*Id.* at § 34 (1) (a).

[115]*Id.* at cl. (c).

[116]*Id.* at cl. (b).

[117]*Id.* at § 35, proviso.

[118]*Cf.* E.V. Rieu, The Rowlatt Act, 4 (1919) where it is defined as "capricious propaganda and agitation with the object of overthrowing the government, upsetting established order and interfering with the administration of the law."

[119]*Cf.* Minattur [21, p. 23] ("It was contended by many Indian lawyers and politicians that there was no concerted action on the part of the people to overthrow the government and that there was no open rebellion to justify the declaration of martial law").

[120]The Martial Law Ordinance, Ordinance 1 of 1919 (Apr. 14, 1919).

[121]*Id.* at §.7. Although the ordinance was promulgated on April 14, 1919, it was stated to apply to persons charged with offences committed on or after April 13, 1919.

[122]By Martial Law (Extension) Ordinance of April 16, 1919 martial law was extended to the District of Gujranwala.

[123]Under the Martial Law (Sentences) Ordinance 1919, a convict could be sentenced to transportation for life, or for a period not less than ten years or to rigorous imprisonment for a period between seven and fourteen years.

law[124] and enhanced further the period retrospectively of the ordinances.[125] The effects of these serious inroads into personal liberty were further exacerbated by the adoption of broad literal canons of interpretation by the courts. The Privy Council, interpreting an amending martial law ordinance,[126] held that it applied to any offence and not only to the offences covered by the Bengal Regulation of 1804 or the first martial law ordinance of 1919.[127] Moreover, Section 65 of the Government of India Act 1915 was held not to be violated as it applied only to law which directly affected the allegiance of the subjects, as by a transfer or qualification of the allegiance or by a modification of the obligations thereby imposed, and did not apply to laws (like the martial law ordinances in question) upon the observation of which a person might conceive of allege that his allegiance depended.[128] In any event, the inconsistency of any part of the ordinance with the 1915 Act would only render that part, to the extent of the repugnancy, void.[129] Similarly, in another decision, the Privy Council, emphasizing the validity of the martial law ordinance, upheld the trial and conviction of a newspaper editor on charges of sedition although the order of the Lieutenant-Governor directing his trial before the Commissioners did not name him.[130]

The agitation of the Moplah peasants in Malabar against increased rent and eviction from tenancy land-holdings erupted into serious disorder in 1921 and led to a large number of martial law ordinances in that year and the next. The first such ordinance entrusted the administration of parts of Malabar to a military commander empowered to make regulations for the public safety and for restoration and maintenance of order.[131] The Commander was empowered to authorize a magistrate or military officer of more than seven years' service to make and issue martial law orders. Summary courts dealt with those criminal matters which attracted penalties of less than five years. No appeal lay from these courts, and although the ordinary law of criminal procedure was normally to be followed, it was not incumbent for the summary courts to do so. Particular cases entrusted to it by the military commander could be tried by the normal courts. Subsequently, provision was made for the constitution of Special Tribunals of three persons for trying any offence which, in the opinion of the local Government, was connected with events which

[124]The Martial Law (Trials Continuance) Ordinance, Ordinance 6 of 1919 (May 27, 1919).

[125]The Martial Law (Further Extension) Ordinance of April 21, 1919, extended the first ordinance to offences committed on or after March 30, 1919.

[126]Martial Law (Further Extension) Ordinance IV of 1919.

[127]Bugga v. Emperor 1920 AIR 29 (Privy Council).

[128]*Id.*

[129]*Id.* § 2 of the Government of India Act 1915, reads: "A law made by any authority in British India and repugnant to any provision of this or any other Act of Parliament shall, to the extent of that repugnancy, but not otherwise be void." *See* The Government of India Act, 1915, 5 & 6 Geo. 5 c. 61, § 2.

[130]Kali Nath Roy v. Emperor 1921 AIR 29 (Privy Council).

[131]Martial Law Ordinance, Ordinance 2 of 1921 (Aug. 26, 1921).

necessitated the enforcement and continuance of martial law.[132] For certain offences specified in a later ordinance, trial by military court was provided, based substantially on the summary procedure of the Indian Army Act 1911.[133] The local government was also authorized to invest any magistrate of the first class of not less than two years' service with powers to try any offence connected with the events necessitating the use of martial law.[134] This connection with martial law was to be determined by the Special Magistrate himself. An explicit provision was made to authorize the sitting of Special Magistrates or summary martial law courts outside the area where martial law was in force,[135] notwithstanding the common law rule to the contrary.[136] However, the Madras High Court was prepared to intervene by habeas corpus if summary courts under the martial law ordinance sought to assume jurisdiction over offences committed outside the area of martial law; as no such thing was actually shown to have been done, habeas corpus was denied.[137] However, in another case, the writ was in fact issued to release detenus who were found to have been tried outside the martial law area by a summary court constituted under the ordinance.[138] As the explicit provision authorizing such trials was inapplicable to the present case, the court issued habeas corpus, noting that "outside the area the ordinary rules of law prevail."[139] A number of martial law ordinances promulgated in 1922,[140] which provided a detailed set of rules for the creation of Special Courts and for the speedy trial of past offences committed during the disorders in the region, complete the regime of martial law instituted to deal with the Malabar agitation. The Courts, however, appeared more inclined to intervene in the aftermath of the disorder, if a violation of the terms of the Ordinances of 1922 could be shown to have occurred. Thus, although the Madras High Court refused to apply the Limitation Act to a case arising under Ordinance of 1922 to excuse delay in filing an appeal,[141] it readily ordered a retrial where it was shown that the trying magistrate did not fulfill the requisite qualifications mentioned in the ordinance,[142]

---

[132]Martial Law (Supplementary) Ordinance, Ordinance 3 of 1921 (Sep. 5 of 1921).

[133]Martial Law (Military Courts) Ordinance, Ordinance 4 of 1921 (Oct. 15, 1921).

[134]Martial Law (Military Courts) Ordinance, Ordinance 4 of 1921 (Oct. 15, 1921).

[135]*Id.*

[136]R. v. Allen (1921) 2 Ir. R. 241; R. (Garde & Ors.) v. Strickland (1921) 2 Ir. R. 317, both of which proceed on the basis that trial would be by military courts sitting in the martial law area.

[137]*In Re* R.K.E. Nair 1972 AIR 215 (Mad).

[138]E.P. Govindan Nair v. Emperor 1922 AIR 499 (Mad).

[139]*Id.* at 500.

[140]These include the Malabar (Restoration of Order) Ordinance, Ordinance 1 of 1922 (Feb. 25, 1922); Malabar (Restoration of Order) Amendment Ordinance, Ordinance 2 of 1922 (Mar. 29, 1922); The Malabar (Completion of Trials) Ordinance, Ordinance 3 of 1922 (Aug. 19, 1922).

[141]Hajee v. Crown 1923 AIR 95 (Mad).

[142]Hameed Haji v. Crown 1923 AIR 598 (Mad). As the magistrate had retired prior to his appointment as Special Magistrate under the Ordinance, it was held that he was not a "Magistrate who (has) exercised the powers of a first class magistrate for not less than two years."

or that, instead of compelling attendance of witnesses, he illegally issued a commission for examination of witnesses.[143]

Bengal also saw the use of some ordinances conferring drastic powers upon the executive. The first, in 1924, empowered the provincial government to direct that persons alleged to be terrorists be tried by special commissions, and also allowed an appeal from the decision of the latter.[144] A later ordinance empowered the provincial government to require any person suspected to be acting in a manner prejudicial to public safety or peace to disclose his identity and to give an account of his movements. Special Judges, Tribunals and Magistrates were also created under this ordinance and wide powers of executive rule-making were conferred.[145]

The year 1930 saw the institution of martial law in Sholapur and in Peshawar. In the former,[146] it was used combat serious disorder which erupted pursuant to the arrest of Mahatma Gandhi on May 5, 1930. The provisions of the ordinance relating to control by the military and issue of regulations were similar to the Ordinance of 1921, which has been discussed earlier. In addition, communication with the "enemy" or collection or publication of any information prejudicial to the restoration and maintenance of order was prohibited and severe punishments were prescribed for those who assisted, relieved, concealed or harbored any "enemy." Regulations issued a few days prior to the promulgation of the ordinance were retrospectively validated by the ordinance. Some of the regulations were of extreme severity. Thus, under the regulations, anyone committing an act likely to be interpreted as the performance or intended performance of the duties of "constituted authority" was made liable to ten years imprisonment and fine.[147] Failure to give information about a relative or dependent who, there was a reason to believe, had joined or was about to join persons actively engaged in the disturbances was made punishable with a sentence up to five years and fine.[148]

In a leading decision on the subject, the Bombay High Court, while dismissing petitions for habeas corpus by detenus held under the 1930 Ordinance, emphatically reaffirmed the judicial power and, indeed, the judicial duty to ascertain that conditions and circumstances justifying the use of martial law do in fact exist.[149] Chief Justice Beaumont said:

> The question whether an emergency exists or not is one of fact which the courts can inquire into . . . I think all that the courts can do is inquire whether there is evidence upon which the Governor-General may reasonably conclude that an emergency exists.[150]

---

[143] *In Re* Pokker & Ors 1924 AIR 243 (Mad).

[144] The Bengal Criminal Law Amendment Ordinance, Ordinance 1 of 1924 (Oct. 25, 1924).

[145] Bengal Emergency Powers Ordinance 1931.

[146] The Sholapur Martial Law Ordinance, Ordinance 4 of 1930, (May 15, 1930).

[147] Minattur [21, p. 31].

[148] *Id.*

[149] Chanappa Shantirappa v. Emperor 1931 AIR 57 (Bom.).

[150] *Id.* at 58 C2–59 C1.

Justice Madgavkar was even more emphatic:

> . . . [L]eave no doubt on the following points: Firstly, a state of war and armed rebellion or insurrection must exist and not merely a state of riot which could be put down with the aid of the military and other citizens. Secondly, neither the military nor citizens can refuse or impose conditions on such aid. Thirdly, the necessity must be proved, not merely of recourse to the military, but also of the impossibility of functioning of the ordinary civil laws and the necessity of their abolition for the time being, and the Courts have power to go into the question whether such necessity existed. Fourthly, it is only when the existence of war, whether against foreigners or rebels, and necessity are established, that the jurisdiction of the Courts ceases . . . The law, however, does not invest the man on the spot with superhuman attributes. Being a man, he may be weak or incapable. He may be out of touch with the people. He may be nervous or even vindictive. He may exaggerate a riot with sticks into an armed insurrection, and disobedience of his own orders into a rebellion. Parliament has not, as far as I know, ordained that the existence of the laws and the working of the Courts should cease on the ipse dixit and at the will of the man on the spot whether District Magistrate, mamlatdar or police patil; or that excesses and breach of peace, arson, or even murder on the part of a small minority of the population should justify the man on the spot into exaggerating disaffection into rebellion, or riot into an armed insurrection and abdicating himself in favour of the military with the abolition of the ordinary law. Such a state is not the first stage in the suppression of any disorder but the last resort of the civil power. It is not a sword hanging over the heads of an entire population by reason of disorder or disobedience by a minority to the man on the spot. It is not a sign of his strength and duty discharged to the end, but rather a confession of helplessness and complete impotence to suppress breaches of the peace and to maintain laws even with the aid of the military. It is only when practically the entire population of a certain area is so widely and so deeply disaffected and so armed that it is able to enforce its own law, and the king's law and writ do not run, that an armed rebellion or insurrection as distinguished from riot can be said to exist and necessity to arise.[151]

Indeed, while the Chief Justice concluded that the prevailing facts and circumstances constituted an emergency,[152] Justice Madgavkar expressed grave doubts about whether the emergency justified martial rule rather than merely asking the military for aid and assistance to the civil authority.[153] However, he did not find it necessary to finally decide the issue as the ordinance, in any event, validated all earlier actions. Similarly, Justice Blackwell was "incline (d) strongly to the view that the court is entitled to look into the matter."[154] The decision provides strong support for the view taken by this author on the issue of judicial review of emergency powers, discussed elsewhere.

With the spread of the Red Shirt movement in the North-West Frontier Province,[155] grave disturbances occurred in Peshawar in April 1930. This was followed in August by an incursion into the city by armed Afridi tribesmen from beyond the frontier. Although the disturbances had died down by August 10, the

---

[151] *Id.* at 63–65.

[152] *Id.* at 60 C1.

[153] *Id.* at 66.

[154] *Id.* at 69.

[155] The movement was led by Khan Abdul Ghaffar Khan, who came to be known as Frontier Gandhi.

Chief Commissioner of the province insisted that it was only the lull before a renewed storm and, on his insistence, Governor-General Irwin instituted martial law by an ordinance on August 15, 1930.[156] Subsequent events support the view that the drastic alternative of martial law was largely unnecessary and superfluous.[157]

Martial law, however, remained in force until January 24, 1931,[158] under this very comprehensive ordinance. Part I provided for a martial law proclamation by the local government, revocable by the Governor-General in Council.[159] The Chief martial law administrator was the GOC-in-C, Northern Command,[160] but he could and did delegate his powers to the Chief Commissioner of the province[161] who in turn appointed Administrators for particular areas.[162] The latter could make and supplement martial law regulations and issue orders[163] provided they were intra vires the regulations made by the primary delegates under the ordinance.[164] The ordinance required that there should be as little interference with the ordinary vocations of life as consistent with the expediencies of the situation,[165] that the Administrator should, if possible, seek the non-binding advice and opinion of the civil authority prior to making the regulations,[166] that the penalty for contravention of the regulations must be specified therein[167] and that the regulation must be published in such a manner as deemed fit to bring it to the notice of those affected.[168] Punishments were prescribed for communication with the "enemy,"[169] for collection, publication or eliciting of information regarding the defence forces and their deployment,[170] for doing acts calculated to hamper, imperil or mislead the success of the defence operations[171] and for assisting protecting or concealing the "enemy" in any manner whatsoever,[172] the enemy being defined to include

[156]The Martial Law Ordinance, Ordinance 8 of 1930 (Aug. 15, 1930).

[157]No serious disorder occurred after mid-August; martial law was used in only one subdivision of the district; no Special Courts, Tribunals or Judges elaborately provided for in the ordinance were in fact constituted and the twenty-one persons convicted under martial law regulations were not sentenced to more than three months rigorous imprisonment. Minattur [21, pp. 35–36].

[158]The Martial Law Ordinance, Ordinance 8 of 1930 (Aug. 15, 1930) § 13.

[159]*Id.* at § 2.

[160]*Id.* at § 4(1).

[161]*Id.* at § 4(3). *See also* statement of Objects and Reasons accompanying the Ordinance.

[162]*Id.* at § 4(2).

[163]*Id.* at § 5(2) and 6(1).

[164]*Id.* at § 5(3) and 6(1) Proviso.

[165]*Id.* at § 5(6) (i).

[166]*Id.* at § 5(6) (i).

[167]*Id.* at § 5(6) (iii).

[168]*Id.* at § 5(7).

[169]*Id.* at § 7(1) (a).

[170]*Id.* at § 7(1) (b).

[171]*Id.* at § 7(2).

[172]*Id.* at § 7(4).

"mutineers, rebels or rioters against whom operations are being carried out."[173] The jurisdiction of the ordinary criminal and civil courts was preserved subject to the jurisdiction of Special Courts,[174] if set up under the ordinance. Limited retrospective effect was given to martial law regulations and orders by validating those issued before the proclamation of martial law[175] and even the sentence of whipping was authorized in certain cases.[176] Acts done under or purportedly under the ordinance for the maintenance of peace and safety in any area, were protected from suit or other legal proceedings provided they were undertaken in good faith and a reasonable belief that such action was necessary for the restoration of peace and order.[177]

Part II of the ordinance, which could be brought into force by notification of the Governor-General in Council in the gazette[178] but was never in fact activated, provided a detailed set of rules for the constitution of Special Courts of the following five classes, viz., Special Tribunals, Special Judges, Special Magistrates, Summary Courts and Military Courts.[179] For each type of special tribunal, rules were specified, inter alia, dealing with the appointment and qualifications of judges, the kinds of offences triable by each tribunal, the procedure applicable during the trial, the sentences imposable and the avenues of appeal available.[180]

---

[173] *Id.* at § 7, Explanation.

[174] *Id.* at §§ 8 & 9.

[175] *Id.* at §§ 11 & 12.

[176] *Id.* at § 10.

[177] *Id.* at § 13

[178] *Id.* at § 1(3)

[179] *Id.* at § 16.

[180] Thus, Special Tribunals were to be manned by three persons appointed by the Local Government with the presiding officer being a sitting or retired judge of the High Court and the other members being persons who had acted as sessions Judge for at least two years (§ 17). They could try such offences as the local government may in writing direct (§ 18) and were to take cognizance without committal (§ 19 (1)) and apply the procedure of warrant cases tried by a Magistrate (*Id.*). An appeal, as in the case of a sessions Court, was provided in case of sentences of death transportation for life or imprisonment of more than ten years (§ 21). The local government was authorized to notify the times and places for the setting of the Tribunals and also its procedure (§ 22). Special Judges, had to be persons who had acted as Sessions Judge for more than 2 years (§ 23), could try offences specified by the local government in writing (§ 24). They had the same power and followed the same procedure of Special Tribunals (§ 24 (2)). Appeals in cases of sentences of death, transportation or imprisonment of more than five years lay as from a Court of Session (§ 25). The Special Magistrate, who had exercised those powers for at least two years (§ 26), could try such offences, except those punishable by death, as specified earlier (§ 28) and the powers similar to that of a Magistrate under the Code of Criminal Procedure (*Id.*). In sentences exceeding two years, an appeal lay to the Special Tribunal (§ 30). The Administrator of martial law in any area was authorized to empower any Magistrate in writing to exercise the powers of summary court (§ 32) to try such offences as the Administrator may direct except those punishable with imprisonment exceeding five years (§ 33). Summary Courts were to follow the procedure for trial of warrant cases (§ 34) but could not impose sentence exceeding two years or one thousand rupees (§ 35). However, it could record merely a memorandum of evidence and dispense with the framing of a formal charge (§ 34, first proviso). Finally, the military courts could also be set up, in

None of the special tribunals could try an offence unless it was committed within an area to which the ordinance applied.[181] After the date of emergency notified by the Governor-General in Council under Section 3 of the ordinance[182] (which, however, could be a date preceding the proclamation of martial law)[183] and was connected with the events necessitating the proclamation or continuance of martial law.[184]

Although this was the last occasion when the legislative provision was made in India on the institution of martial law, there were a large number of other ordinances dealing with a variety of other emergency powers. Thus emergency powers in respect of warrantless arrests, entry, search, imposition of movement, residence and notification restrictions were introduced in Bengal in respect of certain specified offences.[185] A Special Tribunal with special powers was set up for the trial of the so-called Lahore Conspiracy case.[186] Ordinances providing for the use of emergency power in Burma,[187] Bengal[188] and Kashmir[189] were also issued in 1931.[190] Similarly, a variety of ordinances giving emergency and special powers were issued in 1932, especially in respect of Bengal.[191] The most noteworthy and comprehensive

the same manner and applying the same procedure as a Summary General Court Martial under the Indian Army Act 1911, if the Administrator of martial law in an area, or his delegate (not below the rank of Field Officer) so directed in view of the emergencies of a situation (§ 37 (1) and (2)). However, these courts could only try offences under §§ 121, 122 or 302 of the Code or committed under the Ordinance or any offence specified and notified by the local government or any offence specified and notified by the local government with the previous sanction of the Governor-General in Council or any attempts or abetments of such offences (§ 37 (1) (a), (b), (c) and (d)). It is noteworthy that these military courts could award any sentence but death sentences were required to be approved by the General Officer Commanding-in-Chief (§ 37 (3)).

[181]*Id.* at § 38 (1) (a).

[182]*Id.* at § 38 (1) (b).

[183]*Id.* at § 3.

[184]*Id.* at § 38 (1) (c).

[185]The Bengal Criminal Law Amendment Ordinance, Ordinance 1 of 1930 (Apr. 19, 1930).

[186]The Lahore Conspiracy Case Ordinance, Ordinance 3 of 1930 (May 1, 1930).

[187]*See*, *inter alia*, Burma Criminal Law Amendment Ordinance 1, 1931; Burma (Rebellion) Trials Ordinance III of 1931; Burma Emergency Powers Ordinance V of 1931.

[188]Bengal Criminal Law Amendment Ordinance IX of 1931; Bengal Emergency Powers Ordinance XI of 1931.

[189]Kashmir State (Protection Against Disorders) Ordinance X 1931.

[190]Other noteworthy ordinances of 1931 include the United Provinces Emergency Powers Ordinance 1931 and N.W. Frontier Province Emergency Powers Ordinance XIII of 1931.

[191]Those relating to Bengal included: Bengal Emergency Powers (Supplementary) Ordinances 1 of 1932; Bengal Emergency Powers Ordinance IX of 1932; Bengal Emergency Powers (Amendment) Ordinance X of 1932; Bengal Emergency Powers (Second Amendment) Ordinance XII of 1932. Other ordinances of 1932 not relating exclusively to Bengal included the Emergency Powers Ordinance II of 1932; Unlawful Instigation Ordinance 1932; Special Powers Ordinance X of 1932.

of these was undoubtedly the Emergency Powers Ordinance II of 1932 which could be applied to any part of India as notified by the Governor-General in Council.[192]

Upon satisfaction (on reasonable grounds) that a person has acted or is about to act in a manner prejudicial to public safety, it authorized a warrantless arrest,[193] detention up to a maximum of fifteen days[194] and imposition of severe residence and movement restrictions.[195] These powers were supplemented by a large number of other powers ranging from control of the supply of commodities of general use[196] to issue of search warrants.[197] Various penalties were prescribed for violation of the ordinance,[198] including the rather exceptional power of the local government to impose a collective fine on the inhabitants of areas deemed turbulent by the local government.[199] Detailed rules were provided for the creation of special criminal courts, including Special Judges, Special Magistrates and Summary Courts.[200] Provision was also made for arbitration tribunals to decide claims for compensation arising from an action under the ordinance.[201]

The severity of the terms of the ordinance was enhanced by studied judicial non-interference in the exercise of powers under it. Challenges to its validity on the ground of absence of proof of emergency were dismissed by saying that evidence was not adducible before the court "as to whether a state of emergency (justifying the issue of the ordinance) did or did not exist."[202] It is interesting to remember how this principle of judicial restraint in respect of ordinances has undergone a radical transformation in more recent years.[203] At that time, courts not only refused to inquire into the exercise of the ordinance-making power but also upheld the power of the Governor-General to invest a third person with the power to decide when and in what area an ordinance becomes operative[204] and to repetitively issue successive

---

[192] § 1 (2), Ordinance II of 1932.

[193] *Id.* at § 3 (1).

[194] *Id.* at § 3 (2).

[195] *Id.* at § 4(1) (a), (b), (c) and (d).

[196] *Id.* at § 8.

[197] The ordinance also conferred power to take possession of buildings, (*Id.* at § 5), to prohibit or limit access to certain places, (*Id.* at § 6), to prohibit or regulate traffic, (*Id.* at § 7), to take possession of movables, (*Id.* at § 9), to regulate arms and ammunition, (*Id.* at § 11), to employ additional police, (*Id.* at § 12), to require the assistance of certain persons, (*Id.* at § 13), to control public utility services, (*Id.* at § 14), posts and telegraphs (*Id.* at § 15) and use of railways and vessels, (*Id.* at § 16), to secure reports of public meetings, (*Id.* at § 17), and to conger general power of search (*Id.* at § 19).

[198] *Id.* at Chapter III, §§ 21–28.

[199] Further, tampering with public servants with a view to make them disregard their duty (*Id.* at § 23), discussion from enlistment into military service (*Id.* at § 24), dissemination of false rumors (*Id.* at § 25) or the contents of prescribed documents (*Id.* at § 27) were all made offences under the Ordinance.

[200] *Id.* at Chapter IV, §§ 29. 29–52 of the Ordinance.

[201] *Id.* at Chapter V, §§ 53–56.

[202] *In Re* M.K. Ghose and T.K. Biswas 1932 AIR 738 (Cal.).

[203] *But see* A.K. Gopalan v. State of Madras, AIR 1950 SC 27 (India).

[204] B.H. Phansalkar v. Emperor 1933 AIR 1 (Bom.).

ordinances on the same subject.[205] Orders prohibiting publication of articles and penalties for contravention of such orders were readily upheld.[206] An example will suffice to illustrate the severity of these emergency laws. A person, who was required under section 4 of the ordinance to report every day to the police at 6 a.m., 12 noon and 8 p.m., and obeyed the order from January 19 to January 25, 1932,[207] was convicted and sentenced to rigorous imprisonment for two years for failing to report at noon on January 25, 1932. Similarly, a conviction for violating an order under the ordinance prohibiting a particular lady from joining or taking part in any meeting of six or more persons in any public place was upheld.[208] Sometimes, a superior court, despite being shocked by the extraordinary nature of the powers and the triviality of the offence, could do nothing except express helplessness because all appeals were barred by the ordinance[209] and revisions or references were also precluded.[210] Although, occasionally, the judges interfered on the merits of a particular case,[211] they were generally extremely reluctant to apply the beneficial effects of the Criminal Procedure Code[212] or the Statute of Limitations[213] to cases under the ordinance and were ready to continue sentences passed under the ordinance even after the expiry of the ordinance[214]; nor were procedural integralities made a ground for interference.[215] In all this, the judiciary was undoubtedly influenced by the wide amplitude and extensive nature of the ordinance, if not a hands-off attitude engendered by the premises of colonial rule.

Before turning to the Government of India Act of 1935, Section 144 of the Criminal Procedure Code may briefly be mentioned as it was an oft-used source of exercise of emergency power during the 1920s and 1930s. It conferred power to

---

[205] *In Re* A.C. Parihal 1933 AIR 278 (Cal.).

[206] Jethmal Pararam v. Emperor 1933 AIR 278 (Cal.).

[207] R.G. Khadkikar v. Emperor 1933 AIR 58 (Bom.).

[208] High Court Bar Association v. Emperor 1932 AIR 613 (Lah.).

[209] Emperor v. Mulchand Chotiram 1932 AIR 166 (Sind). A man, directed by the District Magistrate under § 4 of Ordinance II of 1932 not to go outside the area of sanitary committee of Buria, convicted and sentenced to six months simple imprisonment and a fine of Rs. 100/- for being found sitting on a bridge at the very limits of the sanitary committee, though he professed that he did not realize that he had marginally crossed the limits by sitting on the bridge. The Sind High Court, though strongly inclined to set aside the conviction, found itself barred by the Ordinances and remarked:

> There is, therefore nothing further which we can do. Nevertheless, since our attention has been drawn to this ordinance, we cannot help observing that extraordinary and very extensive powers have been conferred upon a large body of magistrates. Our experience leads us to suppose that powers of this kind cannot safely be exercised without some sort of supervision. Authority to exercise such supervision has been expressly withheld from us.

[210] M. Kundu v. Emperor 1933 AIR 401 (Cal.).

[211] G. Doshi v. Emperor 1933 AIR 148 (Bom.).

[212] A. Majid v. Emperor 1933 AIR 537 (Cal.).

[213] N.R. Ganguly v. Emperor 1933 AIR 124 (Cal.).

[214] Jogendranath Ray v. Superintendent of Dum Dum Special Jail 1933 AIR 280 (Cal.).

[215] P.C. Chakravarty v. Emperor 1933 AIR 186 (Cal.).

issue an order in urgent cases of nuisance or apprehended danger. Certain specified magistrates could, when of the opinion that immediate prevention or speedy remedy is desirable, direct any person to abstain from a certain act or to take certain action with respect to certain property in his possession or management, if such magistrate considered that such direction is likely to prevent, inter alia, a disturbance of the public tranquility or a riot or an affray.[216] This statutorily conferred and judicially reviewable emergency power of the executive to deal with local emergencies, which is usable both against an individual or the general public, led to a number of cases before independence[217] and continues to be in frequent use in independent India. Judicial determination of the existence of circumstances showing the necessity of immediate action as a condition precedent to the exercise of power under this provision is also well established.[218]

The genesis of many emergency provisions found in independent India's Constitution lies in the Report of the Joint Committee of the British Parliament on Indian Constitutional Reform which submitted its report in 1934.[219] It was this report which formed the basis of the 1935 Act which, in turn, found expression in the Constitution of independent India.

Early in its report, the Joint Committee had occasion to emphasize the "fundamental functions of government": the enforcement of law and order and the maintenance of an upright administration,[220] for the fulfillment of which it deemed the conferment of special responsibilities on the Governor as head of the provincial executive necessary.[221] Underlining the necessity for securing strong executives in the provinces, the Committee said:

> . . . nowhere in the world is there such frequent need for courageous and prompt action as in India and nowhere is the penalty for hesitation and weakness greater.[222]

Hence, an executive power in each province to "step in and save the situation before it is too late" was thought indispensable.[223]

Among the Provincial Governors' special responsibilities, the first was "the prevention of any grave menace to the peace or tranquility of the Province, or any part

---

[216]The Criminal Procedure Code 1973, No. 2 of 1974, CODE CRIM. PROC. § 144 (1) (India).

[217]Reference may be made, *inter alia*, to the following judicial decisions of that time dealing with § 144: Kamini Mohan Das Gupta v. H.K. Sarkar ILR 38 (Mad) 489 (1913); Emperor v. Bhure Mal ILR 45 (Alld.) 526 (1923); Gobind Ram Marwani v. B.L. Marwari ILR 7 (Pat.) 269 (1927); Emperor v. B.N. Sasmal ILR 58 (Cal.) 1037 (1930); S.C. Mukhirty v. L.L. Pal Choudhary ILR 39 (CWN) 1053 (1935); Emperor v. G.V. Mavlankar ILR 55 (Bom.) 322 (1931); Thakin Ba Thaung v. King Emperor ILR 12 (Rangoon) 283 (1935).

[218]Kamini Mohan Das Gupta v. H.K. Sarkar ILR 38 (Mad) 489 (1913); Emperor v. G.V. Mavlankar ILR 55 (Bom.) 322 (1931).

[219]October 31, 1934, hereinafter JT. COMM. (2 Vols.).

[220]*Id.* at ¶ 19.

[221]*Id.*

[222]*Id.* at ¶ 23.

[223]*Id.*

thereof."[224] A proposal to restrict such special responsibility to cases in which the "menace arises from subversive movements or activities tending to crimes of violence" and to confine action by the Governor to the department of law and order was rejected because "terrorism, subversive movements and crimes of violence" do not exhaust the cases in which such menace may occur.[225] In these defined areas of special responsibility, it was thought proper of the Governor to dissent from and even overrule ministerial advice if he deemed it fit.[226] It was also thought imperative to arm the Governor with powers, to combat "terrorism and other activities of revolutionary conspirators."[227] For this, the Governor, it was said, should be able to "to assume charge, to such extent as he may judge requisite, of any branch of the government which he thinks it necessary to employ to combat such activities."[228] In the exercise of these discretionary powers, the Governor was to be answerable to the Governor-General and, through him, to the Secretary of State and the British Parliament. Moreover, it was thought that events since 1919 made it desirable to invest the Governor with power to assume by proclamation all powers vested in any provincial authority if he was satisfied that a situation had arisen which "rendered it impossible for the government of the province to be carried on in accordance with the provisions of the Constitution Act."[229] The similarity of this proposal with article 356 of independent India's constitution is evident. The Governor-General's special responsibilities at the federal level were also stated in terms similar to that of the Provincial Governors[230] and he was also sought to be vested with special powers analogous to those vested in the Governor.[231] A situation where the provincial government may refuse to carry out the directions of the federal government was also envisaged, and overriding powers to allow the Governor-General to direct the provincial Governor to overrule the provincial ministry in such situations were sought to be conferred.[232] It was also thought fit to explicitly state that the ultimate

---

[224] *Id.* at ¶ 78 (a)

[225] *Id.* at ¶ 79.

[226] *Id.* at ¶ 75.

[227] *Id.* at ¶ 96.

[228] *Id.*

[229] *See* Jt. Comm. Rep. ¶ 109:

> ... [T]o give the Governor power at his discretion, if at any time he is satisfied that a situation has arisen which for the time being renders it impossible for the government of the province to be carried on in accordance with the provisions of the Constitution Act, to assume to himself by proclamation all such powers vested in any provincial authority as appear to him to be necessary for the purpose of securing that the Government of the Province shall be carried on effectively. This proclamation will have the same effect as an Act of parliament, and will cease to be in force at the expiration of six months unless previously approved by resolutions of both Houses of Parliament, though it may at any time be revoked by similar resolutions.

[230] *Id.* at ¶¶ 168 & 169.

[231] *Id.* at ¶ 190.

[232] *Id.* at ¶ 221.

responsibility for the peace of India rested upon the Governor-General and for this purpose, he could give any appropriate direction.[233] Finally, and most importantly, the Joint Committee recommended that an express provision in the Constitution Act should not only empower the federal legislature to legislate on any subject during an emergency caused by external aggression, but that it should be able to do so even during a proclamation of emergency caused by internal disturbance and that such laws should override any laws which conflict with them.[234] Such an emergency would, therefore, justify the invasion of even the exclusive provincial sphere.

On the basis of these, six provisions dealing with emergency powers were proposed and are reproduced below. The first three applied to Governor-General at the federal level and authorized him to promulgate ordinances in respect of reserved subjects or his special responsibilities[235]; to do so during an emergency when the legislature is not in session for the "good government" of British India[236]; and to

---

[233] *Id.* at ¶ 222.

[234] *Id.* at ¶ 238.

[235] Clause 53 of the Proposal by the Jt. Committee read:

> The Governor-General will be empowered at his discretion, if at any time he is satisfied that the requirements of the Reserved Departments, or any of the "special responsibilities" with which he is charged by the Constitution Act render it necessary, to make and promulgate such Ordinances as, in his opinion, the circumstances of the case require, containing such provisions as it would have been competent, under the provisions of the Constitution Act, for the Federal Legislature to enact.
>
> An Ordinance promulgated under the proposals contained in this paragraph will continue in operation for such period, not exceeding six months, as may be specified therein; the Governor-General will, however, have power to renew any Ordinance for a second period not exceeding six months, but in that event it will be laid before both Houses of Parliament.
>
> An Ordinance will have the same force and effect; whilst in operation, as an Act of the Federal Legislature; but every such ordinance will be subject of the provisions of the Constitution Act relating to disallowance of Acts, and will be subject to withdrawal at any time by the Governor-General.

[236] Clause 54 read:

> In addition to the powers to be conferred upon the Governor-General at his discretion in the preceding paragraph, the Governor-General will further be empowered, if his ministers are satisfied, at a time when the Federal Legislature is not in session, that an emergency exists which renders such a course necessary, to make and promulgate any such Ordinances for the good government of British India, or any part thereof, as the circumstances of the case require, containing such provisions as, under the Constitution Act, it would have been competent for the Legislature to enact. An Ordinance promulgated under the proposals contained in this paragraph will have, while in operation, the same force and effect as an Act of the Federal Legislature, but every such ordinance—(a) will be required to be laid before the Federal Legislature and will cease to operate at the expiry of six weeks from the date of the reassembly of the Legislature, unless both Chambers have in the meantime disapproved it by Resolution, in which case it will cease to operate forthwith; and (b) will be subject to the provisions of the Constitution Act relating to disallowance as if it were an act of the Federal Legislature; it will also be subject to withdrawal at any time by the Governor-General.

assume the powers of any federal authority "if satisfied that it is impossible" to carry on the government of the federation "in accordance with the Constitution Act."[237] The next three clauses conferred identical powers upon the provincial Governor.[238]

---

[237]Clause 55 read:

> The Governor-General will be empowered at his discretion, if at any time, he is satisfied that a situation has arisen which renders it for the time being impossible for the government of the Federation to be carried on in accordance with the provisions of the Constitution Act, by Proclamation to assume to himself all such powers vested by law in Federal authority of securing that the government of the Federation shall be carried effectively.
>
> A Proclamation so issued will have the same force and effect as an Act of Parliament; will be communicated forthwith to a Secretary of State and laid before Parliament; will cease to operate at the expiry of six months unless, before the expiry of that period, it has been approved by Resolutions of both Houses of Parliament; and may at any time be revoked by Resolutions by both Houses of Parliament.

[238]These were clauses 103, 104 and 105.
Clause 103:

> The Governor will be empowered at his discretion, if at any time he is satisfied that the requirements of any of the "special responsibilities" with which he is charged by the Constitution Act render it necessary, to make and promulgate such Ordinances as, in his opinion, the circumstances of the case require, containing such provisions as it would have been competent, under the provisions of the Constitution Act, for the Provincial Legislature to enact.
>
> An ordinance promulgated under the proposals contained in this paragraph will continue in operation for such period, not exceeding six months, as may be specified therein; the Governor will, however, have the power to renew any Ordinance for a second period not exceeding six months, but in that event it will be laid before both Houses of Parliament.
>
> An Ordinance will have the same force and effect, whilst in operation, as an Act of the Provincial Legislature; but every such Ordinance will be subject to the provisions of the Constitution Act relating to disallowance of Acts and will be subject to withdrawal at any time by the Governor.
>
> Clause 104:
>
> In addition to the powers to be conferred upon the Governor at his discretion in the preceding paragraph, the Governor will further be empowered, if his Ministers are satisfied, at any time when the Legislature exists which renders such a course necessary, to make and promulgate any such Ordinances for the good government of the Province or any part thereof as the circumstances of the case require, containing such provisions as, under the Constitution Act. It would have been competent for the Legislature to enact.
>
> An Ordinance promulgated under the proposals contained in this paragraph will have, while in operation, the same force and effect as an Act of the Provincial Legislature, but every such Ordinance—(a) will be required to be laid before the Provincial Legislature and will cease to operate at the expiry of six weeks from the date of the reassembly of the Legislature (or both Chambers, where two Chambers exist) has disapproved it by Resolution, in which case it will cease to operate forthwith; and (b) will be subject to the provisions of the Constitution Act relating to the disallowance as if it were an Act of the Provincial Legislature; it will also be subject to withdrawal at any time by the Governor.

Those clauses above, which respectively empowered the Governor-General and the provincial Governor to issue ordinances during an emergency for the "good government" of British India or of a province, were reincarnated without change as Sections 45 and 93, respectively, of the 1935 Act,[239] although it is noteworthy that Section 45 was later omitted from the 1935 Act.[240] Additionally, three areas which had been the subject of comment by the joint committee but not the basis of any concrete proposal—provisions as to crimes of violence intended to overthrow the government, power of the federal legislature to legislate if an emergency is proclaimed and power of the Governor-General to give directions to a provincial governor for preventing any grave menace to the peace or tranquility of India found a place in the 1935 Act as Sections 57,[241] 102[242] and 126 (5),[243] respectively. The transformation of these provisions of the 1935 Act into the emergency provisions of the Indian Constitution after the deliberations of the Constituent Assembly has been discussed in detail later and need not be anticipated here.

Section 93 was used by the Provincial Governors to assume powers of the provincial ministries in seven provinces in 1939 when the ministries resigned upon the protest of the Indian National Congress against the use of Indian resources in British wars. A 1939 amendment to the 1935 Act vested the government with special powers in the event of war to coordinate the actions of central and provincial governments including the giving of directions of provincial governments on all executive and legislative matters.[244] Later amendments to the 1935 Act extended the life of ordinances beyond six months[245] and also amended Section 102, first, to

---

Clause 105:

The Governor will be empowered at his discretion, if at any time he is satisfied that a situation has arisen which renders it for the time being impossible for the government of the Province to be carried on in accordance with the provisions of the Constitution Act, by Proclamation to assume to himself all such powers vested by law in any Provincial authority as appears to be necessary for the purpose of securing the government of the Province shall be carried on effectively.

A proclamation so issued will have the same force and effect as an Act of Parliament; will be communicated forthwith to the Governor-General and to a Secretary of State and laid before the Parliament; will cease to operate at the expiry of six months unless approved by Resolutions of both Houses of Parliament; and may at any time be revoked by Resolutions of both Houses of Parliament.

[239]26 Geo V&I Edw VIII c. 1. The Government of India Acts of 1915, 1919 and 1935 are conveniently reproduced in Basu [43].

[240]Omitted by the India (Provisional Constitution) Order 1947.

[241]Government of India Act, 1935, 9 & 10 Geo. 5 c. 101, § 57.

[242]Government of India Act, 1935, 9 & 10 Geo. 5 c. 101, § 102.

[243]Government of India Act, 1935, 9 & 10 Geo. 5 c. 101, § 126 cl. 5.

[244]The Government of India Act, 1939, 2 & 3 Geo 6, c. 66, amending § 126.

[245]India & Burma (Emergency Provisions) Act 1940.

authorize the Centre to make laws on any matter not in any of the three lists of the seventh schedule[246] and, later, to state that laws made by the Centre in exercise of emergency powers would not expire after six months.[247] It is also not noteworthy that the emergency provisions of the 1935 Act were not used for an internal emergency but only to meet the situation arising from the Second World War.

1.6 Second World War and Independence: 1939–47

With the declaration war,[248] an emergency under section 102 of the 1935 Act was proclaimed in India. Although there was no direct legislative entry in respect of laws for the defence of India, the enactment of the Defence of India Ordinance 1939, later converted into an Act,[249] was upheld[250] by reference to legislative entries dealing with the military navy and air force[251] and with preventive detention.[252]

The 1939 Act, broadly patterned upon similar English enactments passed for the war,[253] used the familiar legislative device of delegating a wide area of law-making authority on a large number of issues to the executive, which, in turn, exercised and sub-delegated those powers by making the Defence of India Rules, 1939[254] dealing with a large number of topics.

The most important of these topics was the power to issue detention orders and orders restricting the movement of persons provided for in rule 26. Although the Federal Court held the 1939 Act to be intra vires the legislative competence of the Central legislature,[255] it held rule 26 to be ultra vires Section 2 (x) of the 1939 Act, inter alia, on the ground that while the Act only authorized detention based upon grounds of suspicion which are in fact reasonable, the rule authorized detention on grounds which appear reasonable to the detaining authority.[256] The familiar subjective–objective dichotomy was thus resolved in India in favor of an objective construction, despite the citation, before the Federal Court, of the then recently

---

[246]India (Proclamation of Emergency) Act 1946.

[247]India (Central Government and Legislation) Act 1946.

[248]On Sept. 3, 1939.

[249]The Defense of India Act, No. 35 of 1939, Act of Indian Legislature, 1939, available at http://lawmin.nic.in/legislative/textofcentralacts/1939.pdf.

[250]K. Talpade v. Emperor AIR 1943 FC 1.

[251]*See* Government of India Act, 1935, 9 & 10 Geo. 5 c. 101, entries 1 & 2, list I, Sch. 7.

[252]Government of India Act, 1935, 9 & 10 Geo. 5 c. 101, entry 34, List III.

[253]*Cf.* K. Talpade v. Emperor AIR 1943 FC 1 (Gwyer, C.J.), who thought that the 1939 Act and Rules were patterned after English Legislation "not altogether happily".

[254]The 1939 Act and Rules were conveniently reproduced in THE DEFENSE OF INDIA ACT 1965, (2nd edn.).

[255]K. Talpade v. Emperor AIR 1943 FC 1.

[256]*Id.*

decided case of Liversidge v. Anderson.[257] Chief Justice Gwyer distinguished the latter and said that while the English statute vested the exercise of the detention power absolutely in the discretion of the Secretary of State, the Indian rule did not specify "any particular person or authority" to exercise such power.[258] As the primary safeguard in the English legislation was absent from the Indian one, the Court held the objective construction to be the preferable one.[259]

The ensuing spate of habeas corpus applications after this decision was met by the Central Legislature with the passage of an ordinance[260] which, instead of amending the Rules to bring them into conformity with the Act, did the opposite and amended Section 2 (x) of the Act to authorize the making of rules for detention in respect of persons suspected by the authorities "on grounds appearing to such authority to be reasonable."[261] The ordinance also validated, ex-post facto, the detention orders passed earlier.[262]

The Calcutta High Court, however, issued habeas corpus to various detenus in a subsequent case,[263] inter alia, on the grounds that the Governor-General could not change a legislative enactment (i.e., the 1939 Act) by an ordinance; that as rule 26 had been held to be ultra vires it was void and could not be revalidated by the ordinance and that, even if rule 26 was intra vires, the detention was illegal as it was not shown (in the absence of delegation) that the Governor had personally been satisfied that the impugned detention was necessary. The Federal Court upheld the High Court on the last point and dismissed the appeal.[264] On second appeal, the Privy Council held that rule 26 was not ultra vires Section 2 of the Act (as amended), but dismissed the appeal saying that detention orders were not immune from judicial scrutiny and hold that as the Governor had admittedly not considered the detention orders, the appeal must fail.[265]

Section 2 (xxiv) of the Act and rule 75 A of the Rules providing for requisitioning of property also generated much litigation. In an important decision, the Bombay High Court quashed an order of requisition on the ground that as the legislative power of requisition was not provided in any item of the lists of schedule 7 of the 1935 Act (including items 9 or 21 of the Provincial list), legislation concerning requisition could, despite the proclamation of emergency under Section 102 of the 1935 Act, be made only under the residuary legislative power usable only pursuant to a notification by the Governor-General which was absent in

[257][1942] AC 206.

[258]K. Talpade v. Emperor AIR 1943 FC 1.

[259]*Id.* at 6–7.

[260]Ordinance 14 of 1943.

[261]*Id.* at § 2.

[262]*Id.* at § 3.

[263]Shibnath Banerjee v. Porter, 1943 AIR 377 (Cal.).

[264]Emperor v. Sibnath Banerji, AIR 1943 FC 75 (Federal Court of India).

[265]Emperor v. Sibnath Banerji, AIR 1945 PC 156 (Privy Council).

that case.[266] It is submitted that this detailed and well-considered judgement of Justice Bhagwati reflects the correct, albeit a strict, interpretation of the legislative entries which talk of a compulsory acquisition of land[267] and of land rights over land,[268] but not of the land requisition. A contemporaneous decision of a single judge of the Madras High Court[269] upholding legislation requisitioning property under the entry relating to "trade and commerce within the province"[270] is, as it is submitted, clearly erroneous, while other decisions involving requisitioning of property did not raise the question of the vires of the rule or section but only an application of it.[271] A number of other decisions established the right to compensation for requisitioned property and laid down various principles for calculation of such compensation,[272] although the Act and Rules nowhere explicitly mentioned compensation.[273]

Rule 81, which provided wide and general authority for regulation of industry, led to a plethora of regulatory orders under to but was construed benignly by the courts on the ground that unintentional violation of a whole mass of laws, enacted in quick succession and subject to rapid executive alteration, justified mitigation in the rigor of application.[274]

Similarly, rule 129, providing exceptional powers of arrest and detention was held to impose the burden of proof upon the police officer affecting the arrest to show that his suspicion to do so was reasonable; failing this, the arrest would be illegal.[275] Moreover, if after judicial review, no adequate material could be shown to justify the arrest, the court would be prepared to intervene.[276]

During the war, martial rule was also instituted in 1942 in parts of Sind to combat the growing lawlessness of an allegedly criminal tribe called Hurs.[277] No statute or ordinance was issued but the military commander was instructed by the executive to restore civil authority. For exactly a year, the military commander had complete control of the civil administration and enforced summary justice against

[266]Tan Bug Taim v. Collector Bombay, 1946 AIR 216 (Bom.).

[267]Government of India Act, 1935, 9 & 10 Geo. 5 c. 101, entry 9, List II, sch. 7.

[268]*Id.* entry 21.

[269]*In Re* Venkatasubbier, 1945 AIR 104 (Mad.).

[270]The Government of India Act, 1935, 9 & 10 Geo. 5 c. 101, entry 27, list II, sch. 7.

[271]H.C. Gupta v. Mackertich John, 1946 AIR 140 (Cal.); Municipal Board v. Allah Tala (1951) All. L.J. 145.

[272]Union of India v. Ram Prashad & others, 1952 AIR 116 (Punk.); Collector, Darjeeling v. Mackertich (1950) 54 CWN 853; West Bengal v. Board of Trustees 1946 AIR 416 (Cal.).

[273]*Cf.* Srivastava [22, p. 204] "It appears from these decisions that though DOI Rules did not provide expressly for fair compensation, as were done by the English Defense Regulations, the courts were ready to order payment of fair and reasonable compensation".

[274]Dina Nath v. Emperor 1946 AIR 117 (Alld.). *See also* Roshan Lal v. Emperor 1956 AIR 161 (Alld.).

[275]Emperor v. Vimlabai Deshpande (1946) 73 I.A. 144 (Privy Council).

[276]Teja Singh v. Emperor 1945 AIR 293 (Lah.).

[277]Minattur [21, p. 39].

the Hurs through Special Courts.[278] A subsequent ordinance sought to indemnify all persons against legal proceedings in respect of acts done during martial law … in good faith and in the reasonable belief that it was necessary for the purpose intended to be served thereby."[279] This appears to have been the last known use of martial law within India.

The year 1942 also saw the issue of an ordinance authorizing the setting up of special criminal courts of various types.[280] The ordinance was to come in force in any province only if the provincial government should declare by notification that an emergency existed. It empowered provincial governments to constitute certain classes of special courts, defined the classes of persons who could be appointed to those courts, specified the sentence each of those courts was authorized to impose, prescribed special rules of procedure for the conduct of trials before those courts and made provision for appeals in certain cases.

The Calcutta High Court, however, held the ordinance to be invalid and issued habeas corpus for the release of detenus.[281] On appeal, the federal court upheld the decision of the High Court,[282] firstly on the ground that while the Special Courts under the ordinance could be activated and invested with jurisdiction only by legislative provision, the ordinance delegated power to provincial executive authorities to do so and was therefore invalid and, secondly, on the ground that so long as the Code of Criminal Procedure had not been validly repealed or modified or excluded, a trial could be held only under the Code and not under any special procedure.

The judicial invalidation of the Ordinance of 1942 led to the issue of another ordinance in 1943[283] which, while repealing the earlier ordinance[284] and providing an indemnity for all officers,[285] sought to validate all sentences passed under the repealed ordinance by deeming them to have been passed in a proper trial held under the Code.[286] This validating ordinance was itself challenged as being ultra

---

[278] *Id.*

[279] Martial Law (Indemnity) Ordinance 1943 (XVIII of 1943).

[280] Special Criminal Courts Ordinance 2 of 1942. It authorized the creation of Special Judges, Special Magistrates and Summary Courts.

[281] Benoari Lal Sarma v. Emperor 1943 AIR 285 (Cal.).

[282] Emperor v. Benoari Lal Sarma AIR 1943 FC 36.

[283] Special Criminal Courts (Repeal) Ordinance XIX of 1943.

[284] *Id.* at § 2.

[285] *Id.* at § 5.

[286] *Id.* at § 3.

vires the 1935 Act. The Federal Court,[287] however, upheld the validity of the ordinance and that of the sentences passed under the earlier ordinance, inter alia, on the grounds that legislative entries providing for "administration of justice"[288] and "criminal procedure"[289] authorized the issue of such ordinances, that retrospective legislative validation of earlier legal proceedings was not prohibited by the 1935 Act and that there was no encroachment upon the judicial power by the executive or legislative powers. About a year later, the issue was rendered academic when the Privy Council allowed an appeal from the decision of the federal court invalidating the 1942 ordinance, inter alia, on the grounds that the Governor-General could provide by ordinance for the future setting up of special criminal courts despite the recital of an immediate and imminent emergency and that empowerment of a provincial legislature to set up special criminal courts in the future did not constitute delegated legislation but was instead a manifestation of the "not uncommon legislative arrangement by which the local application of the provision of a statute was determined by the judgement of a local administrative body as to its necessity."[290] The decision seemingly provides support against the theory of judicial review of emergency powers discussed elsewhere, but it is submitted that the remarks of the court denying the power of judges to examine the validity of the Governor-General's view that an emergency exists[291] must be seen in the context of the remarks following immediately thereafter which cite detailed facts and circumstances illustrating the seriousness of the war emergency.[292] It must also be remembered that the existence and severity of the emergency during the Second World War was incontrovertible. A wide variety of other legislative measures were passed during the pendency of the war,[293] sometimes after the cessation of which India achieved independence.

---

[287]Piare Dusadh v. King Emperor (1944) FCR 61.

[288]Government of India Act, 1935, 9 & 10 Geo. 5 c. 101, entry 1, list II, sch. 7.

[289]*Id.* Entry 2, List 2.

[290]Emperor v. Benoari Lal Sarma, AIR 1945 PC 40, 51 C2 (Privy Council).

[291]Emperor v. Benoari Lal Sarma, AIR 1945 PC 48, 50 C1 (Privy Council).

[292]*Id.* at 50 C1.

> In the present instance, such questions are immaterial, for at the date of the ordinance (2nd January 1942) no one could suggest that the situations in India did not constitute an emergency of the most anxious kind. Japan had declared war on the previous 7th December; Rangoon had been bombed by the enemy on 23rd December and again on 25th December: earlier Ordinances had recited that an emergency had arisen which required special provisions being made to maintain essential services, to increase certain penalties, to deal with looting of property left unprotected by evacuation of premises, and so forth.

[293]These include, *inter alia*, Registration Ord. 1939; Requisitioning of Vessels Ord. 1939; Foreigners Ord. 1939; Civil Pioneer Force Ord. 1942 (X of 1942); Women's Habeas Corpus Ord. 1942 (XIII of 1942). Railway Air Raid Precautions Ord. 1942 (XXI of 1942).

2 Emergency Powers in the Indian Constitution

2.1 Introductory

Three types of emergencies are provided for in Part XVIII of the Indian Constitution,[294] *viz.*, those declared on grounds of "war or external aggression or armed rebellion"; those involving "breakdown of constitutional machinery" in the states and those of a financial/economic nature.

Turning to the law as it stood till 1975, the constitutional scheme in respect of the first type of emergency (a scheme which remained unchanged from the creation of the Indian Republic in 1950 up to 1975) empowered the President to proclaim a state of emergency if satisfied "that a grave emergency exists, whereby the security of India or of any part of the territory thereof is threatened, whether by war or external aggression or internal disturbance"[295] or if "there is imminent danger"[296] of such an occurrence. A later proclamation of emergency could revoke an earlier one.[297] *Ex post facto* parliamentary control was the main constitutionally provided restraining factor on the proclaiming power: thus a proclamation had to be laid before Parliament[298] and would automatically expire after two months unless affirmatively approved by resolutions of both Houses[299] although, if the Lower House was not in session or had been dissolved, and the Upper House had approved the proclamation, the latter would expire only if the Lower House did not approve it within thirty days of its reconstituted sitting.[300]

The effects of such a proclamation could be far-reaching. India's quasi-federal structure would be transformed into a unitary one. Parliament could make laws conferring powers or imposing duties even in respect of matters not enumerated in the Union List[301] and the state governments would be subject to executive directions from the Union on all matters.[302] Parliament was also expressly authorized to legislate on subjects under the State List, although such law would cease to have

[294] India Const. art. 352–360. *See also* India Const. art. 250.

[295] India Const. art. 352 § 1.

[296] India Const. art. 352 § 3.

[297] India Const. art. 352 § 2 cl. a.

[298] India Const. art. 352 § 2 cl. b.

[299] India Const. art. 352 § 2 cl. c.

[300] India Const. art. 352 § 2 cl. c., Proviso. The Upper House of the Indian Parliament is never "dissolved" as such, but one third of its members retire every two years: *See* India Const. art. 83.

[301] India Const. art. 353 (b). Parliament has exclusive power to legislate in respect of subjects listed in List I of the Seventh Schedule (the Union List); the States have exclusive power to legislate in respect of List II (the State List); both Parliament and States have legislative power in respect of List 3 (Concurrent List) although the Parliamentary Law would prevail over State Law in case of irreconcilable conflict.

[302] India Const. art. 353 (a).

effect six months after the expiry of the emergency proclamation.[303] The President could suspend all or any of the host of constitutional provisions prescribing in detail the rules governing distribution of revenues between the Union and the States during normal times,[304] although such Presidential order was required to be laid before each House of Parliament[305] and would cease to operate at the expiry of the financial year in which the proclamation of emergency had been made.[306] During the pendency of the emergency proclamation, laws could be enacted as if article 19 (guaranteeing seven fundamental rights[307]) did not exist, although such laws, to the extent that they violate article 19, would cease to have effect after the expiry of the emergency proclamation.[308] Additionally, the President could, by Order, declare that the right to move any court for the enforcement of such of the rights conferred by Part III of the Constitution as may be specified by the Presidential Order shall remain suspended during the emergency proclamation or for a stated shorter period[309] Such Presidential Order was, however, required to be laid before each House of Parliament.[310] Lastly, a provision akin to the Guaranty Clause of the US Constitution provided that it shall be the duty of the Union to protect every state against external aggression and internal disturbance and to ensure that the government of every state is carried on in accordance with the provisions of the Constitution.[311]

2.2 Travaux Preparatoires *Relating to Constitutional Provisions*

Although the Constituent Assembly, which sat from December 1946 to November 1949 to frame a Constitution for independent India, dealt with emergency provisions at various stages of its deliberations, there was, until May 1947, no proposal for comprehensive emergency provisions enabling the Union government to deal

[303] India Const. art. 250.

[304] India Const. art. 354 § 1. *See also* India Const. arts. 268–281 which prescribe in detail the rules governing such distribution of revenues during normal times.

[305] India Const. art. 354 § 2.

[306] India Const. art. 354 § 1.

[307] *See, e.g.*, right to free speech, assembly, association, movement, residence and practice of any trade or profession.

[308] India Const. art. 358.

[309] India Const. art. 359 § 1.

[310] ... protection against deprivation of life or liberty except according to procedure established by law (Art. 21); protection against arrest and detention in certain cases (Art. 22); rights against exploitation (Arts. 23 and 24); rights to freedom of religion (Arts. 25–28); protection of interests of minorities and their cultural and educational rights (Arts. 29–30); right to move the Supreme Court for enforcement of any of the preceding rights (Art. 32).

[311] India Const. art. 359 § 3.

with a national emergency at the central level. The discussion had initially centered upon the nature and scope of the Provincial Governor's emergency powers and revolved around clause 15 of the Provincial Constitution which dealt with the Governor's emergency powers.[312] One amendment sought to empower the Governor, if "satisfied that there is grave menace to the peace and tranquility of the Province or any part thereof," merely to "report" to the President of the Federation.[313] This was vehemently opposed[314] on a variety of grounds: that it gave no substantial power to deal with a grave emergency; that emergencies, by definition, arise suddenly and the man on the spot must be sufficiently well empowered to deal effectively and strongly with them and to ensure public safety; that legislative control and possible impeachment were adequate safeguards against Gubernatorial abuse of the power. For these reasons, an alternative amendment empowering the Governor to assume the functions of any provincial authority very much along the lines of Section 93 of the 1935 Act was proposed, and is reproduced below.[315] Two influential members of the Assembly, one of whom had authored the earlier "reporting" version, objected to this alternative,[316] saying that

---

[312]INDIA CONST. art. 355.

[313]Clause 15 of the memorandum of the Principles of a model Provincial constitution read as follows:

Special responsibilities of Governor:

> (1) In the exercise of his responsibilities, the Governor shall have the following special responsibility, namely, the prevention of any grave menace to the peace and tranquility of the Province or any part thereof.
>
> (2) In the Discharge of his special responsibility, the Governor shall act in his discretion: Provided that if at any time in the discharge of his special responsibility he considers it essential that provisions should be made by legislation, but is unable to secure such legislation, he shall make a report to the President of the Federation who may thereupon take such action as he considers appropriate under his emergency powers.

See 4 CONSTITUENT ASSEMBLY DEBATES, Book 1, 595 (Lok Sabha Secretariat, reprint 2014).

[314]*See* 4 CONSTITUENT ASSEMBLY DEBATES, Book 1, 708 (Lok Sabha Secretariat, reprint 2014) (amendment moved by H.N. Kunzru.)

[315]*See* the discussion at 4 CONSTITUENT ASSEMBLY DEBATES, Book 1, 763–782 (Lok Sabha Secretariat, reprint 2014). The main opposers were B.M. Gupta, K.M. Munshi, T. Prakasam, Pandit L.K. Maitra, B.G. Kher, P.K. Sen, N.G. Ranga, Vallabhbhai Patel.

[316]*See* 4 CONSTITUENT ASSEMBLY DEBATES, Book 1, 709 (Lok Sabha Secretariat, reprint 2014). Moved by K.M. Munshi, the amendment proposed the following clause in place of clause 15:

> (1) Where the Governor of a Province is satisfied in his discretion that a grave situation has arisen which threatens the peace and tranquility of the Province and that it is not possible to carry on the Government of the Province, with the advice of his Ministers in accordance with the provisions of Section 9 he may by proclamation, assume to himself all or any of the functions, of Government and all or any of the powers vested in or exercisable by any Provincial body or authority; and any such consequential provisions as may appear to him to be necessary or desirable for giving effect to the objects of the Proclamation including provisions for suspending in whole or in part of the operation of any provisions of this Act relating to any Provincial body or authority;

the vesting of extraordinary emergency power in the Governor, exercisable in his discretion, would be a subversion of the Cabinet form of Government, and that it would bypass the elected representatives of the people on whose advice alone the Governor should act.[317] It was also doubted if the Governor, who would otherwise be a nominal head of the State Government, would be able to take any effective administrative and executive steps to meet an emergency.[318] However, with Assembly members emphasizing the grave nature of an emergency and referring to the public disorder in West Bengal[319] and Burma (where various prominent Cabinet ministers had been assassinated in the recent past[320]), the alternative amendment giving discretionary emergency power to the Governor for a maximum of two weeks[321] was adopted.

A May 1947 memorandum on principles of the Union Constitution conferred a special responsibility on the President and allowed him to act in his discretion or overrule or ignore the advice of his Ministers for the "prevention of a grave menace to the peace and tranquility of the Union or of any part of it."[322] Another memorandum provided for a proclamation of emergency, due to "war or internal disturbance," where under the Union could legislate in place of the State Legislature and such law would prevail over any contrary state law.[323] A third memorandum entrusted the President with the power to make ordinances valid for six months, to deal with any "sudden emergency like a war, earthquake, epidemic or any other similar natural or man-made calamity."[324] "One member of the Assembly suggested that the President be empowered to maintain the integrity of the Constitution

---

Provided that nothing in this sub-section shall authorize the Governor to assume to himself any of the powers vested in or exercisable by a High Court or to suspend, either in whole or in part, the operation of any provision of the Act relating to High Courts.

(2) The Proclamation shall be forthwith communicated by the Governor to the President of the Union, who may thereupon take such action as he considers appropriate under his emergency powers.

(3) The Proclamation shall cease to operate at the expiration of two weeks, unless revoked earlier by the Governor himself or by the President of the Union.

[317]The "reporting" amendment had been moved by H.N. Kunzru. He was supported by Pandit G. B. Pant and also by Mr. H. Imam. *See* 4 CONSTITUENT ASSEMBLY DEBATES, Book 1, 774–776, 777–778 (Lok Sabha Secretariat, reprint 2014).

[318]*Id.*

[319]*Id.*

[320]*See, e.g.*, 4 CONSTITUENT ASSEMBLY DEBATES, Book 1, 769–70 (Lok Sabha Secretariat, reprint 2014) (T. Prakasa, mentioning the communal disorders of South India).

[321]*See, e.g.*, 4 CONSTITUENT ASSEMBLY D, Book 1, 764, 778, 780 (Lok Sabha Secretariat, reprint 2014) (by B.M. Gupta, N.G. Ranga and Vallabhbhai Patel).

[322]*See* 4 CONSTITUENT ASSEMBLY DEBATES, Book 1, 595 (Lok Sabha Secretariat, reprint 2014).

[323]By B.N. Rau. *See* Shiva Rao [25, p. 806]. *See also* the four volumes of Shiva Rao [26].

[324]By A.K. Ayyar & N.G. Vyyangar. *See*, Shiva Rao [27, p. 546].

and take necessary and sufficient action to meet any emergency that might arise in the Union."[325] Another dealt with the question of conflict between states or between a state and the union and suggested that the President on the advice of the Cabinet should have necessary emergency power to suspend or annul the legislative or executive acts of a provincial government.[326] A third member referred to the anomaly created by the Provincial model Constitution's requirement of reference of emergency action by the Governor to the President and the absence of any consequential Presidential emergency powers in the draft Union Constitution.[327] The provision proposed as an alternative by him,[328] however, dealt only with failure of constitutional machinery in the states (the predecessor of present article 356) rather than with a national emergency created by external or internal disturbance.

It is in the draft Constitution prepared by the constitutional Adviser in October 1947 that the direct genesis of the post-independence emergency provisions is found. Relying strongly upon the provisions of the Government of India Act 1935[329] draft article 182 empowered the federal legislature, during an emergency proclamation, to legislate in respect of matters falling within provincial legislative competence. This article, reproduced below,[330] was similar (though not identical) to the pre-1975 articles 352 and 353 under the Indian Constitution, especially in respect of the grounds for the President's satisfaction, the expanded legislative competence of the central legislature; the provision for revocation of an emergency proclamation, the provision regarding imminent danger and the requirement for affirmative resolutions. Similarly, draft article 191[331] empowered the Federal

---

[325] By K.J. Shah. *See* Shiva Rao [25, p. 806].

[326] By K.M. Pannikar. Shiva Rao [25, p. 806].

[327] By S.P. Mukerjee. *See* Shiva Rao [25, p. 806]. *See also*, Shiva Rao [27, p. 529].

[328] By K. Santhanam, 4 Constituent Assembly Debates, Book 1, 1006 (Lok Sabha Secretariat, reprint 2014).

[329] Santhanam's provision is reproduced in 4 Constituent Assembly Debates, Book 1, 1006 (Lok Sabha Secretariat, reprint 2014).

[330] *See*, Shiva Rao [28, pp. 75–76].

[331] (1) Notwithstanding anything in the preceding sections of this Part, the Federal Parliament shall have power: (a) if the President has declared by proclamation that a grave emergency exists whereby the security of India is threatened, whether by war or internal disturbance, then, to make laws for any province or any part thereof, and (b) if the President has, on receipt of a proclamation issued by the Governor of a Province under Section 160, declared by proclamation under this sub-section that a grave emergency exists whereby the peace and tranquility of that province is threatened, then, to make laws for that province or any part thereof, with respect to any of the matters enumerated in the Provincial Legislative List.

(2) Nothing in this section shall restrict the power of Provincial Legislature to make any law which under this Constitution it has power to make, but if any provision of a Provincial law is repugnant to any provision of a Federal law, which the Federal Parliament has under this section power to make, the Federal law, whether passed before or after the Provincial law shall prevail, and the Provincial law to the extent if the repugnancy, but so long only as the Federal law continues to have effect, be inoperative.

Government to give directions to the provincial executive authorities, as now found in article 353. These provisions were clearly modeled upon the 1935 Act.

The draft constitution presented by the Drafting Committee in January 1948[332] assumed even more closely the form of the post-independence emergency provisions. Draft article 275 was similar to article 352 except that the grounds for a proclamation were "war or domestic violence" and the period for affirmative parliamentary approval was six months. Articles 276, 277, 279 and 280 were mutatis mutandis, similar to articles 353, 354, 358, and 359, although in the last case, the power to suspend rights by Presidential Order did not require specification to the rights the enforcement of which was sought to be suspended.

The focus of the Constituent Assembly discussions was on the federal aspect of the Indian Constitution. Dr. Ambedkar, Chairman of the Drafting Committee, emphasized the flexibility of Indian federalism which would become unitary during an emergency and stressed that this virtue was absent in other federal systems like United States.[333]

It was on August 2, 1949 that Ambedkar proposed two amendments, to article 275 which led to the birth of what was later to be numbered article 352. He substituted "war or external aggression or internal disturbance" in place of "war or domestic violence" as the ground for proclaiming emergency and reduced the period for affirmative parliamentary resolutions from six to two months.[334] The article was then debated at length in the Assembly. Although parallels were drawn with the much abused article 48 of the Weimar Constitution,[335] the necessity for providing emergency powers in the Constitution was largely accepted.[336] Many

---

(3) A proclamation issued under clause (a) of clause (b) of sub-section (1) (in this Constitution referred to as "a Proclamation of Emergency")—(a) may be revoked by subsequent proclamation; (b) shall be laid before each House of the Federal Parliament; (c) shall cease to operate at the expiration of six months, unless before the expiration of that period if it has been approved by resolutions of both houses of the Federal Parliament.

(4) A law made by the Federal Parliament which the Parliament would not but for the issue of a Proclamation of Emergency have been competent to make shall to the extent of the incompetency cease to have effect on the expiration of a period of six months after the proclamation has ceased to operate, except as respects things done or omitted to be done before the expiration of the said period.

(5) A proclamation of Emergency declaring that the security of India is threatened by war or by internal disturbance may be made before the actual occurrence of war or any such disturbance if the President is satisfied that there is imminent danger thereof.

[332] *See*, Shiva Rao [28, p. 79].

[333] *See* Shiva Rao [28, p. 79].

[334] *See* 7 Constituent Assembly Debates, Book 2, 34–35 (Lok Sabha Secretariat, reprint 2014).

[335] 9 Constituent Assembly Debates, Book 4, 104 (Lok Sabha Secretariat, reprint 2014).

[336] 9 Constituent Assembly Debates, Book 4, 105 (Lok Sabha Secretariat, reprint 2014) (H.V. Kamath).

influential members supported the provision as a necessary evil,[337] indispensable for a nascent democracy like India which had yet to build up indigenous democratic institutions and conventions.[338] References were made to the Commander-in-Chief clause in the US Constitution provision for a state of siege.[339] The communal disturbances preceding independence and partition were also relied upon as a justification for residual emergency powers.[340] In respect of the grounds for proclaiming emergency, while some members thought that the specified grounds were not exhaustive enough and suggested alternatives like "economic crisis or subversive movement"[341] or revolt by a state,[342] others objected to the provision, inter alia, on the ground that it gave too broad and undefined a power to proclaim emergency,[343] that "disturbance" was too subjective a word and that it would allow a proclamation of emergency pursuant to a mere quarrel between political parties because of election fever.[344] The clause allowing issue of a proclamation on "imminence" of war or external aggression or "internal disturbance" was both criticized (on the ground that a power exercisable on mere apprehension was too broad and would allow abusive action on mere rumors or on inadequate data)[345] and supported (as necessary to make the emergency power effective).[346] It was suggested that power not only to revoke but also to "vary" a proclamation be given.[347] The proposal[348] to clarify that the President could act under article 275 only on the advice of the Council of Ministers was criticized on the ground that this was already implicit in the Constitution and the Cabinet form of Government and that its specification would imply that in other constitutional areas, the President could act independently of or against such advice.[349] Finally, however, Ambedkar's amended

---

[337] *Id.* at 109–110 (S.L. Saksena); *Id.* at 116 (Naziruddin Ahmed); *Id.* at 118 (Tajaul Hussain); *Id.* at 119 (M. Tyagi); *Id.* at 123 (T.T. Krishnamachari).

[338] *Id.* at 125 (T.T. Krishnamachari).

[339] *Id.* at 116 (N. Ahmed).

[340] *Id.* at 123 (T.T. Krishnamachari).

[341] *Id.* at 116 (Kazi Syed Karimuddin).

[342] *Id.* at 110 (Brajeshwar Prasad).

[343] *Id.* at 120 (M. Tyagi).

[344] *Id.* at 112–113 (K.T. Shah); *Id.* at 115 (Kazi Karimuddin).

[345] *Id.* at 115 (Kazi Karimuddin).

[346] *Id.* at 107 (H.V. Kamath).

[347] *Id.* at 121 (M. Tyagi).

[348] *Id.* at 125 (T.T. Krishnamachari). *Cf.* remarks of W. Ahmed (*Id.* at 117) who felt that the power to revoke a proclamation and issue a new one adequately covered the power to "vary" a proclamation.

[349] By H.V. Kamath (*Id.* at 108); P.S. Deshmukh (*Id.* at 114).

proposal was passed without change, and the three formal amendments by others were negatived.[350]

Article 276 of the draft constitution, later to become article 353 and modeled closely upon section 126-A of the 1935 Act, was adopted without much debate.[351] Two other provisions—articles 277-A and 278—which were later to become articles 355, 356 and 357 and which sought to dilute provincial autonomy during an emergency created by failure of constitutional machinery are discussed in detail in the next chapter.[352]

Article 277, of the Draft Constitution which was to become article 354 of the Constitution of India, was also the subject of much discussion because it allowed the President to modify, by order, any legal agreement or scheme between the Union and any state, for distribution of finances. The provision was vehemently opposed for variety of reasons: that it had no precursor in any other federal constitution in general and in the Government of India Act of 1935 in particular; that it put states at the mercy of the Union suddenly and without warning and thus institutionalized the "undiluted financial autocracy" of the Centre[353]; that it was too drastic a power as it affected not only the discretionary development grants from the Centre to the States but also those funds which the Centre was constitutionally or statutorily obliged to transfer to the States[354]; that such a drastic power would not be necessary even during war and, indeed, had not been required during the Second World War under the 1935 Act[355]; that the provision had not been proposed by either the Provincial or the Union Constitution Committees but was the brainchild of the Drafting Committee for which there was no warrant[356]; that if further strengthened the already excessive powers of the President at the cost of provincial autonomy and thus made a mockery of India's professedly dyarchical constitutional structure[357]; and that it would affect poor states, especially West Bengal, Bihar, Orissa and Assam, very adversely.[358] One member referred to the provision as a "new Frankenstein"[359] and many deemed it unnecessary and fit to be deleted[360];

[350]*See* 9 Constituent Assembly Debates, Book 4, 110 (Lok Sabha Secretariat, reprint 2014) (S.L. Saksena); *id. at* 117 (N. Ahmed); *id. at* 119 (T. Hussain); *id. at* 124 (T.T. Krishnamachari).

[351]*Id.* at 126.

[352]Mr. N. Ahmed's suggestion for transporting the non-obstante portion in the provision to the beginning of the article was not seriously pressed. *See* 9 Constituent Assembly Debates, Book 4, 129–130 (Lok Sabha Secretariat, reprint 2014).

[353]9 Constituent Assembly Debates, Book 4, 514 (Lok Sabha Secretariat, reprint 2014). (Biswanath Das).

[354]*Id.* at 508 (H.N. Kunzru).

[355]*Id.* at 511 (Renuka Ray).

[356]*Id.* at 513 (B. Das).

[357]*Id.* at 517 (B. Das).

[358]*Id.* at 515 (K. Chaha).

[359]*Id.* at 518 (B. Das).

[360]*Id.* at 517 (B. Das).

Kunzru, on the other hand, suggested a modification whereby the President, by Order, could delay the transfer of funds to a State during an emergency, but could not modify or deny (permanently) something agreed to earlier, on the basis of which the state had acted.[361]

Despite such opposition, the provision as proposed by Ambedkar was passed without amendment.[362] Its supporters, including Ambedkar, stressed its emergency nature and it was said that war could not be fought on principles applicable to normal times.[363] Ayyar emphasized[364] that the provision allowed modification which would be inconsistent with abrogation: states could not be starved of funds altogether and exceptions or modifications could not fundamentally alter the rule of distribution of revenues. He also said that Parliament already possessed, even in normal times, the power to vary the financial arrangements by law; they were thus not sacrosanct.[365] A staunch supporter of executive power found the provision necessary to correct the imbalance created by the Constitution in favor of states and said that article 277 was an essential reserve power.[366] The fact that the President would only act on the advice of the Cabinet[367] and the provision requiring laying of a proclamation under article 277 before Parliament were seen as safeguards. A proposal to require that the new financial arrangement be specified in the proclamation itself so that it could also be subjected to parliamentary scrutiny was rejected.[368]

Article 279, of the Draft, later to become article 358, was criticized for four primary reasons: that fundamental rights, by definition, were fundamental and should not be allowed to be suspended or abrogated[369]; that they were already subject to reasonable restrictions and hence their suspension under 279 was superfluous[370]; that, even if they were to be affected during an emergency, this should be permitted only by law made by Parliament and not by mere executive action[371]; and that the power in article 280 to suspend the enforcement of any fundamental right made the preceding article 279, which dealt only with one fundamental right, redundant.[372] Ambedkar, however, successfully piloted the

---

[361] *See, e.g.,* Renuka Ray (*Id.* at 511); B. Das (*Id.* at 513); K. Chahha (*Id.* at 515).

[362] *Id.* at 505–507.

[363] *Id.* at 522–23.

[364] *Id.* at 510 (Ayyar). *See also Id.* at 515–16 (Mrs. Durgabai); *Id.* at 516 (Krishnamoorthy Rao).

[365] *Id.* at 509.

[366] *Id.* at 510.

[367] *Id.* at 514–15 (Mr. Brayeshwar Prasad).

[368] *Id.* at 515–16 (Mrs. Durgabai).

[369] *Id.* at 508 (S.L. Saksena).

[370] *Id.* at 183 (P.S. Deshmukh).

[371] *Id.* at 181 (S.L. Saksena); 183 (H.V. Kamath); 184 (P.S. Deshmukh).

[372] *Id.* at 180 (S.L. Saksena).

provision, reasoning that as Parliament was already authorized during normal times to legislatively affect fundamental rights, provided such action was reasonable, this legislative power could not be denied to it during an emergency.[373] To a query[374] Ambedkar replied that the article did not provide for suspension: that occurred in the following article (viz., article 280). These reasons were not quite accurate because there is a clear difference between allowing Parliament to reasonably restrict fundamental rights, as provided in the various sub clauses of draft article 13 (now article 19), and in allowing Parliament to legislate as if that article did not exist. In the former case, courts can test legislative action on the touchstone of reasonableness and stated constitutional criteria; in the latter case, even an unconstitutional law would be immune from challenge on grounds of violation of draft article 13 (article 19). In any event, the two main amendments—giving Parliament and not the President the power under article 279 and allowing action only by "laws" and not executive action under article 279—were negative and Ambedkar's proposal was approved.

Fierce criticism of draft article 280, the predecessor of article 359, led Ambedkar to make some changes. The earlier version had sought to suspend the right in article 25 (presently article 32) and did not provide for the Presidential Order to be laid before Parliament. The critics argued,[375] inter alia, that no comparable provision could be found in the British, American, French, Italian or, indeed, any other constitution; that article 280 was superfluous as article 279 dealt with the most important fundamental right in draft article 13 (article 19) while many other rights (e.g., against untouchability cultural and educational rights, etc. not covered in article 13) had no relevance to an emergency; that the provision provided for had no parliamentary control; that the judiciary and the courts were one of the greatest hopes and most important for a redress for the citizen in an otherwise oppressive environment and that the provision unjustifiably took away the right to move the courts. Ambedkar made four changes: instead of suspending article 25, he provided for suspension of the enforcement of rights mentioned in the Presidential Order; required the Order to specify the article or rights involved; authorized suspension for the whole or part of India and stipulated that each Presidential Order be laid before Parliament. Although opposition to the provision persisted, the Assembly finally approved Ambedkar's proposal.[376]

---

[373]*Id.* at 182 (H.V. Kamath).

[374]*Id.* at 185 (B.R. Ambedkar).

[375]The critics included H.V. Kamath, S.L. Saksena, H.N. Kunzru, M. Tyagi, K.T. Shah and Thakur Das Bhargava. *See* 9 Constituent Assembly Debates, Book 4, 180–86, 523–554 (Lok Sabha Secretariat, reprint 2014).

[376]9 Constituent Assembly Debates, Book 4, 554 (Lok Sabha Secretariat, reprint 2014).

2.3 *Changes in Emergency Provisions During and After 1975*

In the wake of the declaration of emergency on June 25, 1975, which was qualitatively different from other earlier emergencies, there was a spate of constitutional amendments. The thirty-eighth constitutional amendment passed in that year added three clauses to article 352,[377] authorizing the issuance, by the President, of successive proclamations of emergency, on different times, in spite of the pendency of an earlier emergency proclamation[378]; making the satisfaction of the President recited in the proclamation "final and conclusive" and immune from being questioned in "any court on any ground"[379]; and making it clear that no court (including the Supreme Court) would have jurisdiction to entertain any question on any ground regarding the validity of declaration made by the President of the continued operation of such proclamation.[380] Article 359 was also amended to authorize state action affecting any rights in Part III of the Constitution to be taken in the same way as article 358 authorized state action affecting fundamental rights guaranteed in article 19.[381]

By the forty-second constitutional amendment passed the following year,[382] it was provided, inter alia, that proclamations of emergency could be made for the whole of India or for a specified part of its territory[383]; that a proclamation, apart from being revoked, could also be varied (with the parliamentary approval provisions applying, mutatis mutandis, to the varied proclamation)[384]; and that when emergency was proclaimed in a part of India, executive directions by the Centre to the States under article 353 could be given also to any state where emergency had not been proclaimed if the latter's security was threatened by the activities which had led to the proclamation.[385] Similarly, when emergency was declared only in a

---

377 With effect from Aug 1, 1975.

378 *Id.* cl. 4.

379 *Id.* cl. 5 (a).

380 *Id.* cl. 5 (b).

381 This was done by inserting clause (1A) in article 359, which read:

> (1A) While an order made under clause (1) mentioning any of the rights conferred by Part III is in operation nothing in that Part conferring those rights shall restrict the power of the State as defined in the said Part to make any law or to take any executive action which the State would but for the provisions contained in that Part to make or to take, but any law so made shall, to the extent of the incompetency, cease to have effect as soon as the orders aforesaid ceases to operate, except as respects things done or omitted to be done before the law so ceases to have effect.

382 With effect from December 18, 1976.

383 *Id.* cl. 48 (a).

384 *Id.* cl. 48 (b) and (c).

385 *Id.* cl. 49.

part of India, legislative action infringing article 19 or any other rights under Part III, in respect of a state whose territory was not subject to an emergency proclamation, was explicitly permitted by amending articles 358 and 359.[386]

After the revocation of emergency on March 21, 1977 and the installation of a government which was returned primarily as a vote against the emergency, there began a backtracking process of constitutional amendments[387] by seeking to amend article 352 with a view to make it more difficult to institute or continue a state of emergency. The grounds for a proclamation of emergency were restricted to "war or external aggression or armed rebellion,"[388] the last phrase being substituted in place of "internal disturbance." The President was prohibited from issuing a proclamation of emergency unless the decision of the Cabinet (consisting of the Prime Minister and her Council of Ministers as defined in article 75 of the Constitution) to this effect is communicated to him in writing.[389] This was done to preclude, in future, a repetition of the events on June 25–26, 1975, when, according to the Shah Commission, the then Prime Minister, acting purportedly under a Rule of Business of the Government of India communicated to the President her individual decision to declare emergency, obtained a proclamation of emergency from him shortly before midnight on June 25, 1975 and informed the members of her Cabinet of the declaration the next morning, after various arrests and detentions had already been effected under the emergency laws.[390] The period within which affirmative resolutions of each House are required for the continuance of the proclamation was also reduced from two to one month.[391] It was further added that a second similar and affirmative parliamentary approval would be needed six months after the first approval[392] and that the life of the proclamation could be extended at one time only by six months by successive affirmative resolutions.[393] Further, all such parliamentary resolutions were required to be passed only by a majority of the total membership of either House and by a majority of two-thirds of the members present and voting.[394] Any resolution by the Lower House disapproving of the continuance of the emergency would make it mandatory for the President to revoke the proclamation.[395] Additionally, if not less than a tenth of the total members of the Lower House give notice in writing to the Speaker (when the House is in session) or

---

[386] *Id.* cls. 52 and 53.

[387] With effect from June 10, 1979.

[388] *Id.* cl. 37 (a).

[389] *Id.* cl. 37 (b) inserting article 352(3).

[390] *See generally* the three volumes of the REPORT OF SHAH COMMISSION OF INQUIRY, dated 11/3/78, 26/4/78 and 6/8/78. *See also* 1 REPORT OF SHAH COMMISSION OF INQUIRY (1978) at ¶¶ 5.47, 5.49, 5.51, 5.55, 5.59 & 5.68.

[391] Constitution (Forty-Fourth) Amendment Act, No. 88 of 1978, INDIA CODE, (http://indiacode.nic.in/coiweb/amend/amend44.htm), cl. 37(b), inserting article 352(4).

[392] *See* INDIA CONST. art. 352 § 5.

[393] *See* INDIA CONST. art. 352 § 5 proviso.

[394] *See* INDIA CONST. art. 352 § 6.

[395] *See* INDIA CONST. art. 352 § 7.

to the President (when not in session), of their intention to move a resolution for disapproving an emergency proclamation or its continuance, a special sitting of the House was required mandatorily to be held within fourteen days from the date of the receipt of the notice by the Speaker or the President.[396] Finally, the clause earlier inserted which made the President's emergency proclamation final, conclusive and non-justiciable was deleted.[397] Significant changes were also made in articles 358 and 359. The former, which had allowed legislative and executive action as if article 19 did not exist, was made applicable only when an emergency declaration relating to war or external aggression was in operation.[398] In other words, the drastic powers of article 358 were not available during an internal emergency. Further, even during external emergencies, only those laws (and executive action only under such laws) would be protected from article 19 which contained a recital relating them to the proclamation of emergency in operation.[399] Article 359 was, in turn, amended to prohibit suspension of the rights conferred by articles 20 and 21[400]; previously, any right in Part III of the Constitution could be suspended. Finally, the immunity conferred (by article 359, as amended), upon laws (or executive action taken under laws) was confined only to laws containing a recital relating them to the proclamation of emergency in operation.[401]

2.4 *Some Legal Aspects of Emergency Powers*

2.4.1 Proclamation of Emergency

Discussions about safeguards to regulate the use of emergency powers have invariably focused on parliamentary or judicial controls after the institution of a state of emergency and have ignored the complementary and efficacious role of pre-proclamation safeguards. Prior to 1979, there were no formally prescribed procedures for the declaration of a state of emergency under the Indian Constitution. However, the Rules of Business for the Government of India, framed under article 77 of the Constitution,[402] required that cases specified in its second

[396] *See* INDIA CONST. art. 352 § 8.

[397] Constitution (Forty-Fourth) Amendment Act, No. 88 of 1978, INDIA CODE, (http://indiacode.nic.in/coiweb/amend/amend44.htm), cl. 37(d), inserting article 352(4).

[398] *Id.* cl. 39. *See* also INDIA CONST. art. 358 § 1.

[399] *See* INDIA CONST. art. 358 § 2 cls. a & b.

[400] *See* INDIA CONST. art. 359 § 1.

[401] *See* INDIA CONST. art. 359 § 1B.

[402] *See* INDIA CONST. art. 77 § 3, which reads, "The President shall make rules for more convenient transaction of the business of Government of India, and for the allocation among Ministers of the said business."

schedule should be brought before the cabinet.[403] The second schedule specified, inter alia, "cases relating to the proclamation of emergency under articles 352–360 of the Constitution and other matters related thereto." A practice developed, and it was observed in the 1962 and 1971 wars, whereby the Home Ministry forwarded the proposal for institution of a state of emergency to the Cabinet Secretariat for approval by the Cabinet prior to the issue of an appropriate proclamation under article 352. On June 1975, however, the then Prime Minister in a letter to the President advising an immediate proclamation of emergency, invoked Rule 12 of the Business Rules, which authorized her "in any case or classes of cases to permit or condone a departure from these Rules …".[404]

By doing so, prior Cabinet approval of the decision to issue a proclamation was obviated. The Shah Commission of Inquiry found that the then Prime Minister specifically sought advice from the then Chief Minister of West Bengal (a senior lawyer) on how to take a decision of the proclamation of emergency "without going to the Cabinet"[405]; that, except the Home Minister, no member of their Cabinet was even aware that such action was contemplated[406]; that the President of India and the Home Minister were informed only at 10.30 p.m. on June 25, 1975, and the

---

[403]Rule 7 of Government of India (Transaction of Business) Rules 1961; hereafter Rules of Business of Transaction of Business Rule.

[404]Mrs. Gandhi's letter to President Ahmed, dated 25.6.75, read:

> Dear Rashtrapatiji,
>
> As already explained to you, a little while ago, information has reached us which indicates that there is an imminent danger to the security of India being threatened by internal disturbance. The matter is extremely urgent.
>
> I would have liked to have taken this to Cabinet but unfortunately this is not possible tonight. I am, therefore, condoning or permitting a departure from the Government of India (Transaction of Business) Rule 1961, as amended up-to-date by virtue of my powers Rule 12 thereof. I shall mention the matter to the Cabinet first thing tomorrow morning.
>
> In the circumstances and in case you are so satisfied, a requisite Proclamation under Article 352(1) has become necessary. I am enclosing a copy of the draft Proclamation for your consideration. As you are aware, under Article 352(3) even when there is an imminent danger of such threat, as mentioned by me, the necessary Proclamation under Article 352(1) can be issued.
>
> I recommend that such a Proclamation should be issued tonight, however, late it may be and all arrangements will be made to make it public as early as possible thereafter.
>
> With kindest regards,
>
> Yours Sincerely,
>
> (sd/- Indra Gandhi)

1 Report of Shah Commission of Inquiry, 25 (1978).

[405]1 Report of Shah Commission of Inquiry (1978) at ¶ 5.47.

[406]*Id.* at ¶ 5.68.

proclamation issued shortly thereafter[407]; and that ex post facto Cabinet approval was secured at 6 a.m. the next morning after numerous individuals had already been detained.[408]

While it is clear that the declaration of June 25, 1975 involved a substantial departure from past practice, it is arguable and constitutionally plausible that the Prime Minister's acts were not illegal as Rule 12 was clearly designed to provide for a significant departure necessitated by the exigencies of the situation. Indeed, for this reason, the law was changed by a constitutional amendment in 1979 to require a decision of the Union Cabinet advising emergency rule to be communicated in writing to the President prior to a proclamation under article 352.

The legality of the departure from normal practice in 1975 would depend, in the first instance, upon a showing that reliance upon Rule 12 by the then Prime Minister was not justified by the prevailing facts and circumstances or was done for ulterior motives or on irrelevant considerations.

This presupposes, to some extent, judicial review of the proclamation of emergency, and advises tendered to the President. However, it is not clear whether, assuming that the Business Rules had been violated, the resultant executive action would be void or voidable. Some judicial decisions suggest that Rules for the Transaction of Business of various government departments are merely directory and not mandatory and that their violation does not give rise to any actionable claim.[409] Indeed, article 166 (3) itself, under which Rules of Business for State Governments are framed, has been regarded as directory on the ground that the language of the provision itself, which seeks only to authorize Rules for the "more convenient transaction of the business of the Government of the state," makes it non-mandatory.[410] No distinction can reasonably be made between article 165 (3) dealing with State Governments and article 77 (3) dealing with the Central Government. However, it is noteworthy that the Supreme Court has on one occasion quashed the grant of a forest contract by a government department on the ground that the latter did so without consulting the Finance Department of the State, as was required under the Rules of Business of the Bihar Government framed under article 166 (3).[411] In another decision, the Supreme Court has held Business Rules

---

[407] *Id.* at ¶¶ 5.49 & 5.51.

[408] *Id.* at ¶¶ 5.55 & 5.59.

[409] *See, inter alia*, State of UP v. Om Prakash Gupta AIR 1970 SC 679 (India); Arun Kumar Bhattacharjee v. State of West Bengal 1968 AIR 35 (Cal.); Khirod Saha v. State of Orissa (1982) Cri L.J. 1928 (Orissa HC); Chandrakant Karkharnis v. State of Maharashtra 1977 AIR 193 (Bom.) (Full Bench). A decision of the Supreme Court, Sanjeevi Naidu v. State of Madras AIR 1970 SC 1102 (India), relied upon in the Karkhanis decision, did not directly involve Article 77 (3) or 166 (3).

[410] Chandrakant Karkharnis v. State of Maharashtra 1977 AIR 193 (Bom.) at ¶ 22.

[411] Hardwar Singh v. Bagun Sumbrui AIR 1972 SC 1242 (India). With one exception, this solitary decision of the Supreme Court, which invests Rules of Business with some force, has not been cited in any of the contrary decisions cited earlier. However, in Khirod Saha v. State of Orissa (1982) Cri L.J. 1928 (Orissa HC), Misra, C.J. cited Hardwar Singh's case, but did not discuss it at all, much less distinguish it.

to be binding on the Government.[412] There are several High Court decisions which have relied on the Rules of Business as one of the grounds of invalidating executive action of questionable legality.[413] There is, therefore, some merit in the view that a showing of violation of Business Rules could make the resultant action legally invalid, but the question of justifiability and scrutiny of advice tendered to the President remains intractable.

The question whether a proclamation not revoked by the executive can cease to have effect because circumstances justifying it have ceased to exist is discussed in a later section on judicial review. It is, however, noteworthy that the earlier view expressed in Lakhanpal's case,[414] that a proclamation, once affirmed by parliamentary approval, can cease to have effect only upon Presidential revocation, is no longer applicable because the forty-fourth constitutional amendment requires successive affirmative parliamentary resolutions, each extending the life of the proclamation by not more than six months.[415] It is also noteworthy that the Privy Council has held that mandamus could lie to the Cabinet to revoke an old and obsolete emergency proclamation upon a showing of change of facts and circumstances which no longer justify the continuance of such a proclamation.[416] Although the decision in Lakhanpal's case suggests that it is not necessary to state in the proclamation of an emergency that the President is satisfied about the existence of an emergency,[417] it is submitted that this may be construed as an error and a fundamental defect on the face of the Presidential Order and be subject to invalidity on that account. On the other hand, it may not be correct to suggest, as the "the Constitution . . . does not contemplate the issue of an emergency upon an emergency already existing."[418] There was nothing in the Constitution prior to 1975 to prohibit the issuance of such proclamations. The thirty-eighth amendment's explicit authorization of such action, which was not deleted by the forty-fourth amendment and which continues to exist as article 352(9), further supports this interpretation.

---

[412]Fonseca v. L.C. Gupta AIR 1973 SC 563, 566 (India) (Grover & Mukherjea, JJ.) *See also* Administrator, 24 Parganas v. State of West Bengal, 1970 AIR 346 (Cal.).

[413]Ray v. State of Orissa, 1952 AIR 200 (Orissa) (Order of detention not passed by Home Minister, as required by Rules of Business, quashed); Jay Engg Works v. West Bengal 1968 AIR 407 (Cal.), (Government circular directing police to refer certain law and order questions to Labour Minister and not to intervene directly held invalid, *inter alia*, because Cabinet or Government cannot transfer matters to different Department or Minister in violation of Business Rules; para 189 (Roy, J.), amongst Special Bench of five judges).

[414]P.L. Lakhanpal v. Union of India, AIR 1967 SC 243 (India).

[415]India Const. art. 352 § 5 proviso as it stands present.

[416]Joh Cheng Poh v. Public Prosecutor, Malaysia (1979) 2 WLR 623. *See also* Minerva Mills v. Union of India AIR 1980 SC 1789, 1839–40 (India).

[417]P.L. Lakhanpal v. Union of India, AIR 1967 SC 243 (India).

[418]1 Report of Shah Commission of Inquiry (1978) at ¶ 5.69.

2.4.2 Effects of Emergency

While article 359 requires a Presidential Order to activate it, article 358 comes into operation *ipso jure* by the proclamation of emergency under article 352 and without any further executive or legislative action. The forty-fourth constitutional amendment in 1979 restricted its operation to an external emergency. In effect it allows the state to make laws or take legislative action as if article 19 did not exist. Before the forty-fourth amendment, not only could this drastic suspension of fundamental freedoms occur as a preordained constitutional consequence of the declaration of either internal or external emergency, but article 358 would also protect any executive action taken or law made during an emergency proclamation irrespective of the relation of such law or executive action to the emergency in force. In theory, therefore, a mindless executive order restricting the manufacture of, say, kites or similar trivia could be immunized from challenge on grounds of violation of article 19 (g), although the executive order may not have been passed with the emergency in view or for anything even remotely connected with the emergency. The forty-fourth constitutional amendment obviated this by protecting only those laws (or executive actions under laws) which recite their relationship to the emergency in operation.[419]

Although a whole host of questionable laws and executive actions of dubious validity, many having no relation to the emergency, have been prolonged and given life by article 358 during the subsistence of emergency proclamations between 1962–68 and 1971–77,[420] courts have also devised various doctrines for nullifying the preclusive effect of article 358 and for judicially examining legislative and

---

[419]INDIA CONST. art. 358 § 2.

[420]The following are some decisions upholding laws or executive actions on grounds of Article 358 (the nature of action law protected is given in brackets): Kesho Ram Kale Ram v. State of Punjab, 1964 AIR 307 (Punj.) (Order of Punjab Govt. U/r 125 (2), DOI Rules 1962, prohibiting production of gur); Girdharilal v. State of Punjab (1966) 68 Punj LR 390 (Cancellation of license quota by licensing authority); Himachal Transport Workers Union v. Secy H.P. Govt. 1967 AIR 21 (HP) (Scheme of modification u/Motor Vehicles Act); Devkumarsinghji Kasturichandji v. State 1967 AIR 268 (M.P.) (Constitutionality of § 4(4) of 1964 i.e. M.P. Tax statute); Gangadhar v. Union of India, 1967 AIR 142 (Goa) (Customs Act); Prithvi Cotton Mills v. Broach Borrough Municipality, 1968 AIR 124 (Guj.) (Levy of house tax) (*see* Prithvi Cotton Mills v. Broach Borrough Municipality, AIR 1970 SC 192); Puri v. Asst Controller RBI, 1969 ILR 698 (Del) (§ 18 B Foreign Exchange Regulation Act); Sushil Chander Anand v. State of UP, 1969 AIR 317 (Alld.) (Vritti, Vapar, Aajevika Aur Sevayojan Adhiniyam); Jaichand Lal Sethia v. State of West Bengal, AIR 1967 SC 483 (detention U/DoI Rules 1965); Marikar Motors v. Chief Enforcement Officer Madras, AIR (1973) Ker 2 (Emergency Risks (Goods) Insurance Act 1962); The Mirzapur Electric Supply v. State of Uttar Pradesh 1975 AIR 29 (Alld.) (Mirzapur Electricity (Supply) Act 1948); Shankarappa v. State of Karnataka (1975) 2 Kant LJ 288 (Cinema Rules 1974); Mathura Prasad Singh v. State of Bihar 1975 AIR 295 (Pat.) (Bihar Cooperative Societies (Second Amendment) Ordinance 1975); Gangadhar Sadhashiorao Watane v. State of Maharashtra, 1976 AIR 13 (Bom.) (Maharashtra Raw Cotton (procurement, processing and marketing) Act 1971); Amadalavalasa Cooper v. Union of India, AIR 1976 SC 958 (India) (Emergency (Risks) Goods and factories Insurance Act 1962); Kailashchand Khusalchand Bakliwal v. State of Maharashtra, (1977) 79 Bom. LR 449 (Maharashtra Debt Relief Act).

executive conduct so that there is a set of valuable safeguards. Firstly, only those laws and executive actions "which the state would but for the provisions contained (in article 19) . . . be competent to make or to take" are protected by article 358. Thus, for example, legislative may be challenged as being beyond the legislative competence of Parliament or the State Assembly, despite article 358. Secondly, as article 358 authorizes state action "while a proclamation of emergency is in operation" a law made before the proclamation of emergency is not protected. The leading authority for this proposition is the decisions in *State of Madhya Pradesh v. Thakur Bharat Singh* (1967)[421] where the Supreme Court invalidated a provision of the MP Public Security Act 1959 on the ground that it violated inter alia, article 19, and was not protected by article 356 because it was a pre-emergency statute. The rule has been repeatedly applied,[422] even to subject delegated legislation made during emergency to judicial scrutiny if it is made under pre-emergency primary legislation.[423] The crucial time for treating a law as pre- or post-emergency, would be the date of Presidential assent and not the date of coming into force of the law, if such a date were prescribed. Thirdly, and by an extension of the previous rule, executive actions during an emergency are not protected if they are an emanation of a pre-emergency law.[424] Fourthly, article 358 protects state action only against article 19; all other grounds of constitutional or legal challenge are open, if not otherwise suspended or precluded under article 359. Thus, not only may executive action be challenged for allegedly violating, say, article 301 of the Constitution,[425]

[421]State of Madhya Pradesh v. Thakur Bharat Singh, AIR 1967 SC 1170 (India) (Shah, J.).

[422]S.B. Tewari v. Union of India, 1963 AIR Assam 94 (Rule 149 Indian Railway Establishment Code challengeable as is it pre-emergency); Appukutty v. State of Kerala (1969) Lab IC 30 (Action U/ Essential commodities Act 1955, challengeable as 1955 Act is a pre-emergency statute); Bennett Coleman & Co. v. Union of India, AIR 1973 SC 106 (India) (Newsprint Import Policy of 1972–73, challengeable as it is continuation of earlier policy continued form year to year.); Delhi Police Karamchari Sangh v. Union of India (1974) 2 SLR 574 (Police forces (Restriction of Rights) Act 1966 challengeable as made before 1971 emergency proclamation) (*see also* Delhi Police Non-Gazetted Karamchari Singh v. Union of India, AIR 1987 SC 379, where the Supreme Court dismissed the appeal); Laxmi Touring Talkies v. State of Karnataka, 1975 AIR 37 (Kant) (Cinemas Act 1964) and 1971 Rules U/ it challengeable as pre-emergency law); Sadanand Shenoy v. State of Kerala (1975) KLT 647 (Motor Vehicles Rules 1961 challengeable as pre-emergency law); Pratap Singh Kadian v. State of Punjab, 1975 AIR 324 (P&H) (Punjab Wheat Order 1974 challengeable because it is under pre-emergency 1955 Essential Commodities Act); Bijoy Kumar v. State of Orissa, AIR 1976 SC 138 (India) (Orissa Paddy Procesment (Levy) Order 1974, made during emergency, challengeable as it is under pre-emergency 1955 Act); Dhanna Mal Sehaj Ram v. State of Punjab 1976 AIR 365 (P&H) (Punjab Wheat Dealers Licensing & Price Control (4th Amendment) Order 1974 challengeable as it is under pre-emergency 1955 Act); Shree Meenakshi Mills v. Union of India, 1974 AIR 200 (Alld.) (Executive action u/1955 by-law challengeable as it is pre-emergency law).

[423]*See, inter alia*, Pratap Singh Kadian v. Punjab, 1975 AIR 324 (P&H); Bijoy Kumar v. Orissa, AIR 1976 SC 138 (India); Dhanna Mal Sehaj Ram v. State of Punjab 1976 AIR 365 (P&H).

[424]*See* Bennett Coleman & Co. v. Union of India, AIR 1973 SC 106 (India).

[425]Gordhanlal Ramgopal v. Rajasthan 1976 AIR 151 (Raj.).

but also if it is ultra vires any Act[426] or is mala fide[427] or questionable on any of the usual grounds of judicial review of administrative action.[428] Fifthly, article 19 challenges are not precluded by article 358 during an internal emergency (though they may be so precluded under article 359). Sixthly, only laws containing a recital, as mentioned earlier, are protected and seventhly, executive action only under laws containing such a recital is protected. This last point is noteworthy because it suggests that before any executive action can qualify for immunity under article 358, it must be executive action taken under a law. Prior to the forty-fourth constitutional amendment, this had not been made clear and it was possible to argue, as was done in the Habeas Corpus case discussed in detail later, that executive action taken without authority of any law would be immunized from challenge on grounds of violation or article 19.

Turning to article 359, we find that although it does not automatically suspend any rights but requires, unlike article 358, an enabling Presidential Order in addition to a proclamation of emergency under article 352,[429] it is even wider in scope than article 358. Under article 359, a Presidential Order may suspend the enforcement of any of the articles in part III of the Constitution (except articles 20 and 21) while article 358 applies only to article 19. Prior to the forty-fourth constitutional amendment, even the enforcement of either of articles 20 or 21 could be suspended by Presidential Order under article 359. In practice, the Presidential Orders under article 359, inter alia, on October 26, 1962, December 5, 1971, December 23, 1974 and June 26, 1975 specified articles 14, 21 and 22 for suspension. It is noteworthy that article 359 (and indeed, also article 358) does not seek to "suspend" specified fundamental rights but rather authorizes a declaration that "the right to move any court for the enforcement of (the specified rights) . . . and all proceedings pending in any court for the enforcement of the rights so mentioned shall remain suspended." Although on the basis of this wording, it has been said[430] that article 359 "only" stays a declaration of invalidity during the emergency, what happens in effect is that all challenges on the basis of the specified articles are precluded: statutes, delegated legislation and executive action is all immunized from challenge, even if it be of

[426] District Collector, Hyderabad v. Ibrahim & Co., 1966 AIR 310 (Andhra Pradesh).

[427] Jaichand Lal Sethia v. State of West Bengal AIR 1967 SC 483 (India).

[428] *See* District Collector, Hyderabad v. Ibrahim & Co., 1966 AIR 310 (Andhra Pradesh); Jaichand Lal Sethia v. State of West Bengal AIR 1967 SC 483 (India).

[429] *See, inter alia*, Makhan Singh Tarsikka v. State of Punjab (1964) 4 SCR 797, (India) AIR 1964 SC 381 (India) paras 8 and 9; Union of India v. Bhanudas Gawde AIR 1977 SC 1027, 1041 (India).

[430] M.M. Pathak v. Union of India AIR 1978 SC 803, 811–12 (India) (Beg J.). On nature of Presidential Order under Article 359. *See also* Golak Nath v. Punjab, AIR 1967 SC 1643, 1656 (India); K.P. Singh v. Bihar, 1976 AIR 248 (Pat.).

pre-emergency vintage.[431] For all practical purpose, the specified articles become non-existent during the emergency. Moreover, the operational suspension of articles 14, 21 and 22, affects vital areas of life and liberty and confers an extensive immunity upon action from judicial scrutiny.

Courts have, however, innovatively sought to circumscribe the area of operation of article 359 and have, with one glaring aberration, confined this drastic emergency power to the narrowest limits. The first limiting factor is the language of the Order itself: a conditional Presidential Order, applying only to a specific statute or to one article of the Constitution or for a specified period, would be interpreted by strict adherence to its wording.[432] Thus a Presidential Order precluding challenges arising from the Defence of India Act would not preclude a challenge under MISA, despite the similarity or identity of the challenge. Further, executive action may be challenged as violating mandatory provision of an enactment.[433] For example, a detenu under MISA or COFEPOSA or the DOI Act, under either of which many of the cases involving article 359 arise, may be precluded from invoking article 22 of the Constitution if the latter is specified in an Order under article 359, but may nevertheless argue in a habeas corpus petition that the grounds of detention were not supplied to him in accordance with the relevant provision in the appropriate act. Such a challenge would be open to judicial scrutiny despite Order under article 359.[434] Then again, state action may be challenged on any of the usual grounds of judicial review of administrative action, viz., procedural impropriety, irrationality and illegality. Thus, for example, a detenu may argue that the order of detention is bad in law because it is ultra vires the Act or is vitiated by taking into account irrelevant considerations or by not taking into account relevant considerations or is an abuse of discretion or is so unreasonable that no reasonable man could come to

---

[431]Pre-emergency laws were held unchallengeable because of a Presidential Order U/A 359 in Bhaskay Textile Mills v. Jharsugda Municipality (1977) Tax LR 2177; Bhokta v. Bihar AIR (1976) Patna 345. A number of cases held detentions or other action under DOI Acts or MISA unchallengeable on grounds of violation of Articles 14, 19 or 21, due to the Presidential Order: Mohan Chowdhary v. Chief Commr, U T Tripura, AIR (1964) SC 173; Promode Das Gupta v. Deputy Secretary, West Bengal (1964–65) 69 CWN 913; Acharaj Singh v. Bihar, 1967 AIR 114 (Pat); Karunanidhi v. Raman, 1968 AIR 54 (Mad.); Niaz Khan v. UP (1973) Cri LJ 1344; Thomas v. Kerala, 1976 AIR 94 (Ker.); Patel v. West Bengal (1976) Cri LJ 783; Faridi v. Union of India, 1970 AIR 383 (Alld.); Das v. Union of India (1979) Cri LJ 493; Mali v. Maharashtra (1977) 79 Bom LR 189; Naidu v. AP, AIR 1977 SC 854; Uttarwar v. Maharashtra AIR (1977) Bom 99; Dharmarajan v. Union of India (1977) Cri LJ 230.

[432]Makhan Singh Tarsikka v. State of Punjab AIR 1964 SC 381 (India). On the Constitutionality of the Order, paras 13 & 33; Ghasi Ram v. Rajasthan, AIR (1966) Raj 247; Ananda Nambiar v. Chief Secy. Madras, AIR 1966 SC 657 (India).

[433]Makhan Singh Tarsikka, *id*; Ghatate v. Union of India 1975 AIR 324 (Bom); Joshi v. Maharashtra (1977) 79 Bom. LR 289; Sindha v. Ghosh (1975) 16 Guj LR 642; Milapchand v. Union of India (1975) WLN 750; Ghasi Ram v. Rajasthan AIR (1966) Raj 247; Atma Singh v. Punjab ILR (1976) 1 Punj 879; State of MP v. Thakur Bharat Singh, AIR 1967 SC 1170 (India); Kapoor v. Union of India (1975) Cri LJ 1376; Kasinathan v. Madras 1967 AIR 21 (Mad.); Venkateshamma v. State of A.P. 1976 AIR 1 (AP); Bhagwat Devi Paranjape (1976) Cri LJ 534.

[434]*Id.*

that conclusion.[435] It follows that challenges on grounds of mala fides are not precluded.[436] This includes both factual and legal mala fides, the latter being a much broader concept. Nor are challenges based on fundamental rights precluded. Thus, a detenu's plea that the conditions of his detention are violative of the Prison Rules or of another constitutional provision is not precluded by the Presidential Order suspending articles 14, 21 and 22.[437] A judicial inquiry to determine whether the petition raises any genuine question involving fundamental rights would not be precluded at the threshold by the Presidential Order,[438] especially if the petition alleges mala fides on the part of the detaining authority.[439] Moreover, executive action without the authority of law is not protected: the state may be asked to justify its action as lawful, despite an Order under article 359.[440] Courts normally interpret the 359 Order narrowly and disallow its extension by implication. Thus, challenges based upon constitutional provisions not specified in the Order are not precluded, even if the content of the right involved may overlap with the rights specified in the Order. For example, challenges based on article 16 would not be precluded merely because of the specification of article 14 in the Presidential order under article 359[441] although both articles 14 and 16 involve overlapping rights and freedoms. A detenu may also rely incidentally on article 19 to show that the court hearing his habeas corpus petition has jurisdiction to do so, although no challenge on the merits involving article 19 can be allowed.[442] A Presidential Order is inapplicable where a private party and not the state is involved. Thus a suit by a preemptor (by prior purchase) against the vendor and vendee of land is not affected by article 358 or 359 and can proceed.[443] Appeals to higher courts by respondents who have lost in lower

---

[435]These grounds of invalidity were urged as additional grounds in many of the cases cited in the preceding note and were held not to be excluded by Article 359.

[436]Makhan Singh; Darshan Singh v. State of Punjab (1975) Cri LJ 1974; Ghasi Ram v. Rajasthan AIR (1966) Raj 247; Kapoor v. Union of India (1975) Cri LJ 1376; Ram Manohar Lohia v. State of Bihar AIR 1965 SC 740 (India).

[437]Awasthi v. UP AIR (1976) Alld. 414; Abdulla v. State (1976) Cri LJ 320; Dholakia v. Pillai (1975) LJ 1813; Gordhanla Rangopal v. Rajasthan AIR (1976) Raj 157; Maharashtra v. Sanzgiri AIR 1965 SC 424 (India).

[438]Jamdade v. Maharashtra AIR (1977) Bom. 355. Nene v. Secy. Urban Development AIR (1977) Bom. 367.

[439]Makhan Singh AIR 1964 SC 381, 400 (India) (per Gajendragadkar J.).

[440]Manekben v. Union of India ILR (1975) Del. 820; State of MP v. Thakur Bharat Singh, AIR 1967 SC 1170 (India); Joshi v. Maharashtra (1977) 79 Bom. LR 289; Maharashtra v. Sanzgiri AIR 1965 SC 424 (India); District Collector, Hyderabad v. Ibrahim & Co. AIR 1966 AP 310 (India).

[441]Arjun Singh v. Rajasthan AIR (1975) Raj 217; Iswahrbhai v. Gujarat (1978) Lab IC 235; Lt. Governor v. Dalip Singh (1976) 2 SLR 156; Sahay v. Bihar (1979) 3 SLR 635; Narain v. Bihar (1973) BLJR 122; Rameshwar Pd. v. Union of India (1977) Lab IC (NOC) 31; Sharma v. Director Public Rel. (1977) Lah IC (Noc) 59.

[442]Manjulaben v. Pillay (1976) Cri LJ 889.

[443]Krishen Lal v. Babboo Raj AIR (1977) J&K 58.

courts in cases where the petitioners succeeded on grounds of violation of fundamental rights are not precluded, as the appeals are not proceedings for the enforcement of fundamental rights but rather for their deletion.[444]

The position as far as interim orders are concerned is vexed and complicated, reflecting divergent judicial approaches. According to one view, interim orders obtained before the emergency must be vacated because otherwise it would amount to continued enforcement of fundamental rights.[445] On the same reasoning courts have also refused to grant interim orders during the pendency of a Presidential Order.[446] Another view is that pre-emergency interim orders cannot be varied or vacated. A third view is that interim orders in pre-emergency proceedings may be varied or continued or vacated during the pendency of a Presidential Order but an altogether fresh order is precluded.[447]

Some other ways of avoiding the effects of a Presidential Order have been rejected by the Courts. Challenges on the basis that the law in question has nothing to do with the emergency and therefore ought not to be protected by article 359 have been disallowed.[448] Similarly, an earlier and somewhat remarkable Supreme Court decision[449] subjecting the Presidential Order under article 359 to the test of validity under article 14 was expressly overruled by a later decision,[450] because an Order could not logically be tested on the touchstone of what was suspended.

In *A.D.M. Jabalpur v. Shiv Kant Shukla*,[451] the Supreme Court by a majority of four to one[452] deviated from its earlier approach and departed from established judicial precedents, to allow article 359 to have a blanket preclusive effect on

---

[444] Lt. Governor Dalim Singh (1976) 2 SLR 156; State of Orissa v. Khageshwar Das, AIR 1975 SC 1906 (India).

[445] Kanhaialal Agarwal v. Union of India (1976), 1 Cal LJ 293; K.P. Singh v. Bihar 1976 AIR 248 (Patna); Moyin v. Pathumma (1976) Ker LT 87.

[446] Radha Krishna Agarwal v. Bihar AIR 1977 SC 1496 (India); K.P. Singh v. Bihar 1976 AIR 248 (Patna).

[447] Raj Kr. Rajindra Singh v. Union of India AIR (1976) HP 34. Indeed, if the reason of the only Supreme Court judgement on the subject (Radha Krishna Agarwal v. Bihar AIR 1977 SC 1496 (India)—that the grant of an interim order during Article 359 Presidential Order would amount to enforcement of fundamental right—were extended, it would suggest that pre-existing interim order must be vacated during the pendency of a Presidential Order, otherwise they would amount to indirect enforcement of fundamental rights.

[448] ARN Ct. Firm, Chettiar Bank v. Tamil Nadu (1978) 11 Mad LW 438; Atma Singh v. Punjab ILR (1976) 1 Punj 879; Watane v. Maharashtra AIR (1976) Bom 13.

[449] Ghulam Sarwar v. Union of India, AIR 1967 SC 1335 (Subba Rao, C.J.).

[450] Mohd. Yakub v. J&K AIR (1969) SC 765. See Niaz Khan v. UP (1973) Cri LJ 1344.

[451] A.D.M. Jabalpur v. Shiv Kant Shukla, AIR 1976 SC 1207 (India) (hereafter *Shukla's Case*).

[452] The majority comprised Ray, C.J. Beg, Chandrachud and Bhagwati JJ.; Khanna, J. dissented.

judicial review.[453] The decision has now been expressly overruled by the Supreme Court[454] and it is unlikely that this judicial aberration will ever serve as a precedent for the future more particularly because of the forty-fourth constitutional amendment. The judgement, however, merits analysis not only as an example of grievous judicial error but also for the more positive purpose of providing proper safeguards in an integrated framework of constitutional norms.

A number of detenus who had been detained under MISA 1971 challenged their detentions by writ of habeas corpus on diverse grounds. When the petitions came up for hearing in different High Courts, a preliminary objection was raised on behalf of the States to their maintainability, arguing, inter alia, that in seeking their release on habeas corpus, the petitioners were in substance claiming that they had been deprived of their personal liberty in violation of procedure established by law. As this was a right guaranteed to them only by article 21 of the Constitution, and as the latter, along with articles 14 and 22, had been suspended by a Presidential Order under article 359 issued on June 27, 1975, the petitions, the Government argued, were liable to be dismissed at the threshold. Nine High Courts rejected the government's preliminary objection and held the petitions to be maintainable.[455] Three High Courts upheld the preliminary objection.[456] By a majority of four to one, the Constitution Bench of the Supreme Court held that

> In view of the Presidential Order dated 27th June 1975 no person has any locus standi to move any writ petition under Article 226 before a High Court for habeas corpus or any other writ or order or direction to challenge the legality of an order of detention on the ground that the order is not under or in compliance with the Act or is illegal or is vitiated by mala fides factual or legal or is based on extraneous considerations.[455A]

The judgement and order of the Supreme Court was patently wrong because a number of earlier decisions had upheld a variety of grounds of challenge to a detention order, despite a Presidential Order under article 359. These grounds of challenge accepted earlier by the courts have included violation of the mandatory provisions of the Act under which detention was made: its ultra vires nature, the mala fide nature of the order, excessive delegation etc. It is noteworthy that these various grounds of challenge were unanimously accepted by a seven-judge bench

---

[453]The Court held that during the operation of a Presidential Order under Article 359, detenus under MISA 1971 could challenge their detention only if it was ex facie bad (e.g., not signed by the proper authority or issued for a different purpose) and not on any ground, including mala fides. Even the limited grounds of challenge mentioned above were accepted only on the basis of concession made by the Attorney General on behalf of the State. In view of the preceding discussion showing how courts have often avoided the preclusive effects of an Article 359 Order on other grounds, it is not clear that the decision in Shukla's Case is irreconcilable with earlier precedents.

[454]Justice K.S. Puttaswamy v. Union of India (2017) 10 SCC 1, 419–20.

[455]These were the High Courts of Allahabad, Andhra Pradesh, Bombay, Delhi, Karnataka, Madras, Madhya Pradesh, Punjab & Haryana; and Rajasthan.

[456]These were the High Courts of Kerala and Andhra Pradesh.

[455A] A.D.M. Jabalpur v. Shiv Kant Shukla, AIR 1976 SC 1207, 1392 (India).

of the Supreme Court in *Makhan Singh Tarsikka v. State of Punjab* (1964)[457] which was binding on the bench of five judges in *Shukla*. The inescapable conclusion of the *Makhan Singh* court was circumvented by the *Shukla* court on the most specious pleas, viz., that the Presidential Order under article 359 in issue in *Makhan Singh* was a conditional one, which suspended enforcement of constitutional rights by persons "deprived of any such rights under the Defence of India Ordinance 1962, or any Rule or Order made there under" whereas these words were missing from the Presidential Order in issue in *Shukla*.[458] This distinction between the two Orders did certainly exist, but it could not justify the conclusion reached by the Court in *Shukla*. If a detenu under the DOI Act[459] could challenge his detention despite a conditional Order as in *Makhan Singh*, how could a detenu under MISA be deprived in *Shukla* from doing so on the same grounds? The conditional nature of the Order in *Makhan Singh* only meant that detenus under DOI Acts were precluded from relying upon the suspended articles; as the Presidential Order in *Shukla* did not specify and condition, any detenu (whether under MISA or otherwise) could challenge it on grounds accepted in *Makhan Singh*. Indeed, in one sense, the conditionality of the *Makhan Singh* Order made it more, not less onerous for the detenu; the absence of conditionality in *Shukla* Order made it easier for any detenu (and not only one under DOI Act) to challenge his detention (on the same grounds as in *Makhan Singh*). In other words, the distinction between the two cases related to the kind of detenu eligible to challenge and not to the grounds of challenge.[460]

Makhan Singh was also sought to be distinguished by the Court on the ground that the observations in that case regarding the pleas open to the detenu, despite the 1962 Presidential Order, were obiter dicta. This reason is also fallacious and shows a regrettable recession in the Court's concern for personal liberty in *Shukla*. *Makhan Singh* listed a number of grounds of challenge open to the detenus, despite the 359 Order. These grounds included excessive delegation of legislative power under the detention Act and the detention Act being a colorable piece of legislation. On each of these grounds the *Makhan Singh* held against the detenus on the merits. The consideration of these pleas by the court on the merits shows that they were open to the detenus and were not barred by the Presidential Order. It cannot, therefore, be said that the remarks of the *Makhan Singh* on this issue were merely obiter dicta.

The final operative part of the order in *Shukla*[461] omitted even to mention the one ground of challenge which could be open to the detenus and which was conceded by the Attorney General and accepted by the *Shukla* itself, *viz.*, the case of

---

[457]Makhan Singh Tarsikka v. State of Punjab, AIR 1964 SC 381 (India).

[458]*See* the distinction drawn in A.D.M. Jabalpur v. Shiv Kant Shukla, AIR 1976 SC 1207, 1227 (Ray, C.J.,); *id* at 1341–42 (Chandrachud, J.); 1377–79 (Bhagwati, J.).

[459]That is, Defense of India Act.

[460]On conditionality, *see also* Seervai [30, pp. 1045–1046].

[461]A.D.M. Jabalpur v. Shiv Kant Shukla, AIR 1976 SC 1207, 1392 (India).

a detention order being ex-facie illegal.[462] A judge of the majority bench in Shukla's case said in a later decision that the common order of the majority in *Shukla* was badly drafted and did not accurately reflect the decision of the majority or its individual members.[463]

All the elaborate distinctions drawn in respect of earlier decisions,[464] the grand sentiments expressed in favor of personal liberty,[465] the confident optimism against abuse of State power[466] and the emphatic reassurance about the "maternal care"

[462]It is also submitted that the acceptance of this one ground of challenge is irreconcilable with the acceptance of lawless executive action. As Seervai puts it:

> Once it is admitted that non-compliance with the law in respect of the aforesaid three specified requirements furnishes a ground for setting aside the order of detention, and releasing the detenu on a petition for habeas corpus, there is no justification for limiting illegality to these three grounds … King Canute is said to have bid the waves of the sea "to go thus far and no further". A court must equally fail if it says to illegality "thus far and no further.
>
> Seervai [30, p. 1040].

[463]*See In Re* Shyam Lal, AIR 1978 SC 489, 494–95 (India) (Beg, J.):

> It is true that this Court held that preventive detention was practically removed from judicial supervision during an Emergency. The common statement of a conclusion at the end of the judgements in the Habeas Corpus cases based on the majority view but signed by all the judges, including Khanna J., was perhaps misleading as it gave the impression that no petition at all would lie under either Article 226 or 32 to assert the right of personal liberty because the locus standi of the citizen was suspended.
>
> Had a review petition been filed before us, I would have certainly made it clear that the statement of a conclusion reached by the majority did not accurately set out at least my conclusion which is found at the end of my judgement. It seems to me that the majority conclusion is rather loosely and vaguely expressed at the end of our judgements. A legitimate criticism could, therefore, be that the Court should draft and state its majority conclusions better.

[464]*See, e.g.*, relating to Makhan Singh Tarsikka v. State of Punjab.

[465]*Id.* at 1384–85 (Bhagwati, J.).

> …[T]he rule of law which, since the dawn of political history, both in the India of Brahadaranyaka Upanishad and Greece of Aristotle, has tamed arbitrary exercise of power by the Government and constitutes one of the basic tenets of constitutionalism.

[466]*Id.* at 1349 (Chandrachud, J.).

> Counsel after counsel expressed the fear that during the emergency, the executive may whip and strip and starve the detenu and if this be out judgement even shoot him down. Such misdeeds have not tarnished the record of Free India and I have diamond-bright diamond-hard hope that such things will never come to pass.

bestowed by the state upon its detenus[467] does not salvage the judgement in *Shukla* from being legally and logically indefensible. It formally denied the right to challenge state action on grounds of mala fides,[468] perhaps the only decision of the highest court of any common law country to do so. It is not surprising that *Shukla* has been compared[469] to the majority decision in *Liversidge v. Anderson* by the House of Lords in Great Britain[470] and has been referred to as the "most glaring instance in which the Supreme Court of India has suffered most severely from a self-inflicted wound."[471]

2.5 Post-independence Emergencies

2.5.1 War Emergencies

Although India has faced much by way of external aggression and full-scale wars since the adoption of the Constitution (e.g. China in 1962,[472] and with Pakistan in 1965 and 1971[473]) only two emergency proclamations were issued on grounds of external aggression because the first proclamation of 1962 was revoked only in 1968 and covered the 1965 war.[474] Presidential Orders under article 359 were issued twice during the pendency of the first two proclamations (on November 3,

---

[467] *Id.* at 1319 (Beg, J.)

> Furthermore, we understand that the care and concern bestowed by the state authorities upon the welfare of detenus who are well housed, well fed and well treated, is almost maternal.

[468] *See* A.D.M. Jabalpur v. Shiv Kant Shukla, AIR 1976 SC 1207, 1392 (India).

[469] Seervai [30, p. 1040].

[470] (1941) 3 ALL E.R. 338.

[471] Seervai [30, p. 1048].

[472] The Proclamation issued on October 26, 1962 read:

> In exercise of the powers conferred by clause (1) of Article 352 of the Constitution, I, Sarveplalli Radhakrishnan, President of India, by this proclamation declare that a grave emergency exists whereby the security of India is threatened by external aggression.

It was revoked on Jan 10, 1968.

[473] The Proclamation of the powers conferred by clause (1) of Article 352 of the Constitution, I, V. V. Giri, President of India, by this Proclamation declare that a grave emergency exists whereby the security of India is threatened by external aggression."It was revoked on March 27, 1977.

[474] The third emergency proclamation was issued during peacetime on June 25, 1975 during the subsistence of the second, and both were revoked on March 27, 1977.

1962, and on November 11, 1962). The first suspended the right to move courts for the enforcement of articles 21 and 22 and the second added article 14 to that list.[475] It is noteworthy that no suspension of constitutional rights under article 359 occurred during the 1971 war emergency.

The primary instrument of statutory regulation during the post-independence war emergencies were the Defence of India Act (DOI Act) and the Rules made thereunder. DOI Acts were enacted in 1962 and in 1971 and were modeled primarily on DOI Act 1939 during British rule. The DOI Act 1962 was used for both the 1962 and 1965 conflicts while DOI Act 1971, amended and renamed in 1975 as Defence and Internal Security of India Act 1971,[476] was also used for the 1975 emergency, which is discussed later. These enactments were to continue in force during the pendency of the emergency proclamation and for a period of six months thereafter, after which they would automatically expire.[477] Each enactment had a detailed set of Rules made under its authority. Broadly, the most significant provision of the Act of 1962 was undoubtedly that which empowered the Central Government to make Rules "as appear to it necessary or expedient" for a variety of purposes mentioned in the provision itself.[478] These broad heads of rule-making power comprised defence of India, civil defence, public safety, maintenance of public order, efficient conduct of military operations and maintenance of supplies and services essential to the life of the community.[479] In addition, and without prejudice to the generality of the aforesaid, a list of fifty seven subjects was given concerning which Rules could be made. The subjects covered a wide variety of matters and ranged from the ensuring the safety and welfare of the armed forces[480] to the "control of lights and

---

[475]The first Presidential Order read:

> In exercise of the powers conferred by clause (1) of Article 359 of the Constitution, the President hereby declares that the right any person to move any court for the enforcement of the rights conferred by *Article 21 and Article 22 of the Constitution shall remain suspended for the period during which the Proclamation of Emergency issued under clause (1) of Article 252 on the 26th October, 1962 is in force, if such person has been deprived of any such rights under the Defense of India (Ordinance, 1962 (of 1962)) or any rule or order made thereunder.
>
> *Art. 14 was later added.

[476]By the Defense of India (Amendment) Act, 1975, No. 32, Acts of Parliament, 1975 (India) at § 4.

[477]The Defence of India Act, No. 51 of 1962, GAZETTE OF INDIA, Pt. II sec. 1 (Dec. 12, 1962) at § 1 (3); The Defence of India Act, No. 42 of 1971, GAZETTE OF INDIA, Pt. II sec. 1 (Dec. 4, 1971) at §1 (3).

[478]The Defence of India Act, No. 51 of 1962, GAZETTE OF INDIA, Pt. II sec. 1 (Dec. 12, 1962) at § 3.

[479]*Id.*

[480]*Id.* at § 3(2).

sounds."[481] Parts III,[482] V[483] and VI[484] of the Act dealt, respectively, with Civil Defence, Employment of Technical Personnel in the National Service and Requisitioning and Acquisition of Property. Part IV authorized the setting up of special tribunals to deal with disputes involving, inter alia, any of the fifty seven subjects enumerated in the Act. These tribunals would follow a special and speedier procedure[485] and could exclude the public from their proceedings.[486] Details regarding the composition of the tribunals were also provided.[487] The Rules made under DOI Act 1962[488] dealt more specifically and in greater detail with particular issues. They were grouped subjectwise, and included Rules regarding access to certain premises and areas; control of signaling, telegraphy and postal communication; restriction of movements and activities of persons; prevention of prejudicial acts and control of information; false representations; public safety and order; requisition and acquisition of moveable property; essential supplies and work; transport; imports and exports; trading with the enemy etc. Special sets of rules regarding requisition and acquisition were also issued in 1962 and 1971.

Criminal penalties for violation of the Act or Rules were prescribed. Violation of section 3 of the Act or Rules were prescribed. Violation of section 3 of the Act or any rule or order made thereunder, if done with intent to wage war against India, was made liable to enhanced penalties, including death of life imprisonment or ten-year imprisonment or a fine.[489] Both the Act and the Rules were declared to have effect notwithstanding any other law[490]: the Rules were thus given overriding effect over other statutes. Rules were required to be laid before Parliament "as soon as may be" after their making and Parliament could modify them within thirty days.[491] It is noteworthy that with a few minor changes, the DOI Act 1971 and Rules thereunder were almost identical to the 1962 Act and Rules.

The internal effects of the war emergencies were not particularly far-reaching. Although the DOI Acts of 1962 and 1971 authorized intrusions into civil liberties, there were few such actual invasions and the various fundamental rights and freedoms specified in the Constitution remained substantially unimpaired. Indeed, during the 1971 emergency proclamation, there was no Presidential Order under article 359 of the Constitution. Censorship, drastic controls over rights and freedoms of free expression, of association, of assembly, practicing of trade or

[481] *Id.* at § 3(2) (13).

[482] *Id.* at §§ 7–12.

[483] *Id.* at §§ 19–28.

[484] *Id.* at §§ 29–39.

[485] *Id.* at § 15.

[486] *Id.* at § 16.

[487] *Id.* at § 13.

[488] The Rules can be found, *inter alia*, in Shukla [32].

[489] The Defence of India Act, No. 51 of 1962, Gazette of India, Pt. II sec. 1 (Dec. 12, 1962) at § 5.

[490] *Id.* at § 43.

[491] *Id.* at § 41.

profession, or of movement, were, with one exception, either non-existent or barely noticeable. The exception related to the group of powers found in Rule 30 of DOI Rules 1962, which authorized, inter alia, detention or exclusion or imposition of restrictions on movements of individuals in respect of whom the Central Government is "satisfied that it is necessary to do so" for one of the purposes mentioned in the Rules. It is noteworthy that this power is not found in DOI Act 1971 and detentions after 1971 were resorted to under MISA 1971 of COFEPOSA 1974. During the 1962 and 1971 emergency proclamations, the detention power was carefully circumscribed and the number of detentions was limited.[492]

Indeed, the various decisions discussed earlier which sought to avoid the all-embracing preclusive effects of articles 358 and 359 were evolved in detention cases during the 1960s and early 1970s. Courts emphasized that "satisfied" in the 1962 Act and Rules meant "reasonably satisfied" and the satisfaction must be honest, careful, deliberate and arrived at after exercising due care and caution.[493] Although there were differences on the scope and degree of judicial review, especially of the grounds of detention, some review was widely accepted and mala fides or arbitrary or grossly unreasonable or patently illegal exercise of executive power in respect of detention was clearly liable to be invalidated.[494] Similar principles of judicial review of administrative action were applicable under MISA 1971 or COFEPOSA 1974 prior to the 1975 emergency proclamation. Moreover, various safeguards were available under these enactments prior to the 1975 emergency. Under MISA, the grounds of detention had to be disclosed to persons affected by the order[495] and he had to be afforded the "earliest opportunity" of making a representation.[496] Within thirty days of the date of the detention order, the grounds, along with the representation, if any, were required to be placed before an Advisory Board[497] comprising three persons eligible for appointment as High Court judges and headed by a sitting or former judge of the High Court.[498] The Board could choose to call for further representations or information and was required to submit a report to the Government within ten weeks from the date of detention.[499] The Government was empowered to confirm a detention order, if the Board found, in its opinion, sufficient cause for the detention.[500] But where the Board found to the contrary, the Government was obliged mandatorily to revoke the detention

[492](Blank).

[493]*Re* Venkat Raman AIR (1949) Madras 529; Kamla Kant Azad v. Emperor 1944 AIR 354 (Patna).

[494]Shibnath Banerjee v. Porter AIR (1943) Cal. 377; Prabhakar Kesheo Tare v. Emperor 1943 AIR 26 (Nag).

[495]Maintenance of Internal Security Act, No. 26 of 1971, India Code, § 8 http://indiacode.nic.in/fullact1.asp?tfnm=197126.

[496]*Id.*

[497]*Id.* at § 10.

[498]*Id.* at § 9.

[499]*Id.* at § 11.

[500]*Id.* at § 12 cl. 1.

order.[501] In any event, no one except a foreigner could be detained for longer than one year.[502] This position, combined with judicial assertion of its power to review arbitrary, male fide, unreasonable detention orders, or those made in violation of any mandatory provision of the Act, mentioned earlier, provides an interesting and instructive contrast to the period of the 1975 emergency.

2.5.2 The 1975 Peacetime Emergency

The internal effects of the emergency declared on June 25, 1975,[503] went far beyond anything experienced during the emergencies of the 1960s or of 1971. Clearly, unlike the earlier wartime emergencies, the 1975 declaration involved an extensive countrywide curtailment of civil liberties, a recession in the scope of judicial review and an imposition of strict censorship on the press.[504]

The following account of the emergency is culled from the Shah Commission Report, which with all its shortcomings and infirmities[505] remain the primary source material for that period.[506]

---

[501] *Id.* at § 12 cl. 2.

[502] *Id.* at § 13 read with § 17.

[503] The emergency proclamation read:

> In exercise of the powers conferred by clause (1) of Article 352 of the Constitution, I Fakhruddin Ali Ahmad, President of India by this Proclamation declare that a grave emergency exists whereby the security of India is threatened by internal disturbances.

[504] Summarizing the position existing during the 1975 emergency, a judge of the Supreme Court noted: "(1) That grave emergency was clamped in the whole country; (2) that civil liberties were withdrawn to a great extent; (3) that important fundamental rights of the people were suspended; (4) that strict censorship on the press was placed; and (5) that the judicial powers were crippled to a large extent.") State of Rajasthan v. Union of India, AIR 1977 SC 1361, 1438–39 (India) (Fazl Ali, J.). *See also In Re* Special Courts Bill 1978, (1979) 1 SCC 380, 426–27 (Chandrachud, C.J.).

[505] It must be remembered that the Commission was appointed during a period of national euphoria by a successor government to investigate the alleged malpractices of a predecessor government; that some of its procedures for the collection and analysis of evidence have been found by a single judge of the Delhi High Court to have been contrary to the law and unconstitutional (*See* Indira Nehru Gandhi v. J.C. Shah Commission of Inquiry (ILR (1980) 1 Del 552) and that an inquisitorial Commission of Inquiry is fundamentally different from an "adversarial" court of law. *See also* Jagmohan [33] *passim.*

[506] On the other hand, it equally needs to be remembered that the Commission was headed by a former Chief Justice of India; it conducted both *suo moto* inquiries and also invited statements and other data from those allegedly involved in the acts or events under scrutiny; and it gave reasons and data for its findings.

2.5.3 Detentions

According to the Shah Commission Report there were 34,988 detentions under MISA.[507] Additionally, a large number of arrests were made under the Defense and Internal Security of India Act and Regulations thereunder (DISIA 1971 and DISIR, respectively). The Shah Commission found that these totaled 75,818.[508] There were also some arrests under COFEPOSA but these did not amount to a significant number.

Far-reaching amendments were made to existing detention laws. Thus MISA was amended by introducing section 16A which, after an appropriate declaration by the State Government, made the existing provisions regarding communication of grounds to the detenu and functioning of Advisory Board inapplicable to specified detenus.[509] Section 18 declared that no person "shall have any right to personal liberty by virtues of natural law or common law, if any."[510] Section 16A was amended for a second time[511] to curtail the rights of detenues in a drastic manner.[512] According to the Shah Commission, "These amendments completely metamorphosed the character of MISA."[513] All the significant safeguards against the abuse of the detention power—review of detention by a quasi-judicial Advisory Board, disclosure and communication of grounds of detention and the materials underlying them, opportunity of making representations—were thus jettisoned. The jurisprudence of court decisions on detention was made redundant because there was no mandatory disclosure or communication of grounds and materials. The operation of article 358 during the emergency proclamation and the Presidential Order under article 359 made it difficult to challenge the amendments to MISA on constitutional grounds. The ambiance of judicial self-abnegation created by the *Shukla* left not a vestige of procedural and substantive safeguards. The substitutes

---

[507] *See* 3 Report of Shah Commission of Inquiry, 134 (1978). The figures for individual states varied widely, (*Id.*) with Sikkim and Himachal Pradesh having 4 and 34 detenus respectively, compared to 6956 for Uttar Pradesh and 5620 for Madhya Pradesh. Other states found by Shah Commission to have detained significant numbers of individuals under MISA included Maharashtra (5473), West Bengal (4992), Bihar (2360), Gujarat (1762), Andhra Pradesh (1135), Tamil Nadu (1027) and Delhi (1012).

[508] *Id.* The total detentions under MISA and arrests under DISIR, thus aggregated 1,10,806.

[509] *Id.* at §16A. It was introduced by The Maintenance of Internal Security (Amendment) Act, 1975, No. 39, Act of Parliament, 1975 (India).

[510] *Id.* at§ 18.

[511] By The Maintenance of Internal Security (Amendment) Act, 1976, No. 14, Act of Parliament, 1976 (India).

[512] The section authorized action by the State on the basis of information or material in its possession without affording the detenu any material in its possession without affording the detenu any opportunity to make a representation (§ 16 A (5)). It also treated as confidential the grounds and underlying materials on which a detention order was made and to deem them matters of state not disclosable in the public interest (§ 16 A (9) (b)). Finally, it disallowed communication of any ground or the material on which it was based, to the detenu.

[513] 3 Report of Shah Commission of Inquiry (1978) at ¶ 19.8.

provided by the MISA amendments—review of detentions by the State Government, initially within 15 days and thereafter at 14 monthly intervals—were clearly perfunctory and meager.

According to the Shah Commission, faulted by some as biased and pre-meditated,[514] during the 1975–76 emergency, detention orders were confirmed mechanically by the State Government, without proper scrutiny, and often against the advice of the law or Home Departments of the State; the number of cases where detentions were not confirmed by the State Government were infinitesimal[515]; in several cases, a report by the primary detaining authority, the District Magistrate, was not sent to the State Government within fifteen days.[516] Furthermore, as the Shah Commission Report pointed out, although membership of a banned organization was not per se a ground for detention, many individuals were detained for belonging to such organizations, without any evidence of any prejudicial activity on their part[517]; detentions were sometimes ordered for activities which had occurred more than five years ago, and, in some cases, as long as 15 or 20 years ago[518]; in many cases, activities in respect of which a person had been acquitted of having committed a criminal offence were made the basis of a detention order.[519] Although the Shah Commission's findings cannot be treated as conclusive, they may be dealt with as symptomatic indicators in a state of exception.

2.5.4 The Press and Media

A significant effect of the emergency upon the press was through the practice of censorship for which a detailed legal framework was devised. Although similar powers were available during the two earlier was emergencies, they had not been

---

[514]*See, e.g.*, Jagmohan [33].

[515]*Id.* at ¶ 19.18. For example, non-confirmation occurred only in the following cases: Goa: nil out of 113; Tamil Nadu: 1 out of 1027; Rajasthan 8 out of 542; Haryana: 5 out of 200 etc. (*Id.*).

[516]Report, ¶ 19.15, *Id.* Indeed, in Assam it was found that detentions under § 16A were allowed to continue without confirmation much after fifteen days, allegedly under the un-amended original provisions of MISA (*Id.* at ¶ 19.16).

[517]*Id.* at ¶ 19.23.

[518]*Id.* at ¶ 19.25.

[519]*Id.* at ¶ 19.25 (II). Although it is well established that single offences or isolated acts of crime or illegality cannot be valid grounds for detention, detention orders were passed against single offenders (albeit involved in serious offences like murder and dacoity) and also against minor offenders, e.g., those against railway property (*Id.* at ¶ 19.25 (IV).). Although circulars by the Government of India warning against the use of MISA for ordinary criminal activities not impinging upon the security of state or public order were issued (e.g., Message No. 1372JS (IS)/75 dated (10/9/1975.) such detentions continued to occur (Report, ¶ 19.27.). There was also evidence of detention orders being issued by the detaining authority at the behest of other individuals.

used. The 1975 emergency precluded challenges to press censorship.[520] Section 3 of DISIA 1971, under the preclusive cover of emergency proclamations,[521] empowered the Central Government to make such Rules as appeared to it necessary or expedient to secure the defence of India, "civil defence, internal security, the public safety, the maintenance of public order. The efficient conduct of military operations or the maintenance of supplies and services essential to the life of the community."[522] In addition to the generality this rule making power, the Central Government was specifically empowered by section 3(2) (7) of the Act to provide for:

(a) prohibiting the publishing or printing of any newspaper or document containing matters prejudicial to any of the ground itemized above[523];
(b) demanding security from any press used for publishing or printing documents containing any of the matters mentioned in (a) and forfeiting such documents[524];
(c) forfeiture of such security and the circumstances for ordering of such forfeiture[525];
(d) closing down any press or premises used for publication of documents containing any of the matters itemized above.[526]

In pursuance of this statutory authority, the Central Government made the DISI Rules 1971. Rule 36 gave a detailed list of what is mean by "prejudicial act." Rule 48 dealt specifically with the power to impose censorship. In general, it authorized the Central Government to require that all documents or those of a particular class be submitted for sorting before publication and authorized it to impose conditions for their publication of prohibition of publication in whole or in part.[527] Violation of any order of the Central Government by anyone was made a criminal offence punishable with imprisonment up to a maximum of five years.[528]

---

[520]Although the Indian Constitution guarantees, subject to reasonable restrictions, the right to free speech and expression (under Article 19(1)(a)) and although this has judicially been held to include freedom of press (most recently affirmed by the Supreme Court in Express Newspapers Pvt. Ltd. v. Union of India (1986) 1 SCC 133 (Sen A.P., J.); *see also* Romesh Thapar v. Madras (1950) SCR S 94; Sakal Papers Ltd. v. Union of India (1962) 3 SCR 842; Bennett Coleman & Co. v. Union of India AIR 1973 SC 106 2 SCR 757), the proclamation of emergency under Article 352 and the consequential effects under Articles 358 and 359 precluded challenges based upon this constitutional guarantee.

[521]As the 1971 emergency was in existence when emergency was declared on 25-6-75, the DISIA 1971 Rules thereunder were also in force.

[522]*Id.* at§ 3 (1), DISIA 1971.

[523]*Id.* at§ 3 (2)(7) (a).

[524]*Id.* at§ 3 (7) (b).

[525]*Id.* at§ 3 (2)(7) (c).

[526]*Id.* at§ 3 (2)(7) (d).

[527]Rule 48 (1).

[528]Rules 48(1A) and (3).

In exercise of its power under Rule 48, the Central Government made the Censorship Order on June 26, 1975. The Order allowed publication of certain news items, including those dealing with contravention or alleged contravention of specified Rules of DISIR (a large number of rules were specified),[529] action taken under MIS,[530] the proclamation of emergency,[531] the Presidential Order under article 359,[532] proclamations under article 356 issued in relation to the states of Tamil Nadu and Gujarat,[533] action taken under DISIA,[534] etc., only after prior permission and scrutiny by authorized persons.

Finally, guidelines for the press were also issued on June 26, 1975. These guidelines worded in general terms but they reflect the extended scope of the power to regulate the dissemination of information. They also became the source of certain abuses in respect of press control and censorship.

Although there is no direct pronouncement of the Supreme Court on the issue of press censorship, it is doubtful whether it can be regarded as per se unconstitutional in view of the constitutional authorization for imposition of reasonable restrictions upon press freedom on grounds enumerated in article 19(2).[535]

What happened during the 1975 emergency, however, was that the generality of powers led to an excessive and indiscriminate application of restrictions and those could not be judicially reviewed and corrected because valuable safeguards were dispensed with. The omnibus umbrella of Rule 48[536] and the preclusion of judicial review on the ground of violation of freedom of speech led to a bureaucratic blind alley. Nor could the ground of freedom of trade and commerce throughout India provide any credible remedy or tangible relief because Indian Courts have not

---

[529]Cl. 1(a). Rules specified included Rules of Part III of DISIR Rules 31 and 33 of Pt. IV; Rules 37–39, 43, 46–48, 50–52 of Pt. V; Pt. VIII and Pt. IX.

[530]*Id.* atcl. 1 (c).

[531]*Id.* atcl. 1 (d).

[532]*Id.* atcl. 1 (e).

[533]*Id.* atcl. 1 (f).

[534]*Id.* atcls. 1 (h) & (i).

[535]High Court had, before 1975, adopted the view that pre-censorship is not necessarily unconstitutional and can be justified if it falls within the ambit of Article 19(2); *see* Rama Shankar v. U. P., 1954 AIR 562 (Alld.) 565; Yagnik v. Gujarat, 1963 AIR 259 (Guj.) 264; *In Re* Alavandar, 1957 AIR 427 (Mad.) 430.

[536]A learned writer on press censorship has opined that: "The net cast by Rule 48 is wider and indiscriminate. Even innocuous matters or subjects are brought within its mischief...wide and blanket powers are conferred by clauses (a) and (b) of Rule 48 (1). The touchstone of precision so vital in the sensitive area of free speech is apparent by its absence. The Rule does not contain any of the requisite safeguards. It does not provide for a notice and hearing before any adverse action is taken for prohibiting...publication...does not ensure any effective machinery for redress or correction in respect of an adverse order by way of an appeal or revision and does not cast any obligation to assign reasons in support of the action.... The Censorship Order is open to the same objection of clause (g), it indiscriminately requires all news, comments, rumors or other reports irrespective of their nature and character relating to the matters mentioned in clauses (a) to (f) and (h) to be submitted for scrutiny prior to publication. The Censorship Order also does not provide for the requisite procedural safeguards noticed above."): Sorabjee [44, p. 40].

found it acceptable to extend the freedom of inter-state commerce in the expansive way in which it has been done in United States.[537]

Judicial review, though severely restricted, was, however, not altogether ousted in the initial phase of the 1975 emergency. A division bench of the Bombay High Court in *Rao v. Masani* (1976) charted the somewhat modest but not ineffectual strategy of dealing with censorship orders in the manner of judicial review of administrative action without invoking constitutional guarantee. Administrative law principles were applied to review and relieve the vigors of certain censorship orders.[538]

---

[537]Although constitution challenges based upon Articles 301 or 304 would be open despite the emergency, it is doubtful if they would be of any avail. (The legal viability of such challenges is discussed in Sorabjee, *Id.* at 37–39). Under Article 304, it would be difficult if not impossible to show that the restriction imposed by Rule 48 or the Censorship Order were not in the public interest.

Although interference with the running of a Press or vocation of an editor may conceivably be held to violate the mandate of Article 301 which declares that "trade, commerce and intercourse throughout the territory of India shall be free," it must be remembered that such a challenge would be a very long shot indeed because courts have rarely dealt with press freedom under this provision. *Cf.* S. Ahmed v. State of Mysore, AIR 1975 SC 1443, where restrictions on trade (not press or publication) were tested on the anvil of Article 304.

[538]The Court held: "(1) The Court's scrutiny and review are not totally barred in a case where in the exercise of statutory powers an authority is empowered to make an order in its discretion on its subjective satisfaction. (2) An order made by an authority on its subjective satisfaction can be set aside by the court on the following grounds: (a) Where the authority has not applied its mind; (b) Where the power is exercised dishonestly; (c) where the power is exercised malafide; (d) where the power is exercised for a purpose not contemplated by the statute, that is to say, where it is exercised for a collateral purpose;

(e) Where the authority has acted under the dictate of another body or authority; (f) Where the authority has disabled itself from applying its mind to the facts of each individual case by self-created rules of policy or in any other manner; (g) where the satisfaction of the authority is based on the application of a wrong test; (h) Where the satisfaction of the authority is based on the misconstruction of a statute; (i) where the grounds on which the satisfaction is based are irrelevant to the subject matters of the enquiry and extraneous to the scope and purpose of the statute;

(j) Where the authority has failed to have regard to matters which the statute expressly or by implication requires it to take into consideration; and (k) Where the decision based on subjective satisfaction is such that no reasonable person could possibly arrive at it, that is to say, the satisfaction of the authority is not real and rational. (3) If one of the several grounds relied upon by the authority to support an order passed on subjective satisfaction is vague or irrelevant or bad the whole order must fall because it would not be possible for the court to say whether the impugned order would have been passed in the absence of such ground, though if it were the case of an order passed on objective satisfaction the court might endeavor to uphold the order on surviving grounds.

(4) The authority cannot avoid the scrutiny of the Court by failing to give reasons. In such a case the court can compel the authority to state its reasons. (5) Where the reasons given are bad and the authority has not taken into consideration the relevant matters or real grounds on which the order could have been passed, the Court can direct the authority to reconsider the matter in the light to such relevant matters. (6) Where, however, all the reasons which can be given for upholding the validity of the order have been found by the Court to be bad and unsustainable, the Court will not direct the authority to reconsider the matter, for then there is nothing for the authority to carry out what it has by the impugned order refused to do."

These decisions did not reckon with the reasoning of the later decision in *Shukla* and its sweeping steamroller effect. For, *Shukla* disallowed even that which had always been allowed during an emergency. Normally, Shukla's case would not apply to press freedom because it dealt with suspension of rights by Presidential Order under article 359 whereas press freedom is dealt with by article 19 (1) (a) which is affected only by article 358 and normally not by article 359. But on January 8, 1976, a Presidential Order was issued under article 359 suspending "the right of any person to move any court for the enforcement of the rights conferred by article 19 of the Constitution" and also suspending "all proceedings pending in any court for the enforcement of the above mentioned rights in any court ...". This was in addition to a similar order made on June 27, 1975 in respect of articles 14, 21 and 22. It would thus appear that even if challenged on administrative law grounds had been raised, most of them would have been excluded on the analogy of *Shukla.* The latter had held detentions to be unchallengeable on any ground (with some minor exceptions discussed earlier) on the basis that article 21 was the sole repository of life and liberty and its suspension precluded challenged on other grounds designed substantially to achieve what was denied by its suspensions, viz., liberty of the individual. By analogy, suspension of article 19 would obviate challenged on other grounds designed to achieve what was intended to be denied by its suspension, viz., freedom of press and free speech and expression. This analogy illustrated the draconian and pernicious effects of the decisions in *Shukla.*

The Shah Commission found other additional evidence of abuse of power in respect of the press.[539] Censorship of Parliament and Court proceedings was further facilitated by the repeal of the Parliamentary Proceedings (Protection of Publication) Act 1956 (the 1956 Act), by the enactment of the Prevention of Publication of Objectionable Matters Act 1976 (the 1976 Act) and by the abolition of the Press Council by Ordinance. The 1956 Act had sought to protect bona fide publications of reports of proceedings in the Houses of Parliament or the State Legislature, from being made the subject of civil or criminal proceedings in the Houses of Parliament or the State Legislature, from being made the subject of civil or criminal proceedings in a court of law.[540] In its stead, the 1976 Act authorized the Central Government or competent authority to prohibit publication of material if satisfied that it is necessary for preventing or combating activity prejudicial to the

---

[539]The Shah Commission found that electricity supply was disconnected for a day or so to all newspapers on Bahadur Shah Zafar Marg on June 25, 1975 and in respect of newspapers elsewhere on June 26. *See* 1 REPORT OF SHAH COMMISSION OF INQUIRY (1978) at ¶¶ 6.10.). The Guidelines prevented editors leaving editorial columns blank or filling them with quotes from great works of literature or from national leaders like Mahatma Gandhi and thus arguably violated even the DISIA and DISIR. *Id.* at ¶ 6–14.

[540]A bill was passed repealing the 1956 Act (*See* 1 REPORT OF SHAH COMMISSION OF INQUIRY (1978) at ¶ 6.45). However, the 44th Constitutional Amendment inserted Article 361 into the Constitution which writes into the Constitution the protection originally given by the 1956 Act. *See* Constitution (Forty-Fourth) Amendment Act, No. 88 of 1978, INDIA CODE, (http://indiacode.nic.in/coiweb/amend/amend44.htm).

interests of the country.[541] The Act also sought to define in detail "objectionable matter"[542] and empowered the Government to demand security from presses in certain cases relating to such matter or to forfeit such security.[543] It also empowered the forfeiture of certain publications.[544]

Some other government activities *vis-à-vis* the press, apart from censorship, may now briefly be noticed. The Shah Commission found evidence of discrimination on political grounds for placement of government advertisements.[545] According to its report, a grading list of friendly, neutral and hostile newspapers, with detailed subdivisions, was drawn up and release of government advertisement, usually the primary source of sustenance for newspapers, were structured accordingly.[546]

Property Interests

There were no substantial changes during the 1975 emergency to laws affecting property rights. Section 23 of the DISIA 1971 empowered the Central Government to requisition property, inter alia, for purposes of defence of India, civil defence, public safety, maintenance of public order, efficient conduct of military operations and for maintenance of supplies and services essential to the community. The provision was not widely used, but when it was, the style was peremptory and unmindful of customary legal safeguards. One such case relates to the requisitioning of property in Chanakyapuri in New Delhi, owned by the Vishwa Yuvak Kendra, a trust which had the objective of providing training to social workers of youth organizations. The Shah Commission found[547] that the requisitioning was motivated by irrelevant and oblique considerations.[548]

---

[541] § 5(1) of the 1976 Act.

[542] *Id.* at § 3.

[543] Ch. III, §§ 8–18.

[544] Ch. IV, §§ 19–23. A Censor Room started functioning in Parliament which considerably modified or diluted the news emanating from Parliament. *See* 1 Report of Shah Commission of Inquiry, (1978) at ¶ 6.20. As regards judgements, instructions were often given for publication of operative parts only and aspects meriting publicity or exclusion, as the case may be, were specified. (*Id.* at 6.23). The Shah Commission has given a number of extracts from the Censor's orders on particular matters (*id.* at ¶ 6.80. *See* also Appendix to Ch. 6, *Id.* Vol. I.) and concludes that: "In practice, censorship was for suppressing news unfavorable to the government or to play up news favorable to the Government and to suppress news unfavorable to the supporters of the Congress Party". (*Id.* at ¶ 6–30).

[545] *Id.* at ¶ 6–46, *et seq.*

[546] *Id.* at ¶ 6–49.

[547] Report, Vol. II, Ch. XII, ¶¶ 12–1 to 12–23.

[548] The Commission said that it was done to reconstitute the Board of Trustees and include more government nominees. The Commission also felt that in this case, the initial requisition of the property for purposes of maintenance of public order and services essential to the community, then keeping it vacant for a few months and then allotting it to an organization not connected with maintenance of public order or maintenance of essential supplies (viz. Delhi State Industrial Development Corporation) "were steps not consistent with the provisions of the DISI Act." (*Id.* at ¶ 12–15).

Another aspect relates to demolition of unauthorized structures in Delhi which has long been afflicted with nightmarish chaos affecting the quality and ambiance of life in these areas. The pace and scale of demolition and resettlement activities in Delhi during the emergency, though often actuated by altruistic motives, larger public interest and good intentions, led to an upheaval of disaffection partly because unauthorized squatting had become an accepted way of life. The Shah Commission estimated that the total number of structures demolished by the various municipal agencies of Delhi during the emergency was 1,50,105 and that this amounted to more than eighty times the figure for the thirty months preceding the declaration of emergency in June 1975.[549]

Judiciary

During the 1975 emergency, sixteen High Court judges were transferred without their consent to High Court of other states and a total list of 56 possible transferees was prepared.[550] Prior to the emergency, no judge of the High Court had even been transferred without his consent. Although the Shah Commission did not deal with individual cases of transfer, there is no doubt that during the emergency and thereafter, those non-consensual transfers evoked serious concern and consternation.

In 1978, the Supreme Court had, by a majority, held in *Union of India v. S.H. Sheth*[551] that non-consensual transfers were not per se unconstitutional or violative of the independence of the judiciary. Although in *Sheth* various safeguards to the transfer policy were enumerated, transfers could not be done by way of punishment; they could be done only in the public interest; they could be made only after a full and complete discussion between the Union of India and the Chief Justice of India—the constitutionality of the transfer policy in principle was reaffirmed by a majority of the seven-judge bench of the Supreme Court in the so-called *Judges Case*[552] decided in 1982.[553] During the pendency of proceedings in *Sheth* before the Supreme Court, the Union of India (in the meanwhile the political

[549]*Id.* Ch. XIII, ¶ 13–6. Moreover, the alleged legality of construction of many structures could not be properly investigated under municipal laws; no provision for alternative resettlement was made in some genuine and deserving cases; resettlement facilities, where offered, were sometimes poor and inadequate and located miles away from the place of work of the person uprooted. (*See, e.g., Id.* at ¶ 13–22). Serious allegations of physical brutality during some cases of demolition were also made. (*Id.*). *Cf.* Jagmohan [33], *passim*, where many such allegations are controverted with vehemence.

[550]Seervai [31, pp. 2265–2266].

[551]Union of India v. Sankalchand Himatlal Sheth AIR 1977 SC 2328 (India). On the issue of transfer, the majority comprised Chandrachud, Krishna Iyer and Fazl Ali JJ. Bhagwati and Untwalia dissented.

[552]S.P. Gupta v. Union of India, AIR 1982 SC 149 (India). Only Bhagwati dissented on the transfer issue; six other judges upheld the power of transfer of High Court Judges when exercised in the public interest.

[553]A policy of transfers of judges is also being implemented currently by the government. Although no consensual transfers of High Court judges be criticized in principle, if it can be shown in individual cases that it was actuated by ulterior motives or without appropriate consultation as

complexion of the Union Government had changed) conceded that there was no justification for the transfer of Justice Sheth and said that he would be repatriated to the Gujarat High Court.[554] This appears to be the only case where an individual transfer was judicially found, although mainly on a concession, to be illegal. However, a commentator has opined that the transfer of a judge of the Delhi High Court to Assam High Court was, without "reasonable doubt" a punishment for delivering a judgement critical of the government in the case of journalist.[555]

The Shah Commission considered two other specific incidents relating to the judiciary. It found that a judge of the Delhi High Court[556] and a judge of the Bombay High Court,[557] both additional judges, were not confirmed as permanent judges due to ulterior motives.[558] In the former case, the judge was not made permanent and had to revert as a District and Session Judge although the Chief Justice of Delhi High Court had described him as "an asset to the High Court" and the Chief Justice of India had approved the appointment.[559] In connection with the aforesaid cases, it must be remembered that the Constitution empowers the Central Government to appoint additional judge for two years, and they are then subject to confirmation.[560] Although prior to the 1975 emergency, appointees as additional

---

required by the constitution or by way of punishment, it would be invalidated. The Shah Commission did not deal with evidence of illegal transfers in particular cases.

[554]Union of India v. Sankalchand Himatlal Sheth, AIR 1977 SC 2328, 2329 (India).

[555]Kuldip Nayyar's Case. *See also* Seervai [31, p. 2294]. However, Justice Rangarajan's transfer has not been the subject of judicial pronouncement and has not been separately considered by the Shah Commission.

[556]Mr. Justice Aggarwal.

[557]Mr. Justice Lalit.

[558]1 Report of Shah Commission of Inquiry (1978) at ¶¶ 7.1–7.23.

[559]According to the Shah Commission, this was done primarily because the judge had been a member of the Division Bench which had decided Kuldeep Nayyar's case and which is supposed to have led to the transfer of the presiding judge of that bench. The Government file also noted his alleged connection with an organization known as the RSS during the 1950's and early 1960's. According to the Shah Commission, he was not confirmed on the basis of an order on the file by the Prime Minister herself, which did not state any reasons, and even though there were no adverse reports against the judge.

[560]*See* India Const. art. 224 which reads:

> Appointment of additional and acting Judges: - (1) If by reason of any temporary increase in the business of High Court or by reason of arrears of work therein it appears to the President that the number of Judges of that court should be for the time being increased, the President may appoint duly qualified person to be additional judges of the Court for such period not exceeding two years as he may specify. (2) When any Judge of a High Court other than the Chief Justice is by reason of absence or for any other reason unable to perform the duties of his office or is appointed to act temporarily as Chief Justice, the President may appoint a duly qualified person to act as Judge of that Court until the permanent Judge has resumed his duties. (3) No person appointed as an additional or acting Judge of High Court shall hold office after attaining the age of sixty-two years.

judge to the High Court were, in practice, invariably confirmed as permanent judges, the Constitution clearly does not obligate the Government to do so. In the *First Judges Case*,[561] the Supreme Court upheld the power of the Central Government not to so confirm additional judges after the expiry of two years, although judicial review to examine alleged abuse of the power in individual cases was reaffirmed.

Judicial Review of Emergency Powers

At the outset it may be clarified that the scope of judicial review, in the present context, would be limited to the question whether the decision to proclaim a state of emergency is arbitrary, based on no data, or vitiated by ulterior or oblique motives. There are numerous decision and judicial dicta[562] by Indian courts to the effect that the proclamation of emergency under article 352 or similar statutory or Ordinance grant of emergency power is conclusive and non-reviewable.[563]

The kinds of reasons given in India for the supposed non-reviewability of an emergency proclamation are similar to those found in other jurisdictions. These have been mentioned earlier.

Though overwhelming, the case law to the contrary may appear to be plausible, and somewhat more accurate view appears to be that judicial review of the proclamation of emergency is still an "open" question,[564]

The alleged reasons for non-reviewability are not very convincing and are often inapplicable. They are usually overstated, occasionally misleading and sometimes only a camouflage. They cannot be regarded as absolute or impenetrable. Thus, the political questions doctrine, which is entirely a result of a rigid separation of power in the American Constitution,[565] is inapposite in the Indian context, which is not based upon a separation of powers principle similar in content or degree to the American system. Indeed, the epitaph of the political questions doctrine was written by the Indian Supreme Court as far back as 1971 when Justice Shah said:

---

[561] S.P. Gupta v. Union of India, AIR 1982 SC 149 (India).

[562] The earlier oft cited decisions include Bhagat Singh v. King Emperor AIR (1931) PC 111; Emperor v. Sibnath Banerji AIR (1943) FC 75; Emperor v. Benoari Lal Sarma AIR (1945) PC 48; Lakhi Narayan Das v. Province of Bihar AIR (1950) FC 59. Other decisions supposedly supporting this view include Ghasi Ram v. State, 1966 AIR 247 (Raj.); Rao v. State of AP, 1966 AIR 229 (AP); Ghulam Sarwar v. Union of India, AIR 1967 SC 1335; Rattan Lal v. State, 1969 AIR 5 (J&K); Bhut Nath Mate v. State of West Bengal, AIR 1974 SC 806 (India); Milapchand v. Union of India (1975) WLN 750; Darshan Singh v. State of Punjab (1975) Cri LJ 1974; Manekben v. Union of India ILR (1975) Del 820; Venkateshamma v. State of A.P. AIR (1976) AP 1; Lekhi v. Union of India 1977 AIR 167 (Del.); V.K. Singh v. District Magistrate (1977) Cri L.J. (Noc) 89; A.D.M. Jabalpur v. Shiv Kant Shukla, AIR 1976 SC 1207, 1325 (India) (Chandrachud J.).

[563] Decisions under Article 356 of the Constitution, like State of Rajasthan v. Union of India AIR 1977 SC 1361 (India); Rao Birendra v. Union of India 1968 AIR 41 (Punjab & Haryana) and Sreeramulu's Case 1974 AIR 106 (Andhra Pradesh), may also be referred to.

[564] State of Rajasthan v. Union of India AIR 1977 SC 1361, 1403–04 (India). (Chandrachud J.).

[565] *See e.g.*, Baker v. Carr, 369 U.S. 186 (1962).

> The constitutional mechanism in a democratic polity does not contemplate the existence of any function which may, qua the citizens, be designated as political and orders made in exercise whereof are not liable to be tested for their validity before the legally constituted courts. . . The President is made by the Constitution the repository of the power to recognize the rulers. That power may be exercised consistently with and in aid of the constitutional scheme. A democratic constitution founded on the Rule of Law does not envisage authority in any instrumentality of the Union reminiscent of autocracy . . . President is not invested with any powers transcending the Constitution. Presidential powers arise from and are limited by the Constitution. The validity of the exercise of these powers is always amenable to the jurisdiction of this Court, unless the jurisdiction is by precise enactment excluded. The power of this Court under Article 32 or Article 226 cannot be bypassed under a claim that the President has exercised political power.[566]

This view has recently been emphatically reiterated by the Supreme Court[567] and the ghost of the political questions doctrine needs to be exorcised from Indian constitutional law once and for all.

The privilege argument fares no better. It was exhaustively analyzed in the First Judges Case[568] which emphasized that the doctrine of privilege or public interest immunity must be seen in the context of the necessity and clamor for an open government.[569] It was said that the concept of open government is a direct emanation from the right to know, which is implicit in the right to free speech in article 19 (I) (a) of the Indian Constitution.[570] Secrecy would promote corruption, nepotism and abuse of power, and would militate against a clean and efficient administration.[571] Possibility of subsequent disclosure would check and reduce carelessness, impetuosity, arbitrariness and mala fide.[572] The approach of the Court, it was said, must be to attenuate the area of secrecy as much as possible, consistently with the requirements of public interest.[573] The Court always has a residual power to itself examine the documents for which privilege is claimed and the *ipse dixit* of the executive is not conclusive in this respect.[574] No factors are conclusive or final in determining whether the State is entitled to public interest immunity from disclosure. Apprehensions that disclosure may adversely affect the head of the

---

[566] *See* Madhav Rao Scindia v. Union of India, AIR 1971 SC 531, 565–579 (India) *especially* at ¶¶ 96,110,132, 143.

[567] In A.K. Roy v. Union of India, AIR 1982 SC 710, 724 (India) (Chandrachud, J.) (national Security Ordinance case); and in Minerva Mills v. Union of India AIR 1980 SC 1789, 1836–37 (India) (Bhagwati, J.).

[568] S.P. Gupta v. Union of India, AIR 1982 SC 149 (India).

[569] *Id.* at 233–34 (Bhagwati, J.); *id* at 636–38 (Venkataramiah, J.).

[570] *Id.* at 233–34.

[571] *Id.* at 233.

[572] *Id.* at 251–53.

[573] *Id.* at 233–34.

[574] *Id.* at 234–38, 240–41, 244 (Bhagwati, J.)

department or the department or the Minister or the Government or that it may provoke public criticism or censure in the press are considerations which must be scrupulously excluded while claiming privilege.[575]

Finally, it was held that while the advice tendered by the Council of Ministers to the President is protected against judicial scrutiny in view of the explicit constitutional prohibition contained in article 74, the material on which the advice tendered by the Council of Ministers is based cannot be said to be part of the advice, and correspondence between the constitutional functionaries which constituted the material forming the basis of the decision of the Central Government must therefore be held to be outside the exclusionary rule enunciated in article 74.[576]

Thus, although courts would perhaps accede more readily to claims of privilege in cases involving national security considerations,[577] such factors must manifestly be present and be proved to exist before a plea of non-disclosure is upheld. In any event, this case by case judicial evaluation would be vastly different from a per se ouster of judicial review on the basis of the privilege doctrine: the former upholds an emergency proclamation after judicial review while the latter is premised upon a threshold exclusion of judicial scrutiny.

A proclamation of emergency is based either on well-known and notorious facts and circumstances or on classified and secret information or on a combination of the two or on no data at all. In the first case, a claim of privilege would be superfluous as the Court would be entitled to take judicial notice of such facts and circumstances. In the second case, the claim of privilege would itself be strongly indicative of the existence of sufficient data and would be accepted or rejected, as the case may be upon a perusal of the classified information by the Court. The third case would involve elements of the last two. The fourth case involves a fraud on the constitutional or statutory power by the executive authority and the court, by exercising its discretion and seeing the allegedly privileged documents, would be able to prevent this.

The "means" argument, as also the "expertise," "obstructionist," "expedition" and "discipline" arguments have been discussed earlier and need not be repeated except to mention that Indian judges, like their counterparts elsewhere, have effectively applied the time-tested technique of judicial notice of well-known or notorious facts and circumstances on diverse occasions.[578] It is submitted that so far as "discretion" argument is concerned, judicial review of administrative and

---

[575] *Id.*

[576] *Id.* at 230–31 (Bhagwati, J.)

[577] *Id.* at 221 (Desai, J.). *See* Duncan v. Cammell Laird [1942] AC 124 [U.K.].

[578] Examples of judicial notice of well-known facts and circumstances relating to war in the forties can be found in Emperor v. Sibhath Banerjee AIR (1943) FC 75 and Emperor v. Benoari Lal Sarma AIR (1945) PC 48. In Swadeshi Cotton Mills v. Sales Tax Officer AIR (1965) Alld. 86, para 30, the Allahabad High Court took judicial notice of the proclamation of emergency since 1962.

executive discretion, including ministerial discretion, is a commonplace judicial activity. Indian Courts have always denied the possibility of untendered and undeterred discretion, whether of an administrative official or a minster[579]; nor can Presidential discretion be singled out for immunity from judicial review. Even many constitutionally entrusted Presidential powers have been judicially reviewed.

A most notable example is the judicial assertion of the power of judicial review of the order of the President issued under article 366 (22) of the Constitution derecognizing "Rulers" of princely states.[580] The decision is strong authority against conferral of immunity from judicial review to any executive or political act and asserts the duty of judges to uphold the supremacy of the Constitution by judicial review.

In the analogous area of the President's ordinance-making power under the Constitution, the Supreme Court has indicated that casual, repeated and excessive use of the ordinance-making power may be liable to be struck down as a fraud on the Constitution and has admitted a petition on this issue after hearing both sides at some length.[581]

Turning to a large number of cases which appear to support an exclusionary theory and which have been cited earlier, it is submitted that none of them clearly and conclusively enunciated any blanket rule of exclusion of judicial review of emergency proclamations. Some of them are wartime decisions, decided during a period when the existence of war was undeniable and was judicially noticed.[582] The existence of emergency was not therefore seriously in doubt in these cases. Some others[583] are based upon or given during the existence of the erstwhile article 352 (5), which specifically barred judicial examination of these questions and the subsequent deletion of which, by constitutional amendment, indicates, at least by

---

[579]See the host of cases supporting this preposition, listed and discussed in Jain and Jain [34].

[580]*See* Madhav Rao Scindia v. Union of India AIR 1971 SC 531 (India) (11 judges; 8 in majority; 1 concurring; 1 dissenting on some points; 1 dissenting).

[581]Dr. D.C. Wadhwa v. State of Bihar, AIR 1987 SC 579. The petitioner is the author of the book [35] which shows how Government of Bihar, especially after 1968, has repromulgated Ordinances *en masse* and subverted the principle of rule of law. The Ordinance making powers in the Constitution in Articles 123 and 213 are clearly designed as an exceptional power usable when the legislature is temporarily not in session. In Bihar, Wadhwa shows how the exception has become the rule. For example, between 1971 and 1981, 161 Acts and 1958 Ordinances were passed, i.e., on average 12 Ordinances to each Act. By the device of re-promulgation, used more frequently since 1968, Ordinances with life spaces of 13 years, 11 years, 10 years and 7 years became common. The petition in the Supreme Court is based upon the study by Mr. Wadhwa. *See also*, Seervai [30, pp. 2139–2140].

[582]*See, e.g.*, Emperor v. Sibnath Banerji AIR (1943) FC 75; Emperor v. Benoari Lal Sarma AIR (1945) PC 48.

[583]*See, e.g.*, Milapchand v. Union of India (1975) WLN 750; Darshan Singh v. State of Punjab (1975) Cri LJ 1974; Manekben v. Union of India ILR (1975) Del 820; Venkateshamma v. State of A.P. AIR (1976) AP 1; Lekhi v. Union of India 1977 AIR 167 (Del.); V.K. Singh v. District Magistrate (1977) Cri L.J. (Noc) 89. Although the existence of emergency was not a question in issue in Shukla's case *id.* at 1321–25, Chandrachud, J. relied on the conclusiveness clauses of Article 352 in an obiter upon the non-reviewability of an emergency proclamation.

implication, a willingness to subject these questions to judicial scrutiny. Still other decisions can be explained either on the ground that they followed, without discussion or analysis, one of the earlier mentioned judgements[584] or because they involved the distinguishable article 356,[585] to be discussed later, or because they left the issue open.[586]

On the contrary, courts in different common law jurisdictions, including India, United States and the UK, have repeatedly emphasized the power and duty of courts to decide whether conditions justifying the use of martial law exist.[587] In as much as martial law represents an important type of emergency power, these judicial dicta are equally applicable to judicial review of emergency powers under the Indian Constitution. More direct authority is available in the important decision of the Indian Supreme Court in *Minerva Mills v. Union of India* (1980)[588] where a judge of the Supreme Court, concurring on one issue with the majority, spoke clearly in favor of judicial review of emergency powers. It is therefore necessary to consider this decision in some detail.

Minerva Mills was nationalized under the Sick Textile Undertakings (Nationalization) Act 1974 ("the 1974 Act"). This Act was put in the Ninth Schedule of the Indian Constitution by the thirty-ninth constitutional amendment in 1975.[589] Under article 31B of the Constitution, Acts put in the Ninth Schedule are immune from challenge on grounds of inconsistency with the fundamental rights enumerated in Part III of the Constitution. Further, the 1974 Act also stated that it was in furtherance of Part IV of the Constitution, i.e., Directive Principles of State Policy. Under article 31C, as amended by section 4 of the forty-second constitutional amendment Act in 1977,[590] no law giving effect to the policy of the state toward securing all or any of the principles laid down in Part IV shall be deemed to be void on grounds of inconsistency with any of the fundamental rights in article 14 or 19 of the Constitution. Finally, section 55 of the forty-second constitutional amendment Act inserted finality and conclusiveness clauses in article 368[591] of the Constitution to provide that no amendment of the Constitution, before or after the forty-second

---

[584]*See, e.g.*, Lakhi Narayan Das v. Province of Bihar AIR (1950) FC 59 (India) (relying on Bhagat Singh, Sibnath Banerji and Benoari Lal Sarma).

[585]*See, e.g.*, State of Rajasthan v. Union of India, AIR 1977 SC 1361 (India); Rao Birendra Singh v. Union of India 1968 AIR 441 (Punjab & Haryana); *In Re* Sreeramulu 1974 AIR 106 (Andhra Pradesh).

[586]*See, e.g.*, Ghulam Sarwar v. Union of India, AIR 1967 SC 1335 (India); Bhut Nath Mate v. West Bengal, AIR 1974 SC 806 (India).

[587]A recent Indian decision reaffirming the power and duty of the Court to judicially ascertain the existence of conditions justifying institution of martial law is Chinta Subba Rao v. Supreme Commander, Defense Forces 1980 AIR 172 (Andhra Pradesh).

[588]Minerva Mills v. Union of India, AIR 1980 SC 1789 (India).

[589]With effect from Aug. 10, 1976.

[590]With effect from Dec. 18, 1977.

[591]This provision, in Part XX of the Constitution, provides for the power and procedure to amend the Constitution.

amendment, shall be challenged in any court on any ground. The intended effect of all this was that the 1974 Act would be immunized from challenge on grounds of unconstitutionality and judicial review would be comprehensively barred. The petitioners contended that the 1974 Act was unconstitutional and violated, inter alia, articles 14 and 19 of the Constitution. To challenge the 1974 Act, it was necessary for the petitioners to challenge the insertion of the 1974 Act in the Ninth Schedule by the thirty-ninth constitutional amendment. To do this, it was in turn necessary for them to challenge sections 4 and 55 of the forty-second constitutional amendment which made the thirty-ninth amendment immune from challenge and thus protected the 1974 Act. A majority of four, speaking through Chief Justice Chandrachud, (Justice Bhagwati dissenting) held that section 4 of the forty-second amendment of the Constitution violated the basis structure of the Constitution and therefore struck it down. This was the issue on which Justice Bhagwati dissented. However, section 55 was unanimously held to violate the basic structure of the Constitution and struck down as unconstitutional. The issue regarding judicial review of emergency was touched upon only by Justice Bhagwati.[592]

---

[592]As his discussion of judicial review of emergency powers is inextricably intertwined with his analysis of the constitutionality of § 55, on which there is unanimity, his views on emergency and judicial review cannot be said to be part of a dissent on this issue. It is also noteworthy that Bhagwati J's remarks on this issue arose directly from the grounds of challenge put forth by the petitioners. In challenging §§ 4 and 55 of the forty-second constitutional amendment, one of the arguments raised by the petitioners was that Parliament, in its constituent capacity, was not competent to pass the forty-second constitutional amendment. This, the petitioners argued, was because the amendment was passed by a Parliament whose term of five years had expired earlier, but which had continued to sit illegally beyond five years. The submission of the petitioners was summarized by Bhagwati J., as follows:

> It is no doubt true that the House of People (Extension of Duration) Act 1976 was enacted by Parliament under the proviso to Article 83 (2) (of the constitution) extending the duration of the Lok Sabha for a period of one year, but the argument of the petitioners was that this act was ultra vires and void, because the duration of the Lok Sabha could be extended under the proviso to Article 83(2) only during operation of a proclamation of an Emergency and, in the submission of the petitioners, there was no proclamation of Emergency in operation at the time when the House of People (Extension of Duration) Act 1976 was passed (Minerva Mills v. Union of India, AIR 1980 SC 1789, 1834 (India)....The argument of the petitioners however, was that, though the first proclamation of emergency was validly issued by the President (in 1971) on account of external aggression committed by Pakistan against India, the circumstances changed soon thereafter and the emergency which justified the issue of the proclamation ceased to exist and consequently the continuance of the Proclamation was mala fide and colorable and hence the proclamation though not revoked until 21st March 1977, ceased in law to continue in force and could not be said to be in operation at the material date (of the passage of the 1976 Act). So far as the second proclamation of emergency (in 1975) is concerned it was illegal and void on three grounds:
>
> (1) ....
>
> (2) ....

It appears that the conclusion of Justice Bhagwati rested squarely of the issues urged before him which were directly related to the validity of section 55 of the forty-second constitutional amendment. Justice Bhagwati's remarks connote thus be dismissed as an irrelevant exegesis, though it is possible to suggest that it was unnecessary for the learned judge to rule on this alternative argument as he had already concluded that the finality clauses in article 368 of the Constitution ought to be struck down.[593]

On the aforesaid alternative argument, Justice Bhagwati held that the first proclamation of emergency in 1971 was a valid and subsisting proclamation and satisfied the condition precedent for extension of the life of Parliament. On judicial review the judge said:

> But one thing is certain that if the satisfaction (under article 352) is mala fide or is based on wholly extraneous and irrelevant grounds, the court would have jurisdiction to examine it, because in that case there would be no satisfaction of the President in regard to the matter on which he is required to be satisfied. The satisfaction of the President is a condition precedent to the exercise of the power under article 352 (1) and if it can be shown that there is no satisfaction of the President at all, the exercise of the power would be constitutionally invalid . . . where therefore, the satisfaction is absurd or perverse or mala fide or based on a wholly extraneous and irrelevant ground, it would be no satisfaction at all and it would be liable to be challenged before a Court . . . A proclamation of emergency is undoubtedly amenable to judicial review though on the limited ground that no satisfaction as required by Article 352 was arrived at by the President in law or that the satisfaction was absurd or perverse or mala fide or based on an extraneous or irrelevant ground.[594]

> (3) there was no threat to the security of India on account of internal disturbance, which would justify the issue of a proclamation of emergency, and the second proclamation was issued not for a legitimate purpose sanctioned by clause (1) of Article 352 but with a view to perpetuating the Prime Minister in power and it was clearly mala fide and for collateral purpose and hence outside the power of the President under Article 352(1).

Id. at 1834–35 (Words in brackets supplied).

[593]Bhagwati, J. was aware of this and said: "It may be conceded straightaway that, strictly speaking, it is superfluous and unnecessary to consider this argument, because … we have already held that it is outside the constituent power of the Parliament in so far as it seeks to include sub clauses (4) and (5) an Article 368." (*Id.* at 1834). It is submitted that there is nothing improper about giving a decision on both of the alternative points urged before a court of law, even though the first is sufficient to dispose of the matter, especially where a "long argument… seriously pressing the alternative ground of challenge is addressed to the court." (*Id.* at 1834).

Many of the most important and far reaching judgements have involved just this technique. (*See*, *inter alia*, Marbury v. Madison (1803) 1 Cranch 137, where CJ Marshall "took the engaging position of declining to exercise power which the Constitution withheld from him, by making the occasion an opportunity to assert a far more transcendent power". *See* Corwin [36]. *See also* Shetty v. IAAI, AIR 1979 SC 1028 (Bhagwati, J.) where judicial review of grant of property rights in the form of contracts and leases, was undertaken, although, the applicant was held ineligible for relief on other grounds.

[594]Minerva Mills v. Union of India, AIR 1980 SC 1789, 1838–39 (India).

The learned judge analyzed the argument that there was no justification for the continuance of the first proclamation and it was accepted that the court would issue a mandamus for revoking such an (old) proclamation "in a given case" if the petitioner

> is able to show by placing clear an cogent material before the court that there is no justification of emergency . . . the court could not interfere with the satisfaction of the executive government in this regard unless it is clear on the material on record that there is absolutely no justification for the continuance of the proclamation of emergency and the proclamation is being continued mala fide of for a collateral purpose. The court may, in such a case, if satisfied beyond doubt, grant a writ of mandamus directing the Central Government to revoke the proclamation of emergency.[595]

It is noteworthy that the decision of Justice Bhagwati was given despite the existence of finality and conclusiveness clauses in articles 352 (5) (a) and 5 (b) of the Constitution. The learned judge, however, interpreted these clauses as follows:

> … and that is how I think it must be read-that the immunity from challenge granted by it does not apply where the challenge is not that the satisfaction is improper or unjustified but that there is no satisfaction at all. In such a case, it is not the satisfaction arrived at by the President which is challenged but the existence of the satisfaction itself.[596]

The deletion of these finality clauses by the forty-fourth constitutional amendment[597] would, it is submitted, a fortiori make the judgement and its reasoning intrinsically relevant.

There is, thus, no duly applicable, conclusive and compelling judicial precedent in Indian law altogether denying the possibility of judicial review of emergency proclamations.[598] It is submitted that it is desirable that judicial review of emergency powers, which has often remained a somewhat inarticulate premise or assumption in judicial remarks, be more fully recognized as a useful and desirable principle of law. In an age when parliamentary control is becoming increasingly weak, a residual power of judicial review of emergency proclamations, sparingly and cautiously applied, would more fully help to realize the real intentions of the framers of the Constitution who did not conceive of unfettered executive emergency powers. To attach conclusiveness to executive proclamations would nullify the constitutional mandate of the newly amended article 352, if the conditions precedent to the proclamation of emergency under that article (e.g., "armed rebellion") were mechanically recited but not actually fulfilled. The point is that the phrase "armed rebellion" can be as easily recited in the proclamation as "internal disturbance." Whether the stiffer threshold implicit in the former phrase is actually fulfilled as opposed to the less strict requirement specified in the latter must be a question capable of judicial determination and review. Similarly, even if it be assumed that violation of Business Rules would invalidate resultant executive

---

595 *Id.* at 1839.

596 *Id.* at 1839–40.

597 *Id.* at 1838–39.

598 With effect from June 10, 1979.

action,[599] it would be necessary to show that conditions for the exercise of the extraordinary power in Rule 12 of the Transaction of Business Rules did not exist. It may be added that in the growing ambiance of judicial review in hitherto sheltered areas—but in the read of public interest litigation[600] or of judicial review of conform factors and criteria[600B] or of the ordinance-making power[600C] or of locus stand[600D] or of matters having drastic consequences for the government[600E]—a proper application of judicial review of emergency powers would be neither an aberration nor an innovation.

It must be remembered that these conclusions of a Commission of Inquiry cannot be equated with or be a substitute for the findings reached by a court of law. Indeed, a single Judge of the Delhi High Court in December 1979[601] quashed the proceedings of the Shah Commission against Mrs. Gandhi, former Prime Minister and Mr. P. Mukherjee, former Finance Minister, on the ground that the procedure adopted by the Commission violated mandatory provisions of the Commissions of Inquiry Act, 1952. At the end of a long judgement, Justice Chawla said:

> In my opinion, there can be no doubt that sections 8B and 8C (of the Commissions of Inquiry Act) are mandatory. One might even call them 'statutory Rules of natural justice.' Since they were not complied with in respect of Mrs. Gandhi and Mr. Mukherjee, the proceedings of the Commission become void and ultra vires. The Commission stepped outside its jurisdiction and lost its powers. Therefore, the Chairman was not 'legally competent' to administer the oath to Mrs. Gandhi and Mr. Mukherjee, and in asking them questions he was not exercising his 'legal powers.'[602]

Subject to the foregoing the factual context in which emergency was declared on 25 June, 1975 was dealt with by the Shah Commission of Inquiry,[603] which concluded that:

(a) on the economic front there was nothing alarming[604];
(b) on the law and order front, the fortnightly reports sent to the President of India and the Home Secretary showed that there was no significant deterioration in the period immediately preceding the proclamation of Emergency; the Home

---

[599]Minerva Mills v. Union of India, AIR 1980 SC 1789, 1838–39 (India) (Bhagwati J.).

[600]The tremendous advances made in public interest litigation in India, primarily through a striking application of judicial review, have recently been outlined and discussed in an article by the judge of the Indian Supreme Court mainly responsible for them viz. Bhagwati, P.N.

[600B]Shetty v. IAAI AIR 1979 SC 1028 (India).

[600C]Dr. D.C. Wadhwa v. State of Bihar, AIR 1987 SC 579.

[600D]S.P. Gupta v. Union of India, AIR 1982 SC 149 (India).

[600E]D.S. Nakna v. Union of India (1983) SCC 305 (India).

[601]Indira Nehru Gandhi v. J.C. Shah Commission of Inquiry in 1980 AIR 552 (Del).

[602]*Id.* at 835. Words in brackets supplied. An appeal was filed from this judgement to the Supreme Court but was later withdrawn.

[603]1 Report of Shah Commission of Inquiry (1978) at ¶ 5.61.

[604]On the contrary, the whole-sale price index had declined by 4 percent between December 3, 1974 and the last week of March 1975 as per the Economic Survey 1975–76, a Government of India Publication.

Ministry had not prepared any contingency plans prior to June 25, 1975, with regard to the imposition of internal Emergency;

(c) the Intelligence Bureau had not submitted any report to the Home Ministry any time between June 12 and June 25, 1975, suggesting that the internal situation in the country warranted the imposition of internal Emergency:

(d) the Home Ministry had not submitted any report to the Prime Minister expressing its concern of anxiety about the internal situation in the country. Till after the Emergency was lifted, the Home Ministry did not have on its file the copy of the communication which was sent by the Prime Minister to the President recommending imposition of the Emergency;

(e) while the Director of Intelligence Bureau, the Home Secretary, the Cabinet Secretary and the Secretary to the Prime Minister had not been taken into confidence, Shri R.K. Dhawan, the then Additional Private secretary to the Prime Minister had been associated with the preparation and promulgation of the Emergency right from the early stage;

(f) while the Lt. Governor of Delhi and the Chief Ministers of Haryana, Punjab, Madhya Pradesh, Rajasthan, Karnataka, Andhra Pradesh, Bihar and West Bengal had been given advance intimation by the Prime Minister about the contemplated action, no such advance information was given to the Government of U.P., Maharashtra, Gujarat, Tamil Nadu, J&K, Tripura, Orissa, Kerala, Meghalaya and other Union Territories. In fact, Shri H.N. Bahuguna, the then Chief Minister of Uttar Pradesh has stated in his affidavit that he came to know about the proclamation of Emergency on the morning of June 26, when he was having breakfast along with Shri Uma Shankar Dikshit and Shri Keshav Deo Malaviya, two Central Ministers, and they were as surprised as he was about the promulgation of Emergency.

3 President's Rule: A *Sui Generis* Emergency Power

3.1 Introductory

Apart from the emergency provisions discussed in the preceding part of this chapter, articles 356 and 357 of the Indian Constitution provide for emergency action by the President in case of failure of constitutional machinery in the states. Action under these provisions is often referred to as imposition of "President's Rule" upon a state. Article 355 declares in a centralizing, unitary vein that "it shall be the duty of the Union to protect every State against external aggression and internal disturbance and to ensure that the government of every State is carried on in accordance with the provisions of the Constitution."[605] Article 356 empowers the President, "upon receipt of a report from the Governor of a State or otherwise" and "if satisfied that a situation has arisen in which the government of the state cannot be carried on in accordance with the provisions of this Constitution,"[606] to do, by proclamation, any or all of the following:

(a) assume to himself all or any of the functions of the Government of the State and all powers exercisable by any authority or body in the State except the State Legislature[607];
(b) declare that the powers of the legislature shall be exercisable by or under the authority of Parliament[608];
(c) make such incidental and consequential provisions as appear to him to be necessary or desirable for giving effect to the objects of the proclamation, including provisions for suspending in whole or in part the operation of any provision of the Constitution relating to anybody or authority in the State.[609]

Although the President may revoke or vary an earlier proclamation by a later one,[610] he is specifically debarred from assuming to himself any of the powers vested in or exercisable by the High Court or to suspend in whole or in part any constitutional provision relating to the High Court.[611] Every proclamation under article 356 is required to be laid before each House of Parliament and is given an initial life of two months unless approved by affirmative resolutions of both Houses before the expiry of this period, although if the Lower House is not in session or has been dissolved, and the Upper House has approved the proclamation, the latter would expire only if the Lower house did not approve it within thirty days of its reconstituted sitting.[612] A proclamation, even after such approval, would cease to operate after the expiry of six months from the date of its issue unless further affirmative resolutions for its continuance are passed by both Houses of Parliament, although, again, if the Lower House is not in session or has been dissolved and the Upper House has approved the proclamation, the latter would expire only if the Lower House did not approve it within thirty days of its reconstituted sitting.[613]

---

[605] INDIA CONST. art. 355.
[606] INDIA CONST. art. 356 § 1.
[607] INDIA CONST. art. 356 § 1 cl. a.
[608] INDIA CONST. art. 356 § 1 cl. b.
[609] INDIA CONST. art. 356 § 1 cl. c.
[610] INDIA CONST. art. 356 § 2.
[611] INDIA CONST. art. 356 § 2, proviso.
[612] INDIA CONST. art. 356 § 3.
[613] INDIA CONST. art. 356 § 4.

Such affirmative parliamentary resolutions, providing for the period for which a proclamation is allowed, have to be in force for more than three years in the aggregate despite such periodic resolutions for its continuance.[614] Article 356 prescribes another limitation in this respect. No resolution for the continuance of a proclamation for more than one year from the date of its issue shall be passed by Parliament unless the following two conditions are cumulatively met[615]: (a) a proclamation of emergency (presumably under article 352 or 360) is in force in the whole or in part of India at the time of such resolution[616]; and (b) the Election Commission, an independent constitutionally created body entrusted with the superintendence, direction and control of elections in India, certifies that the continuance in force of the proclamation under article 356 during the period specified in such resolution is necessary on account of difficulties in holding general elections to the legislative Assemble of the State concerned.[617]

Article 357 provides, inter alia, for Parliament to exercise and the President to be vested with the legislative power of the State by means of a parliamentary statute.[618] It also provides for Parliament to delegate certain powers to the President,[619] and for the President to authorize expenditure from the Consolidated Fund of the State pending parliamentary sanction.[620] Laws made by the President or Parliament under article 357 continue to be in force even after the expiry of the proclamation under article 356 and until altered or repealed or amended by a competent (state) legislature or other authority.[621]

3.2 *Constituent Assembly Debates Relating to Articles 355, 356 and 357*

That the genesis of articles 356 and 357 lies in the Government of India Act 1935 (the 1935 Act) becomes clear even from a cursory glance at sections 45 and 93 of that Act. Section 93 sought, inter alia, to empower the provincial Governor to exercise his functions in his discretion and to assume to himself the powers and authority exercisable by any provincial body if satisfied that the "government of the

---

[614]INDIA CONST. art. 356 § 4.

[615]In respect of the proclamation issued under Article 356 on Oct. 6, 1983 for the state of Punjab, this period of one year was increased to two years by the forty eighth constitutional amendment assented to by the President on Aug. 26, 1984. This had to be done because in the then existing state of affairs in Punjab, it was not considered advisable to revoke President's Rule.

[616]INDIA CONST. art. 356 § 5 cl. a.

[617]INDIA CONST. art. 356 § 5 cl. b.

[618]INDIA CONST. art. 357 § 1 cl. a.

[619]INDIA CONST. art. 357 § 1 cl. b.

[620]INDIA CONST. art. 357 § 1 cl. c.

[621]INDIA CONST. art. 357 § 2.

province cannot be carried on in accordance with the provisions of this Act." Section 45 conferred similar powers upon the Governor-General as regards the Government of the federation, in substantially the same language.

The initial debate in the Constituent Assembly centered on the scope of the provincial Governor's powers to act in his discretion if "satisfied that there is grave menace to the peace and tranquility of the province or any part thereof." Santhanam did, however, propose that the President should be empowered to act in an emergency pursuant to a report from a provincial Governor. The draft Constitution proposed by the Constitutional Advisor in October 1947 for the first time drew clearly upon the 1935 Act and included clause 160, broadly similar to section 93 of the 1935 Act but with the important difference that the Governor of the province was empowered to act "if satisfied that a grave emergency has arisen which threatens the peace and tranquility of the province and that it is not possible to carry on the Government of the Province with the advice of his Ministers in accordance with the provisions of this constitution."[622] Clause 160 became draft article 188 in the Draft Constitution prepared by the Drafting Committee and submitted in February 1948.[623] In this document, separate emergency provisions were made: article 188 dealt with the provincial Governor's emergency powers while articles 275 to 280 dealt with emergency powers at the national level, including failure of constitutional machinery and empowered the President to act upon a report of the Governor under article 188. Article 278 thus substantially resembled section 45 of the 1935 Act. When it was decided that provincial Governors were not to be elected but would be appointed by the President, a Special Committee decided on April 11, 1948 that all references to functions to be exercised in their discretion by provincial Governors be omitted from the Constitution.[624] The Constitutional Advisor opined that this would necessitate deletion of article 186 from the Draft Constitution.[625] At the acting of the premiers of various Provinces on July 23, 1846, it was recognized that if Parliament took over the functions of the State Legislature after failure of constitutional machinery, it should be in a position to delegate its legislative authority by law to the President and the President in turn to the Governor.[626] Pandit Pant was of the view that such delegation would allow the Governor to act as an agent of the President carrying out the directions of the Centre rather than a non-elected autocrat acting in his discretion.[627]

---

[622]Clause 160 is reproduced Shiva Rao [26, pp. 65–66].

[623]Clause 188 is reproduced Shiva Rao [29, pp. 587–588].

[624]Shiva Rao [29, p. 411].

[625]*Id.* at 365.

[626]*Id.* at 697.

[627]*Id.*

Taking account of these discussions, the Drafting Committee on August 3, 1949 proposed the deletion of article 188 and the insertion of draft articles 277-A, 278 and 278-A, which eventually became articles 355, 356 and 357 in the Constitution of India.[628]

Speeches on these provisions occupy about fifty pages of the Constituent Assembly Debates.[629] As far as article 277-A is concerned, it is noteworthy that it was included by Ambedkar in March 1948 after representatives from some princely states expressed apprehensions about external aggression or internal violence directed against their states.[630] Interestingly, the provision allows federal intervention in the provinces on the same grounds as article 275 (later to become article 352), viz., "external egression and internal disturbance" but does not mention failure of constitutional machinery.[631] Ambedkar suggested that article 278 was meant to provide the operational machinery to carry out the mandate of article 277-A[632] and was modeled on the US Guaranty Clause and a similar provision of the Australian Constitution.[633]

A proposal[634] to substitute "internal insurrection or chaos" for "internal disturbance" in article 277-A, on the ground that the latter was too broad as "a disturbance of the human organism may range from a little pain in the finger up to hyperpyrexia or coma" was rejected.[635] The provision was justified as being

---

[628] *See* 9 Constituent Assembly Debates, Book 4, 130–32 (Lok Sabha Secretariat, reprint 2014). The scheme proposed by the Drafting Committee contemplated as follows:- (i) the deletion of Article (188); (ii) the insertion of an entirely new Article 277-A (later to become Article 355) declaring that it shall be the duty of the Union to protect every state against external aggression and internal disturbance and to ensure that the government of every state is carried on in accordance with provisions of the Constitution; (iii) the insertion of Article 278 (later Article 356) authorizing Presidential action pursuant to the Governor's report or otherwise if "satisfied that the Government of the state cannot be carried on in accordance with the provisions of the Constitution"; (iv) the insertion of Article 278-A (later Article 357) empowering Parliament to legislate for the State assembly or delegate such legislative power to the President who, in turn, may delegate to the provincial Governor.

[629] *See* 9 Constituent Assembly Debates, Book 4, 180–80 (Lok Sabha Secretariat, reprint 2014).

[630] Shiva Rao [26, pp. 217–220].

[631] This suggests that the provision partakes primarily of the character of the Article 276.

[632] *See* 9 Constituent Assembly Debates, Book 4, 133 (Lok Sabha Secretariat, reprint 2014). *See also* remarks of Raj Bahadur, *Id.* at 148.

[633] *Id.* at 150 (Alladi K. Ayyar). There thus appears to be contradiction in the conception of articles 356 and 357 as being provisions implementing the mandate of Article 355 while the latter is closer in form and substance to Article 352 than to Article 356 and 357.

[634] 9 Constituent Assembly Debates, Book 4, 138 (Lok Sabha Secretariat, reprint 2014) (By H.V. Kamath).

[635] Many speakers, however, criticized Article 277-A as nothing but a pious declaration. *See* 9 Constituent Assembly Debates, Book 4, 147 (Lok Sabha Secretariat, reprint 2014) (P.S. Deshmukh); *id.* at 162–63 (Naziruddin Ahmed); *id.* at 167 (Thakur Das Bhargava).) which arguably had nothing to do with emergency powers and was in any event unnecessarily in view of the other emergency provisions found in the Draft Constitution.

constitutionally necessary in order to authorize temporary dilution of provincial autonomy.[636]

Several voices were also raised in opposition to articles 278 and 278-A.[637] The use of the word "otherwise," was criticized as expanding the ambit of article e278 illimitably and was "mischievous" and "diabolical."[638] The provision was seen as a grave threat to provincial autonomy, inter alia, on the ground that it authorized Central intervention upon the fulfillment of a much lower threshold criterion (failure of constitutional machinery) than that specified for emergencies (external aggression or internal disturbance).[639] Grave apprehensions were expressed that this emergency power would be used casually for political ends, e.g., merely for resolving a ministerial crisis or for allegedly purifying the administration.[640] It was seen by some as being fundamentally violative of the letter and spirit of Federal Government.[641] It was opined that the Governor and not the President should be vested with emergency powers as he is the man on the spot with a deeper and better awareness of local problems.[642] It was also stated that the provision would lead to intolerant action or abuse of power when different political parties were wielding power, respectively, at the Centre and the States.[643] Many speakers found the provisions wholly superfluous in view of the existence of other articles dealing with the use of emergency powers during war, external aggression or internal disturbance.[644] Others deemed it to be the first step toward dictatorship[645] and view it as reducing provincial autonomy to a farce.[646]

Those who supported the proposals of the Drafting Committee were equally articulate. They saw the provisions as a proper and potent antidote to the fissiparous tendencies to which independent India was prone.[647] The importance of reposing greater trust and confidence in both the President and the Governor and the necessity of avoiding excessive legalism or hairsplitting was emphasized.[648] It was opined that Central intervention could be necessitated "otherwise" than by a

---

[636] *Id.* at 133 (B.R. Ambedkar).

[637] These were presented as a composite whole, being merely divisions of the original Article 276. The reason given for the partition into two articles was that "otherwise the whole Article 278 would have been such a mouthful that probably it would have been difficult for Members to follow the various provisions contained therein." (*Id.* at 133–34 (B.R. Ambedkar).).

[638] *Id.* at 140 (H.V. Kamath). *See also id.* at 142–43 (S.L. Saksena).

[639] *Id.* at 152 (B.M. Gupte).

[640] *Id.* at 141 (H.V. Kamath).

[641] *Id.* at 146 (P.S. Deshmukh).

[642] *Id.* at 147 (P.S. Deshmukh); 158 (L. Krishnaswami Bharati).

[643] *Id.* at 154 (K. Santhanam).

[644] *Id.* at 155, 157 (H.N. Kunzru).

[645] *Id.* at 166 (N. Ahmed).

[646] *Id.* at 161(Naziruddin Ahmad).

[647] *Id.* at 145 (B.H.Zaidi).

[648] *Id.* at 146 (B.H.Zaidi).

Governor's Report, e.g.: When the Council of Ministers of a State had collectively resolved that President's Rule is necessary but the Provincial Governor does not think so and does not send a report to this effect to the President.[649] Rapid and successive changes of governments, shaky coalitions and financial emergencies were cited as some of the manifold criteria for intervention and were seen as a justification for inclusion of the word "otherwise" in the provision.[650] It was also said that as the Governor was a non-elected individual, it would be wrong to restrict presidential action only to a Governor's report.[651] Others said that failure of constitutional machinery could only occur when ordinary liberties cannot be enjoyed by the people.[652] Article 278 was therefore seen as a cementing measure.[653] Indeed, a plea was made for the entrustment of all provincial legislative powers to the President including that concerning the High Court.[654] It was felt that the proposed provisions sought to combat evil with good and lawlessness with law.[655] However, some of the supporters of articles 278 and 278-A also expressed the hope that in practice it would either remain a dead letter or be used extremely rarely.[656]

After the debate extending over five hours, the three amendments proposed to article 277-A[657] were negatived and article 277-A, in exactly the same form as present article 255, was adopted.[658]

---

649 *Id.* at 168 (T.D. Bhargava).

650 *Id.* at 149 (Raj Bahadur).

651 *Id.* at 168 (Thakur Das Bhargava).

652 *Id.* at 169 (T.D. Bhargava).

653 *Id.* at 170 (T.D. Bhargava).

654 *Id.* at 170 (Brajeshwar Prasad).

655 *Id.* at 171 (B. Prasad).

656 *Id.* at 152 (B.M. Gupta). However, it was said that mere danger of potential abuse of the constitutional provision should not be a ground for its deletion as every provision in the Constitution can potentially be abused (*Id.* at 168 (T.D. Bhargava); 177 (B.R. Ambedkar).).

657 The proposed amendments are at 9 CONSTITUENT ASSEMBLY DEBATES, Book 4, 135–36 (Lok Sabha Secretariat, reprint 2014) *via* substitution of "Union Government" for "Union," substitution of "or" for "and" where the latter first occurs and substitution of "internal insurrection or chaos" for "internal disturbance."

658 Four amendments were moved in respect of Article 276—two by Mr. Kamath and two by Professor Saksena—but all four were rejected. Mr. Kamath proposed that the word "otherwise" be deleted and that the President be empowered to act only if, additionally, he is satisfied that a "grave emergency has arisen which threatens the peace and tranquility of the state." Professor Saksena wanted "Rajpramukh" in place of "Ruler of a state." *See* 9 CONSTITUENT ASSEMBLY DEBATES, Book 4, 136 (Lok Sabha Secretariat, reprint 2014) (this was later done but deleted by the seventh constitutional amendment with effect from November 1, 1956) and argued for the inclusion of a proviso in Article 278 empowering the President, if he thinks fit, to order dissolution of the State legislature followed by a fresh election and declaring that the proclamation shall cease to have effect from the day on which the newly elected legislature meets in session. (*Id.*).

Rejecting certain amendments, Ambedkar, at the conclusion of the debate, opined that article 278 empowered the President to assume any or all of the powers exercisable by the Governor, which included the power to dissolve the legislature and order elections.[659] He said that the provisions in question were not new or unusual as the counterpart of article 277-A is found in the US Guaranty Clause while articles 278 and 278-A only provided the operational machinery for effectuating the mandate of article 277-A.[660] He went on to differentiate articles 275 and 276 on the one hand and articles 276 and 276-A on the other. The former, he said, is usable during war or internal aggression while the latter "refers to the failure of machinery by reasons other than war or aggression."[661] In his opinion, while under article 275 Parliament could concurrently also legislate on or administer provincial matters, it could not suspend the provincial legislature or act in its stead as it could under article 278.[662] In response to a query, he categorically stated that under article 278, the Centre is not given authority to intervene in provincial affairs for the sake of good government or the provinces.[663] However, he avoided a specific query as to the meaning of the phrase "the provisions of the Constitution" found in article 278, saying that it had been used in the 1935 Act and therefore "everybody must be quite familiar with its de facto and de jure meaning."[664] Just before the voting began, Ambedkar added the following somber, and, in retrospect, prophetic, words:

> In fact I share the sentiments expressed by my honorable friend Mr. Gupta yesterday that the proper thing we ought to expect is that such articles will never be called into operation and that they would remain a dead latter. If a tall they are brought into operation, I hope the President, who is endowed with these powers, will take proper precautions before actually suspending the administration of the provinces. I hope the first thing he will do would be to issue a mere warning to a province that has erred, that things were not happening in the way in which they were intended to happen in the Constitution. If that warning fails, the second thing for him to do will be to order an election allowing the people of the province to settle matters by themselves. It is only in those circumstances he would report to this article. I do not think we could then say that these articles were imported in vain or that the President had acted wantonly.[665]

The provisions were then passed by the Assembly, which also negatived the amendments.

---

[659] *Id.* at 175.

[660] *Id.* at 175–76.

[661] *Id.* at 176.

[662] *Id.*

[663] *Id.* The query was by Mr. H.N. Kunzru.

[664] *Id.* at 177.

[665] *Id.*

3.3 *Post-emergency Changes in Articles 355, 356 and 357*

During the 1975 emergency, articles 356 and 357 were amended on three occasions.[666] In 1975, a new clause (5) making the "satisfaction" of the President mentioned in 356(1) "final and conclusive" and not questionable in "any court on any ground" was inserted. In 1976, the period after which affirmative parliamentary resolutions were required to continue a proclamation under article 356, was increased from six months to one year.[667] These two changes were, however, deleted by the successor Janata Government in 1979 and its period of one year was again brought down to six months.[668] However, one amendment made in 1975,[669] which provided for the continuance in force laws made during the pendency of an article 356 proclamation until altered or repealed by a competent provincial legislature, has not been deleted or modified thereafter and exists presently as article 357(2).[670] Finally, mention may be made of clause (5) added to article 356 in 1979 by the forty-fourth amendment.[671] It prohibits the passing of affirmative parliamentary resolutions for the continuance of an article 356 proclamation beyond one year unless certain conditions, specified above, are satisfied.

3.4 *Some Legal Aspects of President's Rule in India*

3.4.1 Role and Status of President and Governor During an Article 356 Proclamation

In view of the specific authorization found in articles 356 and 357, Presidential enactments for a State, made under authority delegated by Parliament, are valid and constitutional. Thus, a variety of Presidential statutes, made during a 356

[666]Relatively few changes have been made to constitutional provisions dealing with President's Rule in post-independent India. Those that have been made have mostly occurred after the 1975 emergency. Prior to the latter, the only amendment was the innocuous deletion of the word "Rajpramukh" from Article 356(1) in 195 (by the seventh constitutional amendment with effect from 1.11.1956) consequent to the reorganization of states and abolition of the title of "Rajpramukh."

[667]By the forty-second constitutional amendment with effect from December 18, 1976.

[668]By the forty-fourth constitutional amendment with effect from June 10, 1979.

[669]By the thirty eighth constitutional amendment, with effect from Aug. 1, 1975.

[670]The earlier version until 1975 continued in force such laws for a period of one year after the expiry of the proclamation "except as respects things done or omitted to be done before the expiration of the said period."

[671]With effect from June 10, 1979.

proclamation, and ranging from tenancy laws[672] to civil law amendment Acts,[673] have been upheld. As the President acts as a constitutional head and not in his discretion under articles 356 or 357,[674] and as the Supreme Court has categorically declared that Presidential action in name are in substance the actions of the Council of Ministers of the Union Government,[675] the effect of article 357 is that, subject to delegation by Parliament, the Council of Ministers of the Central Government can legislate for a state during a proclamation under article 356. Such central legislation is immune from some of the fetters imposed upon legislation by State Legislatures. For example, in respect of matters listed in the concurrent list,[676] both Parliament and State Legislatures are empowered to legislate, subject to the condition that in case of irreconcilable repugnancy, a parliamentary law would prevail over a state law.[677] However, the latter principle has been held to be inapplicable to a Presidential enactment under article 357[678]: such a law is not considered to be one passed by a State Legislature and is not subordinate, in case of repugnancy, to a Central law. It is, however, submitted that the view that a law made by the President under article 357 is not a state law is not considered to be the one passed by a State Legislature and is not subordinate, in case of repugnancy, to a Central law. It is, however, submitted that the view that a law made by the President under article 357 is not a state law cannot be unduly extended. It must not be forgotten that under article 356 (1) (b), a President is only empowered to declare that the "powers of the legislature of the state 'shall be exercisable by or under the authority of Parliament' and it is only after such declaration that Parliament" and it is only after such declaration that Parliament may, under article 357 (1) (a), proceed to "confer on the President the power of the legislature of the state to make laws." Hence, such laws under article 357 (1) (a), whether made by Parliament or by the President under parliamentary authority, cannot be laws which the State Legislature would itself not be competent to enact, e.g., relating to a matter in the Union List.[679]

The usual practice, when the President issues a proclamation under article 356, is for him to declare both that he has assumed the powers of the Governor and that Parliament shall exercise the powers of the State Legislature.[680] Thereafter, Presidential Orders are usually made delegating all Presidential powers to the Governor, subject to the overall supervision, control and superintendence of the

---

672 Behari Lal v. Kesari Nandan 1970 AIR 201 (Alld.).

673 Debnath v. Radharani Mondal 1971 AIR 534 (Cal.).

674 Bose v. Union of India 1971 AIR 123 (Cal.) at para 5.

675 Shamsher Singh v. Punjab, AIR 1974 SC 2192, 2198 (India).

676 India Const. sch. 7, list 3.

677 India Const. art. 254.

678 Debnath v. Radharani Mondal 1971 AIR 534 (Cal.).

679 India Const. sch. 7, list 7.

680 *See, e.g.*, S. Mohan Singh v. PEPSU, 1954 AIR 136 (PEPSU).

President.[681] Similarly, there may be conferment of state legislative power by Parliament to the President, who in turn may delegate it to the Governor. Such delegation, and indeed re-delegation by the Governor to Advisers or other bureaucrats, is not unconstitutional and is essential to the operation of the constitutional scheme during an article 356 proclamation.[682]

Whether the Governor be called a delegate[683] or the alter ego of the President—courts have even said that he is not a delegate but acts as the President himself[684]—it is clear that he has wide authority to administer the state and that virtually no executive or administrative action of his will be faulted by the courts on the ground that it exceeds the scope of the Presidential delegation. The Governor is seen as a constitutional functionary and authority,[685] who is unfettered in the range of his actions.

Such actions may range from dismissal of a public servant under article 311 of the Constitution[686] to the adoption of Rules for the more convenient transaction of the business of the Government[687] to re-delegation of authority to other individuals or authorities.[688] It is enough that, in theory, the Governor is subject to the superintendence, control and supervision of the President who may revoke such authority at any time.[689]

The conditions laid down by Parliament while delegating legislative powers to the President during President's Rule have varied from time to time and from state to state. Most enactments under which Parliament has made such delegations have required the President (i.e., in effect the Central Government) to consult, except where it is not practicable to do so, a committee whose members are nominated by the Speaker of the Lok Sabha and the Chairman of the Rajya Sabha, prior to making the enactments relating to the state.[690] Such enactments by the President are

---

[681] S. Mohan Singh v. PEPSU, 1954 AIR 136 (PEPSU).; Associated Transports v. Union of India 1978 AIR 173 (Madras).

[682] Behari Lal v. Kesari Nandan 1970 AIR 201 (Alld.); Debnath v. Radharani Mondal 1971 AIR 534 (Cal.).

[683] As he was, e.g., in Sujan Singh Matu Ram v. Punjab 1968 AIR 363 (Punjab and Haryana).

[684] Associated Transports v. Union of India 1978 AIR 173 (Madras).

[685] Burman v. West Bengal (1977) Lab. IC 628.

[686] *Id.*

[687] S. Mohan Singh v. PEPSU, 1954 AIR 136 (PEPSU).

[688] Bose v. Union of India 1971 AIR 123 (Cal.).

[689] Associated Transports v. Union of India 1978 AIR 173 (Madras); Bose v. Union of India 1971 AIR 123 (Cal.); Burman v. West Bengal (1977) Lab. IC 628; Gokulnanda v. Tarapada 1973 AIR 2330 (Cal.).

[690] *See, e.g.*, Patiala and East Punjab States Union Legislature (Delegation of Powers) Act 1953, Gazette of India, pt. II sec. 1 (Nov. 16, 1953). *See also*, Andhra State Legislative (Delegation of Powers) Act 1954, Gazette of India, pt. II sec. 1 (Dec. 7, 1954); Travancore-Cochin State Legislative (Delegation of Powers) Act 1956 Gazette of India, pt. II sec. 2 (May 18, 1956); Kerala State Legislative (Delegation of Powers) Acts 1959, Gazette of India, pt. II sec. 1 (Dec. 17, 1959); Orissa State Legislative (Delegation of Powers) Act 1961, Gazette of India, pt. II sec. 2 (Mar. 29, 1961); Punjab State Legislative (Delegation of Powers) Act 1966.

required to be laid before each House and either House is authorized to direct modifications to the Presidential enactment, by resolution passed within seven days of laying of the enactment before Parliament.[691] A number of variations on this general scheme have occurred from time to time: thus the constitution of the consultative committee has occasionally been dispensed with[692]; its strength has varied from state to state[693]; sometimes "Parliament" and at other times "either House of Parliament" has been authorized to modify the Presidential enactment by resolution.[694] However, the basic structure of the enactments, all of which seek to ensure a measure of parliamentary control over the activities of the Central Government in a state during President's Rule, has remained the same. A noteworthy change resulting from the scheme is that the normal rule of the initiation of legislative proposals in the House of Parliament and their subsequent submission for presidential approval or assent is reversed during President's Rule when Presidential enactments in respect of a State are presented to and are subject to modification by Parliament. This occurs presumably on the promise that the President or the Union Executive functions as a kind of surrogate legislature subject to parliamentary control and supervision.

This reversal of normal legislative practice has been seen as a dilution of Presidential discretion and prerogative to refuse assent to a legislative bill passed by both Houses.[695] Because during President's Rule, the President would possess no power to alter or disagree with the modification proposed by Parliament to a Presidential enactment. It is, however, submitted that the constitutional position of the President in the two situations—as assenter or dissenter to parliamentary bills and as enactor of Presidential enactments for a State during President's Rile—is not the same. In the former case, he acts in his constitutional capacity as the third legislative or as whose assent is necessary to create valid legislation. In the latter case, he acts as a constitutionally directed delegate of Parliament. Moreover, when Parliament specifies conditions, to be fulfilled by Presidential enactments for a state during President's Rule, it does so by an Act of Parliament and such a parliamentary enactment, as all others, must receive Presidential assent before becoming law. Lastly, the scope of the President's discretion regarding assent to bills passed

[691] *Id.*

[692] *See, e.g.*, in The Punjab State Legislature (Delegation of Powers) Act, No. 46 of 1951, Gazette of India, pt. II sec. 1 (Aug. 29, 1951).

[693] E.g., in AP(1954) and PEPSU(1953), the committee consisted of ten members from Lok Sabha and five from Rajya Sabha; in Orissa (1961) it involved fourteen from Lok Sabha and seven from Rajya Sabha; in Kerala (1959) and Punjab (1966 & 1968), it comprised thirty from Lok Sabha and fifteen from Rajya Sabha. This last figure has generally been adhered to in all states after 1959 (barring Orissa in 1961).

[694] *See, e.g.*, The Punjab State Legislature (Delegation of Powers) Act, No. 46 of 1951, Gazette of India, pt. II sec. 1 (Aug. 29, 1951) which mentioned "Parliament," while the Patiala and East Punjab States Union Legislature (Delegation of Powers) Act 1953, Gazette of India, pt. II sec. 1 (Nov. 16, 1953) mentioned "either House of Parliament."

[695] *See* Siwach [37].

by both Houses of Parliament is, in any event, limited by the Constitution. As far as money bills are concerned, he must signify his assent once both houses have passed the measure and cannot refuse to do so.[696] As far as non-money bills are concerned, Presidential discretion is limited to a single referral back to Parliament for reconsideration. If, however, Parliament passes the bill again, the Constitution directs that the "President shall not withhold assent there from."[697] This equation fairly reflects the Constitutional position of the President in a "non-presidential" parliamentary form of government.

3.4.2 Duration of Effects of Action Under an Article

356 Proclamation

It is well established that the life of an enactment passed by the President during an article 356 proclamation is not conterminous with the latter.[698] Prior to the thirty-eighth amendment in 1975, such an enactment would continue to have effect for a period of one year after the expiry of the proclamation[699]; since that amendment, such laws would continue to have effect "until altered or repealed or amended by a competent legislature or other authority."[700] The thirty-eighth amendment is an extraordinary and paternalistic provision in a federal scheme for it puts emergency presidential legislation enacted by the Union Executive for any state under President's rule, permanently on the statute look. The empowerment of the State Legislature to alter, amend or repeal an emergency presidential enactment does not redress the imbalance.

Violation of Constitutional Provisions Relating to Parliamentary Scrutiny

Although the issue remains res Integra in the absence of an authoritative judicial pronouncement, it is submitted that a number of practices relating to the issues of a proclamation under article 356 are open to question. Two particularly objectionable violations of the law, in this respect, occur when, firstly, proclamation under article

---

[696]INDIA CONST. art. 111, proviso.

[697]*Id.*

[698]Mohd. Salim Khan v. Bose AIR 1972 SC 1570 (India); Mondal v. West Bengal AIR (1972) SC 1497 (India).

[699]With effect from Aug. 1, 1985.

[700]INDIA CONST. art. 357 § 2. Under the pre-1975 law, even after the expiry of a year, "things done or omitted to be done" before such expiry would continue to have effect. It was decided in 1966 by the Supreme Court that the question whether actions taken during the pendency of an expiry of one year from the date of expiry of Article 356 proclamation would be dependent on whether the primary delegated legislation in question was intended to last longer than the President's Rule. (Ram Prasad v. State of Punjab (1966) SC 1607). In that case, it was held that the bank of Patiala Regulation and Management Order 1954, under which the petitioner was compulsorily retired, would continue to have effect even after one year from the date of revocation of President's Rule (thus making the petitioner's compulsory retirement permanent) since the 1954 Order was for the better management and regulation of the bank was interned to have effect for a longer period.

356 (not revoking an earlier proclamation) is not placed before Parliament although the latter is sitting and, secondly, when the need for periodic parliamentary approval of the proclamation is obviated by reissuing the proclamation. On the first issue, the Chairman of the Rajya Sabha and a Senior Minister of the Government have accepted, on the floor of Parliament, the obligation of the Government to place on article 356 proclamation on the table of Parliament even if it is intended to continue the proclamation beyond two months.[701] The requirement of laying before the House clearly applies to all kinds of proclamations, whether instituting President's Rule, or varying an earlier proclamation, or extending the life of an existing proclamation or reissuing an expiring proclamation or altogether revoking an earlier proclamation.[702] Occasion when a proclamation has not been placed before Parliament on the day of its issue or has been placed after the Parliament on the day of its issue or has been placed after the lapse of sometime (although before the expiry of two months), have continued to occur[703] and have been met with articulate protests and disapproval.

It is, however, doubtful that non-laying of a proclamation or its laying after some delay, could result in a declaration of illegality. Courts in India have not had occasion to rule on this issue. However, parliamentary procedures may be held to be purely directory rather than mandatory, and consequently, substantial compliance or even non-compliance may not result in retrospective or prospective invalidity. It is submitted that in the event of an absolute and palpable non-compliance (like not laying a 350 proclamation before Parliament) of a constitutional provision, a Presidential proclamation is liable to run the risk of an ex post facto declaration of illegality and impropriety from the courts. There are, however, obvious practical limitations to the judicial process in this respect. Few legal challenges would be adjudicated or decided before the expiry of two moths, by which time the 358 proclamation would either have expired through efflux of time or would have secured parliamentary approval for its continuance. Moreover, it would be

[701] Remarks of Zakhir Hussain speaking during the Rajya Sabha debate on President's Rule in Rajasthan in 1967.

[702] Even a proclamation altogether revoking an earlier one would not appear to be excluded from the requirement of laying before Parliament because Article 356(3) exempts such a revocation of proclamation only from expiring after two months but does not exempt it from the requirement of laying before Parliament. Yet, proclamations under Article 356 have been issued—notably in Orissa on January 11, 1971; January 23, 1971 and March 23, 1971—which were never placed before Parliament. The 11/1/71 proclamation was revoked on 22/1/71 without being placed before Parliament. On the same day (i.e., 23/1/71) a new proclamation was issued which expired on 22/3/71 without being placed before the Lok Sabha, which had already been dissolved. A third proclamation was issued on 23/3/71 re-imposing President's Rule which was revoked on 3/4/71 without being placed before Parliament. Only the last revocation proclamation was placed before Parliament. *See* L.S. Deb. Vol. 1, Nos, 1–12, 1971, col. 151 & Vol. II, No. 1–10, May 24, 1971, col. 159.

[703] *See, e.g.*, Kerala, issued 31/7/59, placed 10/959; AP issued 18/1/73, Parliamentary session commenced 2/2/73, placed 20/2/73; Gujarat issued 9/2/74, session commenced 18/2/74, placed 11/3/74; Nagaland issued 23/3/75, placed in Lok Sabha on 25/3/75 and in Rajya Sabha a day later.

inappropriate to void or invalidate all actions taken under such a proclamation in view of the mandate of article 357 (2) which protects and continues action under the 355 proclamation even after the expiry of the proclamation. The primary result of legal challenge would thus be a declaration, which although largely devoid of any legal penalties, may have political consequences of a signification nature and may well create public awareness and opinion against repetition of such malpractices.

The second possibility of abuse may be explained in terms of a hypothetical example. Suppose an article 356 proclamation is issued; after a few days it is revoked and then immediately replaced by another similar proclamation. Such a succession of proclamations may, in theory, be multiplied endlessly. As long as new proclamation is issued at or prior to the expiry limit of two months, the provisions regarding parliamentary approval or scrutiny can be successfully circumvented. A similar stratagem can be used to avoid a fresh and second parliamentary approval after six months by revoking the existing proclamation and reissuing a new one just before the expiry of the six-month limit. The example is no doubt hypothetical and imaginary but there have been some occasions when parliamentary scrutiny has been avoided by reissuing proclamations rather than submitting them to parliamentary approval.[704]

It would be trite to say that what cannot be done directly cannot be done indirectly. Courts have often treated such indirect executive section as a colorable exercise of power and have even declared the offending action void. Although no such issue has been raised in the courts specifically in relation to article 356, a close parallel can be found in the regrettable practice of successively reissuing ordinances to create legislation by bypassing Parliament. This practice in respect of ordinance has been called a "fraud upon the Constitution."[705] It has been discussed earlier in some detail and need not be repeated except to say that the issue has been before the Supreme Court and awaits a final decision,[706] which would apply to successive article 356 proclamations on a parity of reasoning. A constitutional amendment placing a limit on the total number of proclamations under article 356 within a stipulated period appears to be desirable.

3.4.3 Legality of Suspension of Assembly

Another interesting legal question which may briefly be discussed is the legality of the common practice adopted of suspending the Assembly pursuant to a proclamation under article 356. The political advantages of suspending the Assembly as opposed to dissolving it have been discussed in a later section in the context of the

---

[704]The two-month initial scrutiny was avoided in Orissa in 1971 and in Bihar in 1972. The six-month scrutiny was similarly bypassed in Kerala in 1966 when the existing proclamation issued on September 16, 1961 was revoked on March 24, 1965 and a fresh proclamation was issued the same day.

[705]*See* Wadhwa [35].

[706]Dr. D.C. Wadhwa v. State of Bihar, AIR 1987 SC 579.

use and abuse of the power of President's Rule. On the question of its legality, it is noteworthy that the Constitution nowhere deals explicitly with suspension of the Assembly. Its provisions, even when dealing specifically with the State Assemblies, talk only of dissolution or prorogation.[707] As far as article 356 is concerned, it talks neither of dissolution nor of suspension of the State Assembly. Although the practice of suspension of the Assembly has been severally castigated by many eminent Parliamentarians,[708] and although it may often involve a dilution or even negation of the democratic process by providing breathing time for a party in power to set its house in order and resume the reins of government after revocation of President's Rule without facing the electorate, the Constitution appears, at least impliedly, to permit such a practice. It is arguable, and, indeed, has been argued, that article 356 (1) (a) which allows the President to make incidental and consequential provisions "suspending to whole or in part the operation or any provision of this constitution relating to anybody or authority in state" is applicable to this State Assembly. Hence even if the Assembly may itself not be directly suspendible, a whole host of constitutional provisions necessary for its efficacious functioning may be suspended and may result in the de facto suspension of the Assembly itself. Indeed, many such provisions relating to the Assembly (e.g., articles 151(2), 163-64, 166(3), 167,169, 174-86, 187 (3), 188-89, 195-98, 200-01, 202 (3), 206-11, 232 (2) of the Constitution) have been routinely suspended by the same Presidential proclamation that imposes President's Rule. Moreover, absence of power to suspend the Assembly could imply not only that every article 356 proclamation would result in the automatic dissolution of the Assembly such that the expiry or revolution of such a proclamation would necessitate fresh elections. This would be an onerous burden, and especially so when President's Rule has been introduced soon after or relatively early during the assumption of office by a newly elected government. Implied constitutional minute, political practice and practical convenience would this all suggest that an option to suspend rather than dissolve reflects the correct legal position. It needs, however, to be added that some of the abuses of the suspension power as discussed in a later section underline the need for carefully limiting this power to genuine cases only.

3.4.4 Judicial Review and Article 356

In an earlier section, it was demonstrated how judicial review is not altogether excluded in respect of executive action relating to emergencies arising out of war or

[707] *See, e.g.*, India Const. art. 174 § 2.

[708] L.K. Advani said in Rajya Sabha in 1973: "The new post 1969 theory of suspending legislatures rather than dissolving them is politically dubious and possibly constitutionally bad." *See* Rajya Sabha Deb, Vol. 85, No. 2, July 24, 1973 Col. 79. See remarks to same effect by P.G. Mavlankar, L.S. Deb., 5th Series, Vol. 35, no. 14, March 11, 1974, col. 856.

external aggression or internal disturbance or armed rebellion.[709] The power under article 356 is, in some senses, wider than that found in other provisions of Part XVIII of the Constitution.[710] For instance, the satisfaction required under article 355 is as to a "situation (which) has arisen in which the government of the state cannot be carried on in accordance with the provisions of the constitution…."[711] It is not limited to satisfaction as to the existence of war, external aggression or rebellion, as in article 352, it includes all other features which may give rise to such a "situation," which may arise from a mix of numerous social, legal and political variables. Even the "provisions of this Constitution" referred to in article 356 (7) are not enumerated or specified. The discretion of the executive authority thus appears to be wider and its balancing, decision making and ascertaining role greater. Moreover, the effects of a proclamation under article 356 are more in the realm of administration and politics than directly in relation to citizens and individuals. The proclamation under article 356 has not enhanced the powers of the executive (acting through the Governor) to take action affecting citizens in important areas of life, liberty and property and this may be a factor of underlying judicial reluctance to intervene in respect of action under article 356. Thus, courts have refused to review the power of the President to make incidental and consequential provisions under article 356 (1) (c)[712] or the issue of a proclamation under article 355[713] for a number of policy reasons, many of which have been enumerated in the earlier section on judicial review. Courts tend to take the view that discretion under article 356 is a constitutionally entrusted unreviewable power.[714]

It is submitted that despite various judicial dicta and observations to the contrary, judicial review in respect of article 356 is not altogether excluded. At the outset, it is submitted that violation of any of the mandatory provisions of article 356 or 357 would almost certainly evoke judicial invalidation. Thus, for example, non-observance of any of the time requirements specified, inter alia, in sub clause (3), (4) or 5 of article 356 would undoubtedly lead to judicial review and invalidation of executive action. It may, therefore, be legitimate to ask that if, for example, a filamentary resolution extending the life of an article 356 proclamation beyond one year is passed without satisfying the win conditions specified in clause (5) and leads to judicial observation, how can baseless or male fide or illegal

---

[709]It has been judicially suggested that challenges to exercise of power under article 352 are less likely to succeed than challenges in respect of Article 356: State of Rajasthan v. Union of India AIR 1977 SC 1361, 1389 (Beg CJ). On this reasoning, the conclusions reached earlier in respect of judicial review under Article 352 would apply, a fortori, to Article 356.

[710]*See also* Beg CJ in AIR 1977 SC 1361, 1379–80 (India).

[711]India Const. art. 356 § 1.

[712]Gokulnanda v. Tarapada 1973 AIR 233 (Cal.).

[713]Patnaik v. Orissa, 1974 AIR 52 (Orissa); Rao Birendra Singh v. Union of India 1968 AIR 441 (Punjab & Haryana); *In Re* Sreeramulu, 1974 AIR 106 (Andhra Pradesh).

[714]Although not fully articulated, this promise clearly underlies the decisions. *See* Rao Birendra Singh v. Union of India 1968 AIR 441 (Punjab & Haryana); *In Re* Sreeramulu 1974 AIR 106 (Andhra Pradesh).

satisfaction of the President in respect of failure of institutional machinery in the states be absolutely immune even from judicial scrutiny? Such scrutiny need not be equated to judicial invalidation: it may but often lead to judicial affirmation and legitimation of executive action.

Some of the earlier judicial remarks excluding judicial review[715] were made on the basis of the erstwhile article 356 (5) which, having been specifically inserted by a constitutional amendment, made the satisfaction of the President "final and conclusive" and not challengeable "in any court on any ground." The deletion of this clause by a later constitutional amendment[716] removes that impediment and clears the way for judicial review.

Some decisions have denied the possibility of judicial review on the basis of an erroneous view of the President's role under article 356. The President does not, as these decisions suggest, act under article 356 in his own individual discretion. It is now well settled that he acts as an institutional head and on the advice of the Central Council Ministers.[717] Presidential action under article 356 therefore be subject to judicial review in the same way the ministerial discretions and decisions.

State of Rajasthan v. Union of India

In *State of Rajasthan v. Union of India*[718] (1977), six cases[719] of the Indian Union filed original suits in the Supreme Court against the Union of India under article 131 of the Constitution, praying, inter alia, for an injunction training the Union of India from giving effect to an alleged "directive" and "threat" contained in the letter of the Union Home Minister dated April 18, 1977. This letter was written shortly after Mrs. Gandhi had been defeated at the general elections and the successor

[715] *See, e.g.*, Rao Birendra Singh v. Union of India 1968 AIR 441 (Punjab & Haryana).

[716] Vide the Constitution (Forty-Fourth) Amendment Act, No. 88 of 1978, India Code, (http://indiacode.nic.in/coiweb/amend/amend44.htm), which came in effect on June 20, 1979.

[717] In the leading decision on the nature of President's powers under the Indian Constitution, the Supreme Court said:

> Whenever the Constitution requires the satisfaction of the President or the Governor for the exercise of any power or function or the Governor, as the case may be, as for example in Article 123, 213, 311(2), Proviso (c), 317,352(1),356 and 360, the satisfaction required by the Constitution is not the personal satisfaction of the President or of the Governor but it is the satisfaction of the President or of the Governor in the Constitutional sense under the Cabinet system of Government.

Shamsher Singh v. Punjab AIR 1974 SC 2192, 2198, 2202 (India) (overruling Sardari Lal v. Union of India AIR 1971 SC 1547).

The question has now been settled by a seven judge bench of the Supreme Court dealing specifically with Article 356, where all judges agreed with the view that "there can be no doubt that the decision under Article 356 of the Constitution which is made by the President is a decision of the Council of Ministers". *See* State of Rajasthan v. Union of India, AIR 1977 SC 1361, 1420 (India) (per Goswami, J.).

[718] State of Rajasthan v. Union of India, AIR 1977 SC 1361 (India).

[719] These were: Rajasthan, Madhya Pradesh, Punjab, Bihar, Himachal Pradesh and Orissa.

Janata Government had assumed office. It called upon the Chief Minister of the States which continued to have governments belonging to Mrs. Gandhi's to advise the Governors of their respective states to dissolve the State Assembly in exercise of the power under article 174 (2) (5) and seek a fresh mandate from the electorate.[720]

A seven-member bench of the Supreme Court,[721] proceeding the assumption that the letter contained a "directive" or "threat" that unless the State Legislatures were dissolved a reclamation under article 356 would be issued, unanimously dismissed the suits and rejected the plea for grant of an function. It is noteworthy that at the time of that decision by the Supreme Court, article 356(5), containing the finality and conclusiveness clauses discussed earlier, was present in the Constitution. Despite the finality and conclusiveness clause, the separate judgements of the seven-judge bench in *Rajasthan* upheld the possibility of judicial review under certain circumstances. Thus, for instance, Chief Justice Beg said:

> The amended Article 356 (5) of the Constitution indicates that the Constitution makers did not want such an issue raising a mere question of sufficiency of grounds to be justiciable. Nevertheless, if all the grounds of action taken under Art. 356 (1) of the Constitution are disclosed to the public by the Union Government and its own disclosure of grounds reveals that a constitutionally or legally prohibited or extraneous or collateral purpose is sought to be achieved by a proclamation under Article 356 of the Constitution, this Court will not shirk its duty to act in the manner in which the law may then oblige it to act.[722]

Similarly, Justice Chandrachud, as he then was, said:

> So long as the reasons, if any are disclosed, given for the action proposed or taken, bear a reasonable nexus with the exercise of the particular power, the satisfaction of the President must be treated as conclusive. It will then not be open to judicial scrutiny. If, however, the reasons given are wholly extraneous to the formation of the satisfaction, the proclamation would be open to the attack that it is vitiated by legal mala fides.[723]

Justice Bhagwati was even more explicit:

> The Court cannot in the circumstances, go into the question of correctness or inadequacy of the facts and circumstances on which the satisfaction of the Central Government is based. But one thing is certain that if the satisfaction is mala fide or is based on wholly extraneous and irrelevant grounds, the Court would have jurisdiction to examine it, because in that case there would be (sic-no?) satisfaction of the President in regard to the matter in which he is required to be satisfied. The satisfaction of the President is a condition precedent to the exercise of power under 356, cl. (1) and if it can be shown that there is no satisfaction of the President at all, the exercise of the power would be constitutionally invalid. Of course, by reason of Cl (5) of Article 356, the satisfaction of the President is final and conclusive and cannot be assailed on any ground, but this immunity from attack cannot apply where the challenge is not that the satisfaction is improper or unjustified, but that there is no satisfaction at all. In such a case it is not the satisfaction at all. In such a case it is not the

---

[720]A sample letter to one state is at AIR 1977 SC 1361, 1373 (India).

[721]The judges were: Beg, C.J., Chandrachud, Bhagwati, Goswami, Gupta, Untwalia and Fazl Ali JJ. Each except Gupta, J., delivered a separate judgement; the latter concurred with Bhagwati, J.

[722]State of Rajasthan v. Union of India, AIR 1977 SC 1361, 1390–91 (India).

[723]*Id.* at 1400–01.

satisfaction arrived at by the President which is challenged, but the existence of the satisfaction itself.[724]

Justice Goswami said:

I am not prepared to say that this Court, which is the last recourse for the oppressed and the bewildered, will, for good, refuse to consider when there may be sufficient materials to establish that a proclamation under Article 356 (1) is tainted with mala fides.[725]

Justice Untwalia said:

I, however, must hasten to add that I cannot persuade myself to subscribe to the view that under no circumstances an order of proclamation made by the President under Article 356 can be challenged in a Court of law. And, I am saying so notwithstanding the provision contained in clause (5) of the said Article introduced by the Constitution (38th Amendment Act, 1975.[726]

Justice Fazl Ali remarked:

Even if an issue is not justiciable, if the circumstances relied upon by the executive authority are absolutely extraneous and irrelevant, the Courts have the undoubted power to scrutinize such an exercise of the executive power. Such a judicial scrutiny is one which comes into operation when the exercise of the executive power is colourable or malafide and based on extraneous or irrelevant considerations.[727]

Rajasthan did not involve challenges to a proclamation under article 356 as no such proclamation had in fact been issued.[728] The judges were also undoubtedly influenced by the fact that the impugned letter by the Home Minister sought to dissolve State Assemblies and hold fresh elections. The decision could well have been different had it been decided to impose an indefinite President's Rule rather than the professed search for a new mandate from the electorate.[729] It is, however, arguable that despite the acceptance of a measure of judicial review in principle, the Court's application of that principle was, at best, highly debatable and controversial.

When *Rajasthan* was decided it could have even been said, with some justification, that if no judicial review or judicial intervention was deemed necessary upon the facts and circumstances in *Rajasthan*, it is unlikely that circumstances warranting judicial intervention would ever arise. Rarely, if ever, would the motives and reasons for a proposed proclamation under article 356 be spelt out in detail, as was done in the *Rajasthan case*. Rarely, if ever, would such reasons come as close as they did in the Rajasthan case to being "extraneous" to the exercise of power

---

[724] *Id.* at 1414–15.

[725] *Id.* at 1420.

[726] *Id.* at 1422.

[727] *Id.* at 1437.

[728] *See, e.g.*, Beg, C.J., *Id.* at 1375–76.

[729] *See, e.g.*, remarks of Goswami, J.: "The matter would have been entirely different if there were no proposal, pari passu, for an appeal to the electorate by holding elections to these Assemblies". (*Id.* at 1420).

under article 356. For, in *Rajasthan*, the Union Government in substance sought to support a proposal proclamation under article 366 on the ground that the existence of a large number of State Governments belonging to a political party which had suffered a massive and humiliating defeat in the national elections a few months earlier had led to widespread alienation among the masses, did not reflect the true aspirations of the people and justified the imposition of President's Rule.

Even when *Rajasthan* was decided, it was doubtful if these circumstances or their pretended existence can be said to create a situation "in which the government of the state cannot be carried on in accordance with the provisions of the Constitution."[730] Indeed, the line between the reason given by the Union Government in *Rajasthan* and imposition of President's Rule because of the existence of a different party a power in a state was thin if not non-existent. When Chief Justice Beg suggested that judicial intervention was likely to ensue "if, for example, an authoritative statement on behalf of a Union Government, was issued that a dissolution is proposed only because the Chief Minister or the whole Council of Ministers of a state belongs to a particular caste or creed"[731] he did not perhaps fully appreciate how closely the Union Government action in the case satisfied the criterion spelt out by him. A commentator has said that the *Rajasthan* decision was a reflection of the Supreme Court's quest for populist post-emergency legitimation.[732] The fact remains that even while denying judicial review and relief to the six states in *Rajasthan*, the Court clearly reaffirmed the principle and demarcated areas and angles of judicial review.

S. R. Bommai v. Union of India

Things changed completely in *S. R. Bommai v. Union of India*[733] when a nine-judge bench of the Court was assembled to review proclamations of emergency issued by the President in six states were directly questioned before the Supreme Court as unconstitutional. These were—Karnataka, Meghalaya, Nagaland, Rajasthan, Madhya Pradesh and Himachal Pradesh. Out of these six, three were struck down as unconstitutional (Karnataka, Meghalaya and Nagaland) while the other three were upheld. Since fresh elections had already been ordered in Karnataka, Meghalaya and Nagaland and the State Legislatures had been elected and ministries already installed, the Court refused to order any consequential relief. But the holdings of the Court in *Bommai* were to have effect in several key post *Bommai* decisions where other art. 356 proclamations were questioned, reviewed, struck down, and consequential relief ordered. *Bommai* is a high watermark decision and perhaps one of the greatest contributions of the Supreme Court of India to emergency jurisprudence around the world. One of us have written elsewhere about the emergence of limited state sovereignty and its impact of federalism as understood in India, as a

[730] India Const. art. 356 § 1.

[731] State of Rajasthan v. Union of India, AIR 1977 SC 1361, 1376 (India).

[732] Baxi [38].

[733] S.R. Bommai v. Union of India, (1994) 3 SCC 1 (India).

result of *Bommai*, in Indian constitutional jurisprudence.[734] In this case for the first time, perhaps anywhere in the common law world, it was held that the advice given to the President by his Council of Ministers with the Prime Minister at its head was amendable to judicial review. Though it was not very difficult to come to this conclusion for it was conceded by the Attorney General that the advice of the Council is amenable to judicial review.[735] Furthermore, relying on the majority of Justice Sawant (for himself and Justice Kuldeep Singh), Justice Reddy (for himself and Justice Agrawal), and Justice Ramaswamy, it has been observed that in *Bommai*, "... for the first time, a theory of limited sovereignty of the States within their sphere of operation was accepted, *albeit* by a narrow majority of the Court."[736] Since the federalism aspect of *Bommai* has been examined in detail elsewhere, the same is not being repeated here. Only the part that deals with judicial review of article 356 proclamations is examined as is in keeping with the nature of this work.

Let us first try to understand on facts relating to all these six proclamations that were under question in *Bommai*. Facts are clearly borne out by the lead opinion of Justice Sawant (for himself and Justice Kuldeep Singh, in which a majority of judges had concurred). Focusing first on the Karnataka, Meghalaya and Nagaland proclamations that were struck down, the facts pertinent to these proclamations are reproduced from Justice Sawant's opinion. In context of the Karnataka proclamation the following had transpired:

> The facts were that the Janata Party being the majority party in the State Legislature had formed Government under the leadership of Shri S.R. Bommai on August 30, 1988 following the resignation on August 1, 1988 of the earlier Chief Minister, Shri Hegde who headed the Ministry from March 1985 till his resignation. In September 1988, the Janata Party and Lok Dal (B) merged into a new party called Janata Dal. The Ministry was expanded on April 15, 1989 with addition of 13 members. Within two days thereafter, i.e., on April 17, 1989, one Shri K.R. Molakery, a legislator of Janata Dal defected from the party and presented a letter to the Governor withdrawing his support to the Ministry. On the next day, he presented to the Governor 19 letters allegedly signed by 17 Janata Dal legislators, one independent but associate legislator and one legislator belonging to the

---

[734]Nicholas Aroney & Khagesh Gautam, *Federalism—A Selected Comparison*, in Shaun Star [39].

[735]*See e.g.*, S.R. Bommai v. Union of India, (1994) 3 SCC 1, 80 (India) (Ahmadi, J. for himself, concurring with Ramaswamy, J.) observing that,

> Since it was not disputed before us by the learned Attorney General as well as Mr. Parasaran, the learned counsel for the Union of India, that a Proclamation issued by the President on the advice of his Council of Ministers headed by the Prime Minister, is amenable to judicial review, the controversy narrows down to the determination of the scope and ambit of judicial review i.e. in other words, to the area of justiciability.

See also id. at 93 (Sawant, J. for himself and Kuldeep Singh, J.) observing that,

> It is not disputed before us that the Proclamation issued under Article 356(1) is open to judicial review. All that is contended is that the scope of the review is limited.

[736]Nicholas Aroney & Khagesh Gautam, *Federalism—A Selected Comparison*, in Shaun Star [39].

Bhartiya Janata Party which was supporting the Ministry, withdrawing their support to the Ministry. On receipt of these letters, the Governor is said to have called the Secretary of the Legislature Department and got the authenticity of the signatures on the said letters verified. On April 19, 1989, the Governor sent a report to the President stating therein that there were dissensions in the Janata Party which had led to the resignation of Shri Hegde and even after the formation of the new party, viz., Janata Dal, there were dissensions and defections. In support of his case, he referred to the 19 letters received by him. He further stated that in view of the withdrawal of the support by the said legislators, the Chief Minister, Shri Bommai did not command a majority in the Assembly and, hence, it was inappropriate under the Constitution, to have the State administered by an Executive consisting of Council of Ministers which did not command the majority in the House. He also added that no other political party was in a position to form the Government. He, therefore, recommended to the President that he should exercise power under article 356(1). It is not disputed that the Governor did not ascertain the view of Shri Bommai either after the receipt of the 19 letters or before making his report to the President. On the next day, i.e., April 20, 1989, 7 out of the 19 legislators who had allegedly written the said letters to the Governor sent letters to him complaining that their signatures were obtained on the earlier letters by misrepresentation and affirmed their support to the Ministry. The State Cabinet met on the same day and decided to convene the Session of the Assembly within a week, i.e., on April 27, 1989. The Chief Minister and his Law Minister met the Governor the same day and informed him about the decision to summon the Assembly Session. It is also averred in the petition that they had pointed out to the Governor the recommendation of the Sarkaria Commission that the strength of the Ministry should be tested on the floor of the House. The Chief Minister also offered to prove his majority on the floor of the House even by preponing the Assembly Session, if needed. To the same effect, he sent a telex message to the President. The Governor, however, sent yet another report to the President on the same day, i.e. April 20, 1989, in particular, referring to the letters of 7 members pledging their support to the Ministry and withdrawing their earlier letters. He, however, opined in the report that the letters from the 7 legislators were obtained by the Chief Minister by pressurising them and added that horsetrading was going on and atmosphere was getting vitiated. In the end, he reiterated his opinion that the Chief Minister had lost the confidence of the majority in the House and repeated his earlier request for action under Article 356(1). On that very day, the President issued the Proclamation in question with the recitals already referred to above. The Proclamation was, thereafter approved by Parliament as required by Article 356(3)."[737]

Factual situation was not much different in Meghalaya:

The facts are that the writ petitioner G.S. Massar belonged to a front known as Meghalaya United Parliamentary Party (MUPP) which had a majority in the Legislative Assembly and had formed in March 1990, a Government under the leadership of Shri B.B. Lyngdoh. On July 25, 1991, one Kyndiah Arthree who was at the relevant time, the Speaker of the House, was elected as the leader of the opposition group known as United Meghalaya Parliamentary Forum (UMPF). The majority in this group belonged to the Congress Party. On his election, Shri Arthree claimed support of majority of the members in the Assembly and requested the Governor to invite him to form the Government. Thereupon, the Governor asked the then Chief Minister Shri Lyngdoh to prove his majority on the floor of the House. Accordingly, a special session of the Assembly was convened on August 7, 1991 and a motion of confidence in the Ministry was moved. Thirty legislators supported the motion and 27 voted against it. However, instead of announcing the result of the voting

[737]S.R. Bommai v. Union of India, (1994) 3 SCC 1, 125–26 (Sawant, J., for himself and Kuldeep Singh, J.) (Pandian, J. concurring).

on the motion, the Speaker declared that he had received a complaint against 5 independent MLAs of the ruling coalition front alleging that they were disqualified as legislators under the anti-defection law and since they had become disentitled to vote, he was suspending their right to vote. On this announcement, uproar ensued in the House and it had to be adjourned. On August 11, 1991, the Speaker issued show-cause notices to the alleged defectors, the 5 independent MLAs on a complaint filed by one of the legislators Shri Shylla. The 5 MLAs replied to the notice denying that they had joined any of the parties and contended that they had continued to be independent. On receipt of the replies, the Speaker passed an order on August 17, 1991, disqualifying the 5 MLAs on the ground that 4 of them were Ministers in the then Ministry and one of them was the Deputy Government Chief Whip. Thereafter, again on the Governor's advice, the Chief Minister Shri Lyngdoh summoned the session of the Assembly on September 9, 1991 for passing a vote of confidence in the Ministry. The Speaker however, refused to send the notices of the session to the 5 independent MLAs disqualified by him and simultaneously made arrangements to prohibit their entry into the Assembly. On September 6, 1991, the 5 MLAS, approached this Court. This Court issued interim order staying the operation of the Speaker's orders dated August 7, 1991 and August 17, 1991 in respect of four of them. It appears that one of the members did not apply for such order. The Speaker, thereafter, issued a Press statement in which he declared that he did not accept any interference by any court with his order of August 17, 1991. The Governor, therefore, prorogued the Assembly indefinitely by his order dated September 8, 1991. The Assembly was again convened at the instance of the Governor on October 8, 1991. In the meanwhile, the 4 independent MLAs who had obtained the interim orders moved a contempt petition in this Court against the Speaker who had not only made the declaration in the Press statement defying the interim order of this Court but also taken steps to prevent the independent MLAs from entering the House. On October 8, 1991, this Court passed another order directing that all authorities of the State should ensure the compliance of the Court's interim order of September 6, 1991. Pursuant to this direction, 4 of the 5 independent MLAs received invitation to attend the session of the Assembly convened on October 8, 1991. In all, 56 MLAs including the 4 independent MLAs attended the session. After the motion of confidence in the Ministry was put to vote, the Speaker declared that 26 voted for the motion and 26 against it and excluded the votes of the 4 independent MLAS. Thereafter, declaring that there was a tie in voting, he cast his own vote against the motion and declared that the motion had failed and adjourned the House sine die. However, 30 MLAs, viz., 26 plus 4 independent MLAs who had voted for the motion, continued to stay in the House and elected the Speaker from amongst themselves to conduct the business. The new Speaker declared that the motion of confidence in the Ministry had been carried since 30 MLAs had voted in favour of the Government. They further proceeded to pass a motion of no-confidence in the Speaker. The 30 MLAs thereafter sent a letter to the Governor stating therein that they had voted in favour of the Ministry and had also passed a motion of no-confidence in the Speaker. However, on October 9, 1991, the Governor wrote a letter to the Chief Minister asking him to resign in view of what had transpired in the Session on October 8, 1991. Unfortunately, the Governor in the said letter also proceeded to observe that the non-cognisance by the Speaker of the Supreme Court's orders relating to the 4 independent MLAs was a matter between the Speaker and the Court. The Chief Minister moved this Court, thereafter, against the letter of the Governor, and this Court on October 9, 1991, among other things, asked the Governor to take into consideration the orders of this Court and votes cast by the 4 independent MLAs before taking any decision on the question whether the Government had lost the motion of confidence. In spite of this, the President on October 11, 1991 issued Proclamation under Article 356(1). The Proclamation stated that the President was satisfied on the basis of the report from the Governor and other information received by him that the situation had arisen in which the Government of the State could not be carried on in accordance with the provisions of the Constitution. The Government was dismissed and the

> Assembly was dissolved. This Court by an order of October 12, 1991, set aside the order dated August 17, 1991 of the then Speaker. However, thereafter, both the Houses of Parliament met and approved the Proclamation issued by the President."[738]

And lastly, the facts in Nagaland were also rather similar to the manner in which proclamations in Karnataka and Meghalaya were made:

> The Presidential Proclamation dated August 7, 1988 was issued under Article 356(1) imposing President's rule in the State of Nagaland. At the relevant time, in the Nagaland Assembly consisting of 60 members, 34 belonged to Congress 1, 18 to Naga National Democratic Party, one belonged to Naga Peoples Party and 7 were independent. Shri Sema, the leader of the ruling party was the Chief Minister heading the State Government. On July 28, 1988, 13 out of the 34 MLAs of the ruling Congress I Party informed the Speaker of the Assembly that they had formed a party separate from Congress I ruling party and requested him for allotment of separate seats for them in the House. The session was to commence on August 28, 1988. By his decision of July 30, 1988, the Speaker held that there was a split in the party within the meaning of the Tenth Schedule of the Constitution. On July 31, 1988, Shri Vamuzo, one of the 13 defecting MLAs who had formed a separate party, informed the Governor that he commanded the support of 35 out of the then 59 members in the Assembly and was in a position to form the Government. On October 1988, the Chief Secretary of the State wrote to Shri Vamuzo that cording to his information, Shri Vamuzo had wrongfully confined the MLAs who had formed the new party. Shri Vamuzo denied the said allegation and asked the Chief Secretary to verify the truth from the members themselves. On verification, the members told the Chief Secretary that none of them was confined, as alleged. On August 6, 1988, the Governor sent a report to the President of India about the formation of a new party by the 13 MLAS. He also stated that the said MLAs were allured by money. He further stated that the said MLAs were kept in forcible confinement by Shri Vamuzo and one other person, and that the story of split in the ruling party was not true. He added that the Speaker was hasty in according recognition to the new group of the 13 members and commented that horse-trading was going on in the State. He made a special reference to the insurgency in Nagaland and also stated that some of the members of the Assembly were having contacts with the insurgents. He expressed the apprehension that if the affairs were allowed to continue as they were, it would affect the stability of the State. In the meanwhile, the Chief Minister submitted his resignation to the Governor and recommended the imposition of the President's rule. The President thereafter, issued the impugned Proclamation and dismissed the Government and dissolved the Assembly.[739]

The facts pertinent to proclamations in Rajasthan, Madhya Pradesh and Himachal Pradesh are similar since these assemblies were suspended in the light of the Ram Janmabhumi movement that was underway that time, and will be discussed later.

---

[738] *Id.* at 129–30.

[739] *Id.* at 131–32.

Justice Pandian wrote a short opinion concurring with Justice Sawant and Justice Reddy.[740] Justice Ahmadi wrote a longer opinion concurring with Justice Ramaswamy.[741] Justice Ahmadi made some rather key observations in the context of the British Joint Parliamentary Report discussed above. This Report went on to become the basis for a key provision in the Government of India Act, 1935 that was subsequently adopted in the Indian Constitution as article 356. Whereas the influence of this Report and that of Government of India Act, 1935 on the drafting of article 356 has been discussed earlier, Justice Ahmadi opined that this Report cannot be used to interpret article 356 in the following words:

> Although the emergency provisions found in part XVIII of the Constitution are more or less modeled on the pattern of similar provisions contained in the Government of India Act, 1935, the exercise of that power under the said provisions cannot be compared with its exercise under the Constitution for the obvious reason that they operated under totally different conditions. Under the Government of India Act, 1935, the Governor General and the Governor exercised as representatives of the Crown near absolute powers, only limited powers were given to the elected Governments and those too could be taken away if it was felt that the Government concerned could not be carried on in accordance therewith. So also reference to the British Joint Parliamentary Report is inapposite for the simple reason that the situation under the Constitution is not comparable with that which formed the basis of the Report. The power conferred on the President of India under Article 356 has to be exercised in a wholly different political set-up as compared to that obtaining under the Government of India Act, 1935. The constitutional philosophy of a free country is totally different from the philosophy of a similar law introduced for the governance of a country by its colonial masters.[742]

On the question of a proclamation being issued under article 356 only on the ground that a different political party from the one that is in office in the state has now been elected into office in New Delhi (exactly what had happened on facts in *Rajasthan*), Justice Ahmadi observed, "… the mere defeat of the ruling party at the Centre cannot by itself, without anything more, entitle the newly elected party which comes to power at the Centre to advise the President to dissolve the Assemblies of those States where the party in power is other than the one in power at the Centre. [This] is no ground to hold that 'a situation has arisen in which the Government of the State cannot be carried on in accordance with the provisions of this Constitution'…."[743] On the question of justiciability of the advice of the

---

[740] *Id.* at 65–67 (Pandian, J. for himself, concurring with Sawant, J. and Reddy, J.).

[741] *Id.* at 67–83 (Ahmadi, J. for himself, concurring with Ramaswamy, J.). In the context of the federalism and limited state sovereignty angle mentioned at the start of this part, and discussed in detail elsewhere by one of us, we may note that Ahmadi, J. was in minority on that issue. *See Id.* at 74 (Ahmadi, J. for himself, concurring with Ramaswamy, J.) (observing that, *"Under our Constitution the State as such has no inherent sovereign power or autonomous power which cannot be encroached upon by the Centre.*"), and Nicholas Aroney & Khagesh Gautam, *Federalism—A Selected Comparison*, in Shaun Star [39]. Given the nature of this work, a detailed discussion of the correctness or sustainability of the minority view as represented by Ahmadi, J.'s opinion and any further mentions to the same of other justices who concurred in Ahmadi, J.'s view is omitted.

[742] S.R. Bommai v. Union of India, (1994) 3 SCC 1, 68 (Ahmadi, J. for himself, concurring with Ramaswamy, J.)

[743] *Id.* at 79.

Council of Ministers to the President, Justice Ahmadi held that the bar in article 74 (2) does not prohibit the production of "all the materials on which the ministerial advice was based."[744] It is to be carefully noted that Justice Ahmadi specifically held that the subjective satisfaction that the President has to reach under articles 352, 356 and 360 is beyond judicial review:

> The opinion which the President would form on the basis of the Governor's report or otherwise would be based on his political judgment and it is difficult to evolve judicially manageable norms for scrutinizing such political decisions. It, therefore, seems to me that by the very nature of things which would govern the decision-making under Article 356, it is difficult to hold that the decision of the President is justiciable. ... The temptation to delve into the President's satisfaction may be great but the courts would be well advised to resist the temptation for want to judicially manageable standards. Therefore, in my view, the court cannot interdict the use of constitutional power conferred on the President under article 356 unless the same is shown to be mala fide.[745]

Justice Ahmadi did not concur in striking down on the impugned proclamations in Karnataka, Meghalaya and Nagaland and only observed that the Meghalaya proclamation might be vulnerable to attack. However, since fresh elections had already been conducted, he refused to proceed any further with his review.[746]

Justice Verma (for himself and Justice Dayal) straightaway accepted the proposition that a proclamation issued under article 356 is indeed subject to judicial review and the debate was confined, "... essentially to the scope of judicial review or the area of justiciability in that sphere."[747] Like Justice Ahmadi, Justice Verma also held that when a 356 proclamation in under question, article 74(2) would no bar to production of the materials on which the ministerial advice is based.[748] And like Justice Ahmadi, Justice Verma also cautioned about the lack of judicially manageable standards when the subjective satisfaction of the President under article 356 is in question:

> It would appear that situations wherein the failure of constitutional machinery has to be inferred subjectively from a variety of facts and circumstances, including some imponderables and inferences leading to a subjective political decision, judicial scrutiny of the same is not permissible for want to judicially manageable standards. These political decisions call for judicial hands off envisaging correction only by a subsequent electoral verdict, unless corrected earlier in Parliament.
>
> In other words, only cases which permit application of totally objective standards for deciding whether the constitutional machinery has failed, are amenable to judicial review and the remaining cases wherein there is any significant area of subjective satisfaction dependent on some imponderables or inferences are not justiciable because there are not judicially manageable standards for resolving the controversy; and those cases are subject only to political scrutiny and correction for whatever its value in the existing political scenario. This appears to be constitutional scheme.[749]

---

[744] *Id.* at 80.

[745] *Id.* at 82.

[746] *Id.*

[747] *Id.* at 83 (Verma, J., for himself and Dayal, J.)

[748] *Id.* at 85.

[749] *Id.*

Justice Verma also did not concur in striking down on the impugned proclamations in Karnataka, Meghalaya and Nagaland but when a step ahead on Justice Ahmadi and observed that only the Meghalaya proclamation was justiciable. However, since fresh elections had already been conducted, he observed that there was no occasion to grant any relief and thus stopped his review there.[750]

In our opinion, the most powerful judgement in *Bommai* (also the lead opinion going by the number of concurrences recorded by other justices on the bench in this opinion) was delivered by Justice Sawant (for himself and Justice Kuldeep Singh). Justice Sawant was sensitive to article 356's potential to subvert the "entire constitutional scheme" and observed that it fell upon the judiciary to ensure that no such subversion is allowed.[751] As per Justice Sawant the following questions were presented to the Court:

> The crucial question that falls for consideration in all these matters is whether the President has unfettered powers to issue Proclamation under Article 356(1) of the Constitution. The answer to this question depends upon the answers to the following questions: (a) Is the Proclamation amenable to judicial review? (b) If yes, what is the scope of the judicial review in this respect? and (c) What is the meaning of the expression "a situation has arisen in which the Government of the State cannot be carried on in accordance with the provisions of this Constitution" used in Article 356(1)?[752]

Justice Sawant after an extensive review of Indian and foreign authority on the point, held that the Presidential proclamation under article 356 is subject to judicial review, "... at least to the extent of examining whether the conditions precedent to the issuance of the Proclamation have been satisfied or not."[753] He also held that Presidential satisfaction under article 356 has to be based on objective materials that have to be shown to exist, and the absence whereof can make a 356 proclamation open to challenge.[754] He further held that the prohibition in article 74(2) cannot

---

[750] *Id.* at 87 (Ahmadi, J. for himself, concurring with Ramaswamy, J.).

[751] *Id.* at 112 (Sawant, J. for himself and Kuldeep Singh, J.).

[752] *Id.* at 87.

[753] *Id.* at 102.

[754] *Id.* at 93 (Sawant, J. for himself and Kuldeep Singh, J.) observing that,

> In other words, the President's satisfaction has to be based on objective material. That material may be available in the report sent to him by the Governor or otherwise or both from the report and other sources. Further, the objective material so available must indicate that the Government of the State cannot be carried on in accordance with the provisions of the Constitution. Thus the existence of the objective material showing that the Government of the State cannot be carried on in accordance with the provisions of the Constitution is a condition precedent before the President issues the Proclamation. Once such material is shown to exist, the satisfaction of the President based on the material is not open to question. However, if there is no such objective material before the President, or the material before him cannot reasonably suggest that the Government of the State cannot be carried on in accordance with the provisions of the Constitution, the Proclamation issued is open to challenge.

stand in the way of the Court's inquiry into the existence of these materials.[755] Laying down the scope of judicial review of a 356 proclamation, he held:

> This examination will necessarily involve the scrutiny as to whether there existed material for the satisfaction of the President that a situation had arisen in which the Government of the State could not be carried on in accordance with the provisions of the Constitution. Needless to emphasise that it is not any material but material which would lead to the conclusion that the Government of the State cannot be carried on in accordance with the provisions of the Constitution which is relevant for the purpose. … Hence the material in question has to be such as would induce a reasonable man to come to the conclusion in question. … Hence it is not the personal whim, wish, view or opinion or the *ipse dixit* of the President dehors the material placed before him which is relevant for the purpose. In other words, the President has to be convinced of or has to have sufficient proof of information with regard to or has to be free from doubt or uncertainty about the state of things indicating that the situation in question has arisen. **Although, therefore, the sufficiency or otherwise of the material cannot be questioned, the legitimacy of inference drawn from such material is certainly open to judicial review**. … Hence situations which can be remedied or do not create an impasse, or do not disable or interfere with the governance of the State according to the Constitution, would not merit the issuance of the Proclamation [under article 356]. … When the Proclamation is challenged by making out a prime facie case with regard to its invalidity, the burden would be on Union Government to satisfy that there exists materials which showed that the Government could not be carried on in accordance with the provisions of the Constitution. Since such material would be exclusively within the knowledge of the Union Government, in view of the provisions of Section 106 of the Evidence Act, the burden of proving the existence of such material would be on the Union Government.[756]

The proclamation being subjected to judicial review, and the standard of review being clarified, the next obvious question is what is to be done in the event the proclamation is found unconstitutional and is struck down? Justice Sawant held that in such a situation the suspended State Legislature and State Cabinet shall stand restored since anything less than that and the power of judicial review itself would be rendered

---

[755]*See Id.* at 109 (Sawant, J. for himself and Kuldeep Singh, J.) observing that,

> The courts are not interested in either the advice given by the Ministers to the President or the reasons for such advice. The courts are, however, justified in probing as to whether there was any material on the basis of which the advice was given, and whether it was relevant for such advice and the President could have acted on it. Hence when the courts undertake an enquiry into the existence of such material, the prohibition contained in Article 74(2) does not negate their right to know about the factual existence of any such material. This is not to say that the Union Government cannot raise the plea of privilege under Section 123 of the Evidence Act.

We should note here that on this point Pandian, J., Ahmadi, J., and Verma, J. (for himself and Dayal, J.) also agreed. With the concurrence of Sawant, J. (for himself and Singh, J.) we have a majority of 6 out of 9 judges on this issue.

[756]*Id.* at 103, 109 (Sawant, J. for himself and Kuldeep Singh, J.) (Emphasis Added).

nugatory.[757] Furthermore, it was held that the dissolution of the State Legislature prior to the approval of the proclamation by the Parliament under article 356(3) is *per se* invalid.[758] However, the Supreme Court's power to invalidate a 356 proclamation stands notwithstanding whether the proclamation has been approved by the Parliament or not.[759] As a consequence of a proclamation being declared unconstitutional, the suspended State Legislature and the State Cabinet may be restored, but the grant of this consequential relief will depend on the facts of the case.[760] Having laid down the law as such, Justice Sawant found that the Karnataka,[761] Meghalaya[762] and Nagaland proclamations were unconstitutional. The observations in Karnataka's case (facts have been reproduced above at the beginning of this section—perhaps it would be better for the reader to examine them once again before proceeding forward), made by Justice Sawant are worth careful reading:

> … the Governor … arrogated to himself the task of holding, firstly, that the earlier 19 letters were genuine and were written by the said legislators of their free will and volition. He had not even cared to interview the said legislators, but had merely got the authenticity of the signatures verified through the Legislatures Secretariat. … [I]t is not known from where the Governor got the information that there was horse-trading going on between the legislators. **Even assuming that it was so, the correct and the proper course for him to adopt was to await the test on the floor of the House which test the Chief Minister has willingly undertaken to go through on any day that the Governor chose.** … We are of the view that this is a case where all cannons of propriety were thrown to the wind and the undue haste made

[757] *Id.* at 122 (Sawant, J. for himself and Kuldeep Singh, J.) observing that,

> The question then arises is whether the Council of Ministers and the Legislative Assembly can be restored by the Court when it declares the Proclamation invalid. There is no reason why the Council of Ministers and the Legislative Assembly should not stand restored as a consequence of the invalidation of the Proclamation the same being the normal legal effect of the invalid action. … Unless such result is read, the power of judicial review vested in the judiciary is rendered nugatory and meaningless. To hold otherwise is also tantamount to holding that the Proclamation issued under Article 356(1) is beyond the scope of judicial review. For when the validity of the Proclamation is challenged, the court will be powerless to give relief and would always be met with the *fait accompli.*

[758] *Id.* at 123–24.

[759] *Id.* at 124 (Sawant, J. for himself and Kuldeep Singh, J.).

[760] *Id.*

[761] *Id.* at 128 (Sawant, J. for himself and Kuldeep Singh, J.) observing that,

> … [I]t was incumbent upon the Governor to ascertain whether any other Ministry could be formed. … What is to be ascertained is whether the Governor had proceeded legally and explored all possibilities of ensuring a constitutional Government in the State before reporting that the constitutional machinery had broken down.

[762] *Id.* at 131 (Sawant, J. for himself and Kuldeep Singh, J.) observing that,

> [The facts disclose] in unmistakable terms the Governor's unnecessary anxiety to dismiss the Ministry and dissolve the Assembly and also his failure as a constitutional functionary to realize the binding legal consequence of and give effect to the orders of this Court.

> by the Governor in inviting the President to issue the Proclamation under Article 356(1) clearly smacked of mala fides. ... A duly constituted Ministry was dismissed on the basis of material which was neither tested nor allowed to be tested and was no more than the *ipse dixit* of the Governor. ... **The Proclamation having been basedon the said report and so-called other information which is not disclosed, was therefore liable to be struck down.**[763]

Therefore, the Governor's constitutional obligation is to first make his best possible effort to see if a Government can be made in the State. The only way to do that is allow the State Legislature to convene and go through its motions. In Karnataka's case, the Chief Minister had agreed to defend a no-confidence motion and therefore it was not for the Governor to send a report to the President under article 356 recommending the dissolution of the House. The Governor should have waited for the outcome of the no-confidence motion. This is also borne out by the following observations of Justice Sawant in Nagaland's case:

> On the facts of this case also we are of the view that the Governor should have allowed Shri Vamuzo to test his strength on the floor of the House. This was particularly so because the Chief Minister, Shri Sema had already submitted his resignation to the Governor. ... **Since no opportunity was given to Shri Vamuzo to prove his strength on the floor of the House as claimed by him and to form the Ministry, the Proclamation issued was unconstitutional.**[764]

Having thus struck down the Karnataka, Meghalaya and Nagaland proclamations, Justice Sawant upheld the Rajasthan, Madhya Pradesh and Himachal Pradesh proclamations.[765] The over-arching facts looming large over these three proclamations were very different. Whereas in the cases of Karnataka, Meghalaya and Nagaland, it was mostly about gubernatorial haste in dismissing the State Legislature on questionable grounds, here the facts were in the context of the *Ram Janmabhumi* movement and the mobilization of hundreds of thousands of *kar sevaks* by the BJP across India to move to Ayodhya, the disputed site, to perform *kar seva* in order to build the Ram Temple.[766]

---

[763] *Id.* at 127 (Emphasis added).

[764] *Id.* at 132 (Emphasis added).

[765] *Id.* at 148.

[766] *Id.* at 133 (Sawant, J. for himself and Kuldeep Singh, J.) observing that,

> As a result of the demolition of the structure which was admittedly a mosque standing at the site for about 400 years, there were violent reactions in this country as well as in the neighbouring countries where some temples were destroyed. This in turn created further reactions in this country resulting in violence and destruction of the property. The Union Government tried to cope up with the situation by taking several steps including a ban on several organisations including Rashtriya Swayamsevak Sangh (RSS), Vishva Hindu Parishad (VHP) and Bajrang Dal which had along with BJP given a call for kar sevaks to march towards Ayodhya on December 6, 1992. The ban order was issued on December 10, 1992 under the Unlawful Activities (Prevention) Act, 1967. The dismissal of the State Governments and the State Legislative Assemblies in Madhya Pradesh, Rajasthan and Himachal Pradesh were admittedly a consequence of these developments and were effected by the issuance of Proclamations under Article 356(1), all on December 15, 1992.

In Madhya Pradesh's case, the first report sent by the Governor's noted that the State Government was giving overt and covert support to the communal organization, thus hinting at a breakdown of constitutional machinery. Subsequent reports reported that, "... there was a total failure of the law and order machinery to provide safety and security of life and property in the areas in and around the BHEL factory and the pressure brought on the administration of the factory to accommodate the *kar sevaks* in the BHEL area."[767] The Governor further reported that since the State Government might connive with banned underground organizations the situation demanded urgent action under article 356(1).[768] Facts were pretty much identical in the case of Himachal Pradesh[769] and Rajasthan.[770] Notably a full bench of the Madhya Pradesh High Court had quashed the proclamation on the ground that, "... it was not possible to accept that failure on the part of the State Government to save the lives and properties of citizens in a few cities in the State as a result of sudden outbreaks of violence could reasonably lead to the satisfaction of the President that the Government was unable to function in accordance with the Constitution ...."[771] Justice Sawant found that secularism was a part of the basic structure of the Constitution,[772] and in that light the question before the Court was, "... whether the three Governments when they had to their credit the acts discussed above, could be trusted to carry on the governance of the State in accordance with the provisions of the Constitution and the President's satisfaction based on the said acts could be challenged in law."[773] Finding in the affirmative for the President, Justice Sawant upheld the proclamations since in light of these information and materials, "... it can hardly be argued that there was no material before [the President] to come to the conclusion that the Governments in the three States could not be carried on in accordance with the provisions of the Constitution."[774]

---

[767] *Id.* at 133–34.

[768] *Id.* at 134.

[769] *Id.* at 134–35 (Sawant, J. for himself and Kuldeep Singh, J.) noting that,

> The Governor, however, opined that since the Chief Minister himself was a member of RSS, he was not in a position to implement the directions honestly and effectively and that most of the people in the State felt the same way. ... It is on the basis of this report that the Proclamation in question was issued.

[770] *Id.* at 135.

[771] *Id.* at 142–43 (Sawant, J. for himself and Kuldeep Singh, J.) citing Sunderlal Patwa v. Union of India, 1993 Jab.L.J. 387 (FB).

[772] *Id.* at 149 (Sawant, J. for himself and Kuldeep Singh, J.) (Summary of Conclusions, Conclusion VIII.).

[773] *Id.* at 147.

[774] *Id.* at 148.

Post *Bommai* Developments

Bommai was a decision of momentous proportions by any standard.[775] It heralded a new approach toward judicial review of presidential actions, especially in the area of judicial review of emergency proclamations under article 356[776] by laying down a clear standard of review. The standard, per majority decision of the Court, in simple words lays down that, "… even though the Court could not go into the content of the advice tendered to the President by his council (under the Presidential Aid & Advice Clause), the Court could still examine the materials on the basis of which the advice was tendered to the President."[777] This, and other, principles of law laid down in *Bommai* have had a huge impact on development of our constitutional law in this area. Furthermore, post *Bommai* developments are significant not only for legal and jurisprudential purposes but are even more vital in terms of the constitutional political development of our country. Before elaborating in detail on these legal and constitutional developments, a quick summary of the emerging paradigms may be attempted. This summary however must be read with the cautionary caveat that some of the conclusions are necessarily subjective and have also involved one of the authors actively as counsel.[778]

The emergency provisions of our constitution came into force in 1950. Since then, in a span of approximately 66 years, according to statistics released in 2016 by the Union government's Ministry of Home Affairs ("Home Ministry") article 356 has been invoked, till 2016, a total of 112 times.[779] However, a closer examination of the Home Ministry statistics would show that article 356 proclamations were issued a total of 115 times.[780] *Bommai* was decided on March

---

[775]*See, e.g.*, Sathe [40] (hailing *Bommai* was the most important and politically significant decision given by the Supreme Court of India since *Kesavananda Bharati*).

[776]Mate [41] (noting the use of doctrine of basic structure to review presidential proclamations under article 356).

[777]Gautam [42]. *See also* S.R. Bommai v. Union of India, (1994) 3 SCC 1 at 148.

[778]*See, e.g.*, Harish Chandra Singh Rawat v. Union of India, W.P. (M/S) No. 795 of 2016 (Uttarakhand High Court at Nanital) where one of us appeared for the petitioner.

[779]Ministry of Home Affairs, Govt. of India, *Statement Showing Date of Proclamation and Revocation Regarding President's Rule in State under Article 356 of the Constitution* (on file with authors; hereinafter "Ministry of Home Affairs, *Article 356 Statement*"). The statistics were released by the Ministry of Home Affairs, CS Division, via a response dated May 3, 2016 (in response to two Right to Information (RTI) queries dated April 10, 2016 and April 13, 2016). It might be pertinent to note that this list is restricted to states and does not include the data on union territories.

[780]Ministry of Home Affairs, *Article 356 Statement*, entries 21 and 26 (proclamations were issued three times in Orissa 1971 (on January 11, 1971, January 23, 1971 and March 23, 1971, respectively), and twice in Bihar (on January 9, 1972 and March 9, 1972, respectively)). The problem with computation is that serial numbering of all proclamations is by state where it was issued and the total comes to 112. The document counts all proclamations issues in one state is a single proclamation. But we count the total number of proclamations and count multiple proclamations in one state individually thus increasing the total number by 3 and bringing the total to 115, not 112.

11, 1994.[781] Going by the Home Ministry statistics, before *Bommai* was decided article 356 was proclaimed by the President a total of 94 times[782] but *after* March 11, 1994 (i.e., after *Bommai*) article 356 was proclaimed a total of 21 times.[783] Certainly the most significant post *Bommai* decision given by the Supreme Court has been *Rameshwar Prasad v. Union of India*[784] and this case was decided on January 24, 2006.[785] As per Home Ministry statistics, after *Rameshwar Prasad* article 365 has been invoked a total of 11 times.[786] This would mean that for a 44-year period (1950–1994) article 356 was proclaimed a total of 94 times (a total of 2.13 times per year). Thereafter for a 12-year period (1994–2006) it was proclaimed a total of 10 times (making it 0.83 times per year); and for the subsequent 10-year period (2006–2016) it was proclaimed a total of 11 times (making it 1.1 times per year). For the cumulative 22-year period post *Bommai* (1994–2016) article 356 was proclaimed a total of 21 times (1.04 times per year). Basic arithmetic would seem to clearly indicate that since *Bommai* the use of article 356 proclamations has been cut in half. Though the correlation between *Bommai* and the sudden decline in use of article 356 is for anyone to see, finding causation would require much more industry. In any case, much as one would like to ascribe this to political stability, or to a more cooperative and harmonious polity, that would be a gross oversimplification.

We contend that one of the main reasons for this diminishing invocation of article 356 could be the aggressive judicial review and repeated court interventions in the post *Bommai* period to quash adventurous invocations.[787] More importantly, the result of such court intervention has been achieved in the post *Bommai* era much faster than in the earlier era. Indeed, many post *Bommai* decisions have been contemporaneous and some even prophylactic. Note that the petitions in *Bommai* were filed before the Supreme Court on appeal from Karnataka High Court's decision given in August, 1989 but the decision in *Bommai* was given in March, 1994 (i.e., after 5 years). In every practical sense, the matter by then had become infructuous since assembly terms were largely over, fresh elections had been

---

[781]S.R. Bommai v. Union of India, (1994) 3 SCC 1, 1. The first page of the law report SCC shows the date of decision as March 11, 1994.

[782]Ministry of Home Affairs, *Article 356 Statement*, entries 1–91 (taking into account the method of calculation explained in *supra* note 782).

[783]*Id.* entries 92–112.

[784]Rameshwar Prasad v. Union of India, (2006) 2 SCC 1 (India).

[785]*Id.* at 1. The first page of the law report SCC shows the date of decision as January 24, 2006.

[786]*See* Ministry of Home Affairs, *Article 356 Statement*, entries 102–112.

[787]*See, e.g.*, N.T. Rama Rao v. His Excellency The Governor 1995 (3) ALT 929 (Andhra Pradesh); Jagdimbika Pal v. Union of India (1999) 9 SCC 95; Anil Kumar Jha v. Union of India (2005) 3 SCC 150; Rameshwar Prasad v. Union of India (2006) 2 SCC 1; Yitachu v. Union of India 2008 (2) GLT 284 (Gawahati); Union of India v. Harish Chandra Singh Rawat (2016) 16 SCC 744; Nabam Rebia v. Deputy Speaker (2016) 8 SCC 1; Chandrakant Kavlekar v. Union of India (2017) 3 SCC 758; P. Vetrivel v. P. Dhanabal (Madras) W.P. No. 25260 of 2017; Dr. G. Parmeshwara v. Union of India W.P. (Civil) 536 of 2018.

conducted and ministries installed in all states.[788] Indeed, this had been the pattern in several court interventions in article 356 invocations. In contrast, the petitions in *Rameshwar Prasad* were filed directly before the Supreme Court under article 32 of the Constitution in 2005, the matter was decided in 2006, and actual ground level relief was obtained by the aggrieved parties through a fresh election. Jharkhand, though not an article 356 case, but involving similar paradigms of government change, was even faster.[789] Uttarakhand is an even more compelling example where similar potential regime change was dealt with by the High Court on an expedited fast-track hearing and decided by a very detailed judgement on April 21, 2016, comprehensively analyzing and applying *Bommai* to restore the balance upset by political shenanigans and defections.[790] Last but not the least is the Karnataka example where article 356's invocation was avoided almost entirely by the Supreme Court willing to hear and intervene over a mid-night hearing followed by a hearing 24 hours later followed by the direction to have a floor-test immediately on the very next day without delay.[791]

Some of these examples are admittedly not classic article 356 cases because they did not involve the issuance of an article 356 emergency proclamation. Their importance and relevance lies in the fact that they involved various facets of floor-tests, political adventurism, defections and potential change of government through such means. But for the prompt and result-oriented court intervention in many of the above examples, there would either have been a stalemate inevitably leading to an article 356 proclamation or a regime change by constitutionally suspect and dubious means. Hence, the point that the authors seek to emphasize is that the political practices in India were ultimately reconciled, or at least a definitive step in that direction was taken, with the "rare-exception" nature of article 356 (hoping it to be a "dead-letter" as Dr. Ambedkar had put it) has actually been achieved after almost 44 years (i.e., the date on which *Bommai* was decided) of the adoption of the Constitution. This was achieved in a huge part through the readiness and willingness of both the High Courts and the Supreme Court to understand and appreciate underlying political realities and act, firstly, with unprecedented speed

[788] Indeed, this point was stressed by the Court in *Bommai* itself. *See* S.R. Bommai v. Union of India, (1994) 3 SCC 1, 149 (Conclusion IX in Sawant, J.'s decision where the judge declares proclamations dated August 7, 1988, April 21, 1989, and October 11, 1991 as unconstitutional but still doesn't grant any actual relief to the petitioners since fresh assembly elections had been conducted in these states and ministries had been sworn in).

[789] *See* Anil Kumar Jha v. Union of India (2005) 3 SCC 150. In its interim order, the Supreme Court directed that, "… the only agenda in the assembly … would be to have a floor test between contending political alliances … to see which political party or alliance has a majority in the House."

[790] *See* Harish Chandra Singh Rawat v. Union of India (2016) SCC Online 502 (Utt.). The appeal from Uttarakhand High Court is pending in the Supreme Court and is understood by all parties to be practically completely infructuous but kept alive in the Supreme Court to lay down the law, which, obviously would be of no relevance on the ground since successive governments have changed after that episode.

[791] *See* Dr. G. Parmeshwara v. Union of India, W.P. (Civil) 536 of 2018.

and dispatch, and secondly, with an extremely pragmatic and result-oriented approach. These characteristics of court adjudication in such matters were conspicuous by their absence up to and even including *Bommai*. The inevitable result was that even court invalidations were seen as *ex post facto* homilies and declarations of law with little practical effect leading to the absence of deterrence and fear by the principle actors, viz., the Union Governments, Speakers, Governors, et al.

Even though no consequential relief could be granted in *Bommai* owing to the fact that the fresh elections had been conducted in Karnataka, Meghalaya and Nagaland,[792] the fact that these proclamations were declared unconstitutional was to have great precedential impact in subsequent cases. It is indeed surprising how, in the face of clear law laid down in *Bommai*, the situation in *Rameshwar Prasad v. Union of India*[793] could even arise. Nevertheless, arose it did and luckily *Bommai* and its invalidation of three Presidential proclamations was there to guide the five-judge bench. Chief Justice Sabharwal wrote the majority opinion (for himself, Justice Agrawal and Justice Bhan). The facts of the case simply were that the Bihar State Legislature was dissolved even before the first meeting of the assembly. The Chief Justice noted:

> The challenge in these petitions is to the constitutional validity of the notification dated 23-5-2005 ordering dissolution of the Legislative Assembly of the State of Bihar. It is a unique case. Earlier cases that came up before this Court were those where the dissolutions of Assemblies were ordered on the ground that the parties in power had lost the confidence of the House. The present case is of its own kind where before even the first meeting of the Legislative Assembly, its dissolution has been ordered on the ground that attempts are being made to cobble up a majority by illegal means and lay claim to form the Government in the State and if these attempts continue, it would amount to tampering with constitutional provisions.[794]

The Governor in his report sent to the President in this case, surprisingly referred to *Bommai* and after narrating the facts reported, "I explored all possibilities and from the facts stated above, I am fully satisfied that no political party or coalition of parties or groups is able to substantiate a claim of majority in the Legislative Assembly … a situation has emerged in which no political party or group appears to be able to form a Government commanding a majority in the House. Thus, it is a case of complete inability of any political party to form a stable Government commanding the confidence of the majority members. This is a case of failure of constitutional machinery. …I therefore recommend that the present newly constituted Assembly be kept in suspended animation for the present, and the President of India is requested to take such appropriate action/decision, as required."[795] One month later a second report was sent by the Governor where he reported that, "I am

---

[792]*See Id.* at 149 (Sawant, J. for himself and Kuldeep Singh, J.) (Summary of Conclusions, Conclusion IX).

[793]Rameshwar Prasad v. Union of India, (2006) 2 SCC 1 (India).

[794]*Id.* at 61. (Sabharwal, C.J.).

[795]*Id.* at 64–65 (Sabharwal, C.J.). The entire report dated March 6, 2005 is reproduced at *id.* 62–65 and makes for a very interesting reading.

given to understand that serious attempts are being made by JD(U) and BJP to cobble up a majority and lay claim to form the Government in the State. Contacts in JD(U) and BJP have informed that 16–17 LJP MLAs have been won over by various means and attempt is being made to win over others. The JD(U) is also targeting Congress for creating a split."[796] This is the first time when the Governor reports that attempts to win over MLAs to secure a majority in the House were being made and cited "newspaper reports," certain "other reports gathered through meeting with various party functionaries/leaders" and also "intelligence reports received by me" to support this assertion.[797] Finally, a month thereafter the Governor reported to the President that, "Report has also been received of one of the LJP MLAs, who is General Secretary of the party having resigned today and also 17–18 more perhaps are moving towards JD(U) clearly indicating that various allurements have been offered which is a very disturbing and alarming feature."[798] Thereafter the President invoked article 356(1) and issued a proclamation on May 23, 2005 dissolving the Bihar Assembly that was then challenged before the Court.

The Chief Justice cited with approval the much famed Sarkaria Commission Report that had recommended that the State Assemblies should be dissolved, "... only with the sole object of preservation of the Constitution and not promotion of political interests of one or the other party."[799] The Chief Justice agreed that the evil of political defections are to be denounced but ultimately had no relevance in this matter.[800] On facts it was found that:

> But on facts of the present case, we are unable to accept that the Governor by [his reports] sought to achieve the aforesaid objective [of preventing political defections]. **There was no material, let alone relevant, with the Governor to assume that there was no legitimate realignment of political parties and there was blatant distortion of democracy by induced defections through unfair, illegal, unethical and unconstitutional means.** ... [T]he object was to prevent a particular political party from staking a claim and not the professed object of anxiety not to permit distortion of the political system, as sought to be urged. Such a recourse is nothing but wholly illegal and irregular and has to be described as mala fide. **The recommendation for dissolution of the Assembly to prevent the staking of claim to form the Government purportedly on the ground that the majority was achieved by distortion of the system by allurement, corruption and bribery was based on general assumptions without any material which are quite easy to be made if any political party not gaining absolute majority is to be kept out of governance.** ... Under no circumstances, can the action of the Governor be held to be bona fide when it is intended to prevent a political party to stake claim for formation of the Government.[801]

[796]*Id.* at 66. The entire report dated April 27, 2005 is reproduced *id.* at 66–67.
[797]*Id.* at 67.
[798]The entire report dated May 21, 2005 is reproduced *Id.* at 68–69.
[799]*Id.* at 86.
[800]*Id.* at 90.
[801]*Id.* at 90–91.

Such being the facts of this case, it was clear that this case was squarely covered by *Bommai*,[802] i.e., there was nothing but the *ipse dixit* of the Governor that was behind the recommendation to invoke article 356.[803] It was thus held by the Chief Justice that it is not for the Governor to refuse or prevent a political party from staking its claim to form a government because in his subjective assessment the majority was obtained by illegal or unethical means.[804] The proclamation was thus held unconstitutional[805]; however since fresh elections had already been ordered the Court denied to restore the suspended assembly and allowed the completion of the ongoing election process.[806]

It would thus appear that courts have realized the importance of the old somewhat restricted and private law principle, viz., *ibi jus ibi remedium* applied to the public law arena of article 356, one can ascribe the contemporary focused and prompt court interventions over the last two decades mainly to the realization that a large number of governmental and/or speaker and/or gubernatorial actions, though plainly unconstitutional and challenged immediately and within time, have yielded no effective ground-level relief to the aggrieved party. They have further realized that such absence of practical relief on the ground has emboldened and perhaps even encouraged future egregious action, based on the continuing belief in absence of punitive consequences.

References

1. N. Singh, *Juristic Concepts of Ancient Indian Polity* (1980), pp. 12–13
2. J.W. Spellman, *Political Theory of Ancient India* (1964), p. 4
3. K.P. Jayaswal, *Hindu Policy: A Constitutional History of India in Hindu Times* (1955), pp. 186–187
4. B. Prasad, *Theory of Government in Ancient India* (1968)
5. M.V. Krishna Rao, *Studies of Kautilya* (1953)

---

[802] *Id.* at 111.

[803] *Id.* at 121.

[804] *Id.* at 129 (Sabharwal, C.J.) observing that,

> If a political party with the support of other political party or other MLAs stakes claim to form a Government and satisfies the Governor about its majority to form a stable Government, the Governor cannot refuse formation of the Government and override the majority claim because of his subjective assessment that the majority was cobbled up by illegal and unethical means. No such power has been vested with the Governor. Such a power would be against the democratic principles of majority rule. … The remedy for corruption or similar ills and evils lies elsewhere and not in Article 356(1). In the same vein, it has to be held that the power under the Tenth Schedule for defection lies with the Speaker of the House and not with the Governor.

[805] *Id.* at 130.

[806] *Id.* at 134.

6. I. Hasan, *The Central Structure of the Mughal Empire* (1980)
7. H. Beveridge, *The Akbarnama of Abu-l-Fazl* (1907), pp. 107–108
8. T. Ramaswany, *Essentials of Indian Statecraft* (1962), p. 143
9. J.W. Kaye, *History of the Administration of the East India Company* (1966 ed.) (1853)
10. C. Ilbert, *The Government of Indian Law* (1946)
11. A.B. Keith, *A Constitutional History of India* (1961 photo. reprint) (1936)
12. A.C. Patia, Landmarks in the constitutional history of India. JILI **5**, 81 (1963)
13. M.V. Pylee, *Constitutional History of India* (1972 photo. reprint)
14. M.P. Jain, *Outlines of Indian Legal History* (1966)
15. R. Jois, *Legal and Constitutional History of India* (1984)
16. J.K. Mittal, *Constitutional History of India* (1980)
17. W.M.H. Allen & CO., *The Law Relating to India and the East India Company*, 3rd ed. (1842)
18. G. Eyre, A. Strahan, *A Collection of Charters and Statutes Relating to The East India Company* (1817)
19. A.C. Banerjee, *Indian Constitutional Documents*, vol. 1 (1945)
20. J. Shaw, *Charters Relating to the East India Company from 1600 to 1761* (1887)
21. J. Minattur, *Martial Law in India, Pakistan and Ceylon* (1962)
22. J.K.P Srivastava, *Emergency Provisions in the Constitution of India* (1972), p. 116 (unpublished Ph.D. thesis London University, School of Oriental and African Studies)
23. R. Clarke, *The Regulations of The Government of Fort William in Bengal in Force at the End of 1853,* vol. 2 (1854)
24. D.D. Basu, *Commentary on the Constitution of India,* vol. 6 (1967), pp. 1–18
25. B. Shiva Rao, *The Framing of India's Constitution: A Study* (1968)
26. B. Shiva Rao, *The Framing of India's Constitution: Select Documents* (1961)
27. B. Shiva Rao, *The Framing of India's Constitution: Select Documents,* vol. 2 (1961)
28. B. Shiva Rao, *The Framing of India's Constitution: Select Documents,* vol. 3 (1961)
29. B. Shiva Rao, *The Framing of India's Constitution: Select Documents,* vol. 4 (1961)
30. H.M. Seervai, *Constitution Law of India*, vol. 1, 3rd ed. (1983)
31. H.M. Seervai, *Constitution Law of India*, vol. 2, 3rd ed. (1983)
32. V.N. Shukla, *The Defence of India Act 1962* (1966)
33. Jagmohan, *Island of Truth* (1978)
34. M.P. Jain, S.N. Jain, *Principles of Administrative Law* (1981), pp. 486–512
35. D.C. Wadhwa, *Repromulgation of Ordinances: A Fraud on the Constitution of India* (1983)
36. E. Corwin, The *Doctrine of Judicial Review* (1914), p. 10
37. J.R. Siwach, *Politics of President's Rule in India* (1979), pp. 89–90
38. U. Baxi, *Indian Supreme Court and Politics* (1980)
39. Shaun Star (Ed.), *Australia and India—A Comparative Overview of the Law and Legal Practice* (2016), pp. 1–19
40. S.P. Sathe, *Judicial Activism in India* (2002), p. 152
41. M. Mate, Judicial supremacy in comparative constitutional law. Tul. L. Rev. **92**(393), 426–427 (2017)
42. K. Gautam, Controlled semi-presidentialism: the case for semi-presidentialism under the Indian constitution. Colum. J. Asian L. **29**, 179–201 (2015)
43. D.D. Basu, *Commentary on the Constitution of India*, vol .6, 5th ed. (1966)
44. S.J. Sorabjee, *The Law of Press Censoring in India* (1976), p. 40

Index

A. Singhvi and K. Gautam, *The Law of Emergency Powers*,
https://doi.org/10.1007/978-981-15-2997-9

The manufacturer's authorised representative in the EU is Springer Nature Customer Service Centre GmbH, Europaplatz 3, 69115 Heidelberg, Germany. If you have any concerns regarding our products, please contact ProductSafety@springernature.com

Printed and bound by CPI Group (UK) Ltd, Croydon, CR0 4YY
30/09/2026
02225246-0014